# The Free Flow of Information: Media law and freedom of expression in the United States

First printing 2014
LuLu Press
San Francisco, California
ISBN: 978-1-312-36722-7

ISBN 978-1-312-36722-7      90000

Michael Edward Lenert 2014

i

# Preface

This is the second version of a casebook for an advanced undergraduate course at the University of San Francisco.

Taught by Professor Michael Edward Lenert, the class involves close reading of original legal texts and decisions concerning defamation, privacy, intellectual property and other selected topics.

The primary objectives of this course are (1) to outline the fundamental legal decisions that constitute the framework of media law, (2) to develop the skills to apply this framework to contemporary controversies in media law and ethics (3) to give you practical guidance how to stay out of legal trouble in your career in the media.

Much of this casebook incorporates the work of others and no claim of original authorship of these materials is made. This work constitutes a fair use as provided for in section 107 of the US Copyright Law, and is made available under a Creative Commons Attribution Share-Alike license.

## UNIVERSITY OF SAN FRANCISCO

Department of Media Studies
2130 Fulton St.
San Francisco, CA 94117-1080

*Please feel free to contact the author at melenert@usfca.edu if you have questions, comments or ideas for improvement of this resource.*

# Table of contents

# CHAPTER 1

# What is protected speech?

# The Bill of Rights and the right of freedom of expression (1791)

A constitution is a set of fundamental principles and the supreme law according to which a state or other organization is governed.

Since 1789, the United States Constitution has been amended twenty-seven times, but the first ten amendments were all enacted at the same time and are known collectively as the "Bill of Rights."

Inspired by Thomas Jefferson and written by James Madison in response to calls from several states for greater constitutional protection for individual liberties, the Bill of Rights lists specific prohibitions on governmental power.

The Bill of Rights enumerates freedoms not explicitly indicated in the main body of the Constitution, such as freedom of religion, freedom of speech, a free press, and free assembly; the right to keep and bear arms; freedom from unreasonable search and seizure, security in personal effects, and freedom from warrants issued without probable cause; indictment by a grand jury for any capital or "infamous crime"; guarantee of a speedy, public trial with an impartial jury; and prohibition of double jeopardy.

The right of individuals to speak and publish freely is protected by the wording of the First Amendment: It prohibits Congress from making laws establishing a religion or abridging freedom of speech.

Source: http://billofrightsinstitute.org/founding-documents/bill-of-rights/

**Amendment I**

**Congress shall make no law** respecting an establishment of religion, or prohibiting the free exercise thereof; or **abridging the freedom of speech, or of the press;** or the right of the people peaceably to assemble, and to petition the government for a redress of grievances.

So the question arises, "What speech is protected by the First Amendment?" **Is <u>all</u> speech protected, or just some of it?**

One answer to this question was given in the case of Schenck v. United States (1919).

# Schenck v. United States (1919)

U.S. Supreme Court

249 U.S. 47 (1919)

Decided March 3, 1919

White  McKenna  Holmes  Day  Van  Pitney  McReynolds  Brandeis  Clarke

graphic by http://www.oyez.org

Decision: 9 votes for United States, 0 vote(s) against

**MR. JUSTICE HOLMES delivered the opinion of the court.**

[Mr. Schenck, general secretary of the Socialist party of the USA, was convicted of a] conspiracy to violate the Espionage Act (1917) ... by causing and attempting to cause insubordination ... in the military and naval forces of the United States, and to obstruct the recruiting and enlistment service of the United States, when the United States was at war with the German Empire ...

[The government accused Schenck and the other defendants of having] printed and circulated to men who had been called and accepted for military service under the Act of May 18, 1917, a document ... calculated to cause ... insubordination and obstruction.

Charles Schenck

The defendants were found guilty ... [but argue] the First Amendment to the Constitution forbidding Congress to make any law abridging the freedom of speech, or of the press ...

The document in question, upon its first printed side, recited the first section of the Thirteenth Amendment ... The other ... side of the sheet was headed "Assert Your Rights." It stated reasons for alleging that anyone violated the Constitution when he refused to recognize "your right to assert your opposition to the draft," and went on:

"If you do not assert and support your rights, you are helping to deny or disparage rights which it is the solemn duty of all citizens and residents of the United States to retain."It described the arguments on the other side as coming from cunning politicians and a mercenary capitalist press, and even silent consent to the conscription law as helping to support an infamous conspiracy. It denied the power to send our citizens away to foreign shores to shoot up the people of other lands ...

... We admit that, in many places and in ordinary times, the defendants, in saying all that was said in the circular, would have been within their constitutional rights. But the character of every act depends upon the circumstances in which it is done. *Aikens v. Wisconsin,* 195 U. S. 194 (1904). The most stringent protection of free speech would not protect a man in falsely shouting fire in a theatre and causing a panic. ... The question in every case is whether the words used are

6

used in such circumstances and are of such a nature as to create a clear and present danger that they will bring about the substantive evils that Congress has a right to prevent. It is a question of proximity and degree. When a nation is at war, many things that might be said in time of peace are such a hindrance to its effort that their utterance will not be endured so long as men fight, and that no Court could regard them as protected by any constitutional right. ....

Judgments affirmed.

---

ESPIONAGE.

SECTION 1. That (a) whoever, for the purpose of obtaining information respecting the national defense with intent or reason to believe that the information to be obtained is to be used to the injury of the United States, or to the advantage of any foreign nation, goes upon, enters, flies over, or otherwise obtains information concerning any vessel, aircraft, work of defense, navy yard, naval station, submarine base, coaling station, fort, battery, torpedo station, dockyard, canal, railroad, arsenal, camp, factory, mine, telegraph, telephone, wireless, or signal station, building, office, or other place connected with the national defense, owned or constructed, or in progress of construction by the United States or under the control of the United States, or of any of its

*The Espionage Act (15 June 1917), created by Congress following the U.S. declaration of war on Germany, authorized federal officials to make summary arrests of people whose opinions "threatened national security." The measure prohibited willfully making false reports with intent to interfere with the success of the military or naval forces, inciting insubordination, disloyalty, or mutiny in the military, and obstructing recruitment or the enlistment service of the United States.*

*Congress augmented it with the Sedition Act on 16 May 1918. This set forth eight new criminal offenses, including uttering, printing, writing, or publishing any disloyal, profane, scurrilous, or abusive language intended to cause contempt, scorn, contumely, or disrespect for*

World War I era poster

*the U.S. government or the Constitution.After the Court unanimously found that his speech was not protected by the First Amendment, Schenck served one half year in prison.*

*Source: http://www.answers.com/topic/espionage-and-sedition-acts-of-world-war-i*

# Texas v. Johnson(1989)

U.S. Supreme Court

491 U.S. 397 (1989)

Decided: June 21, 1989

| Brennan | Marshall | Blackmun | Scalia | Kennedy | Rehnquist | White | Stevens | O'Connor |

Decision: 5 votes for Johnson, 4 vote(s) against

**JUSTICE BRENNAN delivered the opinion of the Court.**

After publicly burning an American flag as a means of political protest, Gregory Lee Johnson was convicted of desecrating a flag in violation of Texas law. This case presents the question whether his conviction is consistent with the First Amendment. We hold that it is not.

I

While the Republican National Convention was taking place in Dallas in 1984, respondent Johnson participated in a political demonstration dubbed the "Republican War Chest Tour." As explained in literature distributed by the demonstrators and in speeches made by them, the purpose of this event was to protest the policies of the Reagan administration and of certain Dallas-based corporations. ... The demonstration ended in front of Dallas City Hall, where Johnson unfurled the American flag, doused it with kerosene, and set it on fire. While the flag burned, the protestors chanted, "America, the red, white, and blue, we spit on you." ... No one was physically injured or threatened with injury, though several witnesses testified that they had been seriously offended by the flag burning.

Gregory Lee Johnson

Johnson was charged was the desecration of a venerated object in violation of Tex.Penal Code Ann. § 42.09(a)(3) (1989). [n1] After a trial, he was convicted, sentenced to one year in prison, and fined $2,000. ...

We must first determine whether Johnson's burning of the flag constituted expressive conduct, permitting him to invoke the First Amendment in challenging his conviction. ...The First Amendment literally forbids the abridgment only of "speech," but we have long recognized that
its protection does not end at the spoken or written word. ...

V

Johnson was convicted for engaging in expressive conduct. The State's
interest in preventing breaches of the peace does not support his conviction, because Johnson's conduct did not threaten to disturb the
peace. Nor does the State's interest in preserving the flag as a symbol of
nationhood and national unity justify his criminal conviction for engaging in political expression. The judgment of the Texas Court of Criminal Appeals is therefore

Affirmed.

CHIEF JUSTICE REHNQUIST, with whom JUSTICE WHITE and JUS-
TICE O'CONNOR join, dissenting.

In holding this Texas statute unconstitutional, the Court ignores ... a
uniqueness that justifies a governmental prohibition against flag burning in the way respondent Johnson did here.

...

The Court decides that the American flag is just another symbol, about
which not only must opinions pro and con be tolerated, but for which
the most minimal public respect may not be enjoined ...

...

I cannot agree that the First Amendment invalidates the Act of Congress, and the laws of 48 of the 50 States, which make criminal the public burning of the flag.

**STEVENS, J., Dissenting Opinion**

Surely one of the high purposes of a democratic society is to legislate
against conduct that is regarded as evil and profoundly offensive to the
majority of people -- whether it be murder, embezzlement, pollution,
or flagburning.

The ideas of liberty and equality have been an irresistible force in motivating leaders like Patrick Henry, Susan B. Anthony, and Abraham Lincoln, schoolteachers like Nathan Hale and Booker T. Washington, the
Philippine Scouts who fought at Bataan, and the soldiers who scaled
the bluff at Omaha Beach. If those ideas are worth fighting for -- and
our history demonstrates that they are -- it cannot be true that the flag
that uniquely symbolizes their power is not itself worthy of protection
from unnecessary desecration.

I respectfully dissent.

### What are some examples of "unprotected speech?"

*1) Subversive Advocacy.  For subversive advocacy (speech that advocates lawlessness) to fall outside the protections of the First Amendment the speech must satisfy a two-part test.  The speech must consist of (1) advocacy directed to inciting or producing imminent lawless action and (2) speech that is likely to incite or produce such action. This is known as the Brandenburg test.*

*2) Fighting Words. Fighting words are a narrow category of unprotected speech that are defined as words spoken in a face to face exchange such as personal insults or epithets which by their very utterance are likely to cause the person to whom they are addressed to respond with violence directed at the speaker.*

*3) True Threats. True threats are defined as "statements where the speaker means to communicate a serious expression of an intent to commit an act of unlawful violence to a particular individual or group of individuals."*

*4) Obscenity. As defined by Miller v. California's three prong test, to be obscene material must (1) be a work that the average person, applying contemporary community standards would find, taken as a whole, appeals to the prurient interest and (2) the work must depict or describe, in a patently offensive way, sexual conduct specifically defined by the applicable obscenity law, and (3) the work, taken as a whole, must lack serious literary, artistic, political or scientific value.*

*5) Child Pornography. Under New York v. Ferber, child pornography is an unprotected category of expression and consists of visual depictions of actual children engaged in sexual activity or the lewd exhibition of the genitals. Unlike obscenity, it is not judged by the work taken as a whole and, therefore, can consist of isolated segments of an entire work*

*6) Commercial speech that concerns illegal activity or commercial speech that is false or misleading. Under the Central Hudson test, commercial speech is only protected if it concerns legal activity and if the content is true and not misleading.*

Source: http://www.wneclaw.com/medialaw/unprotectedcategories.html

These words offend for the same reasons that obscenity offends. Their place in the hierarchy of First Amendment values was aptly sketched by Mr. Justice Murphy when he said:

[S]uch utterances are no essential part of any exposition of ideas, and are of such slight social value as a step to truth that any benefit that may be derived from them is clearly outweighed by the social interest in order and morality.

Chaplinsky v. New Hampshire, 315 U.S. at 572.

# Introduction to the US Judicial system

**In a Criminal Case ...**

At the beginning of a federal criminal case, the principal actors are the U.S. attorney (the prosecutor) and the grand jury. The U.S. attorney represents the United States in most court proceedings, including all criminal prosecutions. The grand jury reviews evidence presented by the U.S. attorney and decides whether there is sufficient evidence to require a defendant to stand trial.

The standard of proof in a criminal trial is "beyond a reasonable doubt," which means the evidence must be so strong that there is no reasonable doubt that the defendant committed the crime.

At an initial appearance, a judge advises the defendant of the charges filed, considers whether the defendant should be held in jail until trial, and determines whether there is probable cause to believe that an offense has been committed and the defendant has committed it. Defendants who are unable to afford counsel are advised of their right to a court-appointed attorney. The court may appoint either a federal public defender or a private attorney who has agreed to accept such appointments from the court. In either type of appointment, the attorney will be paid by the court from funds appropriated by Congress. Defendants released into the community before trial may be required to obey certain restrictions, such as home confinement or drug testing, and to make periodic reports to a pretrial services officer to ensure appearance at trial.

The defendant enters a plea to the charges brought by the U.S. attorney at a hearing known as an arraignment. Most defendants — more than

**The U.S. Constitution is the supreme law of the land in the United States.** It creates a federal system of government in which power is shared between the federal government and the state governments. Due to federalism, both the federal government and each of the state governments has its own court system.

Article III of the Constitution invests the judicial power of the United States in the federal court system. Article III, Section 1 specifically creates the U.S. Supreme Court and gives Congress the authority to create the lower federal courts.

Each of the states has its own laws and judicial system. The Constitution and laws of each state establish the state courts. A court of last resort, often known as a supreme court, is usually the highest court in a state. Some states also have an intermediate court of appeals. Below these appeals courts are the state trial courts.

The federal US judicial system is divided into two principal branches. Criminal and civil. Let's look closer at each of these systems.

90% — plead guilty rather than go to trial. If a defendant pleads guilty in return for the government agreeing to drop certain charges or to recommend a lenient sentence, the agreement often is called a "plea bargain." If the defendant pleads guilty, the judge may impose a sentence at that time, but more commonly will schedule a hearing to determine the sentence at a later date. In most felony cases the judge waits for the results of a presentence report, prepared by the court's probation office, before imposing sentence. If the defendant pleads not guilty, the judge will proceed to schedule a trial.

Criminal cases include a limited amount of pretrial discovery proceedings similar to those in civil cases, with substantial restrictions to protect the identity of government informants and to prevent intimidation of witnesses. The attorneys also may file motions, which are requests for rulings by the court before the trial. For example, defense attorneys often file a motion to suppress evidence, which asks the court to exclude from the trial evidence that the defendant believes was obtained by the government in violation of the defendant's constitutional rights.

In a criminal trial, the burden of proof is on the government. Defendants do not have to prove their innocence. Instead, the government must provide evidence to convince the jury of the defendant's guilt. The standard of proof in a criminal trial is proof "beyond a reasonable doubt," which means the evidence must be so strong that there is no reasonable doubt that the defendant committed the crime.

If a defendant is found not guilty, the defendant is released and the government may not appeal. Nor can the person be charged again with the same crime in a federal court. The Constitution prohibits "double jeopardy," or being tried twice for the same offense.

If the verdict is guilty, the judge determines the defendant's sentence according to special federal sentencing guidelines issued by the United States Sentencing Commission.

**In a civil case ...**

Unlike a federal criminal case, a federal civil case involves a legal dispute between two or more parties. To begin a civil lawsuit in federal court, the plaintiff files a complaint with the court and "serves" a copy of the complaint on the defendant. The complaint describes the plaintiff's injury, explains how the defendant caused the injury, and asks the court to order relief. A plaintiff may seek money to compensate for the injury, or may ask the court to order the defendant to stop the conduct that is causing the harm. The court may also order other types of relief, such as a declaration of the legal rights of the plaintiff in a particular situation.

To avoid the expense of having a trial, judges encourage the litigants to try to reach an agreement resolving their dispute.

To prepare a case for trial, the litigants may conduct "discovery." In discovery, the litigants must provide information to each other about the case, such as the identity of witnesses and copies of any documents related to the case. The purpose of discovery is to prepare for trial by requiring the litigants to assemble their evidence and prepare to call witnesses. Each side also may file requests, or "motions," with the court seeking rulings on the discovery of evidence, or on the procedures to be followed at trial.

One common method of discovery is the deposition. In a deposition, a witness is required under oath to answer questions about the case asked by the lawyers in the presence of a court reporter. The court reporter is a person specially trained to record all testimony and produce a word-for-word account called a transcript.

To avoid the expense and delay of having a trial, judges encourage the litigants to try to reach an agreement resolving their dispute. In particular, the courts encourage the use of mediation, arbitration, and other forms of alternative dispute resolution, or "ADR," designed to produce an early resolution of a dispute without the need for trial or other court proceedings. As a result, litigants often decide to resolve a civil lawsuit with an agreement known as a "settlement."

If a case is not settled, the court will schedule a trial. In a wide variety of civil cases, either side is entitled under the Constitution to request a jury trial. If the parties waive their right to a jury, then the case will be heard by a judge without a jury.

At a trial, witnesses testify under the supervision of a judge. By applying rules of evidence, the judge determines which information may be presented in the courtroom. To ensure that witnesses speak from their own knowledge and do not change their story based on what they hear another witness say, witnesses are kept out of the courtroom until it is time for them to testify.

**The Federal Courts**

**The U.S. Supreme Court**
- Reviews the decisions of the federal and state trial and appellate courts

**U.S. Courts of Appeals**
- 13 Appellate Circuits
- Review the decisions of the federal district courts

**U.S. District Courts**
- 94 Judicial Districts
- Trial courts that hear civil and criminal cases
- Specialized courts include bankruptcy, international trade, and federal claims

At the conclusion of the evidence, each side gives a closing argument. In a jury trial, the judge will explain the law that is relevant to the case and the decisions the jury needs to make. The jury generally is asked to determine whether the defendant is responsible for harming the plaintiff in some way, and then to determine the amount of damages that the defendant will be required to pay. If the case is being tried before a judge without a jury, known as a "bench" trial, the judge will decide these issues. In a civil case the plaintiff must convince the jury by a "preponderance of the evidence" (i.e., that it is more likely than not) that the defendant is responsible for the harm the plaintiff has suffered.

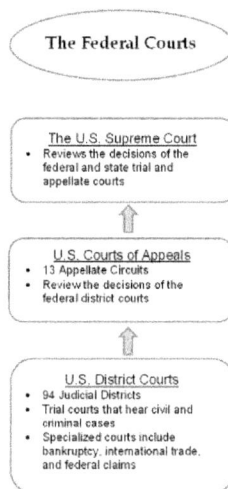

**Three Levels: District Court, Court of Appeals, Supreme Court**

The United States district courts are the trial courts of the federal court system. Within limits set by Congress and the Constitution, the district courts have jurisdiction to hear nearly all categories of federal cases, including both civil and criminal matters. Every day hundreds of people across the nation are selected for jury duty and help decide some of these cases.

There are 94 federal judicial districts, including at least one district in each state, the District of Columbia and Puerto Rico.

The 94 U.S. judicial districts are organized into 12 regional circuits, each of which has a United States court of appeals. A court of appeals hears appeals from the district courts located within its circuit, as well as appeals from decisions of federal administrative agencies.

The United States Supreme Court consists of the Chief Justice of the United States and eight associate justices. At its discretion, and within certain guidelines established by Congress, the Supreme Court each year hears a limited number of the cases it is asked to decide. Those cases may begin in the federal or state courts, and they usually involve important questions about the Constitution or federal law.

The Appeals Process

The losing party in a decision by a trial court in the federal system normally is entitled to appeal the decision to a federal court of appeals. Similarly, a litigant who is not satisfied with a decision made by a federal administrative agency usually may file a petition for review of the agency decision by a court of appeals. Judicial review in cases involving certain federal agencies or programs — for example, disputes over Social Security benefits — may be obtained first in a district court rather than a court of appeals.

In a civil case either side may appeal the verdict. A litigant who files an appeal, known as an "appellant," must show that the trial court or administrative agency made a legal error that affected the decision in the case. The court of appeals makes its decision based on the record of the case established by the trial court or agency. It does not receive additional evidence or hear witnesses. The court of appeals also may review the factual findings of the trial court or agency, but typically may only overturn a decision on factual grounds if the findings were "clearly erroneous."

The court of appeals decision usually will be the last word in a case, unless it sends the case back to the trial court for additional proceedings, or the parties ask the U.S. Supreme Court to review the case.

Appeals are decided by panels of three judges working together. The appellant presents legal arguments to the panel, in writing, in a document called a "brief." In the brief, the appellant tries to persuade the judges that the trial court made an error, and that its decision should be reversed. On the other hand, the party defending against the appeal, known as the "appellee," tries in its brief to show why the trial court decision was correct, or why any error made by the trial court was not significant enough to affect the outcome of the case.

Although some cases are decided on the basis of written briefs alone, many cases are selected for an "oral argument" before the court. Oral argument in the court of appeals is a structured discussion between the appellate lawyers and the panel of judges focusing on the legal principles in dispute. Each side is given a short time — usually about 15 minutes — to present arguments to the court.

The court of appeals decision usually will be the final word in the case, unless it sends the case back to the trial court for additional proceedings, or the parties ask the U.S. Supreme Court to review the case. In some cases the decision may be reviewed en banc, that is, by a larger group of judges (usually all) of the court of appeals for the circuit.

A litigant who loses in a federal court of appeals, or in the highest court of a state, may file a petition for a "writ of certiorari," which is a document asking the Supreme Court to review the case. The Supreme Court, however, does not have to grant review. The Court typically will agree to hear a case only when it involves an unusually important legal principle, or when two or more federal appellate courts have interpreted a law differently. There are also a small number of special circumstances in which the Supreme Court is required by law to hear an appeal. When the Supreme Court hears a case, the parties are required to file written briefs and the Court may hear oral argument.

A party may ask the U.S. Supreme Court to review a decision of the U.S. Court of Appeals, but the Supreme Court usually is under no obligation to do so. The U.S. Supreme Court is the final arbiter of federal constitutional questions.

Source: http://www.uscourts.gov/FederalCourts/UnderstandingtheFederalCourts

# The State Action Requirement and the First Amendment

**State action doctrine** is an important American legal concept that says the protections of the Constitution — such as the Fourteenth and First Amendments — only **apply to the coercive power of the state against the individual**.

In other words, there is no First Amendment protection in the case of an individual versus another individual. For example, a person cannot be criminally prosecuted (that is, prosecuted by the state or federal governments in a criminal case) for making non-threatening racist statements. However, he or she could be 'fired' or legally terminated from his or her profession.

The state action requirement stems from the fact that the constitutional amendments which protect individual rights (especially the Bill of Rights and the 14th Amendment) are **prohibitions against government action.**

A series of United States Supreme Court decisions beginning in the 1920s interpreted the Fourteenth Amendment to "incorporate" the Bill of Rights. This means that the Court found that certain rights, such as "freedom of speech" are fundamental to and implicit in the concept of "ordered liberty." As a consequence, by action of the the Fourteenth Amendment's due process clause, they are valid against both the state and federal governments.

For example, the First Amendment states that "[c]ongress shall make no law" infringing upon the freedoms of speech and religion. Because of this requirement, it is impossible for private parties (citizens or corporations) to violate these amendments, and all lawsuits alleging constitutional violations of this type must show how the government (state or federal) was responsible for the violation of their rights.

Sources: http://rationalwiki.org/wiki/State_action_doctrine and: http://www.law.cornell.edu/wex/state_action_requirement.

AMENDMENT XIV

SECTION 1.

All persons born or naturalized in the United States, and subject to the jurisdiction thereof, are citizens of the United States and of the state wherein they reside. No state shall make or enforce any law which shall abridge the privileges or immunities of citizens of the United States; nor shall any state deprive any person of life, liberty, or property, without due process of law; nor deny to any person within its jurisdiction the equal protection of the laws.

# CHAPTER 2

# Libel: Free press and individual reputation

*The events that led to the 1964 landmark U.S. Supreme Court decision confirming freedom of the press under the First Amendment in New York Times Co. v. Sullivan began in March 1960, after Martin Luther King's supporters published a fundraising appeal on the civil rights leader's behalf. The appeal was in response to King's arrest on perjury charges, and so incensed Alabama officials that they brought suit against several black ministers whose names appeared on the advertisement.*

# New York Times Co. v. Sullivan (1964)

U.S. Supreme Court

Decided March 9, 1964

376 U.S. 254 (1964)

(Together with No. 40, Abernathy et al. v. Sullivan, also on certiorari to the same court, argued January 7, 1964.)

Warren  Black  Douglas  Clark  Harlan  Brennan  Stewart  White  Goldberg

Decision: 9 votes for New York Times, 0 vote(s) against

**MR. JUSTICE BRENNAN delivered the opinion of the Court.**

We are required in this case to determine for the first time the extent to which the constitutional protections for speech and press limit a State's power to award damages in a libel action brought by a public official against critics of his official conduct.

Respondent L. B. Sullivan is one of the three elected Commissioners of the City of Montgomery, Alabama. He testified that he was

"Commissioner of Public Affairs, and the duties are supervision of the Police Department, Fire Department, Department of Cemetery and Department of Scales."

He brought this civil libel action against the four individual petitioners, who are Negroes and Alabama clergymen, and against petitioner the New York Times Company, a New York corporation which publishes the New York Times, a daily newspaper. A jury in the Circuit Court of Montgomery County awarded him damages of $500,000, the full amount claimed, against all the petitioners, and the Supreme Court of Alabama affirmed. 273 Ala. 656, 144 So.2d 25.

Respondent's complaint alleged that he had been libeled by statements in a full-page advertisement that was carried in the New York Times on March 29, 1960. Entitled "Heed Their Rising Voices," the advertisement began by stating that,

"As the whole world knows by now, thousands of Southern Negro students are engaged in widespread nonviolent demonstrations in positive affirmation of the right to live in human dignity as guaranteed by the U.S. Constitution and the Bill of Rights."

It went on to charge that,

> "in their efforts to uphold these guarantees, they are being met by an unprecedented wave of terror by those who would deny and negate that document which the whole world looks upon as setting the pattern for modern freedom. . . ."

Succeeding paragraphs purported to illustrate the "wave of terror" by describing certain alleged events. The text concluded with an appeal for funds for three purposes: support of the student movement, "the struggle for the right to vote," and the legal defense of Dr. Martin Luther King, Jr., leader of the movement, against a perjury indictment then pending in Montgomery.

The text appeared over the names of 64 persons, many widely known for their activities in public affairs, religion, trade unions, and the performing arts. Below these names, and under a line reading "We in the south who are struggling daily for dignity and freedom warmly endorse this appeal," appeared the names of the four individual petitioners and of 16 other persons, all but two of whom were identified as clergymen in various Southern cities. The advertisement was signed at the bottom of the page by the "Committee to Defend Martin Luther King and the Struggle for Freedom in the South," and the officers of the Committee were listed.

Of the 10 paragraphs of text in the advertisement, the third and a portion of the sixth were the basis of respondent's claim of libel. They read as follows:

Third paragraph:

"In Montgomery, Alabama, after students sang 'My Country, 'Tis of Thee' on the State Capitol steps, their leaders were expelled from school, and truckloads of police armed with shotguns and tear-gas ringed the Alabama State College Campus. When the entire student body protested to state authorities by refusing to reregister, their dining hall was padlocked in an attempt to starve them into submission."

Sixth paragraph:

"Again and again, the Southern violators have answered Dr. King's peaceful protests with intimidation and violence. They have bombed his home, almost killing his wife and child. They have assaulted his person. They have arrested him seven times -- for 'speeding,' 'loitering' and similar 'offenses.' And now they have charged him with 'perjury' -- a felony under which they could imprison him for ten years. . . ."

Although neither of these statements mentions respondent by name, he contended that the word "police" in the third paragraph referred to him as the Montgomery Commissioner who supervised the Police Department, so that he was being accused of "ringing" the campus with police. He further claimed that the paragraph would be read as imputing to the police, and hence to him, the padlocking of the dining hall in order to starve the students into submission. As to the sixth paragraph, he contended that, since arrests are ordinarily made by the police, the statement "They have arrested [Dr. King] seven times" would be read as referring to him; he further contended that the "They" who did the arresting would be equated with the "They" who committed the other described acts and with the "Southern violators." Thus, he argued, the paragraph would be read as accusing the Montgomery police, and hence him, of answering Dr. King's protests with "intimidation and violence," bombing his home, assaulting his person, and charging him with perjury. Respondent and six other Montgomery residents testified that they read some or all of the statements as referring to him in his capacity as Commissioner.

It is uncontroverted that some of the statements contained in the two paragraphs were not accurate descriptions of events which occurred in Montgomery. Although Negro students staged a demonstration on the State Capitol steps, they sang the National Anthem and not "My Coun-

try, 'Tis of Thee." Although nine students were expelled by the State Board of Education, this was not for leading the demonstration at the Capitol, but for demanding service at a lunch counter in the Montgomery County Courthouse on another day. Not the entire student body, but most of it, had protested the expulsion, not by refusing to register, but by boycotting classes on a single day; virtually all the students did register for the ensuing semester. The campus dining hall was not padlocked on any occasion, and the only students who may have been barred from eating there were the few who had neither signed a preregistration application nor requested temporary meal tickets. Although the police were deployed near the campus in large numbers on three occasions, they did not at any time "ring" the campus, and they were not called to the campus in connection with the demonstration on the State Capitol steps, as the third paragraph implied. Dr. King had not been arrested seven times, but only four, and although he claimed to have been assaulted some years earlier in connection with his arrest for loitering outside a courtroom, one of the officers who made the arrest denied that there was such an assault.

On the premise that the charges in the sixth paragraph could be read as referring to him, respondent was allowed to prove that he had not participated in the events described. Although Dr. King's home had, in fact, been bombed twice when his wife and child were there, both of

Police Commissioner
L. B. Sullivan

these occasions antedated respondent's tenure as Commissioner, and the police were not only not implicated in the bombings, but had made every effort to apprehend those who were. Three of Dr. King's four arrests took place before respondent became Commissioner. Although Dr. King had, in fact, been indicted (he was subsequently acquitted) on two counts of perjury, each of which carried a possible five-year sentence, respondent had nothing to do with procuring the indictment.

Respondent made no effort to prove that he suffered actual pecuniary loss as a result of the alleged libel. One of his witnesses, a former employer, testified that, if he had believed the statements, he doubted whether he "would want to be associated with anybody who would be a party to such things that are stated in that ad," and that he would not reemploy respondent if he believed "that he allowed the Police Department to do the things that the paper say he did." But neither this witness nor any of the others testified that he had actually believed the statements in their supposed reference to respondent. The cost of the advertisement was approximately $4800, and it was published by the Times upon an order from a New York advertising agency acting for the signatory Committee. The agency submitted the advertisement with a letter from A. Philip Randolph, Chairman of the Committee, certifying that the persons whose names appeared on the advertisement had given their permission. Mr. Randolph was known to the Times' Advertising Acceptability Department as a responsible person, and, in accepting the letter as sufficient proof of authorization, it followed its established practice. There was testimony that the copy of the advertisement which accompanied the letter listed only the 64 names appearing under the text, and that the statement, "We in the south . . . warmly endorse this appeal," and the list of names thereunder, which included those of the individual petitioners, were subsequently added when the first proof of the advertisement was received. Each of the individual petitioners testified that he had not authorized the use of his name, and that he had been unaware of its use until receipt of respondent's demand for a retraction. The manager of the Advertising Acceptability Department testified that he had approved the advertisement for publica-

tion because he knew nothing to cause him to believe that anything in it was false, and because it bore the endorsement of "a number of people who are well known and whose reputation" he "had no reason to question." Neither he nor anyone else at the Times made an effort to confirm the accuracy of the advertisement, either by checking it against recent Times news stories relating to some of the described events or by any other means.

Alabama law denies a public officer recovery of punitive damages in a libel action brought on account of a publication concerning his official conduct unless he first makes a written demand for a public retraction and the defendant fails or refuses to comply. Alabama Code, Tit. 7, § 914. Respondent served such a demand upon each of the petitioners. None of the individual petitioners responded to the demand, primarily because each took the position that he had not authorized the use of his name on the advertisement, and therefore had not published the statements that respondent alleged had libeled him. The Times did not publish a retraction in response to the demand, but wrote respondent a letter stating, among other things, that "we . . . are somewhat puzzled as to how you think the statements in any way reflect on you," and "you might, if you desire, let us know in what respect you claim that the statements in the advertisement reflect on you." Respondent filed this suit a few days later without answering the letter. The Times did, however, subsequently publish a retraction of the advertisement upon the demand of Governor John Patterson of Alabama, who asserted that the publication charged him with

"grave misconduct and . . . improper actions and omissions as Governor of Alabama and Ex-Officio Chairman of the State Board of Education of Alabama."

When asked to explain why there had been a retraction for the Governor but not for respondent, the Secretary of the Times testified:

"We did that because we didn't want anything that was published by The Times to be a reflection on the State of Alabama, and the Governor was, as far as we could see, the embodiment of the State of Alabama and the proper representative of the State, and, furthermore, we had by that time learned more of the actual facts which the and purported to recite and, finally, the ad did refer to the action of the State authorities and the Board of Education, presumably of which the Governor is the ex-officio chairman. . . ."

On the other hand, he testified that he did not think that "any of the language in there referred to Mr. Sullivan."

The trial judge submitted the case to the jury under instructions that the statements in the advertisement were "libelous per se," and were not privileged, so that petitioners might be held liable if the jury found that they had published the advertisement and that the statements were made "of and concerning" respondent. The jury was instructed that, because the statements were libelous per se, "the law . . . implies legal injury from the bare fact of publication itself," "falsity and malice are presumed," "general damages need not be alleged or proved, but are presumed," and "punitive damages may be awarded by the jury even though the amount of actual damages is neither found nor shown." An award of punitive damages -- as distinguished from "general" damages, which are compensatory in nature -- apparently requires proof of actual malice under Alabama law, and the judge charged that

"mere negligence or carelessness is not evidence of actual malice or malice in fact, and does not justify an award of exemplary or punitive damages."

He refused to charge, however, that the jury must be "convinced" of malice, in the sense of "actual intent" to harm or "gross negligence and recklessness," to make such an award, and he also refused to require that a verdict for respondent differentiate between compensatory and punitive damages. The judge rejected petitioners' contention that his rulings abridged the freedoms of speech and of the press that are guaranteed by the First and Fourteenth Amendments.

In affirming the judgment, the Supreme Court of Alabama sustained the trial judge's rulings and instructions in all respects. 273 Ala. 656, 144 So.2d 25. It held that,

"where the words published tend to injure a person libeled by them in his reputation, profession, trade or business, or charge him with an indictable offense, or tend to bring the individual into public contempt,"

they are "libelous per se"; that "the matter complained of is, under the above doctrine, libelous per se, if it was published of and concerning the plaintiff", and that it was actionable without "proof of pecuniary injury . . . . such injury being implied." Id. at 673, 676, 144 So.2d at 37, 41. It approved the trial court's ruling that the jury could find the statements to have been made "of and concerning" respondent, stating:

"We think it common knowledge that the average person knows that municipal agents, such as police and firemen, and others, are under the control and direction of the city governing body, and, more particularly, under the direction and control of a single commissioner. In measuring the performance or deficiencies of such groups, praise or criticism is usually attached to the official in complete control of the body."

Id. at 674-675, 144 So.2d at 39. In sustaining the trial court's determination that the verdict was not excessive, the court said that malice could be inferred from the Times' "irresponsibility" in printing the advertisement while

"the Times, in its own files, had articles already published which would have demonstrated the falsity of the allegations in the advertisement;"

from the Times' failure to retract for respondent while retracting for the Governor, whereas the falsity of some of the allegations was then known to the Times and "the matter contained in the advertisement was equally false as to both parties", and from the testimony of the Times' Secretary that, apart from the statement that the dining hall was padlocked, he thought the two paragraphs were "substantially correct." Id. at 686-687, 144 So.2d at 50-51. The court reaffirmed a statement in an earlier opinion that "There is no legal measure of damages in cases of this character." Id. at 686, 144 So.2d at 50. It rejected petitioners' constitutional contentions with the brief statements that "The First Amendment of the U.S. Constitution does not protect libelous publications," and "The Fourteenth Amendment is directed against State action, and not private action." Id. at 676, 144 So.2d at 40.

Because of the importance of the constitutional issues involved, we granted the separate petitions for certiorari of the individual petitioners and of the Times. 371 U.S. 946. We reverse the judgment. We hold that the rule of law applied by the Alabama courts is constitutionally deficient for failure to provide the safeguards for freedom of speech and of the press that are required by the First and Fourteenth Amendments in a libel action brought by a public official against critics of his official conduct. We further hold that, under the proper safeguards, the evidence presented in this case is constitutionally insufficient to support the judgment for respondent.

I

We may dispose at the outset of two grounds asserted to insulate the judgment of the Alabama courts from constitutional scrutiny. The first is the proposition relied on by the State Supreme Court -- that "The Fourteenth Amendment is directed against State action, and not private action." That proposition has no application to this case. Although this is a civil lawsuit between private parties, the Alabama courts have applied a state rule of law which petitioners claim to impose invalid restrictions on their constitutional freedoms of speech and press.

....

II

Under Alabama law, as applied in this case, a publication is "libelous per se" if the words "tend to injure a person . . . in his reputation" or to "bring [him] into public contempt"; the trial court stated that the standard was met if the words are such as to "injure him in his public office, or impute misconduct to him in his office, or want of official integrity, or want of fidelity to a public trust. . . ." The jury must find that the words were published "of and concerning" the plaintiff, but, where the plaintiff is a public official, his place in the governmental hierarchy is sufficient evidence to support a finding that his reputation has been affected by statements that reflect upon the agency of which he is in charge. Once "libel per se" has been established, the defendant has no defense as to stated facts unless he can persuade the jury that they were true in all their particulars. Alabama Ride Co. v. Vance, 235 Ala. 263, 178 So. 438 (1938); Johnson Publishing Co. v. Davis, 271 Ala. 474, 494 495, 124 So.2d 441, 457-458 (1960). His privilege of "fair comment" for expressions of opinion depends on the truth of the facts upon which the comment is based. Parsons v. Age-Herald Publishing Co., 181 Ala. 439, 450, 61 So. 345, 350 (1913). Unless he can discharge the burden of proving truth, general damages are presumed, and may be awarded without proof of pecuniary injury. A showing of actual malice is apparently a prerequisite to recovery of punitive damages, and the defendant may, in any event, forestall a punitive award by a retraction meeting the statutory requirements. Good motives and belief in truth do not negate an inference of malice, but are relevant only in mitigation of punitive damages if the jury chooses to accord them weight. Johnson Publishing Co. v. Davis, supra, 271 Ala., at 495, 124 So.2d at 458.

The question before us is whether this rule of liability, as applied to an action brought by a public official against critics of his official conduct, abridges the freedom of speech and of the press that is guaranteed by the First and Fourteenth Amendments.

The First Amendment, said Judge Learned Hand,

"presupposes that right conclusions are more likely to be gathered out of a multitude of tongues than through any kind of authoritative selection. To many, this is, and always will be, folly, but we have staked upon it our all."

... [L]ibel can claim no talismanic immunity from constitutional limitations. It must be measured by standards that satisfy the First Amendment.

The general proposition that freedom of expression upon public questions is secured by the First Amendment has long been settled by our decisions. The constitutional safeguard, we have said, "was fashioned to assure unfettered interchange of ideas for the bringing about of political and social changes desired by the people." Roth v. United States, 354 U. S. 476, 354 U. S. 484.

"The maintenance of the opportunity for free political discussion to the end that government may be responsive to the will of the people and that changes may be obtained by lawful means, an opportunity essential to the security of the Republic, is a fundamental principle of our constitutional system."

United States v. Associated Press, 52 F.Supp. 362, 372 (D.C.S.D.N.Y.1943). Mr. Justice Brandeis, in his concurring opinion in Whitney v. California, 274 U. S. 357, 274 U. S. 375-376, gave the principle its classic formulation:

"Those who won our independence believed . . . that public discussion is a political duty, and that this should be a fundamental principle of the American government. They recognized the risks to which all human institutions are subject. But they knew that order cannot be secured merely

Stromberg v. California, 283 U. S. 359, 283 U. S. 369. "[I]t is a prized American privilege to speak one's mind, although not always with perfect good taste, on all public institutions," Bridges v. California, 314 U. S. 252, 314 U. S. 270, and this opportunity is to be afforded for "vigorous advocacy" no less than "abstract discussion." NAACP v. Button, 371 U. S. 415, 371 U. S. 429.

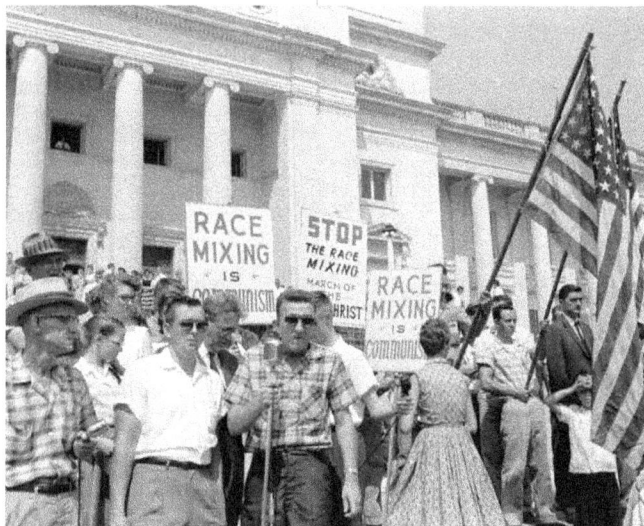

through fear of punishment for its infraction; that it is hazardous to discourage thought, hope and imagination; that fear breeds repression; that repression breeds hate; that hate menaces stable government; that the path of safety lies in the opportunity to discuss freely supposed grievances and proposed remedies, and that the fitting remedy for evil counsels is good ones. Believing in the power of reason as applied through public discussion, they eschewed silence coerced by law -- the argument of force in its worst form. Recognizing the occasional tyrannies of governing majorities, they amended the Constitution so that free speech and assembly should be guaranteed."

Thus, we consider this case against the background of a profound national commitment to the principle that debate on public issues should be uninhibited, robust, and wide-open, and that it may well include vehement, caustic, and sometimes unpleasantly sharp attacks on government and public officials. See Terminiello v. Chicago, 337 U. S. 1, 337 U. S. 4; De Jonge v. Oregon, 299 U. S. 353, 299 U. S. 365. The present advertisement, as an expression of grievance and protest on one of the major public issues of our time, would seem clearly to qualify for the constitutional protection. The question is whether it forfeits that protection by the falsity of some of its factual statements and by its alleged defamation of respondent.

... [E]rroneous statement is inevitable in free debate, and that it must be protected if the freedoms of expression are to have the "breathing space" that they "need . . . to survive," NAACP v. Button, 371 U. S. 415, 371 U. S. 433 ....

...

This is the lesson to be drawn from the great controversy over the Sedition Act of 1798, 1 Stat. 596, which first crystallized a national awareness of the central meaning of the First Amendment. See Levy, Legacy of Suppression (1960), at 258 et seq.; Smith, Freedom's Fetters (1956), at 426, 431, and passim. That statute made it a crime, punishable by a $5,000 fine and five years in prison,

"if any person shall write, print, utter or publish . . . any false, scandalous and malicious writing or writings against the government of the United States, or either house of the Congress . . . or the President . . . with intent to defame . . . or to bring them, or either of them, into contempt or disrepute; or to excite against them, or either or any of them, the hatred of the good people of the United States."

The Act allowed the defendant the defense of truth, and provided that the jury were to be judges both of the law and the facts. Despite these qualifications, the Act was vigorously condemned as unconstitutional in an attack joined in by Jefferson and Madison. In the famous Virginia Resolutions of 1798, the General Assembly of Virginia resolved that it

"doth particularly protest against the palpable and alarming infractions of the Constitution in the two late cases of the 'Alien and Sedition Acts,' passed at the last session of Congress. . . . [The Sedition Act] exercises . . . a power not delegated by the Constitution, but, on the contrary, expressly and positively forbidden by one of the amendments thereto -- a power which, more than any other, ought to produce universal alarm because it is leveled against the right of freely examining public characters and measures, and of free communication among the people thereon, which has ever been justly deemed the only effectual guardian of every other right."

4 Elliot's Debates, supra, pp. 553-554. Madison prepared the Report in support of the protest. His premise was that the Constitution created a form of government under which "The people, not the government, possess the absolute sovereignty." The structure of the government dispersed power in reflection of the people's distrust of concentrated power, and of power itself at all levels. This form of government was "altogether different" from the British form, under which the Crown was sovereign and the people were subjects. "...

The state rule of law is not saved by its allowance of the defense of truth.

...

A rule compelling the critic of official conduct to guarantee the truth of all his factual assertions -- and to do so on pain of libel judgments virtually unlimited in amount -- leads to a comparable "self-censorship." Allowance of the defense of truth, with the burden of proving it on the defendant, does not mean that only false speech will be deterred. Even courts accepting this defense as an adequate safeguard have recognized the difficulties of adducing legal proofs that the alleged libel was true in all its factual particulars. See, e.g., Post Publishing Co. v. Hallam, 59 F. 530, 540 (C.A. 6th Cir. 1893); see also Noel, Defamation of Public Officers and Candidates, 49 Col.L.Rev. 875, 892 (1949). Under such a rule, would-be critics of official conduct may be deterred from voicing their criticism, even though it is believed to be true and even though it is, in fact, true, because of doubt whether it can be proved in court or fear of the expense of having to do so. They tend to make only statements which "steer far wider of the unlawful zone." Speiser v. Randall, supra, 357 U.S. at 357 U. S. 526. The rule thus dampens the vigor and limits the variety of public debate. It is inconsistent with the First and Fourteenth Amendments. The constitutional guarantees require, we think, a federal rule that prohibits a public official from recovering damages for a defamatory falsehood relating to his official conduct unless he proves that the statement was made with "actual malice" -- that is, with knowledge that it was false or with reckless disregard of whether it was false or not.

....

We conclude that such a privilege is required by the First and Fourteenth Amendments.

III

We hold today that the Constitution delimits a State's power to award damages for libel in actions brought by public officials against critics of their official conduct. ....

Since the trial judge did not instruct the jury to differentiate between general and punitive damages, it may be that the verdict was wholly an award of one or the other. But it is impossible to know, in view of the general verdict returned. Because of this uncertainty, the judgment must be reversed and the case remanded. ....

[W]e consider that the proof presented to show actual malice lacks the convincing clarity which the constitutional standard demands, and hence that it would not constitutionally sustain the judgment for respondent under the proper rule of law. The case of the individual petitioners requires little discussion. Even assuming that they could constitutionally be found to have authorized the use of their names on the advertisement, there was no evidence whatever that they were aware of any erroneous statements or were in any way reckless in that regard. The judgment against them is thus without constitutional support.

As to the Times, we similarly conclude that the facts do not support a finding of actual malice. ...

We think the evidence against the Times supports, at most, a finding of negligence in failing to discover the misstatements, and is constitutionally insufficient to show the recklessness that is required for a finding of actual malice.

We also think the evidence was constitutionally defective in another respect: it was incapable of supporting the jury's finding that the allegedly libelous statements were made "of and concerning" respondent. Respondent relies on the words of the advertisement and the testimony of six witnesses to establish a connection between it and himself.

...

But none of [the witnesses] suggested any basis for the belief that respondent himself was attacked in the advertisement beyond the bare fact that he was in overall charge of the Police Department and thus bore official responsibility for police conduct ....

This proposition has disquieting implications for criticism of governmental conduct. For good reason, "no court of last resort in this country has ever held, or even suggested, that prosecutions for libel on government have any place in the American system of jurisprudence."

The present proposition would sidestep this obstacle by transmuting criticism of government, however impersonal it may seem on its face, into personal criticism, and hence potential libel, of the officials of whom the government is composed.

....

Raising as it does the possibility that a good faith critic of government will be penalized for his criticism, the proposition relied on by the Alabama courts strikes at the very center of the constitutionally protected area of free expression. We hold that such a proposition may not constitutionally be utilized to establish that an otherwise impersonal attack on governmental operations was a libel of an official responsible for those operations.

....

The judgment of the Supreme Court of Alabama is reversed, and the case is remanded to that court for further proceedings not inconsistent with this opinion.

Reversed and remanded.

## MR. JUSTICE BLACK, with whom MR. JUSTICE DOUGLAS joins, concurring.

I concur in reversing this half-million-dollar judgment against the New York Times Company and the four individual defendants. In reversing, the Court holds that

"the Constitution delimits a State's power to award damages for libel in actions brought by public officials against critics of their official conduct."

Ante, p. 376 U. S. 283. I base my vote to reverse on the belief that the First and Fourteenth Amendments not merely "delimit" a State's power to award damages to "public officials against critics of their official conduct," but completely prohibit a State from exercising such a power. The Court goes on to hold that a State can subject such critics to damages if "actual malice" can be proved against them. "Malice," even as defined by the Court, is an elusive, abstract concept, hard to prove and hard to disprove. The requirement that malice be proved provides, at best, an evanescent protection for the right critically to discuss public affairs, and certainly does not measure up to the sturdy safeguard embodied in the First Amendment. Unlike the Court, therefore, I vote to reverse exclusively on the ground that the Times and the individual defendants had an absolute, unconditional constitutional right to publish in the Times of the Montgomery agencies and officials. I do not base my vote to reverse on any failure to prove that these individual defendants signed the advertisement or that their criticism of the Police Department was aimed at the plaintiff Sullivan, who was then the Montgomery City Commissioner having supervision of the city's police; for present purposes, I assume these things were proved. Nor is my reason for reversal the size of the half-million-dollar judgment, large as it is. If Alabama has constitutional power to use its civil libel law to impose damages on the press for criticizing the way public officials perform or fail to perform their duties, I know of no provision in the Federal Constitution which either expressly or impliedly bars the State from fixing the amount of damages.

The half-million-dollar verdict does give dramatic proof, however, that state libel laws threaten the very existence of an American press virile enough to publish unpopular views on public affairs and bold enough to criticize the conduct of public officials. The factual background of this case emphasizes the imminence and enormity of that threat. One of the acute and highly emotional issues in this country arises out of efforts of many people, even including some public officials, to continue state-commanded segregation of races in the public schools and other public places despite our several holdings that such a state practice is forbidden by the Fourteenth Amendment. Montgomery is one of the localities in which widespread hostility to desegregation has been manifested. This hostility has sometimes extended itself to persons who favor desegregation, particularly to so-called "outside agitators," a term which can be made to fit papers like the Times, which is published in New York. The scarcity of testimony to show that Commissioner Sullivan suffered any actual damages at all suggests that these feelings of hostility had at least as much to do with rendition of this half-million-dollar verdict as did an appraisal of damages. Viewed realistically, this record lends support to an inference that, instead of being damaged, Commissioner Sullivan's political, social, and financial prestige has likely been enhanced by the Times' publication. Moreover, a second half-million-dollar libel verdict against the Times based on the same advertisement has already been awarded to another Commissioner. There, a jury again gave the full amount claimed. There is no reason to believe that there are not more such huge verdicts lurking just around the corner for the Times or any other newspaper or broadcaster which might dare to criticize public officials. In fact, briefs before us show that, in Alabama, there are now pending eleven libel suits by local and state officials against the Times seeking $5,600,000, and five such suits against the Columbia Broadcasting System seeking $1,700,000.

Moreover, this technique for harassing and punishing a free press -- now that it has been shown to be possible -- is by no means limited to cases with racial overtones; it can be used in other fields where public feelings may make, local as well as out-of-state, newspapers easy prey for libel verdict seekers.

In my opinion, the Federal Constitution has dealt with this deadly danger to the press in the only way possible without leaving the free press open to destruction -- by granting the press an absolute immunity for criticism of the way public officials do their public duty. Compare Barr v. Matteo, 360 U. S. 564. Stopgap measures like those the Court adopts are, in my judgment, not enough. This record certainly does not indicate that any different verdict would have been rendered here whatever the Court had charged the jury about "malice," "truth," "good motives," "justifiable ends," or any other legal formulas which, in theory, would protect the press. Nor does the record indicate that any of these legalistic words would have caused the courts below to set aside or to reduce the half-million-dollar verdict in any amount.

I agree with the Court that the Fourteenth Amendment made the First applicable to the States. This means to me that, since the adoption of the Fourteenth Amendment, a State has no more power than the Federal Government to use a civil libel law or any other law to impose damages for merely discussing public affairs and criticizing public officials. The power of the United States to do that is, in my judgment, precisely nil. Such was the general view held when the First Amendment was adopted, and ever since. Congress never has sought to challenge this viewpoint by passing any civil libel

27

law. It did pass the Sedition Act in 1798, which made it a crime -- "seditious libel" -- to criticize federal officials or the Federal Government. As the Court's opinion correctly points out, however, ante, pp. 376 U. S. 273-276, that Act came to an ignominious end and, by common consent, has generally been treated as having been a wholly unjustifiable and much to be regretted violation of the First Amendment. Since the First Amendment is now made applicable to the States by the Fourteenth, it no more permits the States to impose damages for libel than it does the Federal Government.

We would, I think, more faithfully interpret the First Amendment by holding that, at the very least, it leaves the people and the press free to criticize officials and discuss public affairs with impunity. This Nation of ours elects many of its important officials; so do the States, the municipalities, the counties, and even many precincts. These officials are responsible to the people for the way they perform their duties. While our Court has held that some kinds of speech and writings, such as "obscenity," Roth v. United States, 354 U. S. 476, and "fighting words," Chaplinsky v. New Hampshire, 315 U. S. 568, are not expression within the protection of the First Amendment, freedom to discuss public affairs and public officials is unquestionably, as the Court today holds, the kind of speech the First Amendment was primarily designed to keep within the area of free discussion. To punish the exercise of this right to discuss public affairs or to penalize it through libel judgments is to abridge or shut off discussion of the very kind most needed. This Nation, I suspect, can live in peace without libel suits based on public discussions of public affairs and public officials. But I doubt that a country can live in freedom where its people can be made to suffer physically or financially for criticizing their government, its actions, or its officials.

"For a representative democracy ceases to exist the moment that the public functionaries are by any means absolved from their responsibility to their constituents, and this happens whenever the constituent can be restrained in any manner from speaking, writing, or publishing his opinions upon any public measure, or upon the conduct of those who may advise or execute it. "

An unconditional right to say what one pleases about public affairs is what I consider to be the minimum guarantee of the First Amendment.

I regret that the Court has stopped short of this holding indispensable to preserve our free press from destruction.

**MR. JUSTICE GOLDBERG, with whom MR. JUSTICE DOUGLAS joins, concurring in the result.**

The Court today announces a constitutional standard which prohibits

"a public official from recovering damages for a defamatory falsehood relating to his official conduct unless he proves that the statement was made with 'actual malice' -- that is, with knowledge that it was false or with reckless disregard of whether it was false or not."

Ante at 376 U. S. 279-280. The Court thus rules that the Constitution gives citizens and newspapers a "conditional privilege" immunizing nonmalicious misstatements of fact regarding the official conduct of a government officer. The impressive array of history and precedent marshaled by the Court, however, confirms my belief that the Constitution affords greater protection than that provided by the Court's standard to citizen and press in exercising the right of public criticism.

In my view, the First and Fourteenth Amendments to the Constitution afford to the citizen and to the press an absolute, unconditional privilege to criticize official conduct despite the harm which may flow from excesses and abuses. The prized American right "to speak one's mind," cf. Bridges v California, 314 U. S. 252, 314 U. S. 270, about public officials and affairs needs "breathing space to survive," NAACP v. Button, 371 U. S. 415, 371 U. S. 433. The right should not depend upon a probing by the jury of the motivation of the citizen or press. The theory of our Constitution is that every citizen may speak his mind and every newspaper express its view on matters of public concern, and may not be barred from speaking or publishing because those in control of government think that what is said or written is unwise, unfair, false, or malicious. In a democratic society, one who assumes to act for the citizens in an executive, legislative, or judicial capacity must expect that his official acts will be commented upon and criticized. Such criticism cannot, in my opinion, be muzzled or deterred by the courts at the instance of public officials under the label of libel.

It has been recognized that "prosecutions for libel on government have [no] place in the American system of jurisprudence." City of Chicago v. Tribune Co., 307 Ill. 595, 601, 139 N.E. 86, 88. I fully agree. Government, however, is not an abstraction; it is made up of individuals -- of governors responsible to the governed. In a democratic society, where men are free by ballots to remove those in power, any statement critical of governmental action is necessarily "of and concerning" the governors, and any statement critical of the governors' official conduct is necessarily "of and concerning" the government. If the rule that libel on government has no place in our Constitution is to have real meaning, then libel on the official conduct of the governors likewise can have no place in our Constitution.

We must recognize that we are writing upon a clean slate. As the Court notes, although there have been "statements of this Court to the effect that the Constitution does not protect libelous publications . . . , [n]one of the cases sustained the use of libel laws to impose sanctions upon expression critical of the official conduct of public officials."

Ante at 376 U. S. 268. We should be particularly careful, therefore, adequately to protect the liberties which are embodied in the First and Fourteenth Amendments. It may be urged that deliberately and maliciously false statements have no conceivable value as free speech. That argument, however, is not responsive to the real issue presented by this case, which is whether that freedom of speech which all agree is constitutionally protected can be effectively safeguarded by a rule allowing the imposition of liability upon a jury's evaluation of the speaker's state of mind. If individual citizens may be held liable in damages for strong words, which a jury finds false and maliciously motivated, there can be little doubt that public debate and advocacy will be constrained. And if newspapers, publishing advertisements dealing with public issues, thereby risk liability, there can also be little doubt that the ability of minority groups to secure publication of their views on public affairs and to seek support for their causes will be greatly diminished. Cf. Farmers Educational & Coop. Union v. WDAY, Inc., 360 U. S. 525, 360 U. S. 530. The opinion of the Court conclusively demonstrates the chilling effect of the Alabama libel laws on First Amendment freedoms in the area of race relations. The American Colonists were not willing, nor should we be, to take the risk that "[m]en who injure and oppress the people under their administration [and] provoke them to cry out and complain" will also be empowered to "make that very complaint the foundation for new oppressions and prosecutions." The Trial of John Peter Zenger, 17 Howell's St. Tr. 675, 721-722 (1735) (argument of counsel to the jury). To impose liability for critical, albeit erroneous or even malicious, comments on official conduct would effectively resurrect "the obsolete doctrine that the governed must not criticize their governors." Cf. Sweeney v. Patterson, 76 U.S.App.D.C. 23, 24, 128 F.2d 457, 458.

Our national experience teaches that repressions breed hate, and "that hate menaces stable government." Whitney v. California, 274 U. S. 357,

274 U. S. 375 (Brandeis, J., concurring). We should be ever mindful of the wise counsel of Chief Justice Hughes:

"[I]mperative is the need to preserve inviolate the constitutional rights of free speech, free press and free assembly in order to maintain the opportunity for free political discussion, to the end that government may be responsive to the will of the people and that changes, if desired, may be obtained by peaceful means. Therein lies the security of the Republic, the very foundation of constitutional government."

De Jonge v. Oregon, 299 U. S. 353, 299 U. S. 365.

This is not to say that the Constitution protects defamatory statements directed against the private conduct of a public official or private citizen. Freedom of press and of speech insures that government will respond to the will of the people, and that changes may be obtained by peaceful means. Purely private defamation has little to do with the political ends of a self-governing society. The imposition of liability for private defamation does not abridge the freedom of public speech or any other freedom protected by the First Amendment. This, of course, cannot be said

"where public officials are concerned, or where public matters are involved. . . . [O]ne main function of the First Amendment is to ensure ample opportunity for the people to determine and resolve public issues. Where public matters are involved, the doubts should be resolved in favor of freedom of expression, rather than against it."

Douglas, The Right of the People (1958), p. 41.

In many jurisdictions, legislators, judges and executive officers are clothed with absolute immunity against liability for defamatory words uttered in the discharge of their public duties. See, e.g., Barr v. Matteo, 360 U. S. 564; City of Chicago v. Tribune Co., 307 Ill., at 610, 139 N.E. at 91. Judge Learned Hand ably summarized the policies underlying the rule:

"It does indeed go without saying that an official who is, in fact, guilty of using his powers to vent his spleen upon others, or for any other personal motive not connected with the public good, should not escape liability for the injuries he may so cause; and, if it were possible in practice to confine such complaints to the guilty, it would be monstrous to deny recovery. The justification for doing so is that it is impossible to know whether the claim is well founded until the case has been tried, and that to submit all officials, the innocent as well as the guilty, to the burden of a trial and to the inevitable danger of its outcome would dampen the ardor of all but the most resolute, or the most irresponsible, in the unflinching discharge of their duties. Again and again, the public interest calls for action which may turn out to be founded on a mistake, in the face of which an official may later find himself hard put to it to satisfy a jury of his good faith. There must indeed be means of punishing public officers who have been truant to their duties; but that is quite another matter from exposing such as have been honestly mistaken to suit by anyone who has suffered from their errors. As is so often the case, the answer must be found in a balance between the evils inevitable in either alternative. In this instance, it has been thought in the end better to leave unredressed the wrongs done by dishonest officers than to subject those who try to do their duty to the constant dread of retaliation. . . ."

"The decisions have, indeed, always imposed as a limitation upon the immunity that the official's act must have been within the scope of his powers, and it can be argued that official powers, since they exist only for the public good, never cover occasions where the public good is not their aim, and hence that to exercise a power dishonestly is necessarily to overstep its bounds. A moment's reflection shows, however, that that cannot be the meaning of the limitation without defeating the whole doctrine. What is meant by saying that the officer must be acting within his power cannot be more than that the occasion must be such as would have justified the act, if he had been using his power for any of the purposes on whose account it was vested in him. . . ."

Gregoire v. Biddle, 177 F.2d 579, 581.

If the government official should be immune from libel actions, so that his ardor to serve the public will not be dampened and "fearless, vigorous, and effective administration of policies of government" not be inhibited, Barr v. Matteo, supra, at 360 U. S. 571, then the citizen and the press should likewise be immune from libel actions for their criticism of official conduct. Their ardor as citizens will thus not be dampened, and they will be free "to applaud or to criticize the way public employees do their jobs, from the least to the most important." If liability can attach to political criticism because it damages the reputation of a public official as a public official, then no critical citizen can safely utter anything but faint praise about the government or its officials. The vigorous criticism by press and citizen of the conduct of the government of the day by the officials of the day will soon yield to silence if officials in control of government agencies, instead of answering criticisms, can resort to friendly juries to forestall criticism of their official conduct.

The conclusion that the Constitution affords the citizen and the press an absolute privilege for criticism of official conduct does not leave the public official without defenses against unsubstantiated opinions or deliberate misstatements.

"Under our system of government, counterargument and education are the weapons available to expose these matters, not abridgment . . . of free speech. . . ."

Wood v. Georgia, 370 U. S. 375, 370 U. S. 389. The public official certainly has equal, if not greater, access than most private citizens to media of communication. In any event, despite the possibility that some excesses and abuses may go unremedied, we must recognize that

"the people of this nation have ordained, in the light of history, that, in spite of the probability of excesses and abuses, [certain] liberties are, in the long view, essential to enlightened opinion and right conduct on the part of the citizens of a democracy."

Cantwell v. Connecticut, 310 U. S. 296, 310 U. S. 310. As Mr. Justice Brandeis correctly observed, "sunlight is the most powerful of all disinfectants."

For these reasons, I strongly believe that the Constitution accords citizens and press an unconditional freedom to criticize official conduct. It necessarily follows that, in a case such as this, where all agree that the allegedly defamatory statements related to official conduct, the judgments for libel cannot constitutionally be sustained.

# Milkovich v. Lorain Journal Co. (1990)

U.S. Supreme Court

497 U.S. 1 (1990)

Decided: June 21, 1990

Decision: 7 votes for Milkovich, 2 vote(s) against

**Chief Justice REHNQUIST delivered the opinion of the Court.**

Respondent J. Theodore Diadiun authored an article in an Ohio newspaper implying that petitioner Michael Milkovich, a local high school wrestling coach, lied under oath in a judicial proceeding about an incident involving petitioner and his team which occurred at a wrestling match. Petitioner sued Diadiun and the newspaper for libel, and the Ohio Court of Appeals affirmed a lower court entry of summary judgment against petitioner. This judgment was based in part on the grounds that the article constituted an "opinion" protected from the reach of state defamation law by the First Amendment to the United States Constitution. We hold that the First Amendment does not prohibit the application of Ohio's libel laws to the alleged defamations contained in the article.

...

The column bore the heading "Maple beat the law with the 'big lie,'" beneath which appeared Diadiun's photograph and the words "TD Says." The carryover page headline announced ". . . Diadiun says Maple told a lie." The column contained the following passages:

> . . . a lesson was learned (or relearned) yesterday by the student body of Maple Heights High School, and by anyone who attended the Maple-Mentor wrestling meet of last Feb. 8.
>
> A lesson which, sadly, in view of the events of the past year, is well they learned early.
>
> It is simply this: If you get in a jam, lie your way out. [p5]
>
> If you're successful enough, and powerful enough, and can sound sincere enough, you stand an excellent chance of making the lie stand up, regardless of what really happened.
>
> The teachers responsible were mainly Maple wrestling coach, Mike Milkovich, and former superintendent of schools, H. Donald Scott.
>
> * * * *
>
> Anyone who attended the meet, whether he be from Maple Heights, Mentor, or impartial observer, knows in his heart that Milkovich and Scott lied at the hearing after each having given his solemn oath to tell the truth.

But they got away with it.

Is that the kind of lesson we want our young people learning from their high school administrators and coaches?

I think not.

Thus, where a statement of "opinion" on a matter of public concern reasonably implies false and defamatory facts regarding public figures or officials, those individuals must show that such statements were made with knowledge of their false implications or with reckless disregard of their truth. Similarly, where such a statement involves a private figure on a matter of public concern, a plaintiff must show that the false connotations were made with some level of fault [p21] as required by Gertz. ...

We are not persuaded that, in addition to these protections, an additional separate constitutional privilege for "opinion" is required to ensure the freedom of expression guaranteed by the First Amendment. The dispositive question in the present case then becomes whether or not a reasonable factfinder could conclude that the statements in the Diadiun column imply an assertion that petitioner Milkovich perjured himself in a judicial proceeding. We think this question must be answered in the affirmative. As the Ohio Supreme Court itself observed,

> the clear impact in some nine sentences and a caption is that [Milkovich] "lied at the hearing after . . . having given his solemn oath to tell the truth."

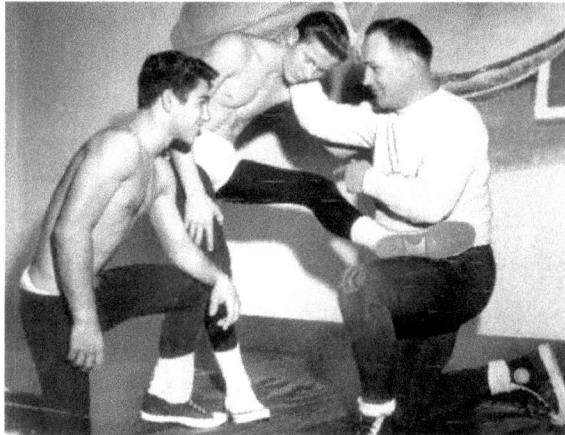

.... This is not the sort of loose, figurative or hyperbolic language which would negate the impression that the writer was seriously maintaining petitioner committed the crime of perjury. Nor does the general tenor of the article negate this impression.

We also think the connotation that petitioner committed perjury is sufficiently factual to be susceptible of being proved true or false. A determination of whether petitioner lied in this instance can be made on a core of objective evidence by comparing, inter alia, petitioner's testimony before the OHSAA board with his subsequent testimony before the trial court. As the Scott court noted regarding the plaintiff in that case, whether or not H. Don Scott did indeed perjure himself is certainly verifiable by a perjury action with evidence adduced from the transcripts and witnesses present at the hearing. Unlike a subjective assertion, the averred defamatory language is an articulation of an objectively verifiable event.

... So too with petitioner Milkovich.

The numerous decisions discussed above establishing First Amendment protection for defendants in defamation actions surely demonstrate the Court's recognition of the Amendment's vital guarantee of free and uninhibited discussion of public issues. But there is also another side to the equation; we have regularly acknowledged the "important social values which underlie the law of defamation," and recognize that "[s]ociety has a pervasive and strong interest in preventing and redressing attacks upon reputation." Rosenblatt v. Baer, 383 U.S. 75, 86 (1966). Justice Stewart in that case put it with his customary clarity:

The right of a man to the protection of his own reputation from unjustified invasion and wrongful hurt reflects no more than our basic concept of the essential dignity and worth of every human being -- a concept at the root of any decent system of ordered liberty.

* * * *

The destruction that defamatory falsehood can bring is, to be sure, often beyond the capacity of the law to redeem. [p23] Yet, imperfect though it is, an action for damages is the only hope for vindication or redress the law gives to a man whose reputation has been falsely dishonored.

Id. at 92-93 (Stewart, J., concurring).

We believe our decision in the present case holds the balance true. The judgment of the Ohio Court of Appeals is reversed, and the case remanded for further proceedings not inconsistent with this opinion.

### Summary of the Court's holding in Milkovich

*1. The First Amendment does not require a separate "opinion" privilege limiting the application of state defamation laws. ... [because] where a media defendant is involved, a statement on matters of public concern must be provable as false before liability can be assessed, thus ensuring full constitutional protection for a statement of opinion having no provably false factual connotation. Next, statements that cannot reasonably be interpreted as stating actual facts about an individual are protected, ... thus assuring that public debate will not suffer for lack of "imaginative expression" or the "rhetorical hyperbole" which has traditionally added much to the discourse of this Nation.*

*2. A reasonable factfinder could conclude that the statements in the Diadiun column imply an assertion that Milkovich perjured himself in a judicial proceeding. The article did not use the sort of loose, figurative, or hyperbolic language that would negate the impression that Diadiun was seriously maintaining Milkovich committed perjury. Nor does the article's general tenor negate this impression. In addition, the connotation that Milkovich committed perjury is sufficiently factual that it is susceptible of being proved true or false by comparing, his testimony before the OHSAA board with his subsequent testimony before the trial court.*

IN SHAKESPEARE'S OTHELLO, IAGO SAYS TO
OTHELLO: (ACT III, SCENE 3)

GOOD NAME IN MAN AND WOMAN, DEAR MY LORD.
IS THE IMMEDIATE JEWEL OF THEIR SOULS.
WHO STEALS MY PURSE STEALS TRASH;
'TIS SOMETHING, NOTHING;
'TWAS MINE, 'TIS HIS, AND HAS BEEN SLAVE TO THOUSANDS;
BUT HE THAT FILCHES FROM ME MY GOOD NAME
ROBS ME OF THAT WHICH NOT ENRICHES HIM,
AND MAKES ME POOR INDEED.

# CHAPTER 3

# Public and private

Gertz v. Robert Welch, Inc. (1974)

U.S. Supreme Court

418 U.S. 323

Decided: June 25, 1974

Stewart  Marshall  Blackmun  Powell  Rehnquist  Burger  Douglas  Brennan  White

Decision: 5 votes for Gertz, 4 vote(s) against

**MR. JUSTICE POWELL delivered the opinion of the Court.**

This Court has struggled for nearly a decade to define the proper accommodation between the law of defamation and the freedoms of speech and press protected by the First Amendment. With this decision we return to that effort. We granted certiorari to reconsider the extent of a publisher's constitutional privilege against liability for defamation of a private citizen. 410 U.S. 925 (1973).

I

In 1968, a Chicago policeman named Nuccio shot and killed a youth named Nelson. The state authorities prosecuted Nuccio for the homicide and ultimately obtained a conviction for murder in the second degree. The Nelson family retained petitioner Elmer Gertz, a reputable attorney, to represent them in civil litigation against Nuccio.

Respondent publishes American Opinion, a monthly outlet for the views of the John Birch Society. Early in the 1960's, the magazine began to warn of a nationwide conspiracy to discredit local law enforcement agencies and create in their stead a national police force capable of supporting a Communist dictatorship. As part of the continuing effort to alert the public to this assumed danger, the managing editor of American Opinion commissioned an article on the murder trial of Officer Nuccio. For this purpose, he engaged a regular contributor to the magazine. In March, 1969, respondent published the resulting article under the title "FRAME-UP: Richard Nuccio And The War On Police." The article purports to demonstrate that the testimony against Nuccio at his criminal trial was false, and that his prosecution was part of the Communist campaign against the police.

In his capacity as counsel for the Nelson family in the civil litigation, petitioner attended the coroner's inquest into the boy's death and initiated actions for damages, but he neither discussed Officer Nuccio with the press nor played any part in the criminal proceeding. Notwithstanding petitioner's remote connection with the prosecution of Nuccio, respondent's magazine portrayed him as an architect of the "frame-up." According to the article, the police file on petitioner took "a big, Irish cop to lift." The article stated that petitioner had been an official of the

Marxist League for Industrial Democracy, originally known as the Intercollegiate Socialist Society, which has advocated the violent seizure of our government.

It labeled Gertz a "Leninist" and a "Communist-fronter." It also stated that Gertz had been an officer of the National Lawyers Guild, described as a Communist organization that "probably did more than any other outfit to plan the Communist attack on the Chicago police during the 1968 Democratic Convention."

These statements contained serious inaccuracies. The implication that petitioner had a criminal record was false. Petitioner had been a member and officer of the National Lawyers Guild some 15 years earlier, but there was no evidence that he or that organization had taken any part in planning the 1968 demonstrations in Chicago. There was also no basis for the charge that petitioner was a "Leninist" or a "Communist-fronter." And he had never been a member of the "Marxist League for Industrial Democracy" or the "Intercollegiate Socialist Society." [p327]

The managing editor of American Opinion made no effort to verify or substantiate the charges against petitioner. Instead, he appended an editorial introduction stating that the author had "conducted extensive research into the Richard Nuccio Case." And he included in the article a photograph of petitioner and wrote the caption that appeared under it: "Elmer Gertz of Red Guild harasses Nuccio." Respondent placed the issue of American Opinion containing the article on sale at newsstands throughout the country and distributed reprints of the article on the streets of Chicago.

*A Chicago Legal Legend*

Sadiya Arbani
*Jamieson School, Chicago*

**B**orn in Chicago in 1906, Elmer Gertz enjoyed a law career that spanned over seven decades. Growing up in the big city, a "famous son" of Maxwell Street, Gertz dealt with nearly every aspect of his profession including corporate cases and murders, the most notable being Jack Ruby and Nathan Leopold. He is best known for his long career as a defender of civil liberties.

*Elmer Gertz gained fame when he won parole for Nathan Leopold, who was convicted of slaying fourteen-year-old Bobby Franks.*

Gertz was born in the area of Roosevelt Road and Blue Island on the city's west side. Of Lithuanian heritage, his parents, Morris and Grace, settled in the area that was at the time the center of Jewish and immigrant culture in the city. He later became a champion for the preservation of the area.

After his mother died when he was ten, Gertz and a younger brother were shipped off to an orphanage in Cleveland. After returning to Chicago in 1920, he attended Crane Technical High School. Acquaintances at that time included Meyer Levin (who later opposed Gertz in a famous court case), Leo Rosten, and Leo Lerner (founder of the Lerner newspaper chain). He went on to the University of Chicago as an undergraduate and then attended law school there. At the university he was exposed to various races and ethnic groups and career aspirations. Often, he and fellow students met in private homes to discuss brotherhood and civil rights because it was not possible for all of his colleagues to dine in designated "white" restaurants.

His years at the University of Chicago Law School helped shape the philosophy that ultimately led to his preference for taking up unpopular cases and protecting the underdog. After graduating, one of his first jobs was with the law firm of Jacob Arvey, where he worked for fourteen years. In the 1940s he became active in the fair-housing movement and in championing the admission of blacks into the local bar association.

In the late 1950s Gertz became a national figure when he won parole (arguing against his old friend Meyer Levin) for Nathan Leopold, a University of Chicago law student convicted with fellow student Richard Loeb in the 1924 slaying of fourteen-year-old Bobby Franks. Leopold was successfully released from prison after having served thirty-four years for his part in the murder. Leopold and Loeb had originally been defended by Gertz's hero, Clarence Darrow, whose twelve-hour plea for the lives of the teenagers from two prominent Chicago families brought tears to the eyes of the presiding judge. At the time, the case was called "the trial of the century." Upon Leopold's release, Gertz walked with him through the gates of Stateville prison in 1958.

Petitioner filed a diversity action for libel in the United States District Court for the Northern District of Illinois. He claimed that the falsehoods published by respondent injured his reputation as a lawyer and a citizen. Before filing an answer, respondent moved to dismiss the complaint for failure to state a claim upon which relief could be granted, apparently on the ground that petitioner failed to allege special damages. But the court ruled that statements contained in the article constituted libel per se under Illinois law, and that, consequently, petitioner need not plead special damages. 306 F.Supp. 310 (1969).

After answering the complaint, respondent filed a pretrial motion for summary judgment, claiming a constitutional privilege against liability for defamation. It asserted that petitioner was a public official or a public figure, and that the article concerned an issue of public interest concern. For these reasons, respondent argued, it was entitled to invoke the privilege enunciated in New York Times Co. v. Sullivan, 376 U.S. 254 (1964). Under this rule, respondent would escape liability unless petitioner could prove publication of defamatory falsehood "with 'actual malice' -- that is, with knowledge that it was false or with reckless disregard of whether it was false or not."

## III

We begin with the common ground. Under the First Amendment, there is no such thing as a false idea. However pernicious an opinion may seem, we depend for its correction not on the conscience of judges and juries, but on the competition of other ideas. But there is no constitutional value in false statements of fact. Neither the intentional lie nor the careless error materially advances society's interest in "uninhibited, robust, and wide-open" debate on public issues. New York Times Co. v. Sullivan, 376 U.S. at 270. They belong to that category of utterances which

are no essential part of any exposition of ideas, and are of such slight social value as a step to truth that any benefit that may be derived from them is clearly outweighed by the social interest in order and morality.

Chaplinsky v. New Hampshire, 315 U.S. 568, 572 (1942).

Although the erroneous statement of fact is not worthy of constitutional protection, it is nevertheless inevitable in free debate. As James Madison pointed out in the Report on the Virginia Resolutions of 1798: "Some degree of abuse is inseparable from the proper use of every thing; and in no instance is this more true than in that of the press." 4 J. Elliot, Debates on the Federal Constitution of 1787, p. 571 (1876). And punishment of error runs the risk of inducing a cautious and restrictive exercise of the constitutionally guaranteed freedoms of speech and press. Our decisions recognize that a rule of strict liability that compels a publisher or broadcaster to guarantee the accuracy of his factual assertions may lead to intolerable self-censorship. Allowing the media to avoid liability only by proving the truth of all injurious statements does not accord adequate protection to First Amendment liberties. As the Court stated in New York Times Co. v. Sullivan, supra, at 279:

Allowance of the defense of truth, with the burden of proving it on the defendant, does not mean that only false speech will be deterred.

The First Amendment requires that we protect some falsehood in order to protect speech that matters.

The need to avoid self-censorship by the news media is, however, not the only societal value at issue. If it were, this Court would have embraced long ago the view that publishers and broadcasters enjoy an unconditional and indefeasible immunity from liability for defamation. See New York Times Co. v. Sullivan, supra, at 293 (Black, J., concurring); Garrison v. Louisiana, 379 U.S. at 80 (DOUGLAS, J., concurring); Curtis Publishing Co. v. Butts, 388 U.S. at 170 (opinion of Black, J.). Such a rule would, indeed, obviate the fear that the prospect of civil liability for injurious falsehood might dissuade a timorous press from the effective exercise of First Amendment freedoms. Yet absolute protection for the communications media requires a total sacrifice of the competing value served by the law of defamation.

The legitimate state interest underlying the law of libel is the compensation of individuals for the harm inflicted on them by defamatory falsehood. We would not lightly require the State to abandon this purpose, for, as MR. JUSTICE STEWART has reminded us, the individual's right to the protection of his own good name

reflects no more than our basic concept of the essential dignity and worth of every human being -- a concept at the root of any decent system of ordered liberty. The protection of private personality, like the protection of life itself, is left primarily to the individual States under the Ninth and Tenth Amendments. But this does not mean that the right is entitled to any less recognition by this Court as a basic of our constitutional system.

Rosenblatt v. Baer, 383 U.S. 75, 92 (1966) (concurring opinion).

Some tension necessarily exists between the need for a vigorous and uninhibited press and the legitimate interest in redressing wrongful injury. As Mr. Justice Harlan stated, some antithesis between freedom of speech and press and libel actions persists, for libel remains premised on the content of speech and limits the freedom of the publisher to express certain sentiments, at least without guaranteeing legal proof of their substantial accuracy.

Curtis Publishing Co. v. Butts, supra, at 152. In our continuing effort to define the proper accommodation between these competing concerns, we have been especially anxious to assure to the freedoms of speech and press that "breathing space" essential to their fruitful exercise. NAACP v. Button, 371 U.S. 415, 433 (1963). To that end, this Court has extended a measure of strategic protection to defamatory falsehood.

The New York Times standard defines the level of constitutional protection appropriate to the context of defamation of a public person. Those who, by reason of the notoriety of their achievements or the vigor and success with which they seek the public's attention, are properly classed as public figures and those who hold governmental office may recover for injury to reputation only on clear and convincing proof that the defamatory falsehood was made with knowledge of its falsity or with reckless disregard for the truth. This standard administers an extremely powerful antidote to the inducement to media self-censorship of the common law rule of strict liability for libel and slander. And it exacts a correspondingly high price from the victims of defamatory falsehood. Plainly, many deserving plaintiffs, including some intentionally subjected to injury, will be unable to surmount the barrier of the New York Times test. Despite this substantial abridgment of the state law right to compensation for wrongful hurt to one's reputation, the Court has concluded that the protection of the New York Times privilege should be available to publishers and broadcasters of defamatory falsehood concerning public officials and public figures. New York Times Co. v. Sullivan, supra; Curtis Publishing Co. v. Butts, supra. We think that these decisions are correct, but we do not find their holdings justified solely by reference to the interest of the press and broadcast media in immunity from liability. Rather, we believe that the New York Times rule states an accommodation between this concern and the lim-

ited state interest present in the context of libel actions brought by public persons. For the reasons stated below, we conclude that the state interest in compensating injury to the reputation of private individuals requires that a different rule should obtain with respect to them.

Theoretically, of course, the balance between the needs of the press and the individual's claim to compensation for wrongful injury might be struck on a case-by-case basis. As Mr. Justice Harlan hypothesized,

it might seem, purely as an abstract matter, that the most utilitarian approach would be to scrutinize carefully every jury verdict in every libel case, in order to ascertain whether the final judgment leaves fully protected whatever First Amendment values transcend the legitimate state interest in protecting the particular plaintiff who prevailed.

Rosenbloom v. Metromedia, Inc., 403 U.S. at 63 (footnote omitted). But this approach would lead to unpredictable results and uncertain expectations, and it could render our duty to supervise the lower courts unmanageable. Because an ad hoc resolution of the competing interests at stake in each particular case is not feasible, we must lay down broad rules of general application: such rules necessarily treat alike various cases involving differences as well as similarities. Thus, it is often true that not all of the considerations which justify adoption of a given rule will obtain in each particular case decided under its authority.

With that caveat, we have no difficulty in distinguishing among defamation plaintiffs. The first remedy of any victim of defamation is self-help -- using available opportunities to contradict the lie or correct the error, and thereby to minimize its adverse impact on reputation. Public officials and public figures usually enjoy significantly greater access to the channels of effective communication, and hence have a more realistic opportunity to counteract false statements than private individuals normally enjoy.{ 418 U.S. 323fn9|9} Private individuals are therefore more vulnerable to injury, and the state interest in protecting them is correspondingly greater.

More important than the likelihood that private individuals will lack effective opportunities for rebuttal, there is a compelling normative consideration underlying the distinction between public and private defamation plaintiffs. An individual who decides to seek governmental office must accept certain necessary consequences of that involvement in public affairs. He runs the risk of closer public scrutiny than might otherwise be the case. And society's interest in the officers of government is not strictly limited to the formal discharge of official duties. As the Court pointed out in Garrison v. Louisiana, 379 U.S. at 77, the public's interest extends to

anything which might touch on an official's fitness for office. . . . Few personal attributes are more germane to fitness for office than dishonesty, malfeasance, or improper motivation, even though these characteristics may also affect the official's private character.

Those classed as public figures stand in a similar position. Hypothetically, it may be possible for someone to become a public figure through no purposeful action of his own, but the instances of truly involuntary public figures must be exceedingly rare. For the most part, those who attain this status have assumed roles of especial prominence in the affairs of society. Some occupy positions of such persuasive power and influence that they are deemed public figures for all purposes. More commonly, those classed as public figures have thrust themselves to the forefront of particular public controversies in order to influence the resolution of the issues involved. In either event, they invite attention and comment.

Even if the foregoing generalities do not obtain in every instance, the communications media are entitled to act on the assumption that public officials and public figures have voluntarily exposed themselves to increased risk of injury from defamatory falsehood concerning them. No such assumption is justified with respect to a private individual. He has not accepted public office or assumed an "influential role in ordering society." Curtis Publishing Co. v. Butts, 388 U.S. at 164 (Warren,

C.J., concurring in result). He has relinquished no part of his interest in the protection of his own good name, and consequently he has a more compelling call on the courts for redress of injury inflicted by defamatory falsehood. Thus, private individuals are not only more vulnerable to injury than public officials and public figures; they are also more deserving of recovery.

For these reasons, we conclude that the States should retain substantial latitude in their efforts to enforce a legal remedy for defamatory falsehood injurious to the reputation of a private individual. The extension of the New York Times test proposed by the Rosenbloom plurality would abridge this legitimate state interest to a degree that we find unacceptable. And it would occasion the additional difficulty of forcing state and federal judges to decide on an ad hoc basis which publications address issues of "general or public interest" and which do not -- to determine, in the words of MR. JUSTICE MARSHALL, "what information is relevant to self-government." Rosenbloom v. Metromedia, Inc., 403 U.S. at 79. We doubt the wisdom of committing this task to the conscience of judges. Nor does the Constitution require us to draw so thin a line between the drastic alternatives of the New York Times privilege and the common law of strict liability for defamatory error. The "public or general interest" test for determining the applicability of the New York Times standard to private defamation actions inadequately serves both of the competing values at stake. On the one hand, a private individual whose reputation is injured by defamatory falsehood that does concern an issue of public or general interest has no recourse unless he can meet the rigorous requirements of New York Times. This is true despite the factors that distinguish the state interest in compensating private individuals from the analogous interest involved in the context of public persons. On the other hand, a publisher or broadcaster of a defamatory error which a court deems unrelated to an issue of public or general interest may be held liable in damages even if it took every reasonable precaution to ensure the accuracy of its assertions. And liability may far exceed compensation for any actual injury to the plaintiff, for the jury may be permitted to presume damages without proof of loss and even to award punitive damages.

We hold that, so long as they do not impose liability without fault, the States may define for themselves the appropriate standard of liability for a publisher or broadcaster of defamatory falsehood injurious to a private individual. This approach provides a more equitable boundary between the competing concerns involved here. It recognizes the strength of the legitimate state interest in compensating private individuals for wrongful injury to reputation, yet shields the press and broadcast media from the rigors of strict liability for defamation. At least this conclusion obtains where, as here, the substance of the defamatory statement "makes substantial danger to reputation apparent." [n11] This phrase places in perspective the conclusion we announce today. Our inquiry would involve considerations somewhat different from those discussed above if a State purported to condition civil liability on a factual misstatement whose content did not warn a reasonably prudent editor or broadcaster of its defamatory potential. Cf. Time, Inc. v. Hill, 385 U.S. 374 (1967). Such a case is not now before us, and we intimate no view as to its proper resolution.

IV

Our accommodation of the competing values at stake in defamation suits by private individuals allows the States to impose liability on the publisher or broadcaster of defamatory falsehood on a less demanding showing than that required by New York Times. This conclusion is not based on a belief that the considerations which prompted the adoption of the New York Times privilege for defamation of public officials and its extension to public figures are wholly inapplicable to the context of private individuals. Rather, we endorse this approach in recognition of the strong and legitimate state interest in compensating private individuals for injury to reputation. But this countervailing state interest extends no further than compensation for actual injury. For the reasons stated below, we hold that the States may not permit recovery of

presumed or punitive damages, at least when liability is not based on a showing of knowledge of falsity or reckless disregard for the truth.

The common law of defamation is an oddity of tort law, for it allows recovery of purportedly compensatory damages without evidence of actual loss. Under the traditional rules pertaining to actions for libel, the existence of injury is presumed from the fact of publication. Juries may award substantial sums as compensation for supposed damage to reputation without any proof that such harm actually occurred. The largely uncontrolled discretion of juries to award damages where there is no loss unnecessarily compounds the potential of any system of liability for defamatory falsehood to inhibit the vigorous exercise of First Amendment freedoms. Additionally, the doctrine of presumed damages invites juries to punish unpopular opinion, rather than to compensate individuals for injury sustained by the publication of a false fact. More to the point, the States have no substantial interest in securing for plaintiffs such as this petitioner gratuitous awards of money damages far in excess of any actual injury.

We would not, of course, invalidate state law simply because we doubt its wisdom, but here we are attempting to reconcile state law with a competing interest grounded in the constitutional command of the First Amendment. It is therefore appropriate to require that state remedies for defamatory falsehood reach no farther than is necessary to protect the legitimate interest involved. It is necessary to restrict defamation plaintiffs who do not prove knowledge of falsity or reckless disregard for the truth to compensation for actual injury. We need not define "actual injury," as trial courts have wide experience in framing appropriate jury instructions in tort actions. Suffice it to say that actual injury is not limited to out-of-pocket loss. Indeed, the more customary types of actual harm inflicted by defamatory falsehood include impairment of reputation and standing in the community, personal humiliation, and mental anguish and suffering. Of course, juries must be limited by appropriate instructions, and all awards must be supported by competent evidence concerning the injury, although there need be no evidence which assigns an actual dollar value to the injury.

We also find no justification for allowing awards of punitive damages against publishers and broadcasters held liable under state-defined standards of liability for defamation. In most jurisdictions jury discretion over the amounts awarded is limited only by the gentle rule that they not be excessive. Consequently, juries assess punitive damages in wholly unpredictable amounts bearing no necessary relation to the actual harm caused. And they remain free to use their discretion selectively to punish expressions of unpopular views. Like the doctrine of presumed damages, jury discretion to award punitive damages unnecessarily exacerbates the danger of media self-censorship, but, unlike the former rule, punitive damages are wholly irrelevant to the state interest that justifies a negligence standard for private defamation actions. They are not compensation for injury. Instead, they are private fines levied by civil juries to punish reprehensible conduct and to deter its future occurrence. In short, the private defamation plaintiff who establishes liability under a less demanding standard than that stated by New York Times may recover only such damages as are sufficient to compensate him for actual injury.

V

Notwithstanding our refusal to extend the New York Times privilege to defamation of private individuals, respondent contends that we should affirm the judgment below on the ground that petitioner is either a public official or a public figure. There is little basis for the former assertion. Several years prior to the present incident, petitioner had served briefly on housing committees appointed by the mayor of Chicago, but, at the time of publication, he had never held any remunerative governmental position. Respondent admits this, but argues that petitioner's appearance at the coroner's inquest rendered him a "de facto public official." Our cases recognize no such concept. Respondent's suggestion would sweep all lawyers under the New York Times rule as officers of the court, and distort the plain meaning of the "public official" category beyond all recognition. We decline to follow it.

Respondent's characterization of petitioner as a public figure raises a different question. That designation may rest on either of two alternative bases. In some instances an individual may achieve such pervasive fame or notoriety that he becomes a public figure for all purposes and in all contexts. More commonly, an individual voluntarily injects himself or is drawn into a particular public controversy, and thereby becomes a public figure for a limited range of issues. In either case, such persons assume special prominence in the resolution of public questions.

42

Petitioner has long been active in community and professional affairs. He has served as an officer of local civic groups and of various professional organizations, and he has published several books and articles on legal subjects. Although petitioner was consequently well known in some circles, he had achieved no general fame or notoriety in the community. None of the prospective jurors called at the trial had ever heard of petitioner prior to this litigation, and respondent offered no proof that this response was atypical of the local population. We would not lightly assume that a citizen's participation in community and professional affairs rendered him a public figure for all purposes. Absent clear evidence of general fame or notoriety in the community, and pervasive involvement in the affairs of society, an individual should not be deemed a public personality for all aspects of his life. It is preferable to reduce the public figure question to a more meaningful context by looking to the nature and extent of an individual's participation in the particular controversy giving rise to the defamation.

In this context, it is plain that petitioner was not a public figure. He played a minimal role at the coroner's inquest, and his participation related solely to his representation of a private client. He took no part in the criminal prosecution of Officer Nuccio. Moreover, he never discussed either the criminal or civil litigation with the press, and was never quoted as having done so. He plainly did not thrust himself into the vortex of this public issue, nor did he engage the public's attention in an attempt to influence its outcome. We are persuaded that the trial court did not err in refusing to characterize petitioner as a public figure for the purpose of this litigation.

We therefore conclude that the New York Times standard is inapplicable to this case, and that the trial court erred in entering judgment for respondent. Because the jury was allowed to impose liability without fault and was permitted to presume damages without proof of injury, a new trial is necessary. We reverse and remand for further proceedings in accord with this opinion.

It is so ordered.

**MR. CHIEF JUSTICE BURGER, dissenting.**

The doctrines of the law of defamation have had a gradual evolution primarily in the state courts. In New York Times Co. v. Sullivan, 376 U.S. 254 (1964), and its progeny this Court entered this field.

Agreement or disagreement with the law as it has evolved to this time does not alter the fact that it has been orderly development with a consistent basic rationale. In today's opinion, the Court abandons the traditional thread so far as the ordinary private citizen is concerned, and introduces the concept that the media will be liable for negligence in publishing defamatory statements with respect to such persons.

**MR. JUSTICE DOUGLAS, dissenting.**

...

With the First Amendment made applicable to the States through the Fourteenth, I do not see how States have any more ability to "accommodate" freedoms of speech or of the press than does Congress.

....

Continued recognition of the possibility of state libel suits for public discussion of public issues leaves the freedom of speech honored by the Fourteenth Amendment a diluted version of First Amendment protection.

....

There can be no doubt that a State impinges upon free and open discussion when it sanctions the imposition of damages for such discussion through its civil libel laws. Discussion of public affairs is often marked by highly charged emotions, and jurymen, not unlike us all, are subject to those emotions. It is indeed this very type of speech which is the reason for the First Amendment, since speech which arouses little emotion is little in need of protection. The vehicle for publication in this case was the American Opinion, a most controversial periodical which disseminates the views of the John Birch Society, an organization which many deem to be quite offensive. The subject matter involved "Communist plots," "conspiracies against law enforcement agencies," and the killing of a private citizen by the police. With any such amalgam of controversial elements pressing upon the jury, a jury determination, unpredictable in the most neutral circumstances, becomes for those who venture to discuss heated issues, a virtual roll of the dice separating them from liability for often massive claims of damage.

It is only the hardy publisher who will engage in discussion in the face of such risk, and the Court's preoccupation with proliferating standards in the area of libel increases the risks.

....

The standard announced today leaves the States free to "define for themselves the appropriate standard of liability for a publisher or broadcaster" in the circumstances of this case. This, of course, leaves the simple negligence standard as an option, with the jury free to impose damages upon a finding that the publisher failed to act as "a reasonable man." With such continued erosion of First Amendment protection, I fear that it may well be the reasonable man who refrains from speaking.

Since, in my view, the First and Fourteenth Amendments prohibit the imposition of damages upon respondent for this discussion of public affairs, I would affirm the judgment below.

**MR. JUSTICE WHITE, dissenting.**

For some 200 years -- from the very founding of the Nation -- the law of defamation and right of the ordinary citizen to recover for false publication injurious to his reputation have been almost exclusively the business of state courts and legislatures. Under typical state defamation law, the defamed private citizen had to prove only a false publication that would subject him to hatred, contempt, or ridicule. Given such publication, general damage to reputation was presumed, while punitive damages required proof of additional facts. The law governing the defamation of private citizens remained untouched by the First Amendment, because, until relatively recently, the consistent view of the Court was that libelous words constitute a class of speech wholly unprotected by the First Amendment, subject only to limited exceptions carved out since 1964.

But now, using that Amendment as the chosen instrument, the Court, in a few printed pages, has federalized major aspects of libel law by declaring unconstitutional in important respects the prevailing defamation law in all or most of the 50 States.

....

The case against razing state libel laws is compelling when considered in light of the increasingly prominent role of mass media in our society and the awesome power it has placed in the hands of a select few.

....

**MR. JUSTICE BRENNAN, dissenting.**

...

I cannot agree, however, that free and robust debate-- so essential to the proper functioning of our system of government -- is permitted adequate "breathing space,

....

[W]e strike the proper accommodation between avoidance of media self-censorship and protection of individual reputations only when we require States to apply the New York Times Co. v. Sullivan, 376 U.S.

254 (1964), "knowing or reckless falsity" standard in civil libel actions concerning media reports of the involvement of private individuals in events of public or general interest.

# Who is a public figure?

## Public Figures

In California, to classify a person as a <u>public figure</u>, the person must have achieved such pervasive fame or notoriety that he becomes a public figure for all purposes and in all contexts. Someone who voluntarily seeks to influence resolution of public issues may also be considered a public figure in California. For example, the following persons have been considered public figures in California:

* A former City Attorney who also represented the city's redevelopment agency;

* A licensed clinical psychologist whose so-called "Nude Marathon" in group therapy is a means of helping people to shed their psychological inhibitions by the removal of their clothes;

* An author and television personality;

* The founder of a Church that has a program for the rehabilitation of drug addicts;

* An associate of Howard Hughes, a famous aviator, movie producer, and billionaire, from approximately 1956 to 1970 who functioned as an "alter ego" and "personal representative" of Mr. Hughes;

* A real-estate developer who was interested in building a housing development near a toxic chemical plant; and

* A "prominent and outspoken feminist author" and anti-pornography advocate.

Limited-Purpose Public Figures

A <u>limited-purpose public figure</u> is a person who voluntarily injects herself or is drawn into a particular public controversy. It is not necessary to show that she actually achieves prominence in public debate; her attempts to thrust herself in front of the public is sufficient. Copp v. Paxton, 52 Cal.Rptr.2d 831, 844 (Cal. Ct. App. 1996). As with all limited-purpose public figures, the alleged defamation must be relevant to the plaintiff's voluntary participation in the public controversy (if the issue requires expertise or specialized knowledge, the plaintiff's credentials as an expert would be relevant).

In California, the following persons have been considered limited-purpose public figures:

* The president of two corporations located in a California village that opposed the rezoning of property adjacent to his property. Kaufman v. Fidelity Fed. Sav. & Loan Ass'n, 189 Cal.Rptr. 818 (Cal. Ct. App. 1983);

* An individual who publicly claimed to be an expert in earthquake safety and a veteran in earthquake rescue operations. Copp v. Paxton, 52 Cal.Rptr.2d 831 (Cal. Ct. App. 1996).

**Actual Malice and Negligence**

In California, a private figure plaintiff bringing a defamation lawsuit must prove that the defendant was at least negligent with respect to the truth or falsity of the allegedly defamatory statements. Public officials, all-purpose public figures, and limited-purpose public figures must prove that the defendant acted with actual malice, i.e., knowing that the statements were false or recklessly disregarding their falsity. See the general page on actual malice and negligence for details on the standards and terminology mentioned in this subsection.

Source:
http://www.dmlp.org/legal-guide/proving-fault-actual-malice-and-negligence#publicFigure

**Examples of public and private figures**

Town Mayor: **Public Official** (A mayor is an elected official and therefore is a public official for purposes of defamation law.)

George W. Bush: **Public Official** (The President of the United States is an elected official and therefore is a public official for purposes of defamation law.)

Laura Bush: **Public Figure** (The President's wife is a person who has pervasive power and influence in society and is therefore a public figure for purposes of defamation law.)

Paris Hilton: **Public Figure** (Well-known celebrities have pervasive power and influence in society and are therefore public figures for purposes of defamation law.)

Bill Gates: **Public Figure** (As the head of a major corporation and one of the richest men in the world, Bill Gates is a public figure for purposes of defamation law.)

Roger Clemens: **Public Figure or Limited-Purpose Public Figure** (Roger Clemens is a well-known athlete and likely to be consid-ered a public figure; at a minimum, he would be a limited-purpose public figure as to issues involving sports.)

Local expert on teen suicide: **Limited-Purpose Public Figure** (The expert would be a limited-purpose public figure because she has distinguished herself in this particular field.)

Church pastor who decries abortion: **Limited-Purpose Public Figure** (The pastor would be a limited-purpose public figure because he thrust himself to the forefront of a particular controversy in order to influence the resolution of the issue.)

Local grocery store manager: **Private Figure** (Individuals who do not qualify as public officials/figures or limited-purpose public figures are private figures.)

Your shy neighbor: **Private figure** (Individuals who do not qualify as public officials/figures or limited-purpose public figures are private figures.)

Source: http://www.dmlp.org/legal-guide/examples-public-and-private-figures

**Sample Brief**

*Curtis Publishing Co. v. Butts*, 388 U.S. 130 (1967)

Issue

Do the constitutional safeguards required by *New York Times v. Sullivan* apply to a 'public figure' who is not a public official?

Facts

In 1962, the *Saturday Evening Post* printed an article accusing Butts, the coach of the University of Georgia football team, of conspiring to fix a Georgia-Alabama game by giving Paul Bryant, the Alabama coach, crucial information about Georgia's offensive strategy. However, at trial it was shown that the magazine assigned the story to a writer who was not a football expert and, among other errors, made no effort to have an expert check the story. The jury awarded Butts $60,000 in general damages and $30,000 in punitive damages

Holding

Yes, the Supreme Court held that a public figure such as a football coach is subject to the same "actual malice" standards for recovery from libel as a public official.

Rationale

The Court held that libel actions concerning public figures are subject to the First Amendment because plaintiff commanded a substantial amount of public interest at the time of the publication. Butts was a public figure who commanded a substantial amount of independent public interest at the times of the publication. Therefore, he had sufficient public interest and sufficient access to the means of public counterargument to be able to expose though discussion the falsehood and fallacies of the defamatory statements in the *Saturday Evening Post* story about him.

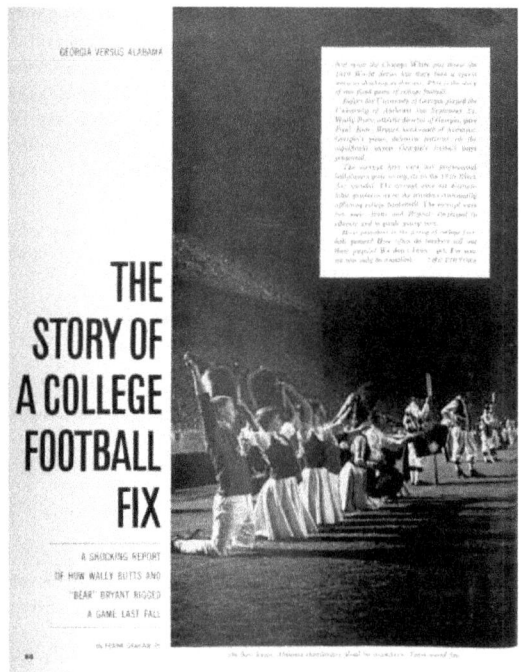

CHAPTER 4

# Right to privacy

*In 2003, Kobe Bryant was arrested after Katelyn Faber, a 19-year-old hotel employee, accused him of sexually assaulting her.*

# Cox Broadcasting Corp. v. Cohn (1975)

U.S. Supreme Court

420 U.S. 469 (1975)

Decided March 3, 1975

Burger   Douglas   Brennan   Stewart   White   Marshall   Blackmun   Powell   Rehnquist

Decision: 8 votes for Cox Broadcasting Corporation, 0 vote(s) against

**MR. JUSTICE WHITE delivered the opinion of the Court.**

The issue before us in this case is whether, consistently with the First and Fourteenth Amendments, a State may extend a cause of action for damages for invasion of privacy caused by the publication of the name of a deceased rape victim which was publicly revealed in connection with the prosecution of the crime.

I

In August, 1971, appellee's 17-year-old daughter was the victim of a rape, and did not survive the incident. Six youths were soon indicted for murder and rape. Although there was substantial press coverage of the crime and of subsequent developments, the identity of the victim was not disclosed pending trial, perhaps because of Ga.Code Ann. § 26-9901 (1972), which makes it a misdemeanor to publish or broadcast the name or identity of a rape victim. In April, 1972, some eight months later, the six defendants appeared in court. Five pleaded guilty to rape or attempted rape, the charge of murder having been dropped. The guilty pleas were accepted by the court, and the trial of the defendant pleading not guilty was set for a later date.

In the course of the proceedings that day, appellant Wassell, a reporter covering the incident for his employer, learned the name of the victim from an examination of the indictments which were made available for his inspection in the courtroom. That the name of the victim appears in the indictments, and that the indictments were public records available for inspection are not disputed. Later that day, Wassell broadcast over the facilities of station WSB-TV, a television station owned by appellant Cox Broadcasting Corp., a news report concerning the court proceedings. The report named the victim of the crime and was repeated the following day.

In May, 1972, appellee brought an action for money damages against appellants, relying on § 26-9901 and claiming that his right to privacy had been invaded by the television broadcasts giving the name of his deceased daughter. Appellants admitted the broadcasts, but claimed that they were privileged under both state law and the First and Fourteenth Amendments. The trial court, rejecting appellants' constitutional claims and holding that the Georgia statute gave a civil remedy to those injured by its violation, granted summary judgment to appellee as to liability, with the determination of damages to await trial by jury.

On appeal, the Georgia Supreme Court, in its initial opinion, held that the trial court had erred in construing 26-9901 to extend a civil cause of action for invasion of privacy, and thus found it unnecessary to consider the constitutionality of the statute. 231 Ga. 60, 200 S.E.2d 127 (1973). The court went on to rule, however, that the complaint stated a cause of action "for the invasion of the appellee's right of privacy, or for the tort of public disclosure" -- a "common law tort ex-ist[ing] in this jurisdiction without the help of the statute that the trial judge in this case relied on." *Id.* at 62, 200 S.E.2d at 130. Although the privacy invaded was not that of the deceased victim, the father was held to have stated a claim for invasion of his own privacy by reason of the publication of his daughter's name. The court explained, however, that liability did not follow as a matter of law, and that summary judgment was improper; whether the public disclosure of the name actually invaded appellee's "zone of privacy," and if so, to what extent, were issues to be determined by the trier of fact. Also,

"in formulating such an issue for determination by the factfinder, it is reasonable to require the appellee to prove that the appellants invaded his privacy with willful or negligent disregard for the fact that reasonable men would find the invasion highly offensive."

*Id.* at 64, 200 S.E.2d at 131. The Georgia Supreme Court did agree with the trial court, however, that the First and Fourteenth Amendments did not, as a matter of law, require judgment for appellants. The court concurred with the statement in *Briscoe v. Reader's Digest Assn., Inc.,* 4 Cal.3d 529, 541, 483 P.2d 34, 42 (1971), that

"the rights guaranteed by the First Amendment do not require total abrogation of the right to privacy. The goals sought by each may be achieved with a minimum of intrusion upon the other."

Upon motion for rehearing, the Georgia court countered the argument that the victim's name was a matter of public interest, and could be published with impunity by relying on § 26-9901 as an authoritative declaration of state policy that the name of a rape victim was not a matter of public concern. This time the court felt compelled to determine the constitutionality of the statute, and sustained it as a "legitimate limitation on the right of freedom of expression contained in the First Amendment." The court could discern

"no public interest or general concern about the identity of the victim of such a crime as will make the right to disclose the identity of the victim rise to the level of First Amendment protection."

231 Ga. at 68, 200 S.E.2d at 134.

* * *

III

Georgia stoutly defends both § 29901 and the State's common law privacy action challenged here. Its claims are not without force, for powerful arguments can be made, and have been made, that however it may be ultimately defined, there s a zone of privacy surrounding every individual, a zone within which the State may protect him from intrusion by the press, with all its attendant publicity. Indeed, the central thesis of the root article by Warren and Brandeis, The Right to Privacy, 4 Harv.L.Rev.193, 196 (1890), was that the press was overstepping its prerogatives by publishing essentially private information, and that there should be a remedy for the alleged abuses.

...

Rather than address the broader question whether truthful publications may ever be subjected to civil or criminal liability consistently with the First and Fourteenth Amendments, or, to put it another way, whether the State may ever define and protect an area of privacy free from unwanted publicity in the press, it is appropriate to focus on the narrower interface between press and privacy that this case presents, namely, whether the State may impose sanctions on the accurate publication of the name of a rape victim obtained from public records -- more specifically, from judicial records which are maintained in connection with a public prosecution and which themselves are open to public inspection. We are convinced that the State may not do so.

In the first place, in a society in which each individual has but limited time and resources with which to observe at first hand the operations of his government, he relies necessarily upon the press to bring to him in convenient form the facts of those operations. Great responsibility is accordingly placed upon the news media to report fully and accurately the proceedings of government, and official records and documents open to the public are the basic data of governmental operations. Without the information provided by the press, most of us and many of our representatives would be unable to vote intelligently or to register opinions on the administration of government generally. With respect to judicial proceedings, in particular, the function of the press serves to guarantee the fairness of trials and to bring to bear the beneficial effects of public scrutiny upon the administration of justice. *See Sheppard v. Maxwell,*384 U. S. 333, 384 U. S. 350 (1966).

. . . .

The special protected nature of accurate reports of judicial proceedings has repeatedly been recognized. This Court, in an opinion written by MR. JUSTICE DOUGLAS, has said:

"A trial is a public event. What transpires in the court room is public property. If a transcript of the court proceedings had been published, we suppose none would claim that the judge could punish the pub-

lisher for contempt. And we can see no difference though the conduct of the attorneys, of the jury, or even of the judge himself, may have reflected on the court. *Those who see and hear what transpired can report it with impunity.* There is no special perquisite of the judiciary which enables it, as distinguished from other institutions of democratic government, to suppress, edit, or censor events which transpire in proceedings before it."

. . .

Thus, even the prevailing law of invasion of privacy generally recognizes that the interests in privacy fade when the information involved already appears on the public record. The conclusion is compelling when viewed in terms of the First and Fourteenth Amendments and in light of the public interest in a vigorous press.

. . . .

By placing the information in the public domain on official court records, the State must be presumed to have concluded that the public interest was thereby being served. Public records, by their very nature, are of interest to those concerned with the administration of government, and a public benefit is performed by the reporting of the true contents of the records by the media. The freedom of the press to publish that information appears to us to be of critical importance to our type of government, in which the citizenry is the final judge of the proper conduct of public business. In preserving that form of government, the First and Fourteenth Amendments command nothing less than that the States may not impose sanctions on the publication of truthful information contained in official court records open to public inspection.

We are reluctant to embark on a course that would make public records generally available to the media but forbid their publication if offensive to the sensibilities of the supposed reasonable man. Such a rule
would make it very difficult for the media to inform citizens about the
public business and yet stay within the law. The rule would invite timidity and self-censorship and very likely lead to the suppression of many
items that would otherwise be published and that should be made available to the public. At the very least, the First and Fourteenth Amendments will not allow exposing the press to liability for truthfully publishing information released to the public in official court records.

. . .

Once true information is disclosed in public court documents open to
public inspection, the press cannot be sanctioned for publishing it. In
this instance, as in others, reliance must rest upon the judgment of
those who decide what to publish or broadcast. *See Miami Herald Publishing Co. v. Tornillo,* 418 U.S. at 418 U. S. 258.

Appellant Wassell based his televised report upon notes taken during
the court proceedings, and obtained the name of the victim from the
indictments handed to him at his request during a recess in the hearing. Appellee has not contended that the name was obtained in an improper fashion, or that it was not on an official court document open to
public inspection. Under these circumstances, the protection of freedom of the press provided by the First and Fourteenth Amendments
bars the State of Georgia from making appellants' broadcast the basis
of civil liability.

Reversed.

# The Florida Star v. B.J.F. (1989)

U.S. Supreme Court

491 U.S. 524

Decided: June 21, 1989.

Brennan | Marshall | Blackmun | Stevens | Scalia | Kennedy | Rehnquist | White | O'Connor

Decision: 6 votes for The Florida Star, 3 vote(s) against

**Justice MARSHALL delivered the opinion of the Court.**

Florida Stat. § 794.03 (1987) makes it unlawful to "print, publish, or broadcast . . . in any instrument of mass communication" the name of the victim of a sexual offense. [1] Pursuant to this statute, appellant The Florida Star was found civilly liable for publishing the name of a rape victim which it had obtained from a publicly released police report. The issue presented here is whether this result comports with the First Amendment. We hold that it does not.

The Florida Star is a weekly newspaper which serves the community of Jacksonville, Florida, and which has an average circulation of approximately 18,000 copies. A regular feature of the newspaper is its "Police Reports" section. That section, typically two to three pages in length, contains brief articles describing local criminal incidents under police investigation.

On October 20, 1983, appellee B.J.F. [2] reported to the Duval County, Florida, Sheriff's Department (Department) that she had been robbed and sexually assaulted by an unknown assailant. The Department prepared a report on the incident which identified B.J.F. by her full name. The Department then placed the report in its pressroom. The Department does not restrict access either to the pressroom or to the reports made available therein.

A Florida Star reporter-trainee sent to the pressroom copied the police report verbatim, including B.J.F.'s full name, on a blank duplicate of the Department's forms. A Florida Star reporter then prepared a one-paragraph article about the crime, derived entirely from the trainee's copy of the police report. The article included B.J.F.'s full name. It appeared in the "Robberies" subsection of the "Police Reports" section on October 29, 1983, one of 54 police blotter stories in that day's edition. The article read:

"B.J.F. reported on Thursday, October 20, she was crossing Brentwood Park, which is in the 500 block of Golfair Boulevard, enroute to her bus stop, when an unknown black man ran up behind the lady and placed a knife to her neck and told her not to yell. The suspect then undressed the lady and had sexual intercourse with her before fleeing the scene with her 60 cents, Timex watch and gold necklace. Patrol efforts have been suspended concerning this incident because of a lack of evidence." In printing B.J.F.'s full name, The Florida Star violated its internal policy of not publishing the names of sexual offense victims.

On September 26, 1984, B.J.F. filed suit in the Circuit Court of Duval County against the Department and The Florida Star, alleging that these parties negligently violated § 794.03. See n. 1, supra. Before trial, the Department settled with B.J.F. for $2,500. The Florida Star moved to dismiss, claiming, inter alia, that imposing civil sanctions on the newspaper pursuant to § 794.03 violated the First Amendment. The trial judge rejected the motion. App. 4.

At the ensuing daylong trial, B.J.F. testified that she had suffered emotional distress from the publication of her name. She stated that she had heard about the article from fellow workers and acquaintances; that her mother had received several threatening phone calls from a man who stated that he would rape B.J.F. again; and that these events had forced B.J.F. to change her phone number and residence, to seek police protection, and to obtain mental health counseling. In defense, The Florida Star put forth evidence indicating that the newspaper had learned B.J.F.'s name from the incident report released by the Department, and that the newspaper's violation of its internal rule against publishing the names of sexual offense victims was inadvertent.

At the close of B.J.F.'s case, and again at the close of its defense, The Florida Star moved for a directed verdict. On both occasions, the trial judge denied these motions. He ruled from the bench that § 794.03 was constitutional because it reflected a proper balance between the First Amendment and privacy rights, as it applied only to a narrow set of "rather sensitive . . . criminal offenses." App. 18-19 (rejecting first motion); see id., at 32-33 (rejecting second motion). At the close of the newspaper's defense, the judge granted B.J.F.'s motion for a directed verdict on the issue of negligence, finding the newspaper per se negligent based upon its violation of § 794.03. Id., at 33. This ruling left the jury to consider only the questions of causation and damages. The judge instructed the jury that it could award B.J.F. punitive damages if it found that the newspaper had "acted with reckless indifference to the rights of others." Id., at 35. The jury awarded B.J.F. $75,000 in compensatory damages and $25,000 in punitive damages. Against the actual damages award, the judge set off B.J.F.'s settlement with the Department.

The First District Court of Appeal affirmed in a three-paragraph per curiam opinion. 499 So.2d 883 (1986). In the paragraph devoted to The Florida Star's First Amendment claim, the court stated that the directed verdict for B.J.F. had been properly entered because, under § 794.03, a rape victim's name is "of a private nature and not to be published as a matter of law." Id., at 884, citing Doe v. Sarasota-Bradenton Florida Television Co., 436 So.2d 328, 330 (Fla.App.1983) (footnote omitted).[3] The Supreme Court of Florida denied discretionary review.

The Florida Star appealed to this Court.[4] We noted probable jurisdiction, 488 U.S. 887, 109 S.Ct. 216, 102 L.Ed.2d 208 (1988), and now reverse.

The tension between the right which the First Amendment accords to a free press, on the one hand, and the protections which various statutes and common-law doctrines accord to personal privacy against the publication of truthful information, on the other, is a subject we have addressed several times in recent years. Our decisions in cases involving government attempts to sanction the accurate dissemination of information as invasive of privacy, have not, however, exhaustively considered this conflict. On the contrary, although our decisions have without exception upheld the press' right to publish, we have emphasized each time that we were resolving this conflict only as it arose in a discrete factual context. 5

The parties to this case frame their contentions in light of a trilogy of cases which have presented, in different contexts, the conflict between truthful reporting and state-protected privacy interests. In Cox Broadcasting Corp. v. Cohn, 420 U.S. 469, 95 S.Ct. 1029, 43 L.Ed.2d 328 (1975), we found unconstitutional a civil damages award entered against a television station for broadcasting the name of a rape-murder victim which the station had obtained from courthouse records. In Oklahoma Publishing Co. v. Oklahoma County District Court, 430 U.S. 308, 97 S.Ct. 1045, 51 L.Ed.2d 355 (1977), we found unconstitutional a state c urt's pretrial order enjoining the media from publishing the name or photograph of an 11-year-old boy in connection with a juvenile proceeding involving that child which reporters had attended. Finally, in Smith v. Daily Mail Publishing Co., 443 U.S. 97, 99 S.Ct. 2667, 61 L.Ed.2d 399 (1979), we found unconstitutional the indictment of two newspapers for violating a state statute forbidding newspapers to publish, without written approval of the juvenile court, the name of any youth charged as a juvenile offender. The papers had learned about a shooting by monitoring a police band radio frequency and had obtained the name of the alleged juvenile assailant from witnesses, the police, and a local prosecutor.

Appellant takes the position that this case is indistinguishable from Cox Broadcasting. Brief for Appellant 8. Alternatively, it urges that our decisions in the above trilogy, and in other cases in which we have held that the right of the press to publish truth overcame asserted interests other than personal privacy, 6 can be distilled to yield a broader First Amendment principle that the press may never be punished, civilly or criminally, for publishing the truth. Id., at 19. Appellee counters that the privacy trilogy is inapposite, because in each case the private information already appeared on a "public record," Brief for Appellee 12, 24, 25, and because the privacy interests at stake were far less profound than in the present case. See, e.g., id., at 34. In the alternative, appellee urges that Cox Broadcasting be overruled and replaced with a categorical rule that publication of the name of a rape victim never enjoys constitutional protection. Tr. of Oral Arg. 44.

We conclude that imposing damages on appellant for publishing B.J.F.'s name violates the First Amendment, although not for either of the reasons appellant urges. Despite the strong resemblance this case bears to Cox Broadcasting, that case cannot fairly be read as controlling here. The name of the rape victim in that case was obtained from courthouse records that were open to public inspection, a fact which Justice WHITE's opinion for the Court repeatedly noted. 420 U.S., at 492, 95 S.Ct., at 1044-45 (noting "special protected nature of accurate reports of judicial proceedings") (emphasis added); see also id., at 493, 496, 95 S.Ct., at 1045, 1046-47. Significantly, one of the reasons we gave in Cox Broadcasting for invalidating the challenged damages award was the important role the press plays in subjecting trials to public scrutiny and thereby helping guarantee their fairness. Id., at 492-493, 95 S.Ct., at 1044-1045. 7 That role is not directly compromised where, as here, the information in question comes from a police report prepared and disseminated at a time at which not only had no adversarial criminal proceedings begun, but no suspect had been identified.

Nor need we accept appellant's invitation to hold broadly that truthful publication may never be punished consistent with the First Amendment. Our cases have carefully eschewed reaching this ultimate question, mindful that the future may bring scenarios which prudence counsels our not resolving anticipatorily. See, e.g., Near v. Minnesota ex rel. Olson, 283 U.S. 697, 716, 51 S.Ct. 625, 75 L.Ed. 1357 (1931) (hypothesizing "publication of the sailing dates of transports or the number and location of troops"); see also Garrison v. Louisiana, 379 U.S. 64, 72, n. 8, 74, 85 S.Ct. 209, 215, n. 8, 216, 13 L.Ed.2d 125 (1964) (endorsing absolute defense of truth "where discussion of public affairs is concerned," but leaving unsettled the constitutional implications of truthfulness "in the discrete area of purely private libels"); Landmark Communications, Inc. v. Virginia, 435 U.S. 829, 838, 98 S.Ct. 1535, 1541, 56 L.Ed.2d 1 (1978); Time, Inc. v. Hill, 385 U.S. 374, 383, n. 7, 87 S.Ct. 534, 539-40, n. 7, 17 L.Ed.2d 456 (1967). Indeed, in Cox Broadcasting, we pointedly refused to answer even the less sweeping question "whether truthful publications may ever be subjected to civil or criminal liability" for invading "an area of privacy" defined by the State. 420 U.S., at 491, 95 S.Ct., at 1044. Respecting the fact that press freedom and privacy rights are both "plainly rooted in the traditions and significant concerns of our society," we instead focused on the less sweeping issue "whether the State may impose sanctions on the accurate publication of the name of a rape victim obtained from public records—more specifically, from judicial records which are maintained in connection with a public prosecution and which themselves are open to public inspection." Ibid. We continue to believe that the sensitivity and significance of the interests presented in clashes between First Amendment and privacy rights counsel relying on limited principles that sweep no more broadly than the appropriate context of the instant case.

In our view, this case is appropriately analyzed with reference to such a limited First Amendment principle. It is the one, in fact, which we articulated in Daily Mail in our synthesis of prior cases involving attempts to punish truthful publication: "If a newspaper lawfully obtains truthful information about a matter of public significance then state officials may not constitutionally punish publication of the information, absent a need to further a state interest of the highest order." 443 U.S., at 103, 99 S.Ct., at 2671. According the press the ample protection provided by that principle is supported by at least three separate considera-

tions, in addition to, of course, the overarching " 'public interest, secured by the Constitution, in the dissemination of truth.' " Cox Broadcasting, supra, 420 U.S., at 491, 95 S.Ct., at 1044, quoting Garrison, supra, 379 U.S., at 73, 85 S.Ct., at 215 (footnote omitted). The cases on which the Daily Mail synthesis relied demonstrate these considerations.

First, because the Daily Mail formulation only protects the publication of information which a newspaper has "lawfully obtained," 443 U.S., at 103, 99 S.Ct., at 2671, the government retains ample means of safeguarding significant interests upon which publication may impinge, including protecting a rape victim's anonymity. To the extent sensitive information rests in private hands, the government may under some circumstances forbid its nonconsensual acquisition, thereby bringing outside of the Daily Mail principle the publication of any information so acquired. To the extent sensitive information is in the government's custody, it has even greater power to forestall or mitigate the injury caused by its release. The government may lassify certain information, establish and enforce procedures ensuring its redacted release, and extend a damages remedy against the government or its officials where the government's mishandling of sensitive information leads to its dissemination. Where information is entrusted to the government, a less drastic means than punishing truthful publication almost always exists for guarding against the dissemination of private facts. See, e.g., Landmark Communications, supra, 435 U.S., at 845, 98 S.Ct., at 1545 ("Much of the risk from disclosure of sensitive information regarding judicial disciplinary proceedings can be eliminated through careful internal procedures to protect the confidentiality of Commission proceedings"); Oklahoma Publishing, 430 U.S., at 311, 97 S.Ct., at 1046-47 (noting trial judge's failure to avail himself of the opportunity, provided by a state statute, to close juvenile hearing to the public, including members of the press, who later broadcast juvenile defendant's name); Cox Broadcasting, supra, 420 U.S., at 496, 95 S.Ct., at 1047 ("If there are privacy interests to be protected in judicial proceedings, the States must respond by means which avoid public documentation or other exposure of private information"). 8

A second consideration undergirding the Daily Mail principle is the fact that punishing the press for its dissemination of information which is already publicly available is relatively unlikely to advance the interests in the service of which the State seeks to act. It is not, of course, always the case that information lawfully acquired by the press is known, or accessible, to others. But where the government has made certain information publicly available, it is highly anomalous to sanction persons other than the source of its release. We noted this anomaly in Cox Broadcasting: "By placing the information in the public domain on official court records, the State must be presumed to have concluded that the public interest was thereby being served." 420 U.S., at 495, 95 S.Ct., at 1046. The Daily Mail formulation reflects the fact that it is a limited set of cases indeed where, despite the accessibility of the public to certain information, a meaningful public interest is served by restricting its further release by other entities, like the press. As Daily Mail observed in its summary of Oklahoma Publishing, "once the truthful information was 'publicly revealed' or 'in the public domain' the court could not constitutionally restrain its dissemination." 443 U.S., at 103, 99 S.Ct., at 2671.

A third and final consideration is the "timidity and self-censorship" which may result from allowing the media to be punished for publishing certain truthful information. Cox Broadcasting, supra, 420 U.S., at 496, 95 S.Ct., at 1046-47. Cox Broadcasting noted this concern with overdeterrence in the context of information made public through official court records, but the fear of excessive media self-suppression is applicable as well to other information released, without qualification, by the government. A contrary rule, depriving protection to those who rely on the government's implied representations of the lawfulness of dissemination, would force upon the media the onerous obligation of sifting through government press releases, reports, and pronouncements to prune out material arguably unlawful for publication. This situation could inhere even where th newspaper's sole object was to reproduce, with no substantial change, the government's rendition of the event in question.

Applied to the instant case, the Daily Mail principle clearly commands reversal. The first inquiry is whether the newspaper "lawfully obtained truthful information about a matter of public significance." 443 U.S., at 103, 99 S.Ct., at 2671. It is undisputed that the news article describing the assault on B.J.F. was accurate. In addition, appellant lawfully obtained B.J.F.'s name. Appellee's argument to the contrary is based on the fact that under Florida law, police reports which reveal the identity of the victim of a sexual offense are not among the matters of "public record" which the public, by law, is entitled to inspect. Brief for Appellee 17-18, citing Fla.Stat. § 119.07(3)(h) (1983). But the fact that state officials are not required to disclose such reports does not make it unlawful for a newspaper to receive them when furnished by the government. Nor does the fact that the Department apparently failed to fulfill its obligation under § 794.03 not to "cause or allow to be . . . published" the name of a sexual offense victim make the newspaper's ensuing receipt of this information unlawful. Even assuming the Constitution permitted a State to proscribe receipt of information, Florida has not taken this step. It is, clear, furthermore, that the news article concerned "a matter of public significance," 443 U.S., at 103, 99 S.Ct., at 2671, in the sense in which the Daily Mail synthesis of prior cases used that term. That is, the article generally, as opposed to the specific identity contained within it, involved a matter of paramount public import: the commission, and investigation, of a violent crime which had been reported to authorities. See Cox Broadcasting, supra (article identifying victim of rape-murder); Oklahoma Publishing Co. v. Oklahoma County District Court, 430 U.S. 308, 97 S.Ct. 1045, 51 L.Ed.2d 355 (1977) (article identifying juvenile alleged to have committed murder); Daily Mail, supra (same); cf. Landmark Communications, Inc. v. Virginia, 435 U.S. 829, 98 S.Ct. 1535, 56 L.Ed.2d 1 (1978) (article identifying judges whose conduct was being investigated).

The second inquiry is whether imposing liability on appellant pursuant to § 794.03 serves "a need to further a state interest of the highest order." Daily Mail, 443 U.S., at 103, 99 S.Ct., at 2671. Appellee argues that a rule punishing publication furthers three closely related interests: the privacy of victims of sexual offenses; the physical safety of such victims, who may be targeted for retaliation if their names become known to their assailants; and the goal of encouraging victims of such crimes to report these offenses without fear of exposure. Brief for Appellee 29-30.

At a time in which we are daily reminded of the tragic reality of rape, it is undeniable that these are highly significant interests, a fact underscored by the Florida Legislature's explicit attempt to protect these interests by enacting a criminal statute prohibiting much dissemination of victim identities. We accordingly do not rule out the possibility that, in a proper case, imposing civil sanctions for publication of the name of a rape victim might be so overwhelmingly necessary to advance these interests as to satisfy the Daily Mail standard. For three independent reasons, however, imposing liability for publication under the circumstances of this case is too precipitous a means of advancing these interests to convince us that there is a "need" within the meaning of the Daily Mail formulation for Florida to take this extreme step. Cf. Landmark Communications, supra (invalidating penalty on publication despite State's expressed interest in nondissemination, reflected in statute prohibiting unauthorized divulging of names of judges under investigation).

First is the manner in which appellant obtained the identifing information in question. As we have noted, where the government itself provides information to the media, it is most appropriate to assume that the government had, but failed to utilize, far more limited means of guarding against dissemination than the extreme step of punishing truthful speech. That assumption is richly borne out in this case. B.J.F.'s identity would never have come to light were it not for the erroneous, if inadvertent, inclusion by the Department of her full name in an incident report made available in a pressroom open to the public. Florida's policy against disclosure of rape victims' identities, reflected in § 794.03, was undercut by the Department's failure to abide by this policy. Where, as here, the government has failed to police itself in disseminating information, it is clear under Cox Broadcasting, Oklahoma Publishing, and Landmark Communications that the imposition of damages against the press for its subsequent publication can hardly be said to be a narrowly tailored means of safeguarding anonymity. See supra, at 534-535. Once the government has placed such information in the public domain, "reliance must rest upon the judgment of those who decide what to publish or broadcast," Cox Broadcasting, 420 U.S., at 496, 95 S.Ct., at 1047, and hopes for restitution must rest upon the willingness of the government to compensate victims for their loss of privacy and to protect them from the other consequences of its mishandling of the information which these victims provided in confidence.

That appellant gained access to the information in question through a government news release makes it especially likely that, if liability were to be imposed, self-censorship would result. Reliance on a news release is a paradigmatically "routine newspaper reporting technique." Daily Mail, supra, at 103, 99 S.Ct., at 2671. The government's issuance of such a release, without qualification, can only convey to recipients that the government considered dissemination lawful, and indeed expected the recipients to disseminate the information further. Had appellant merely reproduced the news release prepared and released by the Department, imposing civil damages would surely violate the First Amendment. The fact that appellant converted the police report into a news story by adding the linguistic connecting tissue necessary to transform the report's facts into full sentences cannot change this result.

A second problem with Florida's imposition of liability for publication is the broad sweep of the negligence per se standard applied under the civil cause of action implied from § 794.03. Unlike claims based on the common law tort of invasion of privacy, see Restatement (Second) of Torts § 652D (1977), civil actions based on § 794.03 require no case-by-case findings that the disclosure of a fact about a person's private life was one that a reasonable person would find highly offensive. On the contrary, under the per se theory of negligence adopted by the courts below, liability follows automatically from publication. This is so regardless of whether the identity of the victim is already known throughout the community; whether the victim has voluntarily called public attention to the offense; or whether the identity of the victim has otherwise become a reasonable subject of public concern—because, perhaps, questions have arisen whether the victim fabricated an assault by a particular person. Nor is there a scienter requirement of any kind under § 794.03, engendering the perverse result that truthful publications challenged pursuant to this cause of action are less protected by the First Amendment than even the least protected defamatory falsehoods: those involving purely private figures, where liability is evaluated under a standard, usually applied by a jury, of ordinary negligence. See Gertz v. Robert Welch, Inc., 418 U.S. 323, 94 S.Ct. 2997, 41 L.Ed.2d 789 (1974). We have previously noted the impermissibility of catego ical prohibitions upon media access where important First Amendment interests are at stake. See Globe Newspaper Co. v. Superior Court of Norfolk County, 457 U.S. 596, 608, 102 S.Ct. 2613, 2620-21, 73 L.Ed.2d 248 (1982) (invalidating state statute providing for the categorical exclusion of the public from trials of sexual offenses involving juvenile victims). More individualized adjudication is no less indispensable where the State, seeking to safeguard the anonymity of crime victims, sets its face against publication of their names.

Third, and finally, the facial underinclusiveness of § 794.03 raises serious doubts about whether Florida is, in fact, serving, with this statute, the significant interests which appellee invokes in support of affirmance. Section 794.03 prohibits the publication of identifying information only if this information appears in an "instrument of mass communication," a term the statute does not define. Section 794.03 does not prohibit the spread by other means of the identities of victims of sexual offenses. An individual who maliciously spreads word of the identity of a rape victim is thus not covered, despite the fact that the communica-

tion of such information to persons who live near, or work with, the victim may have consequences as devastating as the exposure of her name to large numbers of strangers. See Tr. of Oral Arg. 49-50 (appellee acknowledges that § 794.03 would not apply to "the backyard gossip who tells 50 people that don't have to know").

When a State attempts the extraordinary measure of punishing truthful publication in the name of privacy, it must demonstrate its commitment to advancing this interest by applying its prohibition evenhandedly, to the smalltime disseminator as well as the media giant. Where important First Amendment interests are at stake, the mass scope of disclosure is not an acceptable surrogate for injury. A ban on disclosures effected by "instruments of mass communication" simply cannot be defended on the ground that partial prohibitions may effect partial relief. See Daily Mail, 443 U.S., at 104-105, 99 S.Ct., at 2671-2672 (statute is insufficiently tailored to interest in protecting anonymity where it restricted only newspapers, not the electronic media or other forms of publication, from identifying juvenile defendants); id., at 110, 99 S.Ct., at 2674-75 (REHNQUIST, J., concurring in judgment) (same); cf. Arkansas Writers' Project, Inc. v. Ragland, 481 U.S. 221, 229, 107 S.Ct. 1722, 1727-1728, 95 L.Ed.2d 209 (1987); Minneapolis Star & Tribune Co. v. Minnesota Comm'r of Revenue, 460 U.S. 575, 585, 103 S.Ct. 1365, 1371-72, 75 L.Ed.2d 295 (1983). Without more careful and inclusive precautions against alternative forms of dissemination, we cannot conclude that Florida's selective ban on publication by the mass media satisfactorily accomplishes its stated purpose. 9

III

Our holding today is limited. We do not hold that truthful publication is automatically constitutionally protected, or that there is no zone of personal privacy within which the State may protect the individual from intrusion by the press, or even that a State may never punish publication of the name of a victim of a sexual offense. We hold only that where a newspaper publishes truthful information which it has lawfully obtained, punishment may lawfully be imposed, if at all, only when narrowly tailored to a state interest of the highest order, and that no such interest is satisfactorily served by imposing liability under § 794.03 to appella t under the facts of this case. The decision below is therefore

Reversed.

**Justice WHITE, with whom THE CHIEF JUSTICE and Justice O'CONNOR join, dissenting.**

"Short of homicide, rape is the 'ultimate violation of self.' " Coker v. Georgia, 433 U.S. 584, 597, 97 S.Ct. 2861, 2869, 53 L.Ed.2d 982 (1977) (opinion of WHITE, J.). For B.J.F., however, the violation she suffered at a rapist's knifepoint marked only the beginning of her ordeal. A week later, while her assailant was still at large, an account of this assault identifying by name B.J.F. as the victim—was published by The Florida Star. As a result, B.J.F. received harassing phone calls, required mental health counseling, was forced to move from her home, and was even threatened with being raped again. Yet today, the Court holds that a jury award of $75,000 to compensate B.J.F. for the harm she suffered due to the Star's negligence is at odds with the First Amendment. I do not accept this result.

The Court reaches its conclusion based on an analysis of three of our precedents and a concern with three particular aspects of the judgment against appellant. I consider each of these points in turn, and then consider some of the larger issues implicated by today's decision.

* The Court finds its result compelled, or at least supported in varying degrees, by three of our prior cases: Cox Broadcasting Corp. v. Cohn, 420 U.S. 469, 95 S.Ct. 1029, 43 L.Ed.2d 328 (1975); Oklahoma Publishing Co. v. Oklahoma County District Court, 430 U.S. 308, 97 S.Ct.

1045, 51 L.Ed.2d 355 (1977); and Smith v. Daily Mail Publishing Co., 443 U.S. 97, 99 S.Ct. 2667, 61 L.Ed.2d 399 (1979). I disagree. None of these cases requires the harsh outcome reached today.

Cox Broadcasting reversed a damages award entered against a television station, which had obtained a rape victim's name from public records maintained in connection with the judicial proceedings brought against her assailants. While there are similarities, critical aspects of that case make it wholly distinguishable from this one. First, in Cox Broadcasting, the victim's name had been disclosed in the hearing where her assailants pleaded guilty; and, as we recognized, judici l records have always been considered public information in this country. See Cox Broadcasting, supra, 420 U.S., at 492-493, 95 S.Ct., at 1044-1045. In fact, even the earliest notion of privacy rights exempted the information contained in judicial records from its protections. See Warren & Brandeis, The Right to Privacy, 4 Harv.L.Rev. 193, 216-217 (1890). Second, unlike the incident report at issue here, which was meant by state law to be withheld from public release, the judicial proceedings at issue in Cox Broadcasting were open as a matter of state law. Thus, in Cox Broadcasting, the state-law scheme made public disclosure of the victim's name almost inevitable; here, Florida law forbids such disclosure. See Fla.Stat. § 794.03 (1987).

These facts—that the disclosure came in judicial proceedings, which were open to the public—were critical to our analysis in Cox Broadcasting. The distinction between that case and this one is made obvious by the penultimate paragraph of Cox Broadcasting:

"We are reluctant to embark on a course that would make public records generally available to the media but would forbid their publication if offensive. . . . The First and Fourteenth Amendments will not allow exposing the press to liability for truthfully publishing information released to the public in official court records. If there are privacy interests to be protected in judicial proceedings, the States must respond by means which avoid public documentation or other exposure of private information. . . . Once true information is disclosed in public court documents open to public inspection, the press cannot be sanctioned for publishing it." Cox Broadcasting, supra, at 496, 95 S.Ct., at 1047 (emphasis added).

Cox Broadcasting stands for the proposition that the State cannot make the press its first line of defense in withholding private information from the public—it cannot ask the press to secrete private facts that the State makes no effort to safeguard in the first place. In this case, however, the State has undertaken "means which avoid but obviously, not altogether prevent public documentation or other exposure of private information." No doubt this is why the Court frankly admits that "Cox Broadcasting . . . cannot fairly be read as controlling here." Ante, at 532.

Finding Cox Broadcasting inadequate to support its result, the Court relies on Smith v. Daily Mail Publishing Co. as its principal authority.[1] But the flat rule from Daily Mail on which the Court places so much reliance—"If a newspaper lawfully obtains truthful information . . . then state officials may not constitutionally punish publication of the information, absent a need to further a state interest of the highest order"—was introduced in Daily Mail with the cautious qualifier that such a rule was "suggested" by our prior cases, "none of which . . . directly controlled" in Daily Mail. See Daily Mail, 443 U.S., at 103, 99 S.Ct., at 2671. The rule the Court takes as a given was thus offered only as a hypothesis in Daily Mail: it should not be so uncritically accepted as constitutional dogma.

More importantly, at issue in Daily Mail was the disclosure of the name of the perpetrator of an infam us murder of a 15-year-old student. Id.,

at 99, 99 S.Ct., at 2668-69. Surely the rights of those accused of crimes and those who are their victims must differ with respect to privacy concerns. That is, whatever rights alleged criminals have to maintain their anonymity pending an adjudication of guilt—and after Daily Mail, those rights would seem to be minimal—the rights of crime victims to stay shielded from public view must be infinitely more substantial. Daily Mail was careful to state that the "holding in this case is narrow. . . . there is no issue here of privacy." Id., at 105, 99 S.Ct., at 2672 (emphasis added). But in this case, there is an issue of privacy—indeed, that is the principal issue—and therefore, this case falls outside of Daily Mail's "rule" (which, as I suggest above, was perhaps not even meant as a rule in the first place).

Consequently, I cannot agree that Cox Broadcasting, or Oklahoma Publishing, or Daily Mail requires—or even substantially supports—the result reached by the Court today.

II

We are left, then, to wonder whether the three "independent reasons" the Court cites for reversing the judgment for B.J.F. support its result. See ante, at 537-541.

The first of these reasons relied on by the Court is the fact "appellant gained access to B.J.F.'s name through a government news release." Ante, at 538. "The government's issuance of such a release, without qualification, can only convey to recipients that the government considered dissemination lawful," the Court suggests. Ibid. So described, this case begins to look like the situation in Oklahoma Publishing, where a judge invited reporters into his courtroom, but then tried to prohibit them from reporting on the proceedings they observed. But this case is profoundly different. Here, the "release" of information provided by the government was not, as the Court says, "without qualification." As the Star's own reporter conceded at trial, the crime incident report that inadvertently included B.J.F.'s name was posted in a room that contained signs making it clear that the names of rape victims were not matters of public record, and were not to be published. See 2 Record 113, 115, 117. The Star's reporter indicated that she understood that she "was not allowed to take down that information" (i.e., B.J.F.'s name) and that she "was not supposed to take the information from the police department." Id., at 117. Thus, by her own admission the posting of the incident report did not convey to the Star's reporter the idea that "the government considered dissemination lawful"; the Court's suggestion to the contrary is inapt.

Instead, Florida has done precisely what we suggested, in Cox Broadcasting, that States wishing to protect the privacy rights of rape victims might do: "respond to the challenge by means which avoid public documentation or other exposure of private information." 420 U.S., at 496, 95 S.Ct., at 1047 (emphasis added). By amending its public records statute to exempt rape victims names from disclosure, Fla.Stat. § 119.07(3)(h) (1983), and forbidding its officials to release such information, Fla.Stat. § 794.03 (1983), the State has taken virtually every step imaginable to prevent what happened here. This case presents a far cry, then, from Cox Broadcasting or Oklahoma Publishing, where the State asked the news media not to publish information it had made generally available to the public: here, the State is not asking the media to do the State's job in the first instance. Unfortunately, as this case illustrates, mistakes happen: even when States take measures to "avoid" disclosure, sometimes rape victims' names are found out. As I see it, it is not too much to ask the press, in instances such as this, to respect simple standards of decency and refrain from publishing a victims' name, address, and/or phone number. 2

Second, the Court complains that appellant was judged here under too strict a liability standard. The Court contends that a newspaper might be found liable under the Florida courts' negligence per se theory without regard to a newspaper's scienter or degree of fault. Ante, at 539-

540. The short answer to this complaint is that whatever merit the Court's argument might have, it is wholly inapposite here, where the jury found that appellant acted with "reckless indifference towards the rights of others," 2 Record 170, a standard far higher than the Gertz standard the Court urges as a constitutional minimum today. Ante, at 539-540. B.J.F. proved the Star's negligence at trial—and, actually, far more than simple negligence; the Court's concerns about damages resting on a strict liability or mere causation basis are irrelevant to the validity of the judgment for appellee.

But even taking the Court's concerns in the abstract, they miss the mark. Permitting liability under a negligence per se theory does not mean that defendants will be held liable without a showing of negligence, but rather, that the standard of care has been set by the legislature, instead of the courts. The Court says that negligence per se permits a plaintiff to hold a defendant liable without a showing that the disclosure was "of a fact about a person's private life . . . that a reasonable person would find highly offensive." Ibid. But the point here is that the legislature—reflecting popular sentiment—has determined that disclosure of the fact that a person was raped is categorically a revelation that reasonable people find offensive. And as for the Court's suggestion that the Florida courts' theory permits liability without regard for whether the victim's identity is already known, or whether she herself has made it known—these are facts that would surely enter into the calculation of damages in such a case. In any event, none of these mitigating factors was present here; whatever the force of these arguments generally, they do not justify the Court's ruling against B.J.F. in this case.

Third, the Court faults the Florida criminal statute for being underinclusive: § 794.03 covers disclosure of rape victims' names in " 'instruments of mass communication,' " but not other means of distribution, the Court observes. Ante, at 540. But our cases which have struck down laws that limit or burden the press due to their underinclusiveness have involved situations where a legislature has singled out one segment of the news media or press for adverse treatment, see, e.g., Daily Mail (re tricting newspapers and not radio or television), or singled out the press for adverse treatment when compared to other similarly situated enterprises, see, e.g., Minneapolis Star & Tribune Co. v. Minnesota Comm'r of Revenue, 460 U.S. 575, 578, 103 S.Ct. 1365, 1368, 75 L.Ed.2d 295 (1983). Here, the Florida law evenhandedly covers all "instruments of mass communication" no matter their form, media, content, nature, or purpose. It excludes neighborhood gossips, cf. ante, at 540, because presumably the Florida Legislature has determined that neighborhood gossips do not pose the danger and intrusion to rape victims that "instruments of mass communication" do. Simply put: Florida wanted to prevent the widespread distribution of rape victims' names, and therefore enacted a statute tailored almost as precisely as possible to achieving that end.

Moreover, the Court's "underinclusiveness" analysis itself is "underinclusive." After all, the lawsuit against the Star which is at issue here is not an action for violating the statute which the Court deems underinclusive, but is, more accurately, for the negligent publication of appellee's name. See App. to Juris. Statement A10. The scheme which the Court should review, then, is not only § 794.03 (which, as noted above, merely provided the standard of care in this litigation), but rather, the whole of Florida privacy tort law. As to the latter, Florida does recognize a tort of publication of private facts._3 Thus, it is quite possible that the neighborhood gossip whom the Court so fears being left scot free to spread news of a rape victim's identity would be subjected to the same (or similar) liability regime under which appellant was taxed. The Court's myopic focus on § 794.03 ignores the probability that Florida law is more comprehensive than the Court gives it credit for being.

Consequently, neither the State's "dissemination" of B.J.F.'s name, nor the standard of liability imposed here, nor the underinclusiveness of Florida tort law requires setting aside the verdict for B.J.F. And as noted above, such a result is not compelled by our cases. I turn, therefore, to the more general principles at issue here to see if they recommend the Court's result.

III

At issue in this case is whether there is any information about people, which—though true—may not be published in the press. By holding that only "a state interest of the highest order" permits the State to penalize the publication of truthful information, and by holding that protecting a rape victim's right to privacy is not among those state interests of the highest order, the Court accepts appellant's invitation, see Tr. of Oral Arg. 10-11, to obliterate one of the most noteworthy legal inventions of the 20th century: the tort of the publication of private facts. W. Prosser, J. Wade, & V. Schwartz, Torts 951-952 (8th ed. 1988). Even if the Court's opinion does not say as much today, such obliteration will follow inevitably from the Court's conclusion here. If the First Amendment prohibits wholly private persons (such as B.J.F.) from recovering for the publication of the fact that she was raped, I doubt that there remain any "private facts" which persons may assume will not be published in the newspapers or broadcast on television._4

Of course, the right to privacy is not absolute. Even the article widely relied upon in cases vindicating privacy rights, Warren & Brandeis, The Right to Privacy, 4 Harv.L.Rev. 193 (1890), recognized that this right inevitably conflicts with the public's right to know about matters of general concern—and that sometimes, the latter must trump the former. Id., at 214-215. Resolving this conflict is a difficult matter, and I fault the Court not for attempting to strike an appropriate balance between the two, but rather, fault it for according too little weight to B.J.F.'s side of equation, and too much on the other.

I would strike the balance rather differently. Writing for the Ninth Circuit, Judge Merrill put this view eloquently:

"Does the spirit of the Bill of Rights require that individuals be free to pry into the unnewsworthy private affairs of their fellowmen? In our view it does not. In our view, fairly defined areas of privacy must have the protection of law if the quality of life is to continue to be reasonably acceptable. The public's right to know is, then, subject to reasonable limitations so far as concerns the private facts of its individual members." Virgil v. Time, Inc., 527 F.2d 1122, 1128 (1975), cert. denied, 425 U.S. 998, 96 S.Ct. 2215, 48 L.Ed.2d 823 (1976).

Ironically, this Court, too, had occasion to consider this same balance just a few weeks ago, in United States Department of Justice v. Reporters Committee for Freedom of Press, 489 U.S. 749, 109 S.Ct. 1468, 103 L.Ed.2d 774 (1989). There, we were faced with a press request, under the Freedom of Information Act, for a "rap sheet" on a person accused of bribing a Congressman—presumably, a person whose privacy rights would be far less than B.J.F.'s. Yet this Court rejected the media's request for disclosure of the "rap sheet," saying:

"The privacy interest in maintaining the practical obscurity of rapsheet information will always be high. When the subject of such a rap sheet is a private citizen and when the information is in the Government's control as a compilation, rather than as a record of 'what the government is up to,' the privacy interest . . . is . . . at its apex while the . . . public interest in disclosure is at its nadir." Id., at 780, 109 S.Ct., at 1485.

The Court went on to conclude that disclosure of rap sheets "categorically" constitutes an "unwarranted" invasion of privacy. Ibid. The same surely must be true—indeed, much more so for the disclosure of a rape victim's name.

I do not suggest that the Court's decision today is a radical departure from a previously charted course. The Court's ruling has been foreshadowed. In Time, Inc. v. Hill, 385 U.S. 374, 383-384, n. 7, 87 S.Ct. 534, 539-540, n. 7, 17 L.Ed.2d 456 (1967), we observed that—after a brief period early in this century where Brandeis' view was ascendant—the trend in "modern" jurisprudence has been to eclipse an individual's right to maintain private any truthful information that the press

wished to publish. More recently, in Cox Broadcasting, 420 U.S. at 491, 95 S.Ct., at 1044, we acknowledged the possibility that the First Amendment may prevent a State from ever subjecting the publication of truthful but private information to civil liability. Today, we hit the bottom of the slippery slope.

I would find a place to draw the line higher on the hillside: a spot high enough to protect B.J.F.'s desire for privacy and peace-of-mind in the wake of a horrible personal tragedy. There is no public interest in publishing the names, addresses, and phone numbers of persons who are the victims of crime—and no public interest in immunizing the press from liability in the rare cases where a State's efforts to protect a victim's privacy have failed. Consequently, I respectfully dissent.₅

# Privacy overview

SPLC Legal Brief (c) 2011
Invasion of Privacy Law

The legal right of privacy has been defined as the right to be let alone, the right of a person "to withhold himself and his property from public scrutiny if he so chooses."

However, unlike the First Amendment right to free speech, privacy (in the media context) is not a right explicitly guaranteed by the Constitution.

Instead, privacy law has developed over the last 100 years. During that time, four separate kinds of privacy invasion have emerged: (1) **Public Disclosure of Private and Embarrassing Facts, (2) False Light, (3) Intrusion and (4) Misappropriation.**

With all four forms of invasion of privacy, **consent is a valid defense**. However, if you intend to rely on consent as your defense to a privacy claim you must make sure that you obtain the consent from someone with a legal right to give it and be candid with your subject about what information you want to use and how you intend to use it.

## 1. Public Disclosure of Private and Embarrassing Facts

Courts have recognized that certain intimate details about people, even though true, may be "off limits" to the press and public. For example, publishing detailed information about a private person's sexual conduct, medical condition or educational records might result in legal trouble. In order to succeed in this kind of lawsuit, the person suing must show that the information was:

(1) sufficiently private or not already in the public domain,

(2) sufficiently intimate, and

(3) highly offensive to a reasonable person.

The "Newsworthiness" Defense

A news organization will be protected from a private facts privacy claim if it can show that the material published was "newsworthy." Almost any information about a well-known public figure or a public official will be considered newsworthy. Furthermore, reports of recent involvement in criminal behavior will be considered newsworthy for anyone.

## 2. False Light

A false light claim can arise anytime you unflatteringly portray -in words or pictures- a person as something that he or she is not. A typical "false light" problem can arise where a misleading caption is published with a photo (for example, a caption describes a bystander at an unlawful demonstration as a "participant"). The elements of false light, found in the Restatement (Second) of Torts, Sec. 652E are:

(1) the portrayal must be found to be "highly offensive to a reasonable person" and

(2) the actor had knowledge of or acted in reckless disregard as to the falsity of the publicized matter and the false light in which the other would be placed.

The same legal standards that apply to libel apply to false light. The distinction between false light and libel is that in false light claims one need not prove injury or damage to reputation, but only that the statement was highly offensive. Courts in some states have refused to recognize false light claims because of their similarity to libel.

### 3. Intrusion Upon Seclusion

Intrusion is a claim often based on the act of news gathering. A reporter can be sued even when the information obtained is never published. It occurs when a reporter gathers information about a person in a place where that person has a reasonable right to expect privacy. However, newsworthiness can also be a defense to this kind of privacy invasion. As a general rule, reporters are allowed to enter privately owned public places, for example, private school campuses or malls. However, also as a general rule, they must leave when they are asked.

Three most common types of intrusion

(1) Trespass: going onto private property without the owner's consent.

(2) Secret Surveillance: using bugging equipment or hidden cameras. The laws vary by state but as a general rule reporters can legally photograph or record anything from a public area, such as a sidewalk, but they cannot use technology to improve upon what an unaided person would be able to see or hear from that public place.

(3) Misrepresentation: invalid or exceeded consent. Undercover reporting is not necessarily an invasion of privacy as long as the disguise is not used as a means to trespass or engage in an activity that would not otherwise be allowed. For example, it would not be an intrusion for a minority student reporter to pose as a potential pledge to investigate a story about racial discrimination inside a fraternity. The reporter has a right to pledge whether he is serious about it or not.

### 4. Misappropriation of Name or Likeness

Misappropriation is the unauthorized use of a person's name, photograph, likeness, voice or endorsement to promote the sale of a commercial product or service. (For example, using a photo of your school's star athlete in an for a pizza restaurant without her permission.) To avoid problems, publications should routinely have subjects sign a model release form written in simple, straightforward language when using their name or likeness in a commercial ad. Regardless of whether or not a release form has been signed, however, courts have generally allowed the media to reuse editorial photos or clips in its own self-promotion provided there is no suggestion that the person actually endorsed the publication.

CHAPTER 5

# Negligent harm

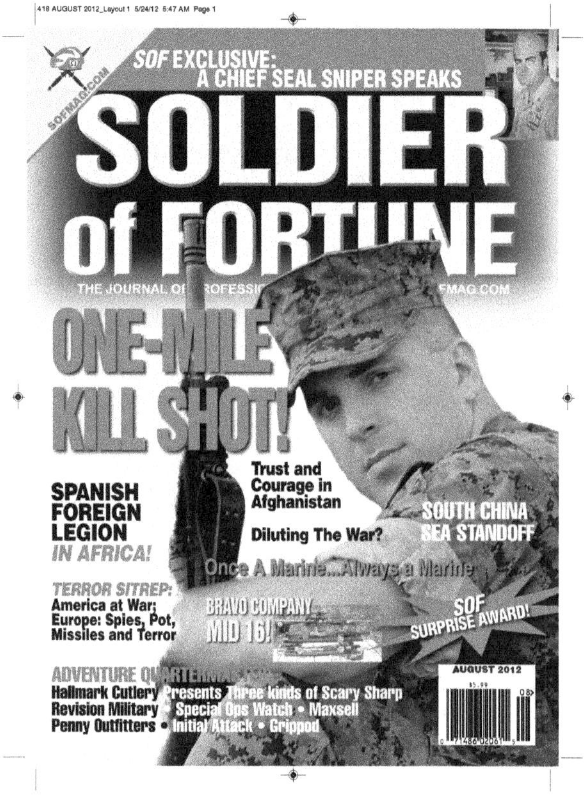

# Eimann v. Soldier of Fortune Magazine, Inc. (1989)

United States Court of Appeals for the Fifth Circuit

880 F.2d 830; 1989
August 17, 1989

**OPINION: W. EUGENE DAVIS, Circuit Judge**

Soldier of Fortune Magazine, Inc. appeals a $ 9.4 million jury verdict against it in a wrongful death action brought by the son and mother of a murder victim. The jury found that Soldier of Fortune acted with negligence and gross negligence in publishing a personal services classified advertisement through which the victim's husband hired an assassin to kill her. We reverse the judgment entered on the jury's verdict.

## I. FACTS

John Wayne Hearn shot and killed Sandra Black at the behest of her husband, Robert, who offered to pay Hearn $ 10,000 for doing so. Robert Black contacted Hearn through a classified advertisement that Hearn ran in Soldier of Fortune Magazine, Inc. (SOF), a publication that focuses on mercenary activities and military affairs.

The ad, which ran in the September, October and November 1984 issues of SOF, read:

EX-MARINES -- 67-69 'Nam Vets, Ex-DI, weapons specialist -- jungle warfare, pilot, M.E., high risk assignments, U.S. or overseas. (404) 991-2684.

Hearn testified that "Ex-DI" meant ex-drill instructor; "M.E." meant multi-engine planes; and "high risk assignments" referred to work as a bodyguard or security specialist. Hearn testified that he and another former Marine placed the ad to recruit Vietnam veterans for work as bodyguards and security men for executives. Hearn's partner testified that they also hoped to train troops in South America. This partner never participated in any ad-related jobs and quit the venture shortly after the ad first ran.

Hearn and his partner testified that they did not place the ad with an intent to solicit criminal employment. However, Hearn stated that about 90 percent of the callers who responded to the ad sought his participation in illegal activities including beatings, kidnappings, jailbreaks, bombings and murders. It also generated at least one lawful inquiry from an oil conglomerate in Lebanon seeking ten bodyguards; Hearn received a commission for placing seven men with the company.

Between early 1982 and January 1984, Black had asked at least four friends or coworkers from Bryan, Texas to kill Sandra Black or help him kill her. All four refused. Black called Hearn in October 1984 after seeing his ad in SOF.

Hearn testified that his initial conversations with Black focused on Black's inquiries about getting bodyguard work through Hearn. In later calls they discussed the sale of Black's gun collection to Hearn. Hearn testified that he traveled from his home in Atlanta to Black's home in Bryan on January 9, 1985 to look at Black's gun collection. Hearn stated that Black discussed his plans for murdering his wife during the meeting and "hinted" that he wanted Hearn to participate, but did not ask Hearn directly to kill his wife. Hearn did not act on the hint and returned to Atlanta.

Black called Hearn repeatedly after Hearn returned to Atlanta. During one call Black spoke with Hearn's girlfriend, Debbie Bannister. Hearn and Bannister met after she called him in response to his SOF ad.

Black proposed directly that Hearn kill his wife during the call to Bannister. She passed the proposal on to Hearn, who called Black and said he would consider doing it. The two talked by phone several times in the following weeks. After an aborted murder attempt about three weeks later -- during which Hearn was to help Black himself kill his wife -- Hearn killed Sandra Black on February 21, 1985. By that time Hearn also had killed the ex-husband of Bannister's sister on January 6, 1985 and Bannister's husband on February 2, 1985.

Neither Hearn, who was sentenced to concurrent life sentences for the murders, nor his partner had criminal records when they placed their ad in SOF. Neither had received a dishonorable discharge from the Marines. Further, Hearn included his real name and correct address in submitting the ad to SOF; the ad itself listed Hearn's correct home telephone number.

Sandra Black's son, Gary Wayne Black, and her mother, Marjorie Eimann, sued SOF and its parent, Omega Group, Ltd., for wrongful death under Texas law on the theory that SOF negligently published Hearn's classified ad.

Eimann introduced into evidence about three dozen personal service classified ads selected from the 2,000 or so classified ads that SOF had printed from its inception in 1975 until September 1984. Some ads of-

Marjorie A. EIMANN, Individually, as Next Friend of Gary Wayne Black, and as Representative of the Estate of Sandra Kay Black, Deceased, and Glenn G. Eimann, Plaintiffs-Appellees,

v.

SOLDIER OF FORTUNE MAGAZINE, INC. and Omega Group, Inc., Defendants-Appellants

fered services as a "Mercenary for Hire," "bounty hunter" or "mechanic"; others promised to perform "dirty work," "high risk contracts" or to "do anything, anywhere at the right price."

Eimann presented evidence that seven and perhaps as many as nine classified ads had been tied to crimes or criminal plots. Eimann introduced stories from sources including the Associated Press, United Press International, The Rocky Mountain News, The Denver Post, Time and Newsweek that reported on links between SOF classified ads and at least five of these crimes.

Eimann also presented evidence that law enforcement officials had contacted SOF staffers during investigations of two crimes linked to SOF personal service classifieds. In one case, SOF had provided correspondence from its files -- along with two affidavits signed by SOF's managing editor -- that were used in the 1982 criminal trial of a Houston man who was convicted of soliciting the murder of his wife; during his effort the man had tried to hire a poisons expert by placing a classified ad in the October 1981 issue of SOF. Eimann also presented testimony from a New Jersey detective, who stated that in April 1984, SOF's advertising manager had helped him to identify a man who placed a classified ad in SOF.

In addition, Eimann presented expert testimony from Dr. Park Dietz, a forensic psychiatrist who had studied SOF, its ads and readership. Dietz testified that an average SOF subscriber -- a male who owns camouflage clothing and more than one gun -- would understand some phrases in SOF's classified ads as solicitations for illegal activity given the "context" of those ads.

That context included other classified ads in SOF, display ads for semi-automatic rifles and books with titles such as "How to Kill," and SOF articles including "Harassing the Bear, New Afghan Tactics Stall Soviet

Victory," "Pipestone Canyon, Summertime in 'Nam and the Dyin' was Easy," and "Night Raiders on Russia's Border." Dietz also described his visit to a SOF convention in summer 1987, where he photographed exhibits of weapons and tactical gear.

Based on his studies, Dietz concluded that the Hearn ad "or any other personal service ad in Soldier of Fortune in 1984 foreseeably is related to the commission of domestic crimes." He suggested that classified ads such as Hearn's would not carry such connotations if they appeared in Esquire or Vanity Fair.

Dietz conceded, however, that he had abandoned an effort to distinguish lawful SOF classified ads from criminal ones on the basis of specific code words such as "gun for hire," "mechanic" and "hunter" because some ads were too ambiguous to assign an illegal meaning to them with any certainty. He also noted that crimes had been linked to SOF classified ads that "seemed relatively innocuous." For example, one ad tied to a kidnapping and extortion plot read:

Recovery and collection. International agents guarantee results on any type of recover[y]. Reply to Delta Enterprises, P.O. Box 5241, Rockford, Illinois 61125.

As Dietz stated, "The code system doesn't work."

SOF relied primarily on the testimony of its president, Robert K. Brown, who stated he did not know or suspect in 1984 that some of the SOF classified ads had been linked to criminal plots. Other SOF staffers and readers echoed these denials. SOF's advertising manager, Joan Steele, testified that she understood the phrase "high risk assignments" in Hearn's ad to mean "gun for hire," but in the sense of a professional bodyguard or security consultant rather than a contract killer.

The district court's first special interrogatory asked the jury whether Hearn's ad "related to" illegal activity. The court's second interrogatory asked, "Did [SOF] . . . know or should it have known from the face or the context of the Hearn advertisement that the advertisement could reasonably be interpreted as an offer to engage in illegal activity?"

The court's instructions charged SOF with knowledge that Hearn's ad reasonably could be interpreted as such an offer when (1) the relation to illegal activity appears on the ad's face; or (2) "the advertisement, embroidered by its context, would lead a reasonable publisher of ordinary prudence under the same or similar circumstances to conclude that the advertisement could reasonably be interpreted" as an offer to commit crimes. The court went on to define "context" as the magazine's (1) "nature"; (2) other advertisements; (3) articles; (4) readership; and (5) knowledge, if any, that other advertisements in the magazine could reasonably be interpreted as an offer to engage in illegal activity.

The jury answered "yes" to the first two interrogatories, and found that SOF's negligence was a proximate cause of Sandra Black's death in response to Interrogatory Three. The court then asked the jury whether SOF's negligence constituted "gross negligence," defined as "conscious indifference." The jury answered "yes" to this interrogatory as well. The jury awarded Eimann $ 1.9 million in compensatory damages and $ 7.5 million in punitive damages; the district court entered judgment on the verdict. SOF appeals.

II. ANALYSIS

A. Overview

Eimann presented this case as a straight-forward negligence action revolving around one primary issue: whether SOF knew or should have known from the face or context of Hearn's ad that it represented an offer to perform illegal acts. Based on evidence that SOF knew of links between other classified ads and other criminal plots, she contends that SOF owed a duty to recognize ads such as Hearn's that reasonably might be interpreted as criminal solicitations and refrain from publishing them.

SOF argues first that no liability can attach under these facts because the criminal activities of Hearn and Robert Black, rather than Hearn's ad, were the proximate cause of Sandra Black's murder. SOF also argues that imposition of tort liability here contravenes first amendment protection for commercial speech because (1) the judgment below impermissibly imposed a duty on publishers to investigate its advertisers and their ads; and (2) the district court's all-encompassing definition of "context," combined with Dietz's testimony, allowed the jury to penalize SOF for the mercenary and military focus of the magazine's articles and other ads.

We need not address SOF's first amendment attacks on the judgment to resolve this appeal. Assuming without deciding that a Texas court would apply general negligence principles to this case, we conclude that no liability can attach under these principles as a matter of law. SOF owed no duty to refrain from publishing a facially innocuous classified advertisement when the ad's context -- at most -- made its message ambiguous.

Under Texas law, negligence liability requires the existence of a duty, breach of that duty, and an injury proximately resulting from that breach. City of Gladewater v. Pike, 727 S.W.2d 514, 517 (Tex. 1987). The existence of a duty presents a threshold question of law for the court; the jury determines breach and proximate cause only after the court concludes that a duty exists. See Otis Engineering Corp. v. Clark, 668 S.W.2d 307, 309 (Tex. 1983); Abalos v. Oil Dev. Co., 544 S.W.2d 627, 633 (Tex. 1976). Our resolution of this case hinges on the initial duty question.

B. Duty

In essence, a duty represents a legally enforceable obligation to conform to a particular standard of conduct. W. Keeton, D. Dobbs, R. Keeton & D. Owen, Prosser and Keeton on Torts § 53 at 356 (5th Ed. 1984). Whether the defendant in a negligence action owes a duty involves consideration of two related issues: (1) whether the defendant owes an obligation to this particular plaintiff to act as a reasonable person would in the circumstances; and (2) the standard of conduct required to satisfy that obligation. Id.

Texas courts have applied risk-utility balancing tests in resolving both aspects of the duty question. Thus, in deciding whether an actor owes a duty of reasonable care to the public at large, the Supreme Court of Texas has weighed the risk, foreseeability and likelihood of injury from certain conduct against the conduct's social utility and the burden of guarding against injury. See Otis Engineering Corp. v. Clark, 668 S.W.2d 307, 309 (Tex. 1983) (employer who exercises control over incapacitated employee owes duty of reasonable care to prevent employee from creating unreasonable risk of harm to the public).

Similarly, Texas courts have applied risk-utility analysis in determining the second duty issue -- whether a defendant who owes an established duty of reasonable care to specified parties must take precautions against particular dangers. See Hendricks v. Todora, 722 S.W.2d 458, 461 (Tex.App. -- Dallas 1986, writ ref'd n.r.e.) (duty of reasonable care did not require lessee restaurant or its lessor to protect business invitee customers against drunken driver who crashed into restaurant's waiting area). Courts have described this aspect of duty as the defendant's obligation to protect those parties against unreasonable risks. Id.; see Prosser & Keeton, supra, § 31. A risk becomes unreasonable when its magnitude outweighs the social utility of the act or omission that creates it. Hendricks, 722 S.W.2d at 461; Restatement (Second) of Torts § 291 (1965).

Our analysis here assumes that SOF owes a duty of reasonable care to the public; we focus on the second prong of the duty issue: whether SOF's decision to print Hearn's ad violated the standard of conduct.

In answering this question we look to Judge Learned Hand's concise expression of these balancing principles in United States v. Carroll Towing, 159 F.2d 169, 173 (2d Cir. 1947). As he described it in algebraic terms, liability turns on whether the burden of adequate precautions, B, is less than the probability of harm, P, multiplied by the gravity of the resulting injury, L. In other words, an actor falls below the standard of conduct and liability attaches when B is less than PL. Conversely, the actor satisfies the obligation to protect against unreasonable risks when the burden of adequate precautions -- examined in light of the challenged action's value -- outweighs the probability and gravity of the threatened harm. See Prosser & Keeton, supra § 31 at 173; Restatement (Second) of Torts § 291; Hendricks, 722 S.W.2d at 461.

We now turn to these individual factors.

1. The Probability and Gravity of the Threatened Harm

In assessing the threatened harm we note that "nearly all human acts . . . carry some recognizable but remote possibility of harm to another." Prosser & Keeton, supra, § 31 at 170. The SOF classified ads presented more than a remote risk. Of the 2,000 or so personal service classified ads that SOF printed between 1975 and 1984, Eimann's evidence established that as many as nine had served as links in criminal plots. Of these nine, the evidence revealed that SOF staffers had participated in at least two police investigations of crimes in which classified ads played a role; other crimes tied to the ads received varying amounts of media coverage.

As noted above, the gravity of the threatened harm may require precautions against even unlikely events. Id. For example, the standard of care may require those who own oil storage tanks to take precautions against fires caused by an unpredictable lightning strike. See, e.g., Tex-Jersey Oil Corp. v. Beck, 292 S.W.2d 803, 807-09 (Tex.Civ.App. -- Texarkana 1956), aff'd in part and rev'd in part on other grounds, 157 Tex. 541, 305 S.W.2d 162 (Tex. 1957), overruled on other grounds in Sanchez v. Schindler, 651 S.W.2d 249, 251 (Tex. 1983). The prospect of ad-inspired crime represents a threat of serious harm. Eimann presented evidence that SOF classified ads played a role in other crimes ranging from extortion to jailbreaks. Sandra Black's murder illustrates one aspect of the crime linked to SOF classified advertisements.

2. The Burden of Preventing the Harm

SOF contends that the standard of conduct applied by the district court impermissibly required the magazine to guard against criminal solicitation by investigating its advertisers and their ads. It relies on a series of cases holding that newspaper publishers owe no duty in tort to investigate their advertisers for the accuracy of ads placed for publication. See Pittman v. Dow Jones & Co., 662 F. Supp. 921, 923 (E.D.La. 1987).

However, in our view the standard of conduct against which the jury measured SOF's actions was more exacting than a duty to investigate; it requires publishers to recognize ads that "reasonably could be interpreted as an offer to engage in illegal activity" based on their words or "context" and refrain from printing them. Based on evidence that SOF knew other ads had been tied to crimes, Eimann's counsel contended at oral argument that SOF should have refrained from publishing Hearn's ad and all other personal service classified ads -- suggestive ones and bland ones alike. This represents an especially heavy burden given (1) the ambiguous nature of Hearn's ad; and (2) the pervasiveness of advertising in our society.

At most, the evidence reveals that Hearn submitted a facially innocuous ad. Standing alone, the phrase "high risk assignments" plausibly encompassed Hearn's professed goal of recruiting candidates for bodyguard jobs. Hearn performed precisely that function for at least one client who contacted him through the ad.

Eimann's effort to portray Hearn's ad as a readily identifiable criminal solicitation falls with Dr. Dietz's repudiation of his effort to identify specific code words signalling criminal intent. At one point in his testimony, Dr. Dietz analyzed a classified ad from the February 1980 issue of SOF. In terms that parallel Hearn's ad, this 1980 ad recruited SOF readers for "exciting high risk undercover stateside work." A court later convicted the individual who submitted it of mailing a threatening communication after he sent a letter instructing someone who had responded to the ad to "terminate" a person in Oklahoma City. Dr. Dietz stated:

In 1984, in my opinion, someone familiar with the classified ads that have been run for years in Soldier of Fortune would be able to recognize from that ad that this is possibly someone who would be willing to be involved in criminal activity; but they might be wrong when they thought that. We knew that sometimes there were honest advertisers, and we know that some of the readers who responded to ads were honest too.

Dr. Dietz's description applies with equal force to Hearn's ad. Its bare terms reveal no identifiable offer to commit crimes, just as a locksmith's ad in the telephone directory reveals nothing about that particular advertiser's willingness to commit burglaries or steal cars.

This ambiguity persists even if we assume that SOF knew other ads had been tied to criminal plots. No evidence linked the other ads and crimes to Hearn. And as Eimann conceded, even if SOF had investigated Hearn and his partner in 1984, it would have discovered no criminal records and no false information that might have aroused suspicion.

Further, Eimann's heavy reliance on "context" cannot compensate for the fundamental ambiguity of Hearn's ad even if we assume that the district court properly defined that context. The presence in SOF of other ads and articles with violent themes provides no realistic method for gauging the likelihood that a particular ad will foster illegal activity. Do ads touting high-performance cars become solicitations for illegal activity when buyers drive them beyond the speed limit? Only when the ads run in Car and Driver magazine? Or, only when the ads run in magazines that also contain ads for radar detectors?

While we do not reach SOF's first amendment arguments, the Supreme Court's recognition of limited first amendment protection for commercial speech nonetheless highlights the important role of such communication for purposes of risk-benefit analysis. As the Court has noted, "The particular consumer's interest in the free flow of commercial information . . . may be as keen, if not keener by far, than his interest in the day's most urgent political debate. . . ." Virginia State Board of Pharmacy v. Virginia Citizens Consumer Council, Inc., 425 U.S. 748, 763, 96 S. Ct. 1817, 1827, 48 L. Ed. 2d 346 (1976). The Supreme Court's subsequent emphasis on the states' interest in regulating commercial speech neither erases this first amendment protection nor alters the fact that advertising is a part of daily life. See Central Hudson Gas & Elec. Corp. v. Public Service Comm'n, 447 U.S. 557, 100 S. Ct. 2343, 65 L. Ed. 2d 341 (1980); Posadas de Puerto Rico Associates v. Tourism Co., 478 U.S. 328, 106 S. Ct. 2968, 92 L. Ed. 2d 266 (1986).

Eimann seeks to discount the importance of SOF's classified ads by stressing that (1) SOF's publisher promoted the ads because they added to the "flavor and mystique" of the magazine; and (2) the jury found that Hearn's ad "relate[d] to" illegal activity. She notes that the Supreme Court has excluded advertising of illegal activity from the scope of first amendment protection. See Pittsburgh Press Co. v. Pittsburgh Commission on Human Relations, 413 U.S. 376, 388-89, 93 S. Ct. 2553, 2560-61, 37 L. Ed. 2d 669 (1973) (newspaper's placement of help-wanted ads in sex-segregated columns violated anti-discrimination ordinance; "Any First Amendment interest which might have been served by advertising an ordinary commercial product . . . is altogether absent when the commercial activity itself is illegal. . . .") However, in the constitutional arena we have noted that the possibility of illegal results does not necessarily strip an ad of its commercial speech protection.

In Dunagin v. City of Oxford, 718 F.2d 738 (5th Cir. 1983) (en banc), this court upheld the constitutionality of a Mississippi law that banned liquor advertising by local, in-state media on grounds that the ban was no broader than necessary to advance the goal of promoting prohibition in the state's dry counties. See Central Hudson, 447 U.S. at 566, 100 S. Ct. at 2351. But in doing so the court rejected arguments that liquor advertising necessarily related to unlawful activity in Mississippi -- even though nearly half of Mississippi's counties are dry, and even though wet counties prohibit alcohol consumption in places such as public schools and colleges. The court stated,

The commercial speech doctrine would disappear if its protection ceased whenever the advertised produce might be used illegally. Peanut butter advertising cannot be banned just because someone might someday throw a jar at the presidential motorcade. Dunagin, 718 F.2d at 743.

Similarly, a standard of conduct that imposes tort liability whenever the advertised product "could reasonably be interpreted as an offer to engage in illegal activity" -- or might "relate to" criminal conduct -- imposes an especially heavy burden. The comments of a court faced with a duty-to-investigate claim apply here:

For the law to permit such exposure to those in the publishing business who in good faith accept paid advertisements for a myriad of products would open the doors "to a liability in an indeterminate amount for an indeterminate time to an indeterminate class." Yuhas v. Mudge, 129 N.J. Super. 207, 322 A.2d 824 (App.Div. 1974) (publisher owes no duty to investigate safety of "inherently dangerous" products advertised in its publication). Relatedly, the publication's editorial content would surely feel the economic crunch from loss of revenue that would result if publishers were required to reject all ambiguous advertisements. See

Walters v. Seventeen Magazine, 195 Cal. App. 3d 1119, 241 Cal. Rptr. 101, 103 (1987).

3. Balancing the Burdens and Risks

We conclude that the standard of conduct imposed by the district court does not strike the proper balance between the risks of harm from ambiguous advertisement and the burden of preventing harm from this source under these facts. The appreciable risk that ads such as Hearn's will cause harm, combined with the gravity of that harm, does not outweigh the onerous burden Eimann asks us to endorse.

Hearn's ad presents a risk of serious harm. But everyday activities, such as driving on high-speed, closed access roadways, also carry definite risks that we as a society choose to accept in return for the activity's usefulness and convenience. See Restatement (Second) of Torts § 291 comment e at 56 (1965). To take a more extreme example, courts have almost uniformly rejected efforts to hold handgun manufacturers liable under negligence or strict liability theories to gunshot victims injured during crimes, despite the real possibility that such products can be used for criminal purposes. See Perkins v. F.I.E. Corp., 762 F.2d 1250, 1275 (5th Cir. 1985) (applying Louisiana law); Armijo v. Ex Cam, Inc., 656 F. Supp. 771, 775 (D.N.M. 1987) (applying New Mexico law); Caveny v. Raven Arms Co., 665 F. Supp. 530, 536 (S.D.Ohio 1987) (applying Ohio law); Patterson v. Gesellschaft, 608 F. Supp. 1206 (N.D.Tex. 1985) (applying Texas law). Given the pervasiveness of advertising in our society and the important role it plays, we decline to impose on publishers the obligation to reject all ambiguous advertisements for products or services that might pose a threat of harm.

III. CONCLUSION

The standard of conduct imposed by the district court against SOF is too high; it allows a jury to visit liability on a publisher for untoward consequences that flow from his decision to publish any suspicious, ambiguous ad that might cause serious harm. The burden on a publisher to avoid liability from suits of this type is too great: he must reject all such advertisements.

The range of foreseeable misuses of advertised products and services is as limitless as the forms and functions of the products themselves. Without a more specific indication of illegal intent than Hearn's ad or its context provided, we conclude that SOF did not violate the required standard of conduct by publishing an ad that later played a role in criminal activity.

The judgment of the district court is REVERSED and RENDERED.

## SECTION 2

# Braun v. Soldier of Fortune Magazine (1992)

United States Court of Appeals, Eleventh Circuit.

968 F.2d 1110 (1992)

Decided: Aug. 13, 1992.

Before ANDERSON and DUBINA, Circuit Judges, and ESCHBACH[*], Senior Circuit Judge.

**ANDERSON, Circuit Judge:**

Soldier of Fortune Magazine, Inc., and its parent, Omega Group, Ltd., (hereinafter collectively referred to as "SOF") appeal a $4,375,000 jury verdict against them in a consolidated tort action brought by Michael and Ian Braun, the sons of a murder victim. The jury found that SOF acted with negligence and malice in publishing a personal service advertisement through which plaintiffs' father's business partner hired an assassin to kill him. We affirm the judgment entered on the jury's verdict.

I. FACTS

In January 1985, Michael Savage submitted a personal service advertisement to SOF. After several conversations between Savage and SOF's advertising manager, Joan Steel, the following advertisement ran in the June 1985 through March 1986 issues of SOF:

GUN FOR HIRE: 37 year old professional mercenary desires jobs. Vietnam Veteran. Discrete [sic] and very private. Body guard, courier, and other special skills. All jobs considered. Phone (615) 436-9785 (days) or (615) 436-4335 (nights), or write: Rt. 2, Box 682 Village Loop Road, Gatlinburg, TN 37738.

Savage testified that, when he placed the ad, he had no intention of obtaining anything but legitimate jobs. Nonetheless, Savage stated that the overwhelming majority of the 30 to 40 phone calls a week he received in response to his ad sought his participation in criminal activity such as murder, assault, and kidnapping. The ad also generated at least one legitimate job as a bodyguard, which Savage accepted.

In late 1984 or early 1985, Bruce Gastwirth began seeking to murder his business partner, Richard Braun. Gastwirth enlisted the aid of another business associate, John Horton Moore, and together they arranged for at least three attempts on Braun's life, all of which were unsuccessful. Responding to Savage's SOF ad, Gastwirth and Moore contacted him in August 1985 to discuss plans to murder Braun.

On August 26, 1985, Savage, Moore, and another individual, Sean Trevor Doutre, went to Braun's suburban Atlanta home. As Braun and his sixteen year-old son Michael were driving down the driveway, Doutre stepped in front of Braun's car and fired several shots into the car with a MAC 11 automatic pistol. The shots hit Michael in the thigh and wounded Braun as well. Braun managed to roll out of the car, but Doutre walked over to Braun and killed him by firing two more shots into the back of his head as Braun lay on the ground.

## II. PROCEEDINGS BELOW

On March 31, 1988, appellees Michael and Ian Braun filed this diversity action against appellants in the United States District Court for the Middle District of Alabama, seeking damages for the wrongful death of their father. Michael Braun also filed a separate action seeking recovery for the personal injuries he received at the time of his father's death. The district court consolidated these related matters.

Trial began on December 3, 1990. Appellees contended that, under Georgia law, SOF was liable for their injuries because SOF negligently published a personal service advertisement that created an unreasonable risk of the solicitation and commission of violent criminal activity, including murder. To show that SOF knew of the likelihood that criminal activity would result from placing an ad like Savage's, appellees introduced evidence of newspaper and magazine articles published prior to Braun's murder which described links between SOF personal service ads and a number of criminal convictions including murder, kidnapping, assault, extortion, and attempts thereof.[1] Appellees also presented evidence that, prior to SOF's acceptance of Savage's ad, law enforcement officials had contacted SOF staffers on two separate occasions in connection with investigations of crimes--a solicitation to commit murder in Houston, Texas, and a kidnapping in New Jersey--linked to SOF personal service ads.

In his trial testimony, SOF president Robert K. Brown denied having any knowledge of criminal activity associated with SOF's personal service ads at any time prior to Braun's murder in August 1985.[2] Both Jim Graves, a former managing editor of SOF, and Joan Steel, the advertising manager who accepted Savage's advertisement, similarly testified that they were not aware of other crimes connected with SOF ads prior to running Savage's ad. Steel further testified that she had understood the term "Gun for Hire" in Savage's ad to refer to a "bodyguard or protection service-type thing," rather than to any illegal activity.

At the end of the five day trial, the district court gave the following instructions on negligence to the jury:

In order to prevail in this case Plaintiffs must prove to your reasonable satisfaction by a preponderance of the evidence that a reasonable reading of the advertisement in this case would have conveyed to a magazine publisher, such as Soldier of Fortune, that this ad presented the clear and present danger of causing serious harm to the public from violent criminal activity. The Plaintiffs must prove that the ad in question contained a clearly identifiable unreasonable risk, that the offer in the ad is one to commit a serious violent crime, including murder.

Now, while Defendants owe a duty of reasonable care to the public, the magazine publisher does not have a duty to investigate every ad it publishes. Defendants owe no duty to the Plaintiffs for publishing an ad if the ad's language on its face would not convey to the reader that it created an unreasonable risk that the advertiser was available to commit such violent crimes as murder.

Now, of course, the tendency to read the advertisement in question in hindsight is hard to avoid, but it must be avoided. The test for you is not how the advertisement in question reads now in light of subsequent events, but rather how the advertisement read to a reasonable publisher at the time of publication. You should view the facts and these instructions with particular care in this case, in view of the First Amendment to the Constitution, which protects the free flow of truthful and legitimate information even when it is of a commercial rather than a political nature.

The district court further instructed that, if the jury found that SOF was negligent and that this negligence was the proximate cause of appellees' father's death, it could "award damages for the value of the life of Richard Braun," but not for mental anguish, emotional distress, or the family's loss of companionship. The court also stated that, if the jury found that SOF was negligent and that this negligence was the proximate cause of appellee Michael Braun's injuries, it could award full compensation, including recovery for both physical pain and mental anguish. The district court also noted that Georgia law permitted punitive damages for appellee Michael Braun's personal injury claim but that, to award punitive damages, the jury must first find that SOF "acted maliciously or with an entire want of care which constitutes conscious indifference to the consequences."

The jury returned a verdict in favor of appellees and awarded compensatory damages on the wrongful death claim in the amount of $2,000,000. The jury also awarded appellee Michael Braun $375,000 in compensatory damages and $10,000,000 in punitive damages for his personal injury claim. The district court entered judgment in accordance with the jury's verdict on December 7, 1990.

On January 23, 1991, the district court denied SOF's motion for judgment notwithstanding the verdict, but ruled that it would grant SOF's motion for a new trial unless there were an agreement to a remittitur reducing the punitive damages awarded to $2,000,000. Appellees agreed to the remittitur, and an amended judgment was entered on February 6, 1991. 757 F.Supp. 1325. SOF appeals.

## III. DISCUSSION

The district court, sitting in Alabama, properly looked to Georgia law in resolving appellees' negligence claims. In Klaxon Co. v. Stentor Electric Mfg. Co., 313 U.S. 487, 494, 61 S.Ct. 1020, 1020, 85 L.Ed. 1477 (1941), the Supreme Court held that "in diversity cases the federal courts must follow conflict of laws rules prevailing in the states in which they sit." Under Alabama law, "the substantive law of the state where the injury occurred is applied when suit is brought in Alabama." Bodnar v. Piper Aircraft Corp., 392 So.2d 1161, 1162 (Ala.1980). Since Richard Braun's murder and appellee Michael Braun's injuries both oc-

curred in Georgia, Alabama conflict of laws rules required that the district court apply Georgia law.

### A. Duty Under Georgia Law

To prevail in an action for negligence in Georgia, a party must establish the following elements:

(1) A legal duty to conform to a standard of conduct raised by the law for the protection of others against unreasonable risks of harm; (2) a breach of this standard; (3) a legally attributable causal connection between the conduct and the resulting injury; and (4) some loss or damage flowing to the plaintiff's legally protected interest as a result of the alleged breach of the legal duty.

Bradley Center, Inc. v. Wessner, 250 Ga. 199, 296 S.E.2d 693, 695 (1982) (citing Lee Street Auto Sales, Inc. v. Warren, 102 Ga.App. 345, 116 S.E.2d 243, 245 (1960)). Under Georgia law, the existence of a legal duty presents a threshold question of law for the court. First Federal Sav. Bank of Brunswick v. Fretthold, 195 Ga.App. 482, 394 S.E.2d 128, 131 (1990). Once a court finds that a legal duty exists, it generally leaves for the jury issues of negligence and proximate cause. Hogan v. Pony Exp. Courier Corp., 195 Ga.App. 592, 394 S.E.2d 391, 392 (1990).

The district court found that publishers like SOF have a duty to the public when they publish an advertisement if "the ad in question contain[s] a clearly identifiable unreasonable risk, that the offer in the ad is one to commit a serious violent crime, including murder." SOF argues that the district court erred in finding that a publisher has a duty "to reject ambiguous advertisements that pose a threat of harm," Brief for Appellants at 24, and contends that a publisher should be held liable for publishing an ad only if the ad explicitly solicits a crime. Since the existence of a duty presents a question of law, we subject the district court's determination to de novo review. Newell v. Prudential Ins. Co. of America, 904 F.2d 644, 649 (11th Cir.1990).

Georgia courts recognize a "general duty one owes to all the world not to subject them to an unreasonable risk of harm." Bradley Center, 296 S.E.2d at 695. Accordingly, the district court properly found that SOF had a legal duty to refrain from publishing advertisements that subjected the public, including appellees, to a clearly identifiable unreasonable risk of harm from violent criminal activity. To the extent that SOF denies that a publisher owes any duty to the public when it publishes personal service ads, its position is clearly inconsistent with Georgia law. We believe, however, that the crux of SOF's argument is not that it had no duty to the public, but that, as a matter of law, the risk to the public presented when a publisher prints an advertisement is "unreasonable" only if the ad openly solicits criminal activity. See Reply Brief for Appellants at 24.

1. Risk-Utility Balancing

To determine whether the risk to others that an individual's actions pose is "unreasonable," Georgia courts generally apply a risk-utility balancing test. See Hanchey v. Hart, 120 Ga.App. 677, 171 S.E.2d 918, 921 (1969); Johnson v. Thompson, 111 Ga.App. 654, 143 S.E.2d 51, 53 (1965); Ely v. Barbizon Towers, Inc., 101 Ga.App. 872, 115 S.E.2d 616, 620 (1960). A risk is unreasonable if it is "of such magnitude as to outweigh what the law regards as the utility of the defendant's alleged negligent conduct." Johnson, 143 S.E.2d at 53. Simply put, liability depends upon whether the burden on the defendant of adopting adequate precautions is less than the probability of harm from the defendant's unmodified conduct multiplied by the gravity of the injury that might result from the defendant's unmodified conduct. United States v. Carroll Towing Co., 159 F.2d 169, 173 (2d Cir.1947).

For the reasons stated below, we find that the district court properly struck the risk-utility balance when it instructed that the jury could hold SOF liable for printing Savage's advertisement only if the advertisement on its face would have alerted a reasonably prudent publisher to the clearly identifiable unreasonable risk of harm to the public that the advertisement posed. Our application of Georgia's risk-utility balancing principles persuades us that the duty of care the district court imposed on publishers was an appropriate reconciliation of Georgia's interest in providing compensation to victims of tortious conduct with the First Amendment concern that state law not chill protected speech. Accordingly, we reject SOF's argument that the district court's instructions "place[d] an intolerable burden upon the press." Brief for Appellants at 20.

SOF relies heavily on Eimann v. Soldier of Fortune Magazine, Inc., 880 F.2d 830 (5th Cir.1989), cert. denied, 493 U.S. 1024, 110 S.Ct. 729, 107 L.Ed.2d 748 (1990), to support its contention that the district court erred in its application of risk-utility balancing to this case. In Eimann, the son and mother of a murder victim brought a wrongful death action under Texas law against SOF, seeking to hold SOF liable for publishing a personal service ad through which the victim's husband hired an assassin to kill her. The advertisement in question read:

EX-MARINES--67-69 'Nam Vets, Ex-DI, weapons specialist-jungle warfare, pilot, M.E., high risk assignments, U.S. or overseas. (404) 991-2684.

Id. at 831. The district court instructed the jury that it could find SOF liable if "(1) the relation to illegal activity appears on the ad's face; or (2) 'the advertisement, embroidered by its context, would lead a reasonable publisher of ordinary prudence under the same or similar circumstances to conclude that the advertisement could reasonably be interpreted' as an offer to commit crimes." Id. at 833 (quoting district court instructions). The jury found for plaintiffs and awarded them $1.9 million in compensatory damages and $7.5 million in punitive damages. Id.

The Fifth Circuit reversed the jury's verdict. After applying Texas risk-utility balancing principles similar to Georgia's, the court concluded that "[t]he standard of conduct imposed by the district court against SOF is too high...." Id. at 838. To impose liability whenever the advertised product "could reasonably be interpreted as an offer to engage in illegal activity" would require a publisher to reject all ambiguous ads. Id. at 837. The court stated: "Without a more specific indication of illegal intent than [this] ad or its context provided, we conclude that SOF did not violate the required standard of conduct by publishing an ad that later played a role in criminal activity." Id. at 838.

SOF's reliance on Eimann is misplaced. We distinguish Eimann from this case based on the instructions to the respective juries. In Eimann, the district court violated risk-utility balancing principles when it allowed the jury to impose liability on SOF if a reasonable publisher would conclude "that the advertisement could reasonably be interpreted" as an offer to commit crimes. 880 F.2d at 833 (emphasis added). The Fifth Circuit correctly observed that virtually anything might involve illegal activity, id. at 837, and that applying the district court's standard would mean that a publisher "must reject all [ambiguous] advertisements," id. at 838 (emphasis in original), or risk liability for any "untoward consequences that flow from his decision to publish" them, id.

In this case, the district court stressed in its instructions that the jury could hold SOF liable only if the ad on its face contained a "clearly identifiable unreasonable risk" of harm to the public. We are convinced that the district court's use of phrases like "clear and present danger" and "clearly identifiable unreasonable risk" properly conveyed to the jury that it could not impose liability on SOF if Savage's ad posed only an unclear or insubstantial risk of harm to the public and if SOF would bear a disproportionately heavy burden in avoiding this risk. The jury instructions in Eimann, in contrast, did not preclude the jury from imposing liability on the basis of an ambiguous advertisement that presented only an unclear risk of harm to the public.

Furthermore, in Eimann, the district court instructed that, even if the face of the ad did not reveal its connection to illegal activity, the jury could hold the publisher liable if a reasonably prudent publisher would discover the connection to crime through investigation of the advertisement's "context." 880 F.2d at 833. It is significant that the district court in this case did not impose such a duty. See infra part III.A.2. The district court here stressed that the jury could find SOF liable only if Savage's ad "on its face" would convey to a reasonable publisher that the ad created a "clearly identifiable unreasonable risk" of harm to the public.

For the foregoing reasons, we conclude that the decision in Eimann is distinguishable.

2. First Amendment Limitations

SOF further argues that the district court erred in instructing the jury to apply a negligence standard because the First Amendment forbids imposing liability on publishers for publishing an advertisement unless the ad openly solicits criminal activity.

....

Based upon the foregoing authorities, we conclude that the First Amendment permits a state to impose upon a publisher liability for compensatory damages for negligently publishing a commercial advertisement where the ad on its face, and without the need for investigation, makes it apparent that there is a substantial danger of harm to the public. ...

Our review of the language of Savage's ad persuades us that SOF had a legal duty to refrain from publishing it. Savage's advertisement (1) emphasized the term "Gun for Hire," (2) described Savage as a "professional mercenary," (3) stressed Savage's willingness to keep his assignments confidential and "very private," (4) listed legitimate jobs involving the use of a gun--bodyguard and courier--followed by a reference to Savage's "other special skills," and (5) concluded by stating that Savage would consider "[a]ll jobs." The ad's combination of sinister terms makes it apparent that there was a substantial danger of harm to the public. [12]

...

[We hold] that the language of Savage's ad should have alerted a reasonably prudent publisher to the clearly identifiable unreasonable risk that Savage was soliciting violent and illegal jobs.

For the foregoing reasons, we AFFIRM the district court's judgment.

AFFIRMED.

**ESCHBACH, Senior Circuit Judge, dissenting:**

This case poses a difficult and specific question of law for which we have little guidance. The First Amendment imposes strict limits on states' ability to subject publishers to tort liability for defamations they publish. Gertz v. Robert Welch, Inc., 418 U.S. 323, 94 S.Ct. 2997, 41 L.Ed.2d 789 (1974); New York Times v. Sullivan, 376 U.S. 254, 84 S.Ct. 710, 11 L.Ed.2d 686 (1964).

...

I remain convinced that the language of the advertisement is ambiguous, rather than patently criminal as the majority believes. I respectfully dissent.

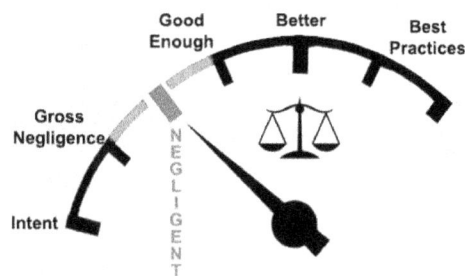

# CHAPTER 6

# Intentional harm

# Hustler Magazine, Inc. v. Falwell (1987)

U.S. Supreme Court

485 U.S. 46 (1987)

Decided: February 24, 1988

Decision: 8 votes for Hustler Magazine, 0 vote(s) against

**CHIEF JUSTICE REHNQUIST delivered the opinion of the Court.**

Petitioner Hustler Magazine, Inc., is a magazine of nationwide circulation. Respondent Jerry Falwell, a nationally known minister who has been active as a commentator on politics and public affairs, sued petitioner and its publisher, petitioner Larry Flynt, to recover damages for invasion of [p48] privacy, libel, and intentional infliction of emotional distress. The District Court directed a verdict against respondent on the privacy claim, and submitted the other two claims to a jury. The jury found for petitioners on the defamation claim, but found for respondent on the claim for intentional infliction of emotional distress and awarded damages. We now consider whether this award is consistent with the First and Fourteenth Amendments of the United States Constitution.

The inside front cover of the November, 1983, issue of Hustler Magazine featured a "parody" of an advertisement for Campari Liqueur that contained the name and picture of respondent and was entitled "Jerry Falwell talks about his first time." This parody was modeled after actual Campari ads that included interviews with various celebrities about their "first times." Although it was apparent by the end of each interview that this meant the first time they sampled Campari, the ads clearly played on the sexual double entendre of the general subject of "first times." Copying the form and layout of these Campari ads, Hustler's editors chose respondent as the featured celebrity and drafted an alleged "interview" with him in which he states that his "first time" was during a drunken incestuous rendezvous with his mother in an outhouse. The Hustler parody portrays respondent and his mother as drunk and immoral, and suggests that respondent is a hypocrite who preaches only when he is drunk. In small print at the bottom of the page, the ad contains the disclaimer, "ad parody -- not to be taken seriously." The magazine's table of contents also lists the ad as "Fiction; Ad and Personality Parody."

Soon after the November issue of Hustler became available to the public, respondent brought this diversity action in the United States District Court for the Western District of Virginia against Hustler Magazine, Inc., Larry C. Flynt, and Flynt Distributing Co., Inc. Respondent stated in his complaint that publication of the ad parody in Hustler entitled him to recover damages for libel, invasion of privacy, and intentional infliction of emotional distress. The case proceeded to trial. At the close of the evidence, the District Court granted a directed verdict for petitioners on the invasion of privacy claim. The jury then found against respondent on the libel claim, specifically finding that the ad parody could not "reasonably be understood as describing actual facts about [respondent] or actual events in which [he] participated." App. to Pet. for Cert. C1. The jury ruled for respondent on the intentional infliction of emotional distress claim, however, and stated that he should be awarded $100,000 in compensatory damages, as well as $50,000 each in punitive damages from petitioners. Petitioners' motion for judgment notwithstanding the verdict was denied.

On appeal, the United States Court of Appeals for the Fourth Circuit affirmed the judgment against petitioners. Falwell v. Flynt, 797 F.2d 1270 (1986). The court rejected petitioners' argument that the "actual malice" standard of New York Times Co. v. Sullivan, 376 U.S. 254 (1964), must be met before respondent can recover for emotional distress. The court agreed that, because respondent is concededly a public figure, petitioners are "entitled to the same level of first amendment protection in the claim for intentional infliction of emotional distress that they received in [respondent's] claim for libel." 797 F.2d at 1274. But this does not mean that a literal application of the actual malice rule is appropriate in the context of an emotional distress claim. In the court's view, the New York Times decision emphasized the constitutional importance not of the falsity of the statement or the defendant's disregard for the truth, but of the heightened level of culpability embodied in the requirement of "knowing . . . or reckless" conduct. Here, the New York Times standard is satisfied by the state law requirement, and the jury's finding, that the defendants have acted intentionally or recklessly. The Court of Appeals then went on to reject the contention that, because the jury found that the ad parody did not describe actual facts about respondent, the ad was an opinion that is protected by the First Amendment. As the court put it, this was "irrelevant," as the issue is "whether [the ad's] publication was sufficiently outrageous to constitute intentional infliction of emotional distress." Id. at 1276. Petitioners then filed a petition for rehearing en banc, but this was denied by a divided court. Given the importance of the constitutional issues in-

volved, we granted certiorari. 480 U.S. 945 (1987).

This case presents us with a novel question involving First Amendment limitations upon a State's authority to protect its citizens from the intentional infliction of emotional distress. We must decide whether a public figure may recover damages for emotional harm caused by the publication of an ad parody offensive to him, and doubtless gross and repugnant in the eyes of most. Respondent would have us find that a State's interest in protecting public figures from emotional distress is sufficient to deny First Amendment protection to speech that is patently offensive and is intended to inflict emotional injury, even when that speech could not reasonably have been interpreted as stating actual facts about the public figure involved. This we decline to do.

At the heart of the First Amendment is the recognition of the fundamental importance of the free flow of ideas and opinions on matters of public interest and concern.

[T]he freedom to speak one's mind is not only an aspect of individual liberty -- and thus a good unto itself -- but also is essential to the common quest for truth and the vitality of society as a whole.

Bose Corp. v. Consumers Union of United States, Inc., 466 U.S. 485, 503-504 (1984). We have therefore been particularly vigilant to ensure that individual expressions of ideas remain free from governmentally imposed sanctions. The First Amendment recognizes no such thing as a "false" idea. Gertz v. Robert Welch, Inc., 418 U.S. 323, 339 (1974). As Justice Holmes wrote,

when men have realized that time has upset many fighting faiths, they may come to believe even more than they believe the very foundations of their own conduct that the ultimate good desired is better reached by free trade in ideas -- that the best test of truth is the power of the thought to get itself accepted in the competition of the market. . . .

Abrams v. United States, 250 U.S. 616, 630 (1919) (dissenting opinion).

The sort of robust political debate encouraged by the First Amendment is bound to produce speech that is critical of those who hold public office or those public figures who are

intimately involved in the resolution of important public questions or, by reason of their fame, shape events in areas of concern to society at large.

Associated Press v. Walker, decided with Curtis Publishing Co. v. Butts, 388 U.S. 130, 164 (1967) (Warren, C.J., concurring in result). Justice Frankfurter put it succinctly in Baumgartner v. United States, 322 U.S. 665, 673-674 (1944), when he said that "[o]ne of the prerogatives of American citizenship is the right to criticize public men and measures." Such criticism, inevitably, will not always be reasoned or moderate; public figures as well as public officials will be subject to "vehement, caustic, and sometimes unpleasantly sharp attacks," New York Times, supra, at 270.

[T]he candidate who vaunts his spotless record and sterling integrity cannot convincingly cry "Foul!" when an opponent or an industrious reporter attempts to demonstrate the contrary.

Monitor Patriot Co. v. Roy, 401 U.S. 265, 274 (1971).

Of course, this does not mean that any speech about a public figure is immune from sanction in the form of damages. Since New York Times Co. v. Sullivan, 376 U.S. 254 (1964), we have consistently ruled that a public figure may hold a speaker liable for the damage to reputation caused by publication of a defamatory falsehood, but only if the statement was made "with knowledge that it was false or with reckless disregard of whether it was false or not." Id. at 279-280. False statements of fact are particularly valueless; they interfere with the truthseeking function of the marketplace of ideas, and they cause damage to an individ- ual's reputation that cannot easily be repaired by counterspeech, however persuasive or effective. See Gertz, 418 U.S. at 340, 344, n. 9. But even though falsehoods have little value in and of themselves, they are "nevertheless inevitable in free debate," id. at 340, and a rule that would impose strict liability on a publisher for false factual assertions would have an undoubted "chilling" effect on speech relating to public figures that does have constitutional value. "'Freedoms of expression require "breathing space."'" Philadelphia Newspapers, Inc. v. Hepps, 475 U.S. 767, 772 (1986) (quoting New York Times, supra, at 272). This breathing space is provided by a constitutional rule that allows public figures to recover for libel or defamation only when they can prove both that the statement was false and that the statement was made with the requisite level of culpability.

Respondent argues, however, that a different standard should apply in this case because, here, the State seeks to prevent not reputational damage, but the severe emotional distress suffered by the person who is the subject of an offensive publication. Cf. Zacchini v. Scripps-Howard Broadcasting Co., 433 U.S. 562 (1977) (ruling that the "actual malice" standard does not apply to the tort of appropriation of a right of publicity). In respondent's view, and in the view of the [p53] Court of Appeals, so long as the utterance was intended to inflict emotional distress, was outrageous, and did in fact inflict serious emotional distress, it is of no constitutional import whether the statement was a fact or an opinion, or whether it was true or false. It is the intent to cause injury that is the gravamen of the tort, and the State's interest in preventing emotional harm simply outweighs whatever interest a speaker may have in speech of this type.

Generally speaking, the law does not regard the intent to inflict emotional distress as one which should receive much solicitude, and it is quite understandable that most, if not all, jurisdictions have chosen to make it civilly culpable where the conduct in question is sufficiently "outrageous." But in the world of debate about public affairs, many things done with motives that are less than admirable are protected by the First Amendment. In Garrison v. Louisiana, 379 U.S. 64 (1964), we held that, even when a speaker or writer is motivated by hatred or ill-will, his expression was protected by the First Amendment:

Debate on public issues will not be uninhibited if the speaker must run the risk that it will be proved in court that he spoke out of hatred; even if he did speak out of hatred, utterances honestly believed contribute to the free interchange of ideas and the ascertainment of truth.

Id. at 73. Thus, while such a bad motive may be deemed controlling for purposes of tort liability in other areas of the law, we think the First Amendment prohibits such a result in the area of public debate about public figures.

Were we to hold otherwise, there can be little doubt that political cartoonists and satirists would be subjected to damages awards without any showing that their work falsely defamed its subject. Webster's defines a caricature as "the deliberately distorted picturing or imitating of a person, literary style, etc. by exaggerating features or mannerisms for satirical effect." Webster's New Unabridged Twentieth Century Dictionary of the English Language 275 (2d ed.1979). The appeal of the political cartoon or caricature is often based on exploitation of unfortunate physical traits or politically embarrassing events -- an exploitation often calculated to injure the feelings

of the subject of the portrayal. The art of the cartoonist is often not reasoned or evenhanded, but slashing and one-sided. One cartoonist expressed the nature of the art in these words:

The political cartoon is a weapon of attack, of scorn and ridicule and satire; it is least effective when it tries to pat some politician on the back. It is usually as welcome as a bee sting, and is always controversial in some quarters.

Long, The Political Cartoon: Journalism's Strongest Weapon, The Quill 56, 57 (Nov.1962). Several famous examples of this type of intentionally injurious speech were drawn by Thomas Nast, probably the greatest American cartoonist to date, who was associated for many years during the post-Civil War era with Harper's Weekly. In the pages of that publication Nast conducted a graphic vendetta against William M. "Boss" Tweed and his corrupt associates in New York City's "Tweed Ring." It has been described by one historian of the subject as "a sustained attack which in its passion and effectiveness stands alone in the history of American graphic art." M. Keller, The Art and Politics of Thomas Nast 177 (1968). Another writer explains that the success of the Nast cartoon was achieved "because of the emotional impact of its presentation. It continuously goes beyond the bounds of good taste and conventional manners." C. Press, The Political Cartoon 251 (1981).

Despite their sometimes caustic nature, from the early cartoon portraying George Washington as an ass down to the present day, graphic depictions and satirical cartoons have played a prominent role in public and political debate. Nast's castigation of the Tweed Ring, Walt McDougall's characterization of Presidential candidate James G. Blaine's banquet with the millionaires at Delmonico's as "The Royal Feast of Belshazzar," and numerous other efforts have undoubtedly had an effect on the course and outcome of contemporaneous debate. Lincoln's tall, gangling posture, Teddy Roosevelt's glasses and teeth, and Franklin D. Roosevelt's jutting jaw and cigarette holder have been memorialized by political cartoons with an effect that could not have been obtained by the photographer or the portrait artist. From the viewpoint of history, it is clear that our political discourse would have been considerably poorer without them.

Respondent contends, however, that the caricature in question here was so "outrageous" as to distinguish it from more traditional political cartoons. There is no doubt that the caricature of respondent and his mother published in Hustler is at best a distant cousin of the political cartoons described above, and a rather poor relation at that. If it were possible by laying down a principled standard to separate the one from the other, public discourse would probably suffer little or no harm. But we doubt that there is any such standard, and we are quite sure that the pejorative description "outrageous" does not supply one. "Outrageousness" in the area of political and social discourse has an inherent subjectiveness about it which would allow a jury to impose liability on the basis of the jurors' tastes or views, or perhaps on the basis of their dislike of a particular expression. An "outrageousness" standard thus runs afoul of our longstanding refusal to allow damages to be awarded because the speech in question may have an adverse emotional impact on the audience. See NAACP v. Claiborne Hardware Co., 458 U.S. 886, 910 (1982) ("Speech does not lose its protected character . . . simply because it may embarrass others or coerce them into action"). And, as we stated in FCC v. Pacifica Foundation, 438 U.S. 726 (1978):

> [T]he fact that society may find speech offensive is not a sufficient reason for suppressing it. Indeed, if it is the speaker's opinion that gives offense, that consequence is a reason for according it constitutional protection. For it is a central tenet of the First Amendment that the government must remain neutral in the marketplace of ideas.

Id. at 745-746. See also Street v. New York, 394 U.S. 576, 592 (1969) ("It is firmly settled that . . . the public expression of ideas may not be prohibited merely because the ideas are themselves offensive to some of their hearers").

Admittedly, these oft-repeated First Amendment principles, like other principles, are subject to limitations. We recognized in Pacifica Foundation that speech that is "'vulgar,' 'offensive,' and 'shocking'" is "not entitled to absolute constitutional protection under all circumstances." 438 U.S. at 747. In Chaplinsky v. New Hampshire, 315 U.S. 568 (1942), we held that a State could lawfully punish an individual for the use of insulting "'fighting' words -- those which by their very utterance inflict injury or tend to incite an immediate breach of the peace." Id. at 571-572. These limitations are but recognition of the observation in Dun & Bradstreet, Inc. v. Greenmoss Builders, Inc., 472 U.S. 749, 758 (1985), that this Court has "long recognized that not all speech is of equal First Amendment importance." But the sort of expression involved in this case does not seem to us to be governed by any exception to the general First Amendment principles stated above.

We conclude that public figures and public officials may not recover for the tort of intentional infliction of emotional distress by reason of publications such as the one here at issue without showing, in addition, that the publication contains a false statement of fact which was made with "actual malice," i.e., with knowledge that the statement was false or with reckless disregard as to whether or not it was true. This is not merely a "blind application" of the New York Times standard, see Time, Inc. v. Hill, 385 U.S. 374, 390 (1967); it reflects our considered judgment that such a standard is necessary to give adequate "breathing space" to the freedoms protected by the First Amendment.

Here it is clear that respondent Falwell is a "public figure" for purposes of First Amendment law. [The jury found against respondent on his libel claim when it decided that the Hustler ad parody could not "reasonably be understood as describing actual facts about [respondent] or actual events in which [he] participated." App. to Pet. for Cert. C1. The Court of Appeals interpreted the jury's finding to be that the ad parody "was not reasonably believable," 797 F.2d at 1278, and, in accordance with our custom, we accept this finding. Respondent is thus relegated to his claim for damages awarded by the jury for the intentional infliction of emotional distress by "outrageous" conduct. But, for reasons heretofore stated, this claim cannot, consistently with the First Amendment, form a basis for the award of damages when the conduct in question is the publication of a caricature such as the ad parody involved here. The judgment of the Court of Appeals is accordingly

Reversed.

JUSTICE KENNEDY took no part in the consideration or decision of this case.

# Rice v. Paladin Enterprises (1977)

United States Court Of Appeals For The Fourth Circuit

128 F.3d 233

November 10, 1997, Decided

**Judge LUTTIG wrote the opinion, in which Judges WILKINS and WILLIAMS joined.**

*A WOMAN RECENTLY ASKED HOW I could, in good conscience, write an instruction book on murder.*

*"How can you live with yourself if someone uses what you write to go out and take a human life?" she whined.*

*I am afraid she was quite offended by my answer.*

*It is my opinion that the professional hit man fills a need in society and is, at times, the only alternative for "personal" justice. Moreover, if my advice and the proven methods in this book are followed, certainly no one will ever know.*

*Almost every man harbors a fantasy of living the life of Mack Bolan or some other fictional hero who kills for fun and profit. They dream of living by their reflexes, of doing whatever is necessary without regard to moral or legal restrictions. But few have the courage or knowledge to make that dream a reality.*

. . . .

I.

On the night of March 3, 1993, readied by these instructions and steeled by these seductive adjurations from *Hit Man: A Technical Manual for Independent Contractors,* a copy of which was subsequently found in his apartment, James Perry brutally murdered Mildred Horn, her eight-year-old quadriplegic son Trevor, and Trevor's nurse, Janice Saunders, by shooting Mildred Horn and Saunders through the eyes and by strangling Trevor Horn. Perry's despicable crime was not one of vengeance; he did not know any of his victims. Nor did he commit the murders in the course of another offense. Perry acted instead as a contract killer, a "hit man," hired by Mildred Horn's ex-husband, Lawrence Horn, to murder Horn's family so that Horn would receive the $2 million that his eight-year-old son had received in settlement for injuries that had previously left him paralyzed for life. At the time of the murders, this money was held in trust for the benefit of Trevor, and, under the terms of the trust instrument, the trust money was to be distributed tax-free to Lawrence in the event of Mildred's and Trevor's deaths.

In soliciting, preparing for, and committing these murders, Perry meticulously followed countless of *Hit Man's* 130 pages of detailed factual instructions on how to murder and to become a professional killer.

Perry, for example, followed many of the book's instructions on soliciting a client and arranging for a contract murder in his solicitation of and negotiation with Lawrence Horn. Cautioning against the placement of advertisements in military or gun magazines, as this might prompt "a personal visit from the FBI," *Hit Man* instructs that "as a beginner" one should solicit business "through a personal acquaintance whom you trust." *Hit Man* at 87. James Perry offered his services as a professional killer to Lawrence Horn through Thomas Turner, a "good friend" of Perry's, and Lawrence Horn's first cousin. *State v. Perry,* 344 Md. 204, 686 A.2d 274, 278 (1996), *cert. denied,* ____ U.S. ___ (1997).

*Hit Man* instructs to request "expense money" from the employer prior to committing the crime, advising the contract killer to get *"all expense money up front." Hit Man* at 92 (emphasis added). The manual goes on to explain that this amount should generally range from five hundred to five thousand dollars, "depending on the type of job and the job location," and that the advance should be paid in cash. *Id.* Prior to commission of the murders, Lawrence Horn paid James Perry three thousand five hundred dollars through a series of wire transfers using phony names. *Perry,* 686 A.2d at 280.

*Hit Man* instructs that the victim's personal residence is the "initial choice" location for a murder and "an ideal place to make a hit," depending on its "layout" and "position." *Hit Man* at 81-82. James Perry murdered the Horns at their place of residence. *Perry,* 686 A.2d at 277.

*Hit Man* instructs its readers to use a rental car to reach the victim's location, *Hit Man* at 98, and to "steal an out-of-state tag" and use it to "replace the rental tag" on the car, explaining that "stolen tags only show up on the police computer of the state in which they are stolen." *Id.* James Perry stole out-of-state tags and affixed them to his rental car before driving it to the Horns' residence on the night of the murders. *Perry,* 686 A.2d at 276.

*Hit Man* instructs the reader to establish a base at a motel in close proximity to the "jobsite" before committing the murders. *Hit Man* at 101.

On the night that he killed Mildred and Trevor Horn and Janice Saunders, James Perry took a room at a Days Inn motel in Rockville, Maryland, a short drive from the Horns' residence. *Perry,* 686 A.2d at 276.

*Hit Man* instructs that one should "use a made-up [license] tag number" when registering at the motel or hotel. *Hit Man* at 102. James

Perry gave a false license tag number when he registered at the Days Inn on the night of the murders. *Perry,* 686 A.2d at 276.

*Hit Man* instructs that a "beginner" should use an AR-7 rifle to kill his victims. *Hit Man* at 21. James Perry used an AR-7 rifle to slay Mildred Horn and Janice Saunders. *Perry,* 686 A.2d at 279.

*Hit Man* instructs its readers where to find the serial numbers on an AR-7 rifle, and instructs them that, prior to using the weapon, they should "completely drill[ ] out" these serial numbers so that the weapon cannot be traced. *Hit Man* at 23. James Perry drilled out the serial numbers of his weapon exactly as the book instructs. *Perry,* 686 A.2d at 280.

*Hit Man* instructs in "explicit detail" (replete with photographs) how to construct, "without [the] need of special engineering ability or machine shop tools," a homemade, "whisper-quiet" silencer from material available in any hardware store. *Hit Man* at 39-51. James Perry constructed such a homemade silencer and used it on the night that he murdered Mildred and Trevor Horn and Janice Saunders. J.A. at 24.

Perry also followed any number of *Hit Man's* instructions on how to commit the murder itself. The manual, for example, instructs its readers to kill their "mark" at close range, so that they will "know beyond any doubt that the desired result has been achieved." *Hit Man* at 24. The book also cautions, however, that the killer should not shoot the victim at point blank range, because "the victim's blood [will] splatter [the killer] or [his] clothing." *Id.* Ultimately, the book recommends that its readers "shoot [their victims] from a distance of three to six feet." *Id.* James Perry shot Mildred Horn and Janice Saunders from a distance of three feet. J.A. at 24.

*Hit Man* specifically instructs its audience of killers to shoot the victim through the eyes if possible:

At least three shots should be fired to insure quick and sure death. . . . Aim for the head--preferably the eye sockets if you are a sharpshooter.

*Hit Man* at 24. James Perry shot Mildred Horn and Janice Saunders two or three times and through the eyes. *Perry,* 686 A.2d at 277.

Finally, Perry followed many of *Hit Man's* instructions for concealing his murders. *Hit Man* instructs the killer to "pick up those empty cartridges that were ejected when you fired your gun." *Hit Man* at 104. Although Perry fired his rifle numerous times during the murders, no spent cartridges were found in the area. Compare *Perry,* 686 A.2d at 277, with *id.* at 280.

*Hit Man* instructs the killer to disguise the contract murder as burglary by "messing the place up a bit and taking anything of value that you can carry concealed." *Hit Man* at 104. After killing Mildred and Trevor Horn and Janice Saunders, James Perry took a Gucci watch, as well as some credit cards and bank cards from Mildred Horn's wallet. *Perry,* 686 A.2d at 278. According to the police report, a few areas of the Horns' residence appeared "disturbed" or "slightly tossed," and "a rug and cocktail table in the living room had been moved." *Id.* at 277.

*Hit Man* instructs that, after murdering the victims, the killer should break down the AR-7 in order to make the weapon easier to conceal. *Hit Man* at 105. James Perry disassembled his weapon after the murders, in accordance with the instructions in *Hit Man. Perry,* 686 A.2d at 280.

*Hit Man* instructs killers to use specified tools to alter specified parts of the rifle. *Hit Man* at 25. The author explains that the described alterations will prevent the police laboratory from matching the bullets recovered from the victims' bodies to the murder weapon. James Perry altered his AR-7 in accordance with these instructions. *Perry,* 686 A.2d at 280.

*Hit Man* also instructs the killer to dispose of the murder weapon by scattering the disassembled pieces of the weapon along the road as he leaves the crime scene. *Hit Man* at 105. And, after killing Mildred and Trevor Horn and Janice Saunders, Perry scattered the pieces of his disassembled AR-7 rifle along Route 28 in Montgomery County. *Perry,* 686 A.2d at 280.

In this civil, state-law wrongful death action against defendant Paladin Enterprises--the publisher of *Hit Man*--the relatives and representatives of Mildred and Trevor Horn and Janice Saunders allege that Paladin aided and abetted Perry in the commission of his murders through its publication of *Hit Man's* killing instructions. For reasons that are here of no concern to the court, Paladin has stipulated to a set of facts which establish as a matter of law that the publisher is civilly liable for aiding and abetting James Perry in his triple murder, unless the First Amendment absolutely bars the imposition of liability upon a publisher for assisting in the commission of criminal acts. As the parties stipulate: "The parties agree that the sole issue to be decided by the Court . . . is whether the First Amendment is a complete defense, as a matter of law, to the civil action set forth in the plaintiffs' Complaint. All other issues of law and fact are specifically reserved for subsequent proceedings." J.A. at 58.

Paladin, for example, has stipulated for purposes of summary judgment that Perry followed the above-enumerated instructions from *Hit Man,* as well as instructions from another Paladin publication, *How to Make a Disposable Silencer, Vol. II,* in planning, executing, and attempting to cover up the murders of Mildred and Trevor Horn and

Janice Saunders. J.A. at 61. Paladin has stipulated not only that, in marketing *Hit Man,* Paladin "intended to attract and assist criminals and would-be criminals who desire information and instructions on how to commit crimes," J.A. at 59, but also that it "intended and had knowledge" that *Hit Man* actually "would be used, *upon receipt,* by criminals and would-be criminals to plan and execute the crime of murder for hire." J.A. at 59 (emphasis added). Indeed, the publisher has even stipulated that, through publishing and selling *Hit Man,* it assisted Perry in particular in the perpetration of the very murders for which the victims' families now attempt to hold Paladin civilly liable. J.A. at 61.

Notwithstanding Paladin's extraordinary stipulations that it not only knew that its instructions might be used by murderers, but that it actually intended to provide assistance to murderers and would-be murderers which would be used by them "upon receipt," and that it in fact assisted Perry in particular in the commission of the murders of Mildred and Trevor Horn and Janice Saunders, the district court granted Paladin's motion for summary judgment and dismissed plaintiffs' claims that Paladin aided and abetted Perry, holding that these claims were barred by the First Amendment as a matter of law.

Because long-established caselaw provides that speech--even speech by the press--that constitutes criminal aiding and abetting does not enjoy the protection of the First Amendment, and because we are convinced that such caselaw is both correct and equally applicable to speech that constitutes civil aiding and abetting of criminal conduct (at least where, as here, the defendant has the specific purpose of assisting and encouraging commission of such conduct and the alleged assistance and encouragement takes a form other than abstract advocacy), we hold, as urged by the Attorney General and the Department of Justice, that the First Amendment does not pose a bar to a finding that Paladin is civilly liable as an aider and abetter of Perry's triple contract murder. We also hold that the plaintiffs have stated against Paladin a civil aiding and abetting claim under Maryland law sufficient to withstand Pala-

din's motion for summary judgment. For these reasons, which we fully explain below, the district court's grant of summary judgment in Paladin's favor is reversed and the case is remanded for trial.

II.

A.

In the seminal case of *Brandenburg v. Ohio,* 395 U.S. 444 (1969), the Supreme Court held that abstract advocacy of lawlessness is protected speech under the First Amendment. Although the Court provided little explanation for this holding in its brief per curiam opinion, it is evident the Court recognized from our own history that such a right to advocate lawlessness is, almost paradoxically, one of the ultimate safeguards of liberty. Even in a society of laws, one of the most indispensable freedoms is that to express in the most impassioned terms the most passionate disagreement with the laws themselves, the institutions of, and created by, law, and the individual officials with whom the laws and institutions are entrusted. Without the freedom to criticize that which constrains, there is no freedom at all.

However, while even speech advocating lawlessness has long enjoyed protections under the First Amendment, it is equally well established that speech, which, in its effect, is tantamount to legitimately proscribable nonexpressive conduct, may itself be legitimately proscribed, punished, or regulated incidentally to the constitutional enforcement of generally applicable statutes. Cf . *Cohen v. Cowles Media Co.,* 501 U.S. 663, 669 (1991) (noting "well-established line of decisions holding that generally applicable laws do not offend the First Amendment simply because their enforcement against the press has incidental effects on its ability to gather and report the news"). As no less a First Amendment absolutist than Justice Black wrote for the Supreme Court almost fifty years ago in *Giboney v. Empire Storage & Ice Co.,* in rejecting a First Amendment challenge to an injunction forbidding unionized distributors from picketing to force an illegal business arrangement:

It rarely has been suggested that the constitutional freedom for speech and press extends its immunity to speech or writing used as an integral part of conduct in violation of a valid criminal statute. We reject the contention now. . .

. . .

. . . It is true that the agreements and course of conduct here were as in most instances brought about through speaking or writing. But it has never been deemed an abridgment of freedom of speech or press to make a course of conduct illegal merely because the conduct was in part initiated, evidenced, or carried out by means of language, either spoken, written, or printed. Such an expansive interpretation of the constitutional guaranties of speech and press would make it practically impossible ever to enforce laws against agreements in restraint of trade as well as many other agreements and conspiracies deemed injurious to society.

336 U.S. 490, 498, 502 (1949) (citations omitted). And as the Court more recently reaffirmed:

Although agreements to engage in illegal conduct undoubtedly possess some element of association, the State may ban such illegal agreements without trenching on any right of association protected by the First Amendment. The fact that such an agreement necessarily takes the form of words does not confer upon it, or upon the underlying conduct, the constitutional immunities that the First Amendment extends to speech. While a solicitation to enter into an agreement arguably crosses the sometimes hazy line distinguishing conduct from pure speech, such a solicitation, even though it may have an impact in the political arena, remains in essence an invitation to engage in an illegal exchange for private profit, and may properly be prohibited.

*Brown v. Hartlage,* 456 U.S. 45, 55 (1982); see also *Osborne v. Ohio,* 495 U.S. 103, 110 (1990) (quoting *Giboney,* 336 U.S. at 498); *New York v. Ferber,* 458 U.S. 747, 761-62 (1982) (same); *Ohralik v. Ohio State Bar Ass'n,* 436 U.S. 447, 456 (1978) (quoting *Giboney,* 336 U.S. at 502); *National Organization for Women v. Operation Rescue,* 308 U.S. App. D.C. 349, 37 F.3d 646, 656 (D.C. Cir. 1994) ("That 'aiding and abetting' of an illegal act may be carried out through speech is no bar to its illegality."); *United States v. Varani,* 435 F.2d 758, 762 (6th Cir. 1970) ("Speech is not protected by the First Amendment when it is the very vehicle of the crime itself."); Laurence H. Tribe, American Constitutional Law 837 (2d ed. 1988) ("The law need not treat differently the crime of one man who sells a bomb to terrorists and that of another who publishes an instructional manual for terrorists on how to build their own bombs out of old Volkswagen parts.").

Were the First Amendment to bar or to limit government regulation of such "speech brigaded with action," *Brandenburg,* 395 U.S. at 456 (Douglas, J., concurring), the government would be powerless to protect the public from countless of even the most pernicious criminal acts and civil wrongs. See, e.g., Model Penal Code § 223.4 (extortion or blackmail); *id.* § 240.2 (threats and other improper influences in official and political matters); *id.* § 241 (perjury and various cognate crimes); *id.* § 5.02 and § 2.06(3)(a)(i) (criminal solicitation); 18 U.S.C. § 871 (threatening the life of the President); Model Penal Code § 5.03 (conspiracy); *id.* § 250.4(harassment); *id.* § 224.1 (forgery); *id.* § 210.5(2) (successfully soliciting another to commit suicide); *id.* § 250.3 (false public alarms); and the like. As Professor Greenawalt succinctly summarized:

The reasons of ordinary penal policy for covering communicative efforts to carry out ordinary crimes are obvious, and the criminal law sensibly draws no distinction between communicative and other acts. Although assertions of fact generally fall within a principle of freedom of speech, what these sorts of factual statements contribute to the general understanding of listeners is minimal, and the justifications for free speech that apply to speakers do not reach communications that are simply means to get a crime successfully committed.

Greenawalt, Speech, Crime, and the Uses of Language at 85 (1989).

In particular as it concerns the instant case, the speech-act doctrine has long been invoked to sustain convictions for aiding and abetting the commission of criminal offenses. Indeed, every court that has addressed the issue, including this court, has held that the First Amendment does not necessarily pose a bar to liability for aiding and abetting a crime, even when such aiding and abetting takes the form of the spoken or written word.

Thus, in a case indistinguishable in principle from that before us, the Ninth Circuit expressly held in *United States v. Barnett,* 667 F.2d 835 (9th Cir. 1982), that the First Amendment does not provide publishers a defense as a matter of law to charges of aiding and abetting a crime through the publication and distribution of instructions on how to make illegal drugs. In rejecting the publisher's argument that there could be no probable cause to believe that a crime had been committed because its actions were shielded by the First Amendment, and thus a fortiori there was no probable cause to support the search pursuant to which the drug manufacturing instructions were found, the Court of Appeals explicitly foreclosed a First Amendment defense not only to the search itself, but also to a later prosecution:

To the extent . . . that Barnett appears to contend that he is immune from search or *prosecution* because he uses the printed word in encouraging and counseling others in the commission of a crime, we hold expressly that the first amendment does not provide a defense as a matter of law to such conduct.

*Id.* at 843 (emphasis in original); see also *id.* at 842 ("The first amendment does not provide a defense to a criminal charge simply because the actor uses words to carry out his illegal purpose. Crimes, including that of aiding and abetting, frequently involve the use of speech as part of the criminal transaction."). The Ninth Circuit derided as a "specious syllogism" with "no support in the law" the publisher's argument that the First Amendment protected his sale of the instruction manual simply because the First Amendment protects the written word. *Id.* at 842.

The principle of *Barnett,* that the provision of instructions that aid and abet another in the commission of a criminal offense is unprotected by the First Amendment, has been uniformly accepted, and the principle has been applied to the aiding and abetting of innumerable crimes.

Notably, then-Judge Kennedy, in express reliance upon *Barnett,* invoked the principle in *United States v. Freeman* to sustain convictions for the aiding and abetting of tax fraud. 761 F.2d 549, 552-53 (9th Cir. 1985), *cert. denied,* 476 U.S. 1120 (1986). In *Freeman,* the Ninth Circuit concluded that the defendant could be held criminally liable for counseling tax evasion at seminars held in protest of the tax laws, even though the speech that served as the predicate for the conviction "sprang from the anterior motive to effect political or social change." 761 F.2d at 551. Said the court:

The First Amendment is quite irrelevant if the intent of the actor and the objective meaning of the words used are so close in time and purpose to a substantive evil as to become part of the ultimate crime itself. In those instances, where speech becomes an integral part of the crime, a First Amendment defense is foreclosed even if the prosecution rests on words alone.

*Id.* at 552 (citations omitted). Thus, the court held that a First Amendment instruction was required only for those counts as to which there was evidence that the speaker "directed his comments at the unfairness of the tax laws generally, without soliciting or counseling a violation of the law in an immediate sense [and] made statements that, at least arguably, were of abstract generality, remote from advice to commit a specific criminal act." *Id.* at 551-52. For those counts as to which the defendant, through his speech, directly assisted in the preparation and review of false tax returns, the court held that the defendant was not entitled to a First Amendment instruction at all. *Id.* at 552. See also *United States v. Mendelsohn*, 896 F.2d 1183, 1186 (9th Cir. 1990) (holding *Brandenburg* inapplicable to a conviction for conspiring to transport and aiding and abetting the interstate transportation of wagering paraphernalia, where defendants disseminated a computer program that assisted others to record and analyze bets on sporting events; program was "too instrumental in and intertwined with the performance of criminal activity to retain first amendment protection").

Our own circuit, and every other circuit to address the issue, has likewise concluded that the First Amendment is generally inapplicable to charges of aiding and abetting violations of the tax laws. See, e.g., *United States v. Kelley*, 769 F.2d 215 (4th Cir. 1985); *United States v. Rowlee*, 899 F.2d 1275 (2d Cir. 1990), *cert. denied*, 498 U.S. 828 (1990); *United States v. Moss*, 604 F.2d 569 (8th Cir. 1979), *cert. denied*, 444 U.S. 1071 (1980); *United States v. Buttorff*, 572 F.2d 619, 623-24 (8th Cir. 1978) (holding that tax evasion speeches were not subject to *Brandenburg* because, although they did not "incite the type of imminent lawless activity referred to in criminal syndicalism cases," they did "go beyond mere advocacy of tax reform"), *cert. denied*, 437 U.S. 906 (1978).

Thus, in *Kelley*, we held that a defendant who "participated" in the preparation of false tax forms for others by telling listeners "what to do and how to prepare the forms" and by supplying forms and materials was not entitled to the protections of the First Amendment, 769 F.2d at 217, even though the defendant offered his advice in a meeting of a group concededly dedicated to the political belief "that the federal income tax is unconstitutional as applied to wages," *id.* at 216. We observed, as the Ninth Circuit did with respect to the claim made in *Barnett*, that, the claim of First Amendment protection of [Kelley's] speech is frivolous. His was no abstract criticism of income tax laws. His listeners were not urged to seek congressional action to exempt wages from income taxation. Instead, they were urged to file false returns, with every expectation that the advice would be heeded.

The cloak of the First Amendment envelops critical, but abstract, discussions of existing laws, but lends no protection to speech which urges the listeners to commit violations of current law. *Brandenburg v. Ohio*, 395 U.S. 444; *United States v. Buttorff*, 572 F.2d 619 (8th Cir. 1978). It was no theoretical discussion of non-compliance with laws; action was urged; the advice was heeded, and false forms were filed.

*Kelley*, 769 F.2d at 217. Analogously, we held in *United States v. Fleschner*, 98 F.3d 155 (4th Cir. 1996), *cert. denied*, 117 S. Ct. 2484 (1997), that defendants who instructed and advised meeting attendees to file unlawful tax returns were not entitled to a First Amendment jury instruction on the charge of conspiracy to defraud the United States of income tax revenue because "the defendants' words and acts were not remote from the commission of the criminal acts." 98 F.3d at 158-59.

Indeed, as the Department of Justice recently advised Congress, the law is now well established that the First Amendment, and *Brandenburg's* "imminence" requirement in particular, generally poses little obstacle to the punishment of speech that constitutes criminal aiding and abetting, because "culpability in such cases is premised, not on defendants' 'advocacy' of criminal conduct, but on defendants' successful efforts to assist others by detailing to them the means of accomplishing the crimes." Department of Justice, "Report on the Availability of Bombmaking Information, the Extent to Which Its Dissemination is Controlled by Federal Law, and the Extent to Which Such Dissemination May Be Subject to Regulation Consistent with the First Amendment to the United States Constitution" 37 (April 1997) (footnote omitted) [hereinafter "DOJ Report"]; see also *id.* ("The question of whether criminal conduct is 'imminent' is relevant for constitutional purposes only where, as in *Brandenburg* itself, the government attempts to restrict advocacy, as such."). And, while there is considerably less authority on the subject, we assume that those speech acts which the government may criminally prosecute with little or no concern for the First Amendment, the government may likewise subject to civil penalty or make subject to private causes of action. Compare *Garrison v. Louisi-*

*ana,* 379 U.S. 64 (1964) (applying the same "actual malice" standard to both criminal libel prosecutions and private defamation actions) with *New York Times Co. v. Sullivan,* 376 U.S. 254 (1964). Cf. *Cohen,* 501 U.S. 663 (finding in civil promissory estoppel case that First Amendment does not bar liability for newspaper's publication of confidential source's name); *Zacchini v. Scripps-Howard Broadcasting Co.,* 433 U.S. 562 (1977) (First Amendment does not bar liability for common law tort of unlawful appropriation of "right to publicity" where television station broadcast "human cannonball" act in its entirety without plaintiff's authorization); *Harper & Row, Publishers, Inc. v. Nation Enterprises,* 471 U.S. 539 (1985) (rejecting First Amendment defense to copyright infringement action against magazine for printing unauthorized presidential memoir excerpts). Even if this is not universally so, we believe it must be true at least where the government's interest in preventing the particular conduct at issue is incontrovertibly compelling.

## B.

We can envision only two possible qualifications to these general rules, neither of which, for reasons that we discuss more extensively below, is of special moment in the context of the particular aiding and abetting case before us.

### 1.

The first, which obviously would have practical import principally in the civil context, is that the First Amendment may, at least in certain circumstances, superimpose upon the speech-act doctrine a heightened intent requirement in order that preeminent values underlying that constitutional provision not be imperiled. See, e.g., *New York Times,* 376 U.S. 254; cf. *United States v. Aguilar,* 515 U.S. 593, 605

(1995) (rejecting defendant's First Amendment construction in part because "the statute here in question does not impose such a restriction [on the disclosure of wiretap authorizations] generally, but only upon those who disclose wiretap information *in order to* obstruct, impede, or prevent' a wiretap interception" (emphasis added)); *Haig v. Agee,* 453 U.S. 280, 308-09 (1981) ("[The defendant's] disclosures, among other things, have the *declared purpose* of obstructing intelligence operations and the recruiting of intelligence personnel. They are clearly not protected by the Constitution." (emphasis added)); *United States v. Featherston,* 461 F.2d 1119, 1122 (5th Cir. 1972) (rejecting First Amendment challenge to federal statute criminalizing the teaching or demonstration of the making of any explosive device after construing statute to require "intent or knowledge that the information disseminated would be used in the furtherance of a civil disorder"), *cert. denied,* 409 U.S. 991 (1972); *National Mobilization Committee to End the War in Viet Nam v. Foran,* 411 F.2d 934, 937 (7th Cir. 1969). That is, in order to prevent the punishment or even the chilling of entirely innocent, lawfully useful speech, the First Amendment may in some contexts stand as a bar to the imposition of liability on the basis of mere foreseeability or knowledge that the information one imparts could be misused for an impermissible purpose. Where it is necessary, such a limitation would meet the quite legitimate, if not compelling, concern of those who publish, broadcast, or distribute to large, undifferentiated audiences, that the exposure to suit under lesser standards would be intolerable. See discussion *infra,* Part IV. At the same time, it would not relieve from liability those who would, for profit or other motive, intentionally assist and encourage crime and then shamelessly seek refuge in the sanctuary of the First Amendment. Like our sister circuits, at the very least where a speaker--individual or media--acts with the purpose of assisting in the commission of crime, we do not believe that the First Amendment insulates that speaker from responsibility for his actions simply because he may have disseminated his message to a wide audience. See, e.g., *Barnett,* 667 F.2d 835 (holding that drug manufacturing instructions mailed to countless customers with whom the defendant had no personal contact could give rise to aiding and abetting conviction); *Mendelsohn,* 896 F.2d 1183 (holding that First Amendment did not forbid prosecution of aiding and abetting interstate transportation of wagering paraphernalia where computer programs for recording and analyzing illegal wagers were distributed generally and widely to the public); *Buttorff,* 572 F.2d at 622-23 (affirming, despite First Amendment challenges, convictions for providing tax-evasion information at "large public gatherings" to participants whom the defendants did not personally meet); *Kelley,* 769 F.2d 215 (similar); *Moss,* 604 F.2d 569 (similar); *Freeman,* 761 F.2d 549 (similar). This is certainly so, we are satisfied, where not only the speaker's dissemination or marketing strategy, but the nature of the speech itself, strongly suggest that the audience both targeted and actually reached is, in actuality, very narrowly confined, as in the case before us. See discussion *infra* at 39-44. Were the First Amendment to offer protection even in these circumstances, one could publish, by traditional means or even on the internet, the necessary plans and instructions for assassinating the President, for poisoning a city's water supply, for blowing up a skyscraper or public building, or for similar acts of terror and mass destruction, with the specific, indeed even the admitted, purpose of assisting such crimes--all with impunity.

We need not engage in an extended discussion of the existence or scope of an intent-based limitation today, however, because we are confident that the First Amendment poses no bar to the imposition of civil (or criminal) liability for speech acts which the plaintiff (or the prosecution) can establish were undertaken with specific, if not criminal, intent. See DOJ Report at 42-43 (advising that "the government may punish publication of dangerous instructional information where that publication is motivated by a desire to facilitate the unlawful [conduct as to which the instructions inform, or] at the very least, publication with such an improper intent should not be constitutionally protected where it is foreseeable that the publication will be used for criminal purposes . . . ."). In fact, this conclusion would seem to follow a fortiori from the Supreme Court's holding in New York Times, 376 U.S. 254, allowing the imposition of civil tort liability on a media defendant for reputational injury caused by mere reckless disregard of the truth of its published statements. And, here, as previously noted, see also discussion *infra* at 37-38, Paladin has stipulated that it provided its assistance to Perry with both the knowledge and the intent that the book would immediately be used by criminals and would-be criminals in the solicitation, planning, and commission of murder and murder for hire, and even absent the stipulations, a jury could reasonably find such specific intent, see discussion *infra* at 38-42. Thus, Paladin has stipulated to an intent, and a jury could otherwise reasonably find that Paladin acted with a kind and degree of intent, that would satisfy any heightened standard that might be required by the First Amendment prerequisite to the imposition of liability for aiding and abetting through speech conduct.

2.

The second qualification is that the First Amendment might well (and presumably would) interpose the same or similar limitations upon the imposition of civil liability for abstract advocacy, without more, that it interposes upon the imposition of criminal punishment for such advocacy. In other words, the First Amendment might well circumscribe the power of the state to create and enforce a cause of action that would permit the imposition of civil liability, such as aiding and abetting civil liability, for speech that would constitute pure abstract advocacy, at least if that speech were not "directed to inciting or producing imminent lawless action, and . . . likely to incite or produce such action." *Brandenburg*, 395 U.S. at 447. The instances in which such advocacy might give rise to civil liability under state statute would seem rare, but they are not inconceivable. Cf. *Schenck v. United States*, 249 U.S. 47 (1919) (criminal conspiracy prosecution predicated upon subversive advocacy); *Frohwerk v. United States*, 249 U.S. 204 (1919) (same); *Debs v. United States*, 249 U.S. 211 (1919) (criminal attempt prosecution predicated upon such advocacy). Again, however, an exhaustive analysis of this likely limitation is not required in this case.

Here, it is alleged, and a jury could reasonably find, see discussion *infra* Part III.A, that Paladin aided and abetted the murders at issue through the quintessential speech act of providing step-by-step instructions for murder (replete with photographs, diagrams, and narration) so comprehensive and detailed that it is as if the instructor were literally present with the would-be murderer not only in the preparation and planning, but in the actual commission of, and follow-up to, the murder; there is not even a hint that the aid was provided in the form of speech that might constitute abstract advocacy. As the district court itself concluded, *Hit Man* "merely teaches what must be done to implement a professional hit." J.A. at 218. Moreover, although we do not believe such would be necessary, we are satisfied a jury could readily find that the provided instructions not only have no, or virtually no, noninstructional communicative value, but also that their only instructional communicative "value" is the indisputably illegitimate one of training persons how to murder and to engage in the business of murder for hire. See *id.*; see also *id.* at 221 ("This Court, quite candidly, personally finds *Hit Man* to be reprehensible and devoid of any significant redeeming social value").

Aid and assistance in the form of this kind of speech bears no resemblance to the "theoretical advocacy," *Scales v. United States*, 367 U.S. 203, 235 (1961), the advocacy of "principles divorced from action," *Yates v. United States*, 354 U.S. 298, 320 (1957), overruled on other grounds, *Burks v. United States*, 437 U.S. 1 (1978), the "doctrinal justification," 354 U.S. at 321, "the mere abstract teaching [of] the moral propriety or even moral necessity for a resort to force and violence," *Brandenburg*, 395 U.S. at 448 (quoting *Noto v. United States*, 367 U.S. 290, 297-98 (1961)), or any of the other forms of discourse critical of government, its policies, and its leaders, which have always animated, and to this day continue to animate, the First Amendment. Indeed, this detailed, focused instructional assistance to those contemplating or in the throes of planning murder is the antithesis of speech protected under *Brandenburg*. It is the teaching of the "techniques" of violence, *Scales*, 367 U.S. at 233, the "advocacy and teaching of concrete action," *Yates*, 354 U.S. at 320, the "preparation . . . for violent action and [the] steeling . . . to such action," *Brandenburg*, 395 U.S. at 448 (quoting *Noto*, 367 U.S. at 297-98). It is the instruction in the methods of terror of which Justice Douglas spoke in *Dennis v. United States*, when he said, "If this were a case where those who claimed protection under the First Amendment were teaching the techniques of sabotage . . . I would have no doubts. The freedom to speak is not absolute; the teaching of methods of terror . . . should be beyond the pale . . . ." 341 U.S. 494, 581 (1951) (Douglas, J., dissenting). As such, the murder instructions in *Hit Man* are, collectively, a textbook example of the type of speech that the Supreme Court has quite purposely left unprotected, [250] and the prosecution of which, criminally or civilly, has historically been thought subject to few, if any, First Amendment constraints. Accordingly, we hold that the First Amendment does not pose a bar to the plaintiffs' civil aiding and abetting cause of action against Paladin Press. If, as precedent uniformly confirms, the states have the power to regulate speech that aids and abets crime, then certainly they have the power to regulate the speech at issue here.

III.

The district court's contrary conclusion, reached in an initial and then an amended opinion, must be attributed ultimately, we believe, to that court's failure at the time of its initial ruling to realize that Maryland does recognize a civil cause of action for aiding and abetting. Once the court's error with respect to the existence in Maryland of a civil aiding and abetting cause of action was brought to the court's attention by the parties on motion for reconsideration, it appears that the court was simply unprepared to revisit its decision, issued only the week before, in order to address the above-discussed cases, which the district court itself had observed are "factually similar" to the case at hand, J.A. at 156, but which the court had distinguished on the ground that they involved *criminal* prosecutions for aiding and abetting and Maryland does not provide a *civil* cause of action for aiding and abetting. J.A. at 155 ("Plaintiffs are asking the Court to allow the Defendants to be subjected to civil liability for murder, based on a theory of civil aiding and abetting--*a claim that does not exist under Maryland law.*" (emphases added)). Perhaps

ironically, this unwillingness foreordained what was, as we explain below, the district court's second error in the interpretation of Maryland law--its holding, on reconsideration, that Maryland would not recognize aiding and abetting liability under the facts as stipulated by the parties to this litigation, or on the facts as they appear from the record.

Whatever doubts the district court may have harbored about its interpretation of Maryland aiding and abetting law were almost certainly eased because it concluded alternatively (albeit in dicta) that *Hit Man* is entitled to the protections of *Brandenburg* in any event because it is a mere instructional manual for, and not an incitement to, murder. However, in this conclusion the district court erred as well, misunderstanding the Supreme Court's decision in *Brandenburg* to protect not just abstract advocacy of lawlessness and the open criticism of government and its institutions, but also the teaching of the technical methods of criminal activity--in this case, the technical methods of murder.

A.

In its initial memorandum opinion, the district court rejected the plaintiffs' principal argument, that the First Amendment does not bar the imposition of liability for the aiding and abetting of murder, on the ground that the State of Maryland does not recognize a civil cause of action for aiding and abetting:

Plaintiffs argue that *Hit Man* is not protected by the First Amendment because the First Amendment does not protect communication aiding and abetting murder. This argument must fail, however, because Plaintiffs do not cite, nor has the Court located, any reported decision that suggests that Maryland recognizes the tort of aiding and abetting. A federal court sitting in diversity cannot create new causes of action. There-

101

fore, the Court cannot create a cause of action for aiding and abetting under Maryland law . . . .

J.A. at 153-54 (footnote and citations omitted). In response to submissions by both parties filed the very next day informing the court that Maryland does recognize civil aiding and abetting, the district court was obliged to amend its memorandum opinion to acknowledge the overwhelming authority that Maryland does, in fact, recognize such a cause of action. However, rather than address then the numerous precedents holding that the First Amendment offers little protection against claims of aiding and abetting criminal conduct, which in its initial opinion the court had agreed were similar to the instant case, the district court thereafter merely added to its original memorandum opinion the single conclusory footnote sentence (together with the necessary conforming changes to the relevant paragraph from its initial opinion) that, "although Maryland appears to recognize aider and abetter tort liability, it has never been applied to support liability in this context." J.A. at 205 n.2 (internal citation deleted). In this holding, as with its original holding that Maryland did not recognize a cause of action for civil aiding and abetting, the district court erred.

Maryland's highest court has held that a defendant may be liable in tort if he "by any means (words, signs, or motions) encourages, incites, aids or abets the act of the direct perpetrator of the tort." *Alleco Inc. v. Harry & Jeanette Weinberg Foundation,* 340 Md. 176, 665 A.2d 1038, 1049 (1995) (quoting *Duke v. Feldman,* 245 Md. 454, 226 A.2d 345, 347 (1967)). It further appears that generally Maryland defines the tort of aiding and abetting in the same way that it defines the crime of aiding and abetting. The state defines "aider" as one who "assists, supports or supplements the efforts of another," and defines "abettor" as "one who instigates, advises or encourages the commission of a crime." *Anello v. State,* 201 Md. 164, 93 A.2d 71, 72-73 (Md. 1952). The Court of Appeals has explained that in order for a conviction to stand, "it is not essential that there be a prearranged concert of action, although, in the absence of such action, it is essential that [the defendant] should in

some way advocate or encourage the commission of the crime." *Id.* And, recently, the court has reiterated that criminal aiding and abetting "may be predicated upon counseling or encouraging" a criminal act, even if there is no agreement between the principal and the aider or abettor, and also that "it is well settled that aiding and abetting does not always require a conspiracy." *Apostoledes v. State,* 323 Md. 456, 593 A.2d 1117, 1121 (1991).

The primary, and possibly only, difference between Maryland's civil and criminal laws of aiding and abetting is the intent requirement. As Judge Learned Hand explained in discussing generally the difference between civil and criminal aiding and abetting laws, the intent standard in the civil tort context requires only that the criminal conduct be the "natural consequence of [one's] original act," whereas criminal intent to aid and abet requires that the defendant have a "purposive attitude" toward the commission of the offense. *United States v. Peoni,* 100 F.2d 401, 402 (2d Cir. 1938); see also *Nye & Nissen v. United States,* 336 U.S. 613, 619 (1949) (adopting Judge Hand's view of the criminal intent requirement). We assume that Maryland prescribes a higher intent standard for the imposition of criminal liability than it does for civil liability.

Especially in light of the caselaw discussed above, we are satisfied not only that the Maryland courts would conclude that an aiding and abetting cause of action would lie in the circumstances of this case, but also that plaintiffs have, by way of stipulation and otherwise, established a genuine issue of material fact as to each element of that cause of action. Perhaps most importantly in this regard, we conclude that plaintiffs have more than met their burden of establishing a genuine issue of material fact as to Paladin's intent, even assuming that the First Amendment erects a heightened standard from that required under Maryland state law.

Paladin itself has stipulated that "Perry followed a number of instructions outlined in *Hit Man"* in preparing for and in murdering Mildred and Trevor Horn and Janice Saunders. J.A. at 61. In fact, as noted, the publisher has actually stipulated that it assisted Perry in the "perpetration of the murders." *Id.*

Even without these express stipulations of assistance, however, a reasonable jury could conclude that Paladin assisted Perry in those murders, from the facts that Perry purchased and possessed *Hit Man* and that the methods and tactics he employed in his murders of Mildred and Trevor Horn and Janice Saunders so closely paralleled those prescribed in the book. As discussed above, see discussion *supra* Part I, Perry followed, in painstaking detail, countless of the book's instructions in soliciting, preparing for, and carrying out his murders. Without repeating these in detail here, Perry faithfully followed the book's instructions in making a home-made silencer, using a rental car with stolen out-of-state tags, murdering the victims in their own home, using an AR-7 rifle to shoot the victims in the eyes from point blank range, and concealing his involvement in the murders. The number and extent of these parallels to the instructions in *Hit Man* cannot be consigned, as a matter of law, to mere coincidence; the correspondence of techniques at least creates a jury issue as to whether the book provided substantial assistance, if it does not conclusively establish such assistance.

A jury likewise could reasonably find that Perry was encouraged in his murderous acts by Paladin's book. *Hit Man* does not merely detail how to commit murder and murder for hire; through powerful prose in the second person and imperative voice, it encourages its readers in their specific acts of murder. It reassures those contemplating the crime that they may proceed with their plans without fear of either personal failure or punishment. And at every point where the would-be murderer might yield either to reason or to reservations, *Hit Man* emboldens the killer, confirming not only that he should proceed, but that he must proceed, if he is to establish his manhood. See discussion *infra* at 54-56. The book is so effectively written that its protagonist seems actually to be present at the planning, commission, and cover-up of the murders

the book inspires. Illustrative of the nature and duration of the criminal partnership established between *Hit Man* and its readers who murder is the following "dialogue" that takes place when the murderer returns from his first killing:

I'm sure your emotions have run full scale over the past few days or weeks.

There was a fleeting moment just before you pulled the trigger when you wondered if lightning would strike you then and there. And afterwards, a short burst of panic as you looked quickly around you to make sure no witnesses were lurking.

But other than that, you felt absolutely nothing. And you are shocked by that nothingness. You had expected this moment to be a spectacular point in your life. . . .

The first few seconds of nothingness give you an almost uncontrollable urge to laugh out loud. You break into a wide grin. Everything you have been taught about life and its value was a fallacy.

*Hit Man* at 107. As this and other cases reveal, the book is arrestingly effective in the accomplishment of its objectives of counseling others to murder and assisting them in its commission and cover-up.

Finally, and significantly, Paladin also has stipulated to an intent that readily satisfies that required under Maryland law or the First Amendment. Even if the First Amendment imposes a heightened intent-based limitation on the state's ability to apply the tort of aiding and abetting to speech, see discussion *supra* at II.B.1, we are confident that, at the very least, the aiding and abetting of a malum in se crime such as murder with the specific purpose of assisting and encouraging another or others in that crime would satisfy such a limitation. Paladin has stipulated not only that it had knowledge that its publication would be used upon receipt by murderers and other criminals in the commission of murder, but that it even intended that the book be so used. Thus, the publisher stipulated, "defendants intended and had knowledge that their publications would be used, upon receipt, by criminals and would-be criminals to plan and execute the crime of murder for hire." J.A. at 59. Paladin has even stipulated that it "engaged in a marketing strategy intended to attract and assist criminals and would-be criminals who desire information and instructions on how to commit crimes." *Id.* These stipulations are more than sufficient to foreclose an absolute First Amendment defense to plaintiffs' suit. See DOJ Report at 43 & 44-45 n.71 ("We believe that the district court in *Rice v. Paladin* erred insofar as it concluded that *Brandenburg* bars liability for dissemination of[instructions on murder] *regardless* of the publisher's intent. . . . [Defendant Paladin's] concessions would, for purposes of summary judgment, seem to foreclose a constitutional defense . . .").

The district court was never required to consider the intent requirement under Maryland's law of aiding and abetting, much less whether the First Amendment imposes a heightened intent standard in the context of authorizing liability for speech acts, because of its mistaken conclusion that Maryland does not recognize a civil cause of action for aiding and abetting. In analogizing this case to the copycat cases (and seemingly in order to permit the analogy), however, the district court accepted Paladin's post hoc "clarification" that it meant by its stipulation only that it was reasonably foreseeable to the publisher that, once the book was published and publicly available, it would be used by murderers to plan and to commit murder. Thus, in accepting the defendants' belated clarification, the district court said:

Defendants conceded that they intended that their publications would be used by criminals to plan and execute murder as instructed in the manual. . . . However, Defendants clarify their concession by explaining that when they published, advertised and distributed both *Hit Man* and *Silencers,* they knew, and in that sense "intended," that the books would be purchased by all of the categories of readers previously de-

scribed and used by them for the broad range of purposes previously described.

J.A. at 215-16 (citations omitted). Of course, the district court was without authority to allow Paladin to alter the parties' stipulation unilaterally, particularly given that Paladin was the party moving for summary judgment. If anything, the stipulation should have been, and in any event must now be, interpreted in the light most favorable to the plaintiffs.

Furthermore, even if the stipulation only established knowledge, summary judgment was yet inappropriate because a trier of fact could still conclude that Paladin acted with the requisite intent to support civil liability. Wholly apart from Paladin's stipulations, there are four bases upon which, collectively, if perhaps not individually, a reasonable jury could find that Paladin possessed the intent required under Maryland law, as well as the intent required under any heightened First Amendment standard. Compare DOJ Report, at 45 n.71 ("Even assuming arguendo that the defendants' own construction of the 'intent' stipulation were correct, that still would not justify the grant of summary judgment, since it would leave unanswered the question whether Paladin also had the specific purpose of facilitating murder.").

First, the declared purpose of *Hit Man* itself is to facilitate murder. Consistent with its declared purpose, the book is subtitled "A Technical Manual for Independent Contractors," and it unabashedly describes itself as "an instruction book on murder," *Hit Man* at ix. A jury need not, but plainly could, conclude from such prominent and unequivocal statements of criminal purpose that the publisher who disseminated the book intended to assist in the achievement of that purpose.

Second, the book's extensive, decided, and pointed promotion of murder is highly probative of the publisher's intent, and may be considered as such, whether or not that promotion, standing alone, could serve as the basis for liability consistent with the First Amendment. See *Wisconsin v. Mitchell,* 508 U.S. 476, 489 (1993) ("The First Amendment . . .

does not prohibit the evidentiary use of speech to establish the elements of a crime or to prove motive or intent."); cf. Noto, 367 U.S. at 299. [note 7] After carefully and repeatedly reading *Hit Man* in its entirety, we are of the view that the book so overtly promotes murder in concrete, nonabstract terms that we regard as disturbingly disingenuous both Paladin's cavalier suggestion that the book is essentially a comic book whose "fantastical" promotion of murder no one could take seriously, and *amici's* reckless characterization of the book as "almost avuncular," see Br. of Amici at 8-9. The unique text of *Hit Man* alone, boldly proselytizing and glamorizing the crime of murder and the "profession" of murder as it dispassionately instructs on its commission, is more than sufficient to create a triable issue of fact as to Paladin's intent in publishing and selling the manual.

Third, Paladin's marketing strategy would more than support a finding of the requisite intent. Cf. *Direct Sales v. United States,* 319 U.S. 703, 712-13 (1943) (holding that jury may infer intent to assist a criminal operation based upon a drug distributor's marketing strategy). It is known through Paladin's stipulations that it "engaged in a marketing strategy intended to attract and assist criminals and would be criminals who desire information and instructions on how to commit crimes." J.A. at 59. But an inference as to such a strategy would be permitted from Paladin's catalogue advertisement of *Hit Man*. The publisher markets the book as follows, invoking a disclaimer which, the district court's characterization notwithstanding, a jury could readily find to be transparent sarcasm designed to intrigue and entice:

Learn how a pro gets assignments, creates a false identity, makes a disposable silencer, leaves the scene without a trace, watches his mark unobserved and more. Feral reveals how to get in, do the job and get out without getting caught. *For academic study only!*

Paladin Press Catalog, Vol. 26, No. 2 at 41 (emphasis in original). See also *infra* note 10. From this statement by the publisher in its own promotional sales catalogue, a jury could conclude that Paladin marketed *Hit Man* directly and even primarily to murderers and would-be criminals, and, from this permissible conclusion, in turn conclude that Paladin possessed the requisite intent necessary to support liability.

Certainly, such a conclusion would be reasonable based upon this promotional description coupled with the singular character of *Hit Man,* which is so narrowly focused in its subject matter and presentation as to be effectively targeted exclusively to criminals. In other words, despite the fact that Paladin may technically offer the book for sale to all comers, we are satisfied that a jury could, based upon *Hit Man's* seemingly exclusive purpose to assist murderers in the commission of murder, reasonably conclude that Paladin essentially distributed *Hit Man* only to murderers and would-be murderers--that its conduct was not, at least in law, different from that of a publisher (or anyone else) who delivered *Hit Man* to a specific person or group of persons whom the publisher knew to be interested in murder. And even Paladin effectively concedes that it could be liable were such a finding permissibly made. Paladin's Memorandum in Support of Summary Judgment at 33 n.24.

A conclusion that Paladin directed *Hit Man* to a discrete group rather than to the public at large would be supported, even if not established, by the evidence that *Hit Man* is not generally available or sold to the public from the bookshelves of local bookstores, but, rather, is obtainable as a practical matter only by catalogue. Paladin Press is a mail order company, and for the most part does not sell books through retail outlets. In order to procure a copy of *Hit Man,* the prospective reader must first obtain a copy of Paladin's catalogue, typically by completing a request form reprinted in one of Paladin's advertisements in specialized magazines such as *Soldier of Fortune.* After obtaining that catalogue, the reader must scan the list of book titles and read the accompanying descriptions. Once the reader finds the book he desires, he must then complete and mail another form to order the book.

From the requirements of this process, together with the book's character, a jury need not, but could, permissibly find that *Hit Man* is not at all distributed to the general public and that, instead, it is available only to a limited, self-selected group of people interested in learning from and being trained by a self-described professional killer in various methods of killing for money, individuals who are then contemplating or highly susceptible to the commission of murder.

Finally, a jury could reasonably conclude that Paladin specifically intended to assist Perry and similar murderers by finding, contrary to Paladin's demurs, as would we, that *Hit Man's* only genuine use is the unlawful one of facilitating such murders. Cf. J.A. at 221 (observation by district court that *Hit Man* is "devoid of any significant redeeming social value"). Although before us Paladin attempts to hypothesize lawful purposes for *Hit Man,* and it would doubtless advance the same hypotheses before a jury, at some point hypotheses are so implausible as to be deserving of little or no weight. The likelihood that *Hit Man* actually is, or would be, used in the legitimate manners hypothesized by Paladin is sufficiently remote that a jury could quite reasonably reject them altogether as alternative uses for the book. If there is a publication that could be found to have no other use than to facilitate unlawful conduct, then this would be it, so devoid is the book of any political, social, entertainment, or other legitimate discourse. Cf. *Miller v. California,* 413 U.S. 15 (1973) (distinguishing obscene from nonobscene material in part on basis of "whether the work, taken as a whole, lacks serious literary, artistic, political, or scientific value"). Thus, for example, a jury would certainly not be unreasonable in dismissing (in fact, it arguably would be unreasonable in accepting) Paladin's contention that *Hit Man* has significant social value in that the book, in the course of instructing murderers how to murder, incidentally informs law enforcement on the techniques that the book's readers will likely employ in the commission of their murders. Likewise, a reasonable jury could simply refuse to accept Paladin's contention that this purely factual, instructional manual on murder has entertainment value to law-abiding citizens. And, just as a permissible inference as to Paladin's marketing

strategy would be supportable by evidence as to the specialized process by which one acquires *Hit Man,* either of these conclusions as to the absence of lawful purpose could be reinforced by the same evidence.

In summary, a reasonable jury clearly could conclude from the stipulations of the parties, and, apart from the stipulations, from the text of *Hit Man* itself and the other facts of record, that Paladin aided and abetted in Perry's triple murder by providing detailed instructions on the techniques of murder and murder for hire with the specific intent of aiding and abetting the commission of these violent crimes.

B.

Any argument that *Hit Man* is abstract advocacy entitling the book, and therefore Paladin, to heightened First Amendment protection under *Brandenburg* is, on its face, untenable. Although the district court erred in its alternative conclusion that the speech of *Hit Man* is protected advocacy, see discussion *infra* at III.B.2, even that court expressly found that "the book merely teaches what must be done to implement a professional hit." J.A. at 217-18; *id.* at 218 n.4 (discussing "instructive nature" of book). Indeed, Paladin's protests notwithstanding, this book constitutes the archetypal example of speech which, because it methodically and comprehensively prepares and steels its audience to specific criminal conduct through exhaustively detailed instructions on the planning, commission, and concealment of criminal conduct, finds no preserve in the First Amendment. To the extent that confirmation of this is even needed, given the book's content and declared purpose to be "an instruction book on murder," *Hit Man* at ix, that confirmation is found in the stark contrast between this assassination manual and the speech heretofore held to be deserving of constitutional protection.

1.

Through its stipulation that it intended *Hit Man* to be used by criminals and would-be criminals to commit murder for hire in accordance with the book's instructions, Paladin all but concedes that, through those instructions, *Hit Man* prepares and steels its readers to commit the crime of murder for hire. But even absent the publisher's stipulations, it is evident from even a casual examination of the book that the prose of *Hit Man* is at the other end of the continuum from the ideation at the core of the advocacy protected by the First Amendment.

The cover of *Hit Man* states that readers of the book will "learn how a pro makes a living at this craft [of murder] without landing behind bars" and, how he gets hit assignments, creates a false working identity, makes a disposable silencer, leaves the scene without a trace of evidence, watches his mark unobserved, and more . . . how to get in, do the job, and get out--without getting caught.

In the first pages of its text, *Hit Man* promises, consistent with its title as *"A Technical Manual for Independent Contractors,"* that the book will prepare the reader, step by step, to commit murder for hire:

Within the pages of this book you will learn one of the most successful methods of operation used by an independent contractor. You will follow the procedures of a man who works alone, without backing of organized crime or on a personal vendetta. Step by step you will be taken from research to equipment selection to job preparation to successful job completion. You will learn where to find employment, how much to charge, and what you can, and cannot, do with the money you earn.

But deny your urge to skip about, looking for the "good" parts. Start where any amateur who is serious about turning professional will start--at the beginning.

*Hit Man* at x-xi. And, faithful to these promises, in the successive chapters of the 130 pages that follow, *Hit Man* systematically and in meticu-

lous detail instructs on the gruesome particulars of every possible aspect of murder and murder for hire. The manual instructs step-by-step on building and using fertilizer bombs, constructing silencers, picking locks, selecting and using poisons, sinking corpses, and torturing victims. It teaches would-be assassins how to arrive at, and conduct surveillance of, a potential victim's house, and it instructs on the use of a fake driver's license and registration at a motel, the placement of stolen out-of-state license plates on rental cars, and the deception of the postal service into delivering weapons to the murder scene. The book instructs the reader in murder methods, explaining in dispassionate and excruciatingly graphic detail how to shoot, stab, poison, and incinerate people, and in gory detail it expounds on which methods of murder will best ensure the death of the victims. The book schools the reader on how to escape the crime scene without detection, and how to foil police investigations by disassembling and discarding the murder weapon, altering the ballistics markings of that weapon, stealing and switching license plates, and disguising the reader's physical appearance. And it counsels on how to manipulate the legal system, if caught.

At the risk of belaboring the obvious, but in order to appreciate the encyclopedic character of *Hit Man's* instructions, one need only consider the following chapter-by-chapter synopsis. [257]

Chapter One of *Hit Man,* entitled "The Beginning--Mental and Physical Preparation," starts by outlining the "essential" steps to becoming a professional killer. *Hit Man* at 9. The book urges the reader to read other books from publishers such as Paladin Press, but it cautions that "books on subjects related to the professional hit man are hard to find [and that] there are only a few publishers out there who have the backbone to provide those . . . who take life seriously with the necessary educational materials." *Hit Man* at 9-10. The book goes on to recommend that one read articles in magazines such as *Soldier of Fortune,* and military newsletters in order to "stay abreast of new trends and developments [in weapons and techniques of killing] as well as new gadgets and inventions as they become available." *Hit Man* at 9. It also encourages the reader to comb fictional accounts of murder, on the off chance that, for example, "the warped imagination of a fiction writer will point out an obvious but somehow never before realized method of pacification or body disposal." *Id.* at 10. It instructs its readers to study their local newspapers carefully "to see who in your area might be your next employer . . . or victim," and to use the classified advertisements, among other things, to find "new toys and pick them up from private owners to avoid registering your weapons." *Id.* The book provides indepth advice on using a variety of publicly available reference materials to locate weapons and other "equipment," gather information about victims, and plan murders for hire. For example, the book instructs its readers to go to the auto tag department of the county courthouse and "look up the mark by last name or tag number for address," because books containing such information are often "left out for public use." *Id.* at 12. Similarly, the book instructs the readers in how to use the postal service to "track down the last known address of anyone you choose as a function of the Freedom of Information Act," *id.* at 14, and to send weapons safely to the location of a planned murder, *id.* at 13.

In addition, *Hit Man* instructs its readers to become familiar with local law enforcement techniques, for example by obtaining law enforcement handbooks, and it provides practical advice on how to obtain these books, either from "any college bookstore where law enforcement courses are taught," *id.* at 14, or by theft. The book also offers the readers practical tips on diet, fitness, combat training, ("Veterans with wartime experience and the ability to kill are first choice instructors." *Id.* at 17), and observational skills. Although much of the information in this chapter is not explicit in outlining the methods of terror, it is explicit in advising the would-be assassin where to turn for additional information beyond that found between the covers of the book.

Chapter Two of the book, entitled "Equipment--Selection and Purpose," imparts a wealth of information on the "basic equipment" the "beginner" will need as tools of his trade, *id.*at 21, and provides detailed instructions as to the equipment's use. For example, the book first instructs the reader to obtain, inter alia, an AR-7 rifle, hollowpoint bullets, disposable silencers, liquid poison, disposable rubber gloves, a double-edged knife with a six-inch blade, handcuffs, and a ski mask. See *id.*at 21-22. The book next provides precise instructions on how to kill, using each of the various weapons. The manual recommends "close kills," and teaches that:

When using a small caliber weapon like the 22, it is best to shoot from a distance of three to six feet. You will not want to be at point-blank range to avoid having the victim's blood splatter you or your clothing. At least three shots should be fired to ensure quick and sure death. You can judge when death has occurred by observing the wound. When the blood ceases to flow, the heart has stopped working. Check for pulse at both the wrist and throat as an added precaution.

at 24. The book goes on to teach which weapons to avoid and why, explaining, for example, that,

although revolvers are often depicted as being a favorite tool among hit men, they are not recommended by this pro. Revolvers cannot be effectively silenced. The open cylinder allows gases to escape, thus making noise. When fired, gas is forced around the cylinder in a 360 degree circle, thereby throwing powder all over the person who fires the gun.

An automatic, on the other hand, is tightly sealed so that when it is fired almost all the powder residue is forced into the silencer, where it is trapped. This prevents the powder from escaping and covering the person who fired the shot. . . . If a shell catcher is used, the powder residue will become trapped inside the catch bag.

at 26. The manual further instructs how to kill efficiently at close-range with a knife:

The knife you carry should have a six-inch blade with a serrated section for making efficient, quiet kills. . . .

The knife should have a double-edged blade. This double edge, combined with the serrated section and six-inch length, will insure a deep, ragged tear, and the wound will be difficult, if not impossible, to close without prompt medical attention.

Make your thrusts to a vital organ and twist the knife before you withdraw it. If you hit bone, you will have to file the blade to remove the marks left on the metal when it struck the victim's bone.

at 27-28. The book also instructs on alternatives to the close-range kill, including instructions such as the following:

If you must do your shooting from a distance, use a rifle with a good scope and silencer and aim for the head--preferably the eye sockets if you are a sharpshooter. Many people have been shot repeatedly, even in the head, and survived to tell about it.

at 24. Finally, the chapter includes a host of other instructions on how to use basic tools, ranging from handcuffs, to lock picks, to surveillance equipment, in the commission of murder. For instance, the book teaches the need for a hit man to always wear gloves and it discusses glove choice, recommending surgical gloves because,

leather gloves are not to be considered as a job tool. The leather has the same individual, distinct characteristics as the human fingerprint. If you have to use leather gloves, destroy them immediately after the job. If found in your possession, they can convict you as quickly as a set of your own fingerprints.

at 27. The chapter continues in like vein.

Chapter Three, entitled "The Disposable Silencer--A Poor Man's Access to a Rich Man's Toy," teaches the reader, with step-by-step instructions and accompanying photographic illustration, how to construct a "whisper-quiet," "inexpensive," and "effective" disposable silencer that is "reusable for over four hundred rounds." *Id.* at 47, 51. These directions are designed to allow the "amateur" to construct disposable silencers, which, the book explains, are "one of the most important tools a professional will ever have." *Id.* at 38. As the book explains, these "same directions can be followed successfully to construct a silencer for any weapon, with only the size of the drill rod used for alignment changed. . . ." *Id.* at 39.

*Hit Man's* Chapter Four, entitled "More Than One Way To Kill a Rabbit--The Direct Hit is Not Your Only Alternative," includes discursive instructions on numerous additional methods of killing and torture. If "several marks will be together in one place at the same time," the book teaches, one can kill all of the "marks" with a fertilizer bomb, and it goes on to teach the reader, through step-by-step instructions, how to build such a bomb. *Id.* at 54-55. The chapter teaches the reader how to kill by arson, admonishing and instructing, "Don't ever use gasoline or other traceable materials to start your fire. [Specified substance] is your best starter because it burns away all traces." *Id.* at 56. In addition, the chapter includes instructions such as that, "[a] fire victim will have smoke present in his lungs. Therefore, if this is your choice of extermination, your mark should be unconscious, but breathing, when the fire is set. Make sure no scratches or bruises point to foul play." Later in the chapter, *Hit Man* discusses poisons. After teaching an elaborate method for obtaining hard-to-find poisons through impersonation, the manual explains how one can successfully use substances such as tetrodotoxin, oleander, nicotine, and jessamine to kill his victims. See *id.* at 58-63. The chapter's discussion of torture techniques provides explicit advice on how to inflict sufficient pain to ensure that "people will tell you anything you want to know, even when they are sure they are about to die." *Id.* at 64. In what is offered as a helpful example, the book illustrates from the author's own experience:

We [the book's author and his accomplice, referred to only as "the Indian"] subdued the [victim], stripped him to the waist and tied him into a wooden chair

. . .

The Indian pulled an ice pick from his hip pocket

. . .

Suddenly he stopped and inserted the tip of the pick into the [victim's] upper arm about a quarter of an inch. When he withdrew the pick, there was a sickening little popping sound as blood spurted from the wound for a second, then stopped.

. . .

Several stabs later, the [victim] was quivering like a jellyfish, his body like a pin cushion, while the Indian was getting more and more excited and more and more into his work.

. . . With a malicious grin, [the Indian] pulled a pair of pliers from his other hip pocket and gave me a sly wink. Pointedly, methodically, he began with the [victim's] little finger on his left hand and crunched each knuckle slowly with the pliers. It seemed to take no effort at all on his part as the soft bone gave way under the force of the simple tool. He had only gotten to the third finger when the victim began to cry like a baby and spill his guts.

*Id.* at 65-66. The chapter concludes with instructions for disposing of human corpses without detection, providing directions for, *inter alia,* hiding the bodies in a river:

. . . .

I

Indeed, one finds in *Hit Man* little, if anything, even remotely characterizable as the abstract criticism that *Brandenburg* jealously protects. *Hit Man's* detailed, concrete instructions and adjurations to murder stand in stark contrast to the vague, rhetorical threats of politically or socially motivated violence that have historically been considered part and parcel of the impassioned criticism of laws, policies, and government indispensable in a free society and rightly protected under *Brandenburg*. The speech of *Hit Man* defies even comparison with the Klansman's chilling, but protected, statement in *Brandenburg* itself that, "[the Ku Klux Klan is] not a revengent organization, but if our President, our Congress, our Supreme Court, continues to suppress the white, Caucasian race, it's possible that there might have to be some revengeance taken," 395 U.S. at 446; the protestor's inciteful, but protected, chant in United *States v. Hess,* 414 U.S. 105, 108 (1973) that "we'll take the fucking street again"; the NAACP speaker's threat, rhetorical in its context, to boycott violators that "if we catch any of you going in any of them racist stores, we're gonna break your damn neck," which was held to be protected in *NAACP v. Claiborne Hardware Co.,* 458 U.S. 886, 902 (1982); or the draft protestor's crude, but protected, blustering in Watts that "if they ever make me carry a rifle the first man I want to get in my sights is L.B.J," *Watts v. United States,* 394 U.S. 705, 706 (1969).

Plaintiffs observed in their submissions before the district court that,

*Hit Man* is not political manifesto, not revolutionary diatribe, not propaganda, advocacy, or protest, not an outpouring of conscience or credo.

. . .

It contains no discussion of ideas, no argument, no information about politics, religion, science, art, or culture . . . it offers no agenda for self-governance, no insight into the issues of the day . . . .

Appellant's Br. at 32; Memorandum of Points and Authorities in Support of Plaintiffs' Opposition to Defendant's Motion for Summary Judgment at 31-32. And, this is apt observation. *Hit Man* is none of this. Ideas simply are neither the focus nor the burden of the book. To the extent that there are any passages within *Hit Man's* pages that arguably are in the nature of ideas or abstract advocacy, those sentences are so very few in number and isolated as to be legally of no significance whatsoever. *Kois v. Wisconsin,* 408 U.S. 229, 231 (1972) ("A quotation from Voltaire in the flyleaf of a book will not constitutionally redeem an otherwise obscene publication."); see also *Miller,* 413 U.S. at 24; *Penthouse International, Ltd. v. McAuliffe,* 610 F.2d 1353 (5th Cir. 1980), *cert. dismissed,* 447 U.S. 931 (1980). *Hit Man* is, pure and simple, a step-by-step murder manual, a training book for assassins. There is nothing even arguably tentative or recondite in the book's promotion of, and instruction in, murder. To the contrary, the book directly and unmistakably urges concrete violations of the laws against murder and murder for hire and coldly instructs on the commission of these crimes. The Supreme Court has never protected as abstract advocacy speech so explicit in its palpable entreaties to violent crime.

2.

In concluding that *Hit Man* is protected "advocacy," the district court appears to have misperceived the nature of the speech that the Supreme Court held in *Brandenburg* is protected under the First Amendment. In particular, the district court seems to have misunderstood the Court in *Brandenburg* as having distinguished between "advocating or teaching" lawlessness on the one hand, and "inciting or encouraging" lawlessness on the other, any and all of the former being entitled to First Amendment protection. The district court thus framed the issue before it as "whether *Hit Man* merely advocates or teaches murder or whether it incites or encourages murder." J.A. at 212. And, finding that *Hit Man*

"merely teaches" in technical fashion the fundamentals of murder, it concluded that "the book does not cross that line between permissible advocacy and impermissible incitation to crime or violence." *Id.* at 218.

The Court in *Brandenburg,* however, did not hold that "mere teaching" is protected; the Court never even used this phrase. And it certainly did not hold, as the district court apparently believed, that *all* teaching is protected. Rather, however inartfully it may have done so, the Court fairly clearly held only that the "mere *abstract* teaching" of principles, *id.* at 447-48 (quoting *Noto,* 367 U.S. at 297-98) (emphasis added), and "mere *advocacy,*" 395 U.S. at 448-49 (emphasis added), are protected. In the final analysis, it appears the district court simply failed to fully appreciate the import of the qualification to the kind of "teaching" that the Supreme Court held to be protected in *Brandenburg.* See J.A. at 217 (defining "advocacy" as "mere teaching" rather than "mere abstract teaching" but citing to *Brandenburg,* 395 U.S. at 448 (quoting *Noto,* 367 U.S. at 297-98)). As the Supreme Court's approving quotation from its opinion in Noto confirms, it is not teaching simpliciter, but only "the mere abstract teaching . . . *of the moral propriety or even moral necessity*" for resort to lawlessness, or its equivalent, that is protected under the commands of *Brandenburg,* 367 U.S. at 297-98 (emphasis added).

Although we believe the district court's specific misreading of *Brandenburg* was plainly in error, we cannot fault the district court for its confusion over the opinion in that case. The short per curiam opinion in *Brandenburg* is, by any measure, elliptical.

In particular, the Court unmistakably draws the distinction discussed above, between "the mere abstract teaching. . . of the moral propriety or even moral necessity for a resort to force and violence" on one hand, 395 U.S. at 448, and the "preparation [of] a group for violent action

and steeling it to such action" on the other. *Id.* And it then recites in the very next sentence that "[a] statute which fails to draw *this* distinction," *id.* (emphasis added)--a seeming reference to the distinction between "mere abstract teaching" and "preparing and steeling"--is unconstitutional under the First Amendment. In the succeeding paragraph and a later footnote, however, the Court distinguishes between "mere advocacy" and "incitement to imminent lawless action," a distinction which, as a matter of common sense and common parlance, appears different from the first distinction drawn, because "preparation and steeling" can occur without "incitement," and vice-versa. See *id.* at 448 ("Neither the indictment nor the trial judge's instructions to the jury in any way refined the statute's bald definition of the crime in terms of mere advocacy not distinguished from incitement to imminent lawless action." (footnote omitted)); *id.* at 449 n.4 ("Statutes affecting the right of assembly, like those touching on freedom of speech, must observe the established distinctions between mere advocacy and incitement to imminent lawless action . . . ." ).

It would have been natural, based upon its prior cases, for the Court actually to have contemplated and intended both distinctions, and to have developed the latter only, because the case before it turned exclusively on that distinction. It is more likely, however, that the Court did not focus at all on the seeming facial incongruity between the first and the latter two of these distinctions. The Court, therefore, may well have intended to equate the preparation and steeling of a group to violent action with speech that is directed to inciting imminent lawless action and likely to produce such action. In other words, the Court may well have meant to imply that one prepares and steels another or others for violent action only when he does so through speech that is "directed to inciting or producing imminent lawless action and . . . [that is] likely to incite or produce such action," *id.* at 447, and thus that preparation and steeling is not per se unprotected. Compare *id.* at 447-48 ("As we said in *Noto.* . . .") with *Noto,* 367 U.S. at 298 (describing preparation and steeling through "a call to violence"). Assuming that it did so mean to imply, however, we are confident it meant to do so only in the con-

text of advocacy--speech that is part and parcel of political and social discourse--which was the only type of speech at issue in *Brandenburg, Noto,* and the other cases relied upon by the Court. See, e.g., *44 Liquormart v. Rhode Island,* 517 U.S. 484 (1996) (Stevens, J., for plurality) (describing *Brandenburg* as setting forth "test for suppressing political speech"). The Court even so defined its own holding: "These later decisions have fashioned the principle that the constitutional guarantees of free speech and free press do not permit a State to forbid or proscribe advocacy of the use of force or of law violation except where such advocacy is directed to inciting or producing imminent lawless action and is likely to incite or produce such action." 395 U.S. at 447 (footnote omitted; emphases added). For, as this case reveals, and as the Court itself has always seemed to recognize, one obviously can prepare, and even steel, another to violent action not only through the dissident "call to violence," but also through speech, such as instruction in the methods of terror or other crime, that does not even remotely resemble advocacy, in either form or purpose. And, of course, to understand the Court as addressing itself to speech other than advocacy would be to ascribe to it an intent to revolutionize the criminal law, in a several paragraph per curiam opinion, by subjecting prosecutions to the demands of *Brandenburg's* "imminence" and "likelihood" requirements whenever the predicate conduct takes, in whole or in part, the form of speech--an intent that no lower court has discerned and that, this late in the day, we would hesitate to impute to the Supreme Court.

Accordingly, we hold that plaintiffs have stated, sufficient to withstand summary judgment, a civil cause of action against Paladin Enterprises for aiding and abetting the murders of Mildred and Trevor Horn and Janice Saunders on the night of March 3, 1993, and that this cause of action is not barred by the First Amendment to the United States Constitution.

IV.

Paladin, joined by a spate of media *amici*, including many of the major networks, newspapers, and publishers, contends that any decision recognizing even a potential cause of action against Paladin will have far-reaching chilling effects on the rights of free speech and press. See Br. of *Amici* at 3, 22 ("Allowing this lawsuit to survive will disturb decades of First Amendment jurisprudence and jeopardize free speech from the periphery to the core. . . . No expression--music, video, books, even newspaper articles--would be safe from civil liability."). That the national media organizations would feel obliged to vigorously defend Paladin's assertion of a constitutional right to intentionally and knowingly assist murderers with technical information which Paladin admits it intended and knew would be used immediately in the commission of murder and other crimes against society is, to say the least, breathtaking. But be that as it may, it should be apparent from the foregoing that the indisputably important First Amendment values that Paladin and *amici* argue would be imperiled by a decision recognizing potential liability under the peculiar facts of this case will not even arguably be adversely affected by allowing plaintiffs' action against Paladin to proceed. In fact, neither the extensive briefing by the parties and the numerous *amici* in this case, nor the exhaustive research which the court itself has undertaken, has revealed even a single case that we regard as factually analogous to this case.

Paladin and *amici* insist that recognizing the existence of a cause of action against Paladin predicated on aiding and abetting will subject broadcasters and publishers to liability whenever someone imitates or "copies" conduct that is either described or depicted in their broadcasts, publications, or movies. This is simply not true. In the "copycat" context, it will presumably never be the case that the broadcaster or publisher actually intends, through its description or depiction, to assist another or others in the commission of violent crime; rather, the information for the dissemination of which liability is sought to be imposed will actually have been misused vis-a-vis the use intended, not,

as here, used precisely as intended. It would be difficult to overstate the significance of this difference insofar as the potential liability to which the media might be exposed by our decision herein is concerned.

And, perhaps most importantly, there will almost never be evidence proffered from which a jury even could reasonably conclude that the producer or publisher possessed the actual intent to assist criminal activity. In only the rarest case, as here where the publisher has stipulated in almost taunting defiance that it intended to assist murderers and other criminals, will there be evidence extraneous to the speech itself which would support a finding of the requisite intent; surely few will, as Paladin has, "stand up and proclaim to the world that because they are publishers they have a unique constitutional right to aid and abet murder." Appellant's Reply Br. at 20. Moreover, in contrast to the case before us, in virtually every "copycat" case, there will be lacking in the speech itself any basis for a permissible inference that the "speaker" intended to assist and facilitate the criminal conduct described or depicted. Of course, with few, if any, exceptions, the speech which gives rise to the copycat crime will not directly and affirmatively promote the criminal conduct, even if, in some circumstances, it incidentally glamorizes and thereby indirectly promotes such conduct.

Additionally, not only will a political, informational, educational, entertainment, or other wholly legitimate purpose for the description or depiction be demonstrably apparent; but the description or depiction of the criminality will be of such a character that an inference of impermissible intent on the part of the producer or publisher would be unwarranted as a matter of law. So, for example, for almost any broadcast, book, movie, or song that one can imagine, an inference of unlawful motive from the description or depiction of particular criminal conduct therein would almost never be reasonable, for not only will there be (and demonstrably so) a legitimate and lawful purpose for these communications, but the contexts in which the descriptions or depictions appear will themselves negate a purpose on the part of the producer or publisher to assist others in their undertaking of the described or depicted conduct. Compare Miller, 413 U.S. 15.

Paladin contends that exposing it to liability under the circumstances presented here will necessarily expose broadcasters and publishers of the news, in particular, to liability when persons mimic activity either reported on or captured on film footage and disseminated in the form of broadcast news. Appellee's Br. at 26 n.17. This contention, as well, is categorically wrong. News reporting, we can assume, no matter how explicit it is in its description or depiction of criminal activity, could never serve as a basis for aiding and abetting liability consistent with the First Amendment. It will be self-evident in the context of news reporting, if nowhere else, that neither the intent of the reporter nor the purpose of the report is to facilitate repetition of the crime or other conduct reported upon, but, rather, merely to report on the particular event, and thereby to inform the public.

A decision that Paladin may be liable under the circumstances of this case is not even tantamount to a holding that all publishers of instructional manuals may be liable for the misconduct that ensues when one follows the instructions which appear in those manuals. Admittedly, a holding that Paladin is not entitled to an absolute defense to the plaintiffs' claims here may not bode well for those publishers, if any, of factually detailed instructional books, similar to *Hit Man,* which are devoted exclusively to teaching the techniques of violent activities that are criminal per se. But, in holding that a defense to liability may not inure to publishers for their dissemination of such manuals of criminal conduct, we do not address ourselves to the potential liability of a publisher for the criminal use of published instructions on activity that is either entirely lawful, or lawful or not depending upon the circumstances of its occurrence. Assuming, as we do, that liability could not be imposed in these circumstances on a finding of mere foreseeability or knowledge that the instructions might be misused for a criminal purpose, the chances that claims arising from the publication of instructional manuals like these can withstand motions for summary judg-

ment directed to the issue of intent seem to us remote indeed, at least absent some substantial confirmation of specific intent like that that exists in this case.

Thus, while the "horribles" paraded before us by Paladin and *amici* have quite properly prompted us to examine and reexamine the established authorities on which plaintiffs' case firmly rests, we regard them ultimately as but anticipatory of cases wholly unlike the one we must decide today.

Paladin Press in this case has stipulated that it specifically targeted the market of murderers, would-be murderers, and other criminals for sale of its murder manual. Paladin has stipulated both that it had knowledge and that it intended that *Hit Man* would immediately be used by criminals and would-be criminals in the solicitation, planning, and commission of murder and murder for hire. And Paladin has stipulated that, through publishing and selling *Hit Man,* it "assisted" Perry in particular in the perpetration of the brutal triple murders for which plaintiffs now seek to hold the publisher liable. Beyond these startling stipulations, it is alleged, and the record would support, that Paladin assisted Perry through the quintessential speech act of providing Perry with detailed factual instructions on how to prepare for, commit, and cover up his murders, instructions which themselves embody not so much as a hint of the theoretical advocacy of principles divorced from action that is the hallmark of protected speech. And it is alleged, and a jury could find, that Paladin's assistance assumed the form of speech with little, if any, purpose beyond the unlawful one of facilitating murder.

Paladin's astonishing stipulations, coupled with the extraordinary comprehensiveness, detail, and clarity of *Hit Man's* instructions for criminal activity and murder in particular, the boldness of its palpable exhortation to murder, the alarming power and effectiveness of its peculiar form of instruction, the notable absence from its text of the kind of ideas for the protection of which the First Amendment exists, and the book's evident lack of any even arguably legitimate purpose beyond the promotion and teaching of murder, render this case unique in the law. In at least these circumstances, we are confident that the First Amendment does not erect the absolute bar to the imposition of civil liability for which Paladin Press and *amici* contend. Indeed, to hold that the First Amendment forbids liability in such circumstances as a matter of law would fly in the face of all precedent of which we are aware, not only from the courts of appeals but from the Supreme Court of the United States itself. *Hit Man* is, we are convinced, the speech that even Justice Douglas, with his unrivaled devotion to the First Amendment, counseled without any equivocation "should be beyond the pale" under a Constitution that reserves to the people the ultimate and necessary authority to adjudge some conduct--and even some speech-- fundamentally incompatible with the liberties they have secured unto themselves.

The judgment of the district court is hereby reversed, and the case remanded for trial.

It is so ordered.

*Epilogue: On May 21, 1999, Paladin Press' insurance company agreed to settle the case out-of-court, against the wishes of Paladin Press themselves, who were confident that they would prevail in court. Paladin's insurance company refused to go court again, figuring expenses for a lengthy trial in federal court, plus the posting of a bond in case they lost and appealed, would have cost much more than the settlement. Under this settlement, Paladin's insurance policy paid several million dollars to the families of those killed by the murderer, while also agreeing to destroy the remaining 700 copies of the book in their possession and surrendering any rights they had to publish and reproduce the work.*

# CHAPTER 7

# Commercial speech

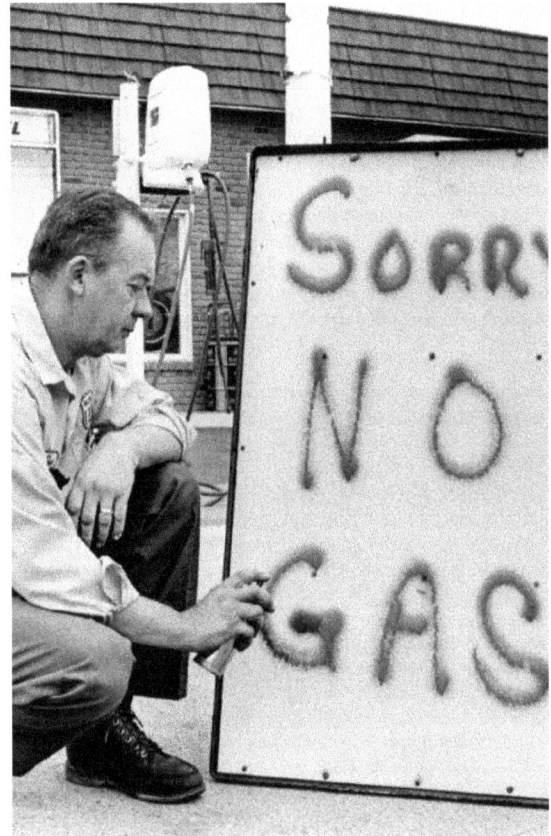

# Central Hudson Gas & Electric Corp. v. Public Service Commission of New York (1980)

U.S. Supreme Court

447 U.S. 557 (1980)

Decided: June 20, 1980

Burger    Brennan    Stewart    White    Marshall    Blackmun    Powell    Stevens    Rehnquist

Decision: 8 votes for Central Hudson Gas & Elec., 1 vote(s) against

**MR. JUSTICE POWELL delivered the opinion of the Court.**

This case presents the question whether a regulation of the Public Service Commission of the State of New York violates the First and Fourteenth Amendments because it completely bans promotional advertising by an electrical utility.

I

In December, 1973, the Commission, appellee here, ordered electric utilities in New York State to cease all advertising that "promot[es] the use of electricity." App. to Juris.Statement 31a. The order was based on the Commission's finding that "the interconnected utility system in New York State does not have sufficient fuel stocks or sources of supply to continue furnishing all customer demands for the 1973-1974 winter." Id. at 26a.

Three years later, when the fuel shortage had eased, the Commission requested comments from the public on its proposal to continue the ban on promotional advertising. Central Hudson Gas & Electric Corp., the appellant in this case, opposed the ban on First Amendment grounds. App. A10. After reviewing the public comments, the Commission extended the prohibition in a Policy Statement issued on February 25, 1977.

The Policy Statement divided advertising expenses

into two broad categories: promotional -- advertising intended to stimulate the purchase of utility services -- and institutional and informational, a broad category inclusive of all advertising not clearly intended to promote sales.

1 App. to Juris.Statement 35a. The Commission declared all promotional advertising contrary to the national policy of conserving energy. It acknowledged that the ban is not a perfect vehicle for conserving energy. For example, the Commission's order prohibits promotional advertising to develop consumption during periods when demand for electricity is low. By limiting growth in "off-peak" consumption, the ban limits the "beneficial side effects" of such growth in terms of more efficient use of existing powerplants. Id. at 37a. And since oil dealers are not under the Commission's jurisdiction and thus remain free to advertise, it was recognized that the ban can achieve only "piecemeal conservationism." Still, the Commission adopted the restriction because it

117

was deemed likely to "result in some dampening of unnecessary growth" in energy consumption. Ibid.

The Commission's order explicitly permitted "informational" advertising designed to encourage "shifts of consumption" from peak demand times to periods of low electricity demand. Ibid. (emphasis in original). Informational advertising would not seek to increase aggregate consumption, but would invite a leveling of demand throughout any given 24-hour period. The agency offered to review "specific proposals by the companies for specifically described [advertising] programs that meet these criteria." Id. at 38a.

When it rejected requests for rehearing on the Policy Statement, the Commission supplemented its rationale for the advertising ban. The agency observed that additional electricity probably would be more expensive to produce than existing output. Because electricity rates in New York were not then based on marginal cost, the Commission feared that additional power would be priced below the actual cost of generation. The additional electricity would be subsidized by all consumers through generally higher rates. Id. at 57a-58a. The state agency also thought that promotional advertising would give "misleading signals" to the public by appearing to encourage energy consumption at a time when conservation is needed. Id. at 59a.

Appellant challenged the order in state court, arguing that the Commission had restrained commercial speech in violation of the First and Fourteenth Amendments. The Commission's order was upheld by the trial court and at the intermediate appellate level. The New York Court of Appeals affirmed. It found little value to advertising in "the noncompetitive market in which electric corporations operate." Consolidated Edison Co. v. Public Service Comm'n, 47 N.Y.2d 94, 110, 390 N.E.2d

749, 757 (1979). Since consumers "have no choice regarding the source of their electric power," the court denied that "promotional advertising of electricity might contribute to society's interest in 'informed and reliable' economic decisionmaking." Ibid. The court also observed that, by encouraging consumption, promotional advertising would only exacerbate the current energy situation. Id. at 110, 390 N.E.2d at 758. The court concluded that the governmental interest in the prohibition outweighed the limited constitutional value of the commercial speech at issue. We noted probable jurisdiction, 111 U.S. 962 (1979), and now reverse.

## II

The Commission's order restricts only commercial speech, that is, expression related solely to the economic interests of the speaker and its audience. Virginia Pharmacy Board v. Virginia Citizens Consumer Council, 425 U.S. 748, 762 (1976); Bates v. State Bar of Arizona, 433 U.S. 350, 363-364 (1977); Friedman v. Rogers, 440 U.S. 1, 11 (1979). The First Amendment, as applied to the States through the Fourteenth Amendment, protects commercial speech from unwarranted governmental regulation. Virginia Pharmacy Board, 425 U.S. at 761-762. Commercial expression not only serves the economic interest of the speaker, but also assists consumers and furthers the societal interest in the fullest possible dissemination of information. In applying the First Amendment to this area, we have rejected the "highly paternalistic" view that government has complete power to suppress or regulate commercial speech.

[P]eople will perceive their own best interests if only they are well enough informed, and . . . the best means to that end is to open the channels of communication, rather than to close them. . . .

Id. at 770; see Linmark Associates, Inc. v. Willingboro, 431 U.S. 85, 92 (1977). Even when advertising communicates only an incomplete ver-

118

sion of the relevant facts, the First Amendment presumes that some accurate information is better than no information at all. Bates v. State Bar of Arizona, supra at 374.

Nevertheless, our decisions have recognized

the "common sense" distinction between speech proposing a commercial transaction, which occurs in an area traditionally subject to government regulation, and other varieties of speech.

Ohralik v. Ohio State Bar Assn., 436 U.S. 447, 455-456 (1978); see Bates v. State Bar of Arizona, supra at 381; see also Jackson & Jeffries, Commercial Speech: Economic Due Process and the First Amendment, 65 Va.L.Rev. 1, 38-39 (1979). The Constitution therefore accords a lesser protection to commercial speech than to other constitutionally guaranteed expression. 436 U.S. at 456, 457. The protection available for particular commercial expression turns on the nature both of the expression and of the governmental interests served by its regulation.

The First Amendment's concern for commercial speech is based on the informational function of advertising. See First National Bank of Boston v. Bellotti, 435 U.S. 765, 783 (1978). Consequently, there can be no constitutional objection to the suppression of commercial messages that do not accurately inform the public about lawful activity. The government may ban forms of communication more likely to deceive the public than to inform it, Friedman v. Rogers, supra at 13, 15-16; Ohralik v. Ohio State Bar Assn., supra at 464-465, or commercial speech related to illegal activity, Pittsburgh Press Co. v. Human Relations Comm'n, 413 U.S. 376, 388 (1973).

If the communication is neither misleading nor related to unlawful activity, the government's power is more circumscribed. The State must assert a substantial interest to be achieved by restrictions on commercial speech. Moreover, the regulatory technique must be in proportion to that interest. The limitation on expression must be designed carefully to achieve the State's goal. Compliance with this requirement may be measured by two criteria. First, the restriction must directly advance the state interest involved; the regulation may not be sustained if it provides only ineffective or remote support for the government's purpose. Second, if the governmental interest could be served as well by a more limited restriction on commercial speech, the excessive restrictions cannot survive.

Under the first criterion, the Court has declined to uphold regulations that only indirectly advance the state interest involved. In both Bates and Virginia Pharmacy Board, the Court concluded that an advertising ban could not be imposed to protect the ethical or performance standards of a profession. T he Court noted in Virginia Pharmacy Board that "[t]he advertising ban does not directly affect professional standards one way or the other." 425 U.S. at 769. In Bates, the Court overturned an advertising prohibition that was designed to protect the "quality" of a lawyer's work.] "Restraints on advertising . . . are an ineffective way of deterring shoddy work." 433 U.S. at 378.

The second criterion recognizes that the First Amendment mandates that speech restrictions be "narrowly drawn." In re Primus, 436 U.S. 412, 438 (1978). The regulatory technique may extend only as far as the interest it serves. The State cannot regulate speech that poses no danger to the asserted state interest, see First National Bank of Boston v. Bellotti, supra at 794-795, nor can it completely suppress information when narrower restrictions on expression would serve its interest as well. For example, in Bates, the Court explicitly did not "foreclose the possibility that some limited supplementation, by way of warning or disclaimer or the like, might be required" in promotional materials. 433 U.S. at 384. See Virginia Pharmacy Board, supra at 773. And in Carey v. Population Services International, 431 U.S. 678, 701-702 (1977), we held that the State's "arguments . . . do not justify the total suppression of advertising concerning contraceptives." This holding left open the possibility that the State could implement more carefully drawn restrictions. See id. at 712 (POWELL, J., concurring in part and in judgment); id. at 716-717 (STEVENS, J., concurring in part and in judgment).

In commercial speech cases, then, a four-part analysis has developed. At the outset, we must determine whether the expression is protected by the First Amendment. For commercial speech to come within that provision, it at least must concern lawful activity and not be misleading. Next, we ask whether the asserted governmental interest is substantial. If both inquiries yield positive answers, we must determine whether the regulation directly advances the governmental interest asserted, and whether it is not more extensive than is necessary to serve that interest.

### III

We now apply this four-step analysis for commercial speech to the Commission's arguments in support of its ban on promotional advertising.

### A

The Commission does not claim that the expression at issue either is inaccurate or relates to unlawful activity. Yet the New York Court of Appeals questioned whether Central Hudson's advertising is protected commercial speech. Because appellant holds a monopoly over the sale of electricity in its service area, the state court suggested that the Commission's order restricts no commercial speech of any worth. The court stated that advertising in a "noncompetitive market" could not improve the decisionmaking of consumers. 47 N.Y.2d at 110, 390 N.E.2d at 757. The court saw no constitutional problem with barring commercial speech that it viewed as conveying little useful information.

This reasoning falls short of establishing that appellant's advertising is not commercial speech protected by the First Amendment. Monopoly over the supply of a product provides no protection from competition with substitutes for that product. Electric utilities compete with suppli-

ers of fuel oil and natural gas in several markets, such as those for home heating and industrial power. This Court noted the existence of interfuel competition 45 years ago, see West Ohio as Co. v. Public Utilities Comm'n, 294 U.S. 63, 72 (1935). Each energy source continues to offer peculiar advantages and disadvantages that may influence consumer choice. For consumers in those competitive markets, advertising by utilities is just as valuable as advertising by unregulated firms.

Even in monopoly markets, the suppression of advertising reduces the information available for consumer decisions, and thereby defeats the purpose of the First Amendment. The New York court's argument appears to assume that the providers of a monopoly service or product are willing to pay for wholly ineffective advertising. Most businesses -- even regulated monopolies -- are unlikely to underwrite promotional advertising that is of no interest or use to consumers. Indeed, a monopoly enterprise legitimately may wish to inform the public that it has developed new services or terms of doing business. A consumer may need information to aid his decision whether or not to use the monopoly service at all, or how much of the service he should purchase. In the absence of factors that would distort the decision to advertise, we may assume that the willingness of a business to promote its products reflects a belief that consumers are interested in the advertising. Since no such extraordinary conditions have been identified in this case, appellant's monopoly position does not alter the First Amendment's protection for its commercial speech.

### B

The Commission offers two state interests as justifications for the ban on promotional advertising. The first concerns energy conservation. Any increase in demand for electricity -- during peak or off-peak periods -- means greater consumption of energy. The Commission argues, and the New York court agreed, that the State's interest in conserving energy is sufficient to support suppression of advertising designed to increase consumption of electricity. In view of our country's dependence on energy resources beyond our control, no one can doubt the importance of energy conservation. Plainly, therefore, the state interest asserted is substantial.

The Commission also argues that promotional advertising will aggravate inequities caused by the failure to base the utilities' rates on marginal cost. The utilities argued to the Commission that, if they could promote the use of electricity in periods of low demand, they would improve their utilization of generating capacity. The Commission responded that promotion of off-peak consumption also would increase consumption during peak periods. If peak demand were to rise, the absence of marginal cost rates would mean that the rates charged for the additional power would not reflect the true costs of expanding production. Instead, the extra costs would be borne by all consumers through higher overall rates. Without promotional advertising, the Commission stated, this inequitable turn of events would be less likely to occur. The choice among rate structures involves difficult and important questions of economic supply and distributional fairness. The State's concern that rates be fair and efficient represents a clear and substantial governmental interest.

C

Next, we focus on the relationship between the State's interests and the advertising ban. Under this criterion, the Commission's laudable concern over the equity and efficiency of appellant's rates does not provide a constitutionally adequate reason for restricting protected speech. The link between the advertising prohibition and appellant's rate structure is, at most, tenuous. The impact of promotional advertising on the equity of appellant's rates is highly speculative. Advertising to increase off-peak usage would have to increase peak usage, while other factors that directly affect the fairness and efficiency of appellant's rates remained constant. Such conditional and remote eventualities simply cannot justify silencing appellant's promotional advertising.

In contrast, the State's interest in energy conservation is directly advanced by the Commission order at issue here. There is an immediate connection between advertising and demand for electricity. Central Hudson would not contest the advertising ban unless it believed that promotion would increase its sales. Thus, we find a direct link between the state interest in conservation and the Commission's order.

D

We come finally to the critical inquiry in this case: whether the Commission's complete suppression of speech ordinarily protected by the First Amendment is no more extensive than necessary to further the State's interest in energy conservation. The Commission's order reaches all promotional advertising, regardless of the impact of the touted service on overall energy use. But the energy conservation rationale, as important as it is, cannot justify suppressing information about electric devices or services that would cause no net increase in total energy use. In addition, no showing has been made that a more limited restriction on the content of promotional advertising would not serve adequately the State's interests.

Appellant insists that, but for the ban, it would advertise products and services that use energy efficiently. These include the "heat pump," which both parties acknowledge to be a major improvement in electric heating, and the use of electric heat as a "backup" to solar and other heat sources. Although the Commission has questioned the efficiency of electric heating before this Court, neither the Commission's Policy Statement nor its order denying rehearing made findings on this issue. In the absence of authoritative findings to the contrary, we must credit as within the realm of possibility the claim that electric heat can be an efficient alternative in some circumstances.

The Commission's order prevents appellant from promoting electric services that would reduce energy use by diverting demand from less efficient sources, or that would consume roughly the same amount of energy as do alternative sources. In neither situation would the utility's advertising endanger conservation or mislead the public. To the extent that the Commission's order suppresses speech that in no way impairs the State's interest in energy conservation, the Commission's order violates the First and Fourteenth Amendments, and must be invalidated. See First National Bank of Boston v. Bellotti, 435 U.S. 765 (1978).

The Commission also has not demonstrated that its interest in conservation cannot be protected adequately by more limited regulation of appellant's commercial expression. To further its policy of conservation, the Commission could attempt to restrict the format and content of Central Hudson's advertising. It might, for example, require that the advertisements include information about the relative efficiency and expense of the offered service, both under current conditions and for the foreseeable future. Cf. Banzhaf v. FCC, 132 U.S.App.D.C. 14, 405 F.2d 1082 (1968), cert. denied sub nom. Tobacco Institute, Inc. v. FCC, 396 U.S. 842 (1969).  In the absence of a showing that more limited speech regulation would be ineffective, we cannot approve the complete suppression of Central Hudson's advertising.

IV

Our decision today in no way disparages the national interest in energy conservation. We accept without reservation the argument that conservation, as well as the development of alternative energy sources, is an imperative national goal. Administrative bodies empowered to regulate electric utilities have the authority -- and indeed the duty -- to take appropriate action to further this goal. When, however, such action involves the suppression of speech, the First and Fourteenth Amendments require that the restriction be no more extensive than is necessary to serve the state interest.

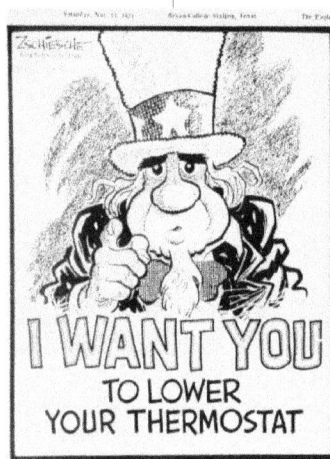

In this case, the record before us fails to show that the total ban on promotional advertising meets this requirement.

Accordingly, the judgment of the New York Court of Appeals is

Reversed.

**MR. JUSTICE REHNQUIST, dissenting.**

The Court today invalidates an order issued by the New York Public Service Commission designed to promote a policy that has been declared to be of critical national concern. ...

The Court's analysis, in my view, is wrong in several respects. Initially, I disagree with the Court's conclusion that the speech of a state-created monopoly, which is the subject of a comprehensive regulatory scheme, is entitled to protection under the First Amendment....

The state-created monopoly status of a utility arises from the unique characteristics of the services that a utility provides. As recognized in Cantor v. Detroit Edison Co., 428 U.S. 579, 595-596 (1976), public utility regulation typically assumes that the private firm is a natural monopoly, and that public controls are necessary to protect the consumer from exploitation.

The consequences of this natural monopoly, in my view, justify much more wide-ranging supervision and control of a utility under the First Amendment ....

And a state regulatory body charged with the oversight of these types of services may reasonably decide to impose on the utility a special duty to conform its conduct to the agency's conception of the public interest. Thus I think it is constitutionally permissible for it to decide that promotional advertising is inconsistent with the public interest in energy conservation.

....

I remain of the view that the Court unlocked a Pandora's Box when it "elevated" commercial speech to the level of traditional political speech by according it First Amendment protection in Virginia Pharmacy Board v. Virginia Citizens Consumer Council, 425 U.S. 748 (1976). ....

For the foregoing reasons, I would affirm the judgment of the New York Court of Appeals.

# Lorillard Tobacco Co. et al. v. Reilly, Attorney General of Massachusetts (2001)

U.S. Supreme Court

533 U.S. 525 (2001)

Decided June 28, 2001*

Decision: 5 votes for Lorillard Tobacco, 4 vote(s) against

**Justice O'Connor delivered the opinion of the Court.**

In January 1999, the Attorney General of Massachusetts promulgated comprehensive regulations governing the advertising and sale of cigarettes, smokeless tobacco, and cigars. 940 Code of Mass. Regs. §§21.01-21.07, 22.01-22.09 (2000). Petitioners, a group of cigarette, smokeless tobacco, and cigar manufacturers and retailers, filed suit in Federal District Court claiming that the regulations violate federal law and the United States Constitution. In large measure, the District Court determined that the regulations are valid and enforceable. The

United States Court of Appeals for the First Circuit affirmed in part and reversed in part, concluding that the regulations are not pre-empted by federal law and do not violate the First Amendment. The first question presented for our review is whether certain cigarette advertising regulations are pre-empted by the Federal Cigarette Labeling and Advertising Act (FCLAA), 79 Stat. 282, as amended, 15 U. S. C. §1331 et seq. The second question presented is whether certain regulations governing the advertising and sale of tobacco products violate the First Amendment.

I

In November 1998, Massachusetts, along with over 40 other States, reached a landmark agreement with major manufacturers in the cigarette industry. The signatory States settled their claims against these companies in exchange for monetary payments and permanent injunctive relief. See App. 253-258 (Outline of Terms for Massachusetts in National Tobacco Settlement); Master Settlement Agreement (Nov. 23, 1998), http://www.naag.org. At the press conference covering Massachusetts' decision to sign the agreement, then-Attorney General Scott Harshbarger announced that as one of his last acts in office, he would create consumer protection regulations to restrict advertising and sales practices for tobacco products. He explained that the regulations were necessary in order to "close holes" in the settlement agreement and "to stop Big Tobacco from recruiting new customers among the children of Massachusetts." App. 251.

In January 1999, pursuant to his authority to prevent unfair or deceptive practices in trade, Mass. Gen. Laws, ch. 93A, §2 (1997), the Massachusetts Attorney General (Attorney General) promulgated regulations governing the sale and advertisement of cigarettes, smokeless tobacco, and cigars. The purpose of the cigarette and smokeless tobacco regulations is "to eliminate deception and unfairness in the way cigarettes and smokeless tobacco products are marketed, sold and distributed in Massachusetts in order to address the incidence of cigarette

124

smoking and smokeless tobacco use by children under legal age .... [and] in order to prevent access to such products by underage consumers." 940 Code of Mass. Regs. §21.01 (2000). The similar purpose of the cigar regulations is "to eliminate deception and unfairness in the way cigars and little cigars are packaged, marketed, sold and distributed in Massachusetts [so that] ... consumers may be adequately informed about the health risks associated with cigar smoking, its addictive properties, and the false perception that cigars are a safe alternative to cigarettes ... [and so that] the incidence of cigar use by children under legal age is addressed ... in order to prevent access to such products by underage consumers." Ibid. The regulations have a broader scope than the master settlement agreement, reaching advertising, sales practices, and members of the tobacco industry not covered by the agreement. The regulations place a variety of restrictions on outdoor advertising, point-of-sale advertising, retail sales transactions, transactions by mail, promotions, sampling of products, and labels for cigars.

The cigarette and smokeless tobacco regulations being challenged before this Court provide:

"(2) Retail Outlet Sales Practices. Except as otherwise provided in [§21.04(4)], it shall be an unfair or deceptive act or practice for any person who sells or distributes cigarettes or smokeless tobacco products through a retail outlet located within Massachusetts to engage in any of the following retail outlet sales practices:

. . . .

"(5) Advertising Restrictions. Except as provided in [§21.04(6)], it shall be an unfair or deceptive act or practice for any manufacturer, distributor or retailer to engage in any of the following practices:

"(a) Outdoor advertising, including advertising in enclosed stadiums and advertising from within a retail establishment that is directed toward or visible from the outside of the establishment, in any location that is within a 1,000 foot radius of any public playground, playground area in a public park, elementary school or secondary school;

"(b) Point-of-sale advertising of cigarettes or smokeless tobacco products any portion of which is placed lower than five feet from the floor of any retail establishment which is located within a one thousand foot radius of any public playground, playground area in a public park, elementary school or secondary school, and which is not an adult-only retail establishment." §§21.04(5)(a)-(b).

. . . .

Before the effective date of the regulations, February 1, 2000, members of the tobacco industry sued the Attorney General in the United States District Court for the District of Massachusetts. Four cigarette manufacturers (Lorillard Tobacco Company, Brown & Williamson Tobacco Corporation, R. J. Reynolds Tobacco Company, and Philip Morris Incorporated), a maker of smokeless tobacco products (U. S. Smokeless Tobacco Company), and several cigar manufacturers and retailers claimed that many of the regulations violate the Commerce Clause, the Supremacy Clause, the First and Fourteenth Amendments, ...

[T]he District Court considered the claim that the Attorney General's regulations violate the First Amendment. 84 F. Supp. 2d, at 183-196. Rejecting petitioners' argument that strict scrutiny should apply, the court applied the four-part test of Central Hudson Gas & Elec. Corp. v. Public Serv. Comm'n of N. Y., 447 U. S. 557 (1980), for commercial speech. The court reasoned that the Attorney General had provided an

125

adequate basis for regulating cigars and smokeless tobacco as well as cigarettes because of the similarities among the products. The court held that the outdoor advertising regulations, which prohibit outdoor advertising within 1,000 feet of a school or playground, do not violate the First Amendment because they advance a substantial government interest and are narrowly tailored to suppress no more speech than necessary. The court concluded that the sales practices regulations, which restrict the location and distribution of tobacco products, survive scrutiny because they do not implicate a significant speech interest. The court invalidated the point-of-sale advertising regulations, which require that indoor advertising be placed no lower than five feet from the floor, finding that the Attorney General had not provided sufficient justification for that restriction. The District Court's ruling with respect to the cigar warning requirements and the Commerce Clause is not before this Court.

. . .

With respect to the First Amendment, the Court of Appeals applied the Central Hudson test. 447 U. S. 557 (1980). The court held that the outdoor advertising regulations do not violate the First Amendment. The court concluded that the restriction on outdoor advertising within 1,000 feet of a school or playground directly advances the State's substantial interest in preventing tobacco use by minors. The court also found that the outdoor advertising regulations restrict no more speech than necessary, reasoning that the distance chosen by the Attorney General is the sort of determination better suited for legislative and executive decisionmakers than courts. The Court of Appeals reversed the District Court's invalidation of the point-of-sale advertising regulations, again concluding that the Attorney General is better suited to determine what restrictions are necessary. The Court of Appeals also held that the sales practices regulations are valid under the First Amendment. The court found that the regulations directly advance the State's interest in preventing minors' access to tobacco products and that the regulations are narrowly tailored because retailers have a variety of other means to present the packaging of their products and to allow customers to examine the products.

. . . .

II

Before reaching the First Amendment issues, we must decide to what extent federal law pre-empts the Attorney General's regulations. The cigarette petitioners contend that the [The Federal Cigarette Labeling and Advertising Act]FCLAA, 15 U. S. C. §1331 et seq., pre-empts the Attorney General's cigarette advertising regulations.

A

Article VI of the United States Constitution commands that the laws of the United States "shall be the supreme Law of the Land; ... any Thing in the Constitution or Laws of any State to the Contrary notwithstanding."

....

In the FCLAA, Congress has crafted a comprehensive federal scheme governing the advertising and promotion of cigarettes.

. . . .

Viewed in light of the context in which the current pre-emption provision was adopted, we must determine whether the FCLAA pre-empts Massachusetts' regulations governing outdoor and point-of-sale advertising of cigarettes.

B

The Court of Appeals acknowledged that the FCLAA pre-empts any "requirement or prohibition based on smoking and health ... with respect to the advertising or promotion of ... cigarettes," 15 U. S. C.

§1334(b), but concluded that the FCLAA does not nullify Massachusetts' cigarette advertising regulations.

. . . .

In sum, we fail to see how the FCLAA and its pre-emption provision permit a distinction between the specific concern about minors and cigarette advertising and the more general concern about smoking and health in cigarette advertising, especially in light of the fact that Congress crafted a legislative solution for those very concerns. We also conclude that a distinction between state regulation of the location as opposed to the content of cigarette advertising has no foundation in the text of the pre-emption provision. Congress pre-empted state cigarette advertising regulations like the Attorney General's because they would upset federal legislative choices to require specific warnings and to impose the ban on cigarette advertising in electronic media in order to address concerns about smoking and health. Accordingly, we hold that the Attorney General's outdoor and point-of-sale advertising regulations targeting cigarettes are pre-empted by the FCLAA.

. . . .

III

By its terms, the FCLAA's pre-emption provision only applies to cigarettes. Accordingly, we must evaluate the smokeless tobacco and cigar petitioners' First Amendment challenges to the State's outdoor and point-of-sale advertising regulations. The cigarette petitioners did not raise a pre-emption challenge to the sales practices regulations. Thus, we must analyze the cigarette as well as the smokeless tobacco and cigar petitioners' claim that certain sales practices regulations for tobacco products violate the First Amendment.

A

For over 25 years, the Court has recognized that commercial speech does not fall outside the purview of the First Amendment. See, e.g., Virginia Bd. of Pharmacy, supra, at 762. Instead, the Court has afforded commercial speech a measure of First Amendment protection " `commensurate' " with its position in relation to other constitutionally guaranteed expression. See, e.g., Florida Bar v. Went For It, Inc., 515 U. S. 618, 623 (1995) (quoting Board of Trustees of State Univ. of N. Y. v. Fox, 492 U. S. 469, 477 (1989)). In recognition of the "distinction between speech proposing a commercial transaction, which occurs in an area traditionally subject to government regulation, and other varieties of speech," Central Hudson, supra, at 562 (internal quotation marks omitted), we developed a framework for analyzing regulations of commercial speech that is "substantially similar" to the test for time, place, and manner restrictions, Board of Trustees of State Univ. of N. Y. v. Fox, supra, at 477. The analysis contains four elements:

"At the outset, we must determine whether the expression is protected by the First Amendment. For commercial speech to come within that provision, it at least must concern lawful activity and not be misleading. Next, we ask whether the asserted governmental interest is substantial. If both inquiries yield positive answers, we must determine whether the regulation directly advances the governmental interest asserted, and whether it is not more extensive than is necessary to serve that interest." Central Hudson, supra, at 566.

Petitioners urge us to reject the Central Hudson analysis and apply strict scrutiny. They are not the first litigants to do so. See, e.g., Greater New Orleans Broadcasting Assn., Inc. v. United States, 527 U. S. 173, 184 (1999). Admittedly, several Members of the Court have expressed doubts about the Central Hudson analysis and whether it should apply in particular cases. See, e.g., Greater New Orleans, supra, at 197 (Thomas, J., concurring in judgment); 44 Liquormart, Inc. v. Rhode Island, 517 U. S. 484, 501, 510-514 (1996) (joint opinion of Stevens, Kennedy, and Ginsburg, JJ.); id., at 517 (Scalia, J. concurring in part and concurring in judgment); id., at 518 (Thomas, J., concurring in part and concurring in judgment). But here, as in Greater New Orleans, we see "no need to break new ground. Central Hudson, as applied in our more recent commercial speech cases, provides an adequate basis for decision." 527 U. S., at 184.

Only the last two steps of Central Hudson's four-part analysis are at issue here. The Attorney General has assumed for purposes of summary judgment that petitioners' speech is entitled to First Amendment protection. 218 F. 3d., at 43; 84 F. Supp. 2d, at 185-186. With respect to the second step, none of the petitioners contests the importance of the State's interest in preventing the use of tobacco products by minors. Brief for Petitioners Lorillard Tobacco Co. et al. in No. 00-596, p. 41; Brief for Petitioner U. S. Smokeless Tobacco Co. in Nos. 00-596 and 00-597, at 16; Brief for Petitioners Altadis U. S. A. Inc. et al. in No. 00-597, p. 8.

The third step of Central Hudson concerns the relationship between the harm that underlies the State's interest and the means identified by the State to advance that interest. It requires that

"the speech restriction directly and materially advanc[e] the asserted governmental interest. `This burden is not satisfied by mere speculation or conjecture; rather, a governmental body seeking to sustain a restriction on commercial speech must demonstrate that the harms it recites are real and that its restriction will in fact alleviate them to a material degree.' " Greater New Orleans, supra, at 188 (quoting Edenfield v. Fane, 507 U. S. 761, 770-771 (1993)).

We do not, however, require that "empirical data come ... accompanied by a surfeit of background information... [W]e have permitted litigants to justify speech restrictions by reference to studies and anecdotes pertaining to different locales altogether, or even, in a case applying strict scrutiny, to justify restrictions based solely on history, consensus, and `simple common sense.' " Florida Bar v. Went For It, Inc., 515 U. S., at 628 (citations and internal quotation marks omitted).

The last step of the Central Hudson analysis "complements" the third step, "asking whether the speech restriction is not more extensive than necessary to serve the interests that support it." Greater New Orleans, supra, at 188. We have made it clear that "the least restrictive means" is not the standard; instead, the case law requires a reasonable " `fit between the legislature's ends and the means chosen to accomplish those ends, ... a means narrowly tailored to achieve the desired objective.' " Went For It, Inc., supra, at 632 (quoting Board of Trustees of State Univ. of N. Y. v. Fox, 492 U. S., at 480). Focusing on the third and fourth steps of the Central Hudson analysis, we first address the outdoor advertising and point-of-sale advertising regulations for smokeless tobacco and cigars. We then address the sales practices regulations for all tobacco products.

B

The outdoor advertising regulations prohibit smokeless tobacco or cigar advertising within a 1,000-foot radius of a school or playground. 940 Code of Mass. Regs. §§21.04(5)(a), 22.06(5)(a) (2000). The District Court and Court of Appeals concluded that the Attorney General had identified a real problem with underage use of tobacco products, that limiting youth exposure to advertising would combat that problem, and that the regulations burdened no more speech than necessary to accomplish the State's goal. 218 F. 3d, at 44-53; 84 F. Supp. 2d, at 186-193. The smokeless tobacco and cigar petitioners take issue with all of these conclusions.

The smokeless tobacco and cigar petitioners contend that the Attorney General's regulations do not satisfy Central Hudson's third step. They maintain that although the Attorney General may have identified a problem with underage cigarette smoking, he has not identified an equally severe problem with respect to underage use of smokeless tobacco or cigars. The smokeless tobacco petitioner emphasizes the "lack of parity" between cigarettes and smokeless tobacco. Brief for Petitioner U. S. Smokeless Tobacco Co. in Nos. 00-596 and 00-597, at 19; Reply Brief for Petitioner U. S. Smokeless Tobacco Co. in Nos. 00-596 and 00-597, pp. 4, 10-11. The cigar petitioners catalogue a list of differences between cigars and other tobacco products, including the characteristics of the products and marketing strategies. Brief for Petitioners Altadis U. S. A. Inc. et al. in No. 00-597, at 9-11. The petitioners finally contend that the Attorney General cannot prove that advertising has a causal link to tobacco use such that limiting advertising will materially alleviate any problem of underage use of their products. Brief for Petitioner U. S. Smokeless Tobacco Co. in Nos. 00-596 and 00-597, at 20-22; Brief for Petitioners Altadis U. S. A. Inc. et al. in No. 00-597, at 9-16.

In previous cases, we have acknowledged the theory that product advertising stimulates demand for products, while suppressed advertising may have the opposite effect. See Rubin, 514 U. S., at 487; United States v. Edge Broadcasting Co., 509 U. S. 418, 434 (1993); Central Hudson,
447 U. S., at 568-569. The Attorney General cites numerous studies to support this theory in the case of tobacco products.

The Attorney General relies in part on evidence gathered by the Food and Drug Administration (FDA) in its attempt to regulate the advertising of cigarettes and smokeless tobacco. See Regulations Restricting the Sale and Distribution of Cigarettes and Smokeless Tobacco Products to Protect Children and Adolescents, FDA Proposed Rule, 60

Fed. Reg. 41314 (1995); Regulations Restricting the Sale and Distribution of Cigarettes and Smokeless Tobacco to Protect Children and Adolescents, FDA Final Rule, 61 Fed. Reg. 44396 (1996). The FDA promulgated the advertising regulations after finding that the period prior to adulthood is when an overwhelming majority of Americans first decide to use tobacco products, and that advertising plays a crucial role in that decision. FDA Final Rule, 61 Fed. Reg., at 44398-44399. We later held that the FDA lacks statutory authority to regulate tobacco products. See FDA v. Brown & Williamson Tobacco Corp., 529 U. S. 120 (2000). Nevertheless, the Attorney General relies on the FDA's proceedings and other studies to support his decision that advertising affects demand for tobacco products. Cf. Erie v. Pap's A. M., 529 U. S. 277, 296 (2000) (plurality opinion) (cities and localities may rely on evidence from other jurisdictions to demonstrate harmful secondary effects of adult entertainment and to justify regulation); Barnes v. Glen Theatre, Inc., 501 U. S. 560, 583-584 (1991) (Souter, J., concurring in judgment) (same); Renton v. Playtime Theatres, Inc., 475 U. S. 41, 50-52 (1986) (same). See also Nixon v. Shrink Missouri Government PAC, 528 U. S. 377, 393, and n. 6 (2000) (discussing evidence of corruption and the appearance of corruption in campaign finance).

In its rulemaking proceeding, the FDA considered several studies of tobacco advertising and trends in the use of various tobacco products. The Surgeon General's report and the Institute of Medicine's report found that "there is sufficient evidence to conclude that advertising and labeling play a significant and important contributory role in a young person's decision to use cigarettes or smokeless tobacco products." 60 Fed. Reg. 41332. See also Pierce et al., Tobacco Industry Promotion of Cigarettes and Adolescent Smoking, 279 JAMA 511, 514 (1998).

For instance, children smoke fewer brands of cigarettes than adults, and those choices directly track the most heavily advertised brands, unlike adult choices, which are more dispersed and related to pricing. FDA Proposed Rule, 60 Fed. Reg. 41332. Another study revealed that 72% of 6 year olds and 52% of children ages 3 to 6 recognized "Joe

Camel," the cartoon anthropomorphic symbol of R. J. Reynolds' Camel brand cigarettes. Id., at 41333. After the introduction of Joe Camel, Camel cigarettes' share of the youth market rose from 4% to 13%. Id., at 41330. The FDA also identified trends in tobacco consumption among certain populations, such as young women, that correlated to the introduction and marketing of products geared toward that population. Id., at 41333.

The FDA also made specific findings with respect to smokeless tobacco. The FDA concluded that "[t]he recent and very large increase in the use of smokeless tobacco products by young people and the addictive nature of these products has persuaded the agency that these products must be included in any regulatory approach that is designed to help prevent future generations of young people from becoming addicted to nicotine-containing tobacco products." Id., at 41318. Studies have analyzed smokeless tobacco use by young people, discussing trends based on gender, school grade, and locale. See, e.g., Boyd et al., Use of Smokeless Tobacco among Children and Adolescents in the United States, 16 Preventative Medicine 402-418 (1987), Record, Doc. No. 38, Exh. 63.

Researchers tracked a dramatic shift in patterns of smokeless tobacco use from older to younger users over the past 30 years. See, e.g., FDA Proposed Rule, 60 Fed. Reg., at 41317; Tomar et al., Smokeless tobacco brand preference and brand switching among

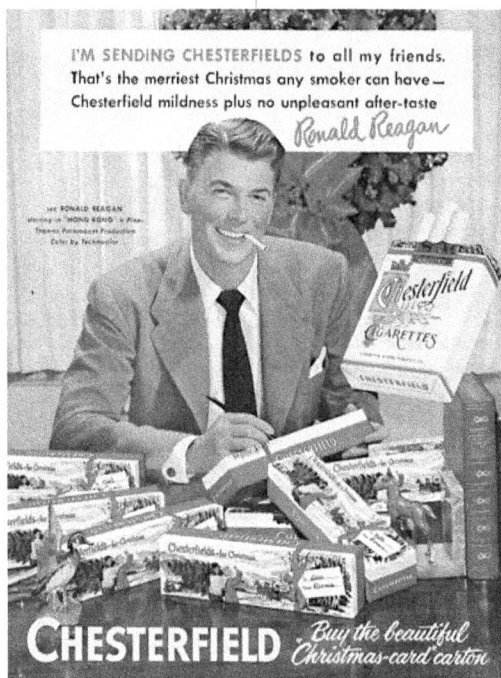

US adolescents and young adults, 4 Tobacco Control 67 (1995), Record, Doc. No. 38, Exh. 62; Department of Health and Human Services, Preventing Tobacco Use Among Young People: A Report of the Surgeon General 163 (1994), Record, Doc. No. 36, Exh. 1. In particular, the smokeless tobacco industry boosted sales tenfold in the 1970s and 1980s by targeting young males. FDA Proposed Rule, 60 Fed. Reg., at 41331. See also National Cancer Institute, Cigars: Health Effects and Trends, Smoking and Tobacco Control Monograph No. 9, p. 16 (1998), Record, Doc. No. 39, Exh. 67. Another study documented the targeting of youth through smokeless tobacco sales and advertising techniques. Ernster, Advertising and Promotion of Smokeless Tobacco Products, National Cancer Institute Monograph No. 8, pp. 87-93 (1989), Record, Doc. No. 38, Exh. 66.

The Attorney General presents different evidence with respect to cigars. There was no data on underage cigar use prior to 1996 because the behavior was considered "uncommon enough not to be worthy of examination." Smoking and Tobacco Control Monograph No. 9, at 13; FTC Report to Congress: Cigar Sales and Advertising and Promotional Expenses for Calendar Years 1996 and 1997, p. 9 (1999), Record, Doc. No. 39, Exh. 71. In 1995, the FDA decided not to include cigars in its attempted regulation of tobacco product advertising, explaining that "the agency does not currently have sufficient evidence that these products are drug delivery devices ... . FDA has focused its investigation of its authority over tobacco products on cigarettes and smokeless tobacco products, and not on pipe tobacco or cigars, because young people predominantly use cigarettes and smokeless tobacco products." 60 Fed. Reg. 41322.

More recently, however, data on youth cigar use has emerged. The National Cancer Institute concluded in its 1998 Monograph that the rate of cigar use by minors is increasing and that, in some States, the cigar use rates are higher than the smokeless tobacco use rates for minors. Smoking and Tobacco Control Monograph No. 9, at 19, 42-51. In its 1999 Report to Congress, the FTC concluded that "substantial numbers of adolescents are trying cigars." FTC Report to Congress, at 9. See also Department of Health and Human Services, Office of Inspector General, Youth Use of Cigars: Patterns of Use and Perceptions of Risk (1999), Record, Doc. No. 39, Exh. 78.

Studies have also demonstrated a link between advertising and demand for cigars. After Congress recognized the power of images in advertising and banned cigarette advertising in electronic media, television advertising of small cigars "increased dramatically in 1972 and 1973," "filled the void left by cigarette advertisers," and "sales ... soared." Smoking and Tobacco Control Monograph No. 9, at 24. In 1973, Congress extended the electronic media advertising ban for cigarettes to little cigars. Little Cigar Act, §3, Pub. L. 93-109, 87 Stat. 352, as amended, 15 U. S. C. §1335. In the 1990s, cigar advertising campaigns triggered a boost in sales. Smoking and Tobacco Control Monograph No. 9, at 215.

Our review of the record reveals that the Attorney General has provided ample documentation of the problem with underage use of smokeless tobacco and cigars. In addition, we disagree with petitioners' claim that there is no evidence that preventing targeted campaigns and limiting youth exposure to advertising will decrease underage use of smokeless tobacco and cigars. On this record and in the posture of summary judgment, we are unable to conclude that the Attorney General's decision to regulate advertising of smokeless tobacco and cigars in an effort to combat the use of tobacco products by minors was based on mere "speculation [and] conjecture." Edenfield v. Fane, 507 U. S., at 770.

2

Whatever the strength of the Attorney General's evidence to justify the outdoor advertising regulations, however, we conclude that the regulations do not satisfy the fourth step of the Central Hudson analysis. The final step of the Central Hudson analysis, the "critical inquiry in this case," requires a reasonable fit between the means and ends of the regulatory scheme. 447 U. S., at 569. The Attorney General's regulations do not meet this standard. The broad sweep of the regulations indicates that the Attorney General did not "carefully calculat[e] the costs and benefits associated with the burden on speech imposed" by the regulations. Cincinnati v. Discovery Network, Inc., 507 U. S. 410, 417 (1993) (internal quotation marks omitted).

The outdoor advertising regulations prohibit any smokeless tobacco or cigar advertising within 1,000 feet of schools or playgrounds. In the District Court, petitioners maintained that this prohibition would prevent advertising in 87% to 91% of Boston, Worchester, and Springfield, Massachusetts. 84 F. Supp. 2d, at 191. The 87% to 91% figure appears to include not only the effect of the regulations, but also the limitations imposed by other generally applicable zoning restrictions. See App. 161-167. The Attorney General disputed petitioners' figures but "concede[d] that the reach of the regulations is substantial." 218 F. 3d, at 50. Thus, the Court of Appeals concluded that the regulations prohibit advertising in a substantial portion of the major metropolitan areas of Massachusetts. Ibid.

The substantial geographical reach of the Attorney General's outdoor advertising regulations is compounded by other factors. "Outdoor" advertising includes not only advertising located outside an establishment, but also advertising inside a store if that advertising is visible from outside the store. The regulations restrict advertisements of any size and the term advertisement also includes oral statements. 940 Code of Mass. Regs §§21.03, 22.03 (2000).

In some geographical areas, these regulations would constitute nearly a complete ban on the communication of truthful information about smokeless tobacco and cigars to adult consumers. The breadth and scope of the regulations, and the process by which the Attorney General adopted the regulations, do not demonstrate a careful calculation of the speech interests involved.

First, the Attorney General did not seem to consider the impact of the 1,000-foot restriction on commercial speech in major metropolitan areas. The Attorney General apparently selected the 1,000-foot distance based on the FDA's decision to impose an identical 1,000-foot restriction when it attempted to regulate cigarette and smokeless tobacco advertising. See FDA Final Rule, 61 Fed. Reg. 44399; Brief for Respondents 45, and n. 23. But the FDA's 1,000-foot regulation was not an adequate basis for the Attorney General to tailor the Massachusetts regulations. The degree to which speech is suppressed--or alternative avenues for speech remain available--under a particular regulatory scheme tends to be case specific. See, e.g., Renton, 475 U. S., at 53-54. And a case specific analysis makes sense, for although a State or locality may have common interests and concerns about underage smoking and the effects of tobacco advertisements, the impact of a restriction on speech will undoubtedly vary from place to place. The FDA's regulations would have had widely disparate effects nationwide. Even in Massachusetts, the effect of the Attorney General's speech regulations will vary based on whether a locale is rural, suburban, or urban. The uniformly broad sweep of the geographical limitation demonstrates a lack of tailoring.

In addition, the range of communications restricted seems unduly broad. For instance, it is not clear from the regulatory scheme why a ban on oral communications is necessary to further the State's interest. Apparently that restriction means that a retailer is unable to answer inquiries about its tobacco products if that communication occurs outdoors. Similarly, a ban on all signs of any size seems ill suited to target the problem of highly visible billboards, as opposed to smaller signs. To the extent that studies have identified particular advertising and promotion practices that appeal to youth, tailoring would involve targeting those practices while permitting others. As crafted, the regulations make no distinction among practices on this basis.

The Court of Appeals recognized that the smokeless tobacco and cigar petitioners' concern about the amount of speech restricted was "valid," but reasoned that there was an "obvious connection to the state's interest in protecting minors." 218 F. 3d, at 50. Even on the premise that Massachusetts has demonstrated a connection between the outdoor advertising regulations and its substantial interest in preventing underage tobacco use, the question of tailoring remains. The Court of Appeals failed to follow through with an analysis of the countervailing First Amendment interests.

The State's interest in preventing underage tobacco use is substantial, and even compelling, but it is no less true that the sale and use of tobacco products by adults is a legal activity. We must consider that tobacco retailers and manufacturers have an interest in conveying truthful information about their products to adults, and adults have a corresponding interest in receiving truthful information about tobacco products. In a case involving indecent speech on the Internet we explained that "the governmental interest in protecting children from harmful materials ... does not justify an unnecessarily broad suppression of speech addressed to adults." Reno v. American Civil Liberties Union, 521 U. S. 844, 875 (1997) (citations omitted). See, e.g., Bolger v. Youngs Drug Products Corp., 463 U. S. 60, 74 (1983) ("The level of discourse reaching a mailbox simply cannot be limited to that which would be suitable for a sandbox"); Butler v. Michigan, 352 U. S. 380, 383 (1957) ("The incidence of this enactment is to reduce the adult population ... to reading only what is fit for children"). As the State protects children from tobacco advertisements, tobacco manufacturers and retailers and their adult consumers still have a protected interest in communication. Cf. American Civil Liberties Union, supra, at 886-889 (O'Connor, J., concurring in judgment in part and dissenting in part) (discussing the creation of "adult zones" on the Internet).

In some instances, Massachusetts' outdoor advertising regulations would impose particularly onerous burdens on speech. For example, we disagree with the Court of Appeals' conclusion that because cigar manufacturers and retailers conduct a limited amount of advertising in comparison to other tobacco products, "the relative lack of cigar advertising also means that the burden imposed on cigar advertisers is correspondingly small." 218 F. 3d, at 49. If some retailers have relatively small advertising budgets, and use few avenues of communication, then the Attorney General's outdoor advertising regulations potentially place a greater, not lesser, burden on those retailers' speech. Furthermore, to the extent that cigar products and cigar advertising differ from that of other tobacco products, that difference should inform the inquiry into what speech restrictions are necessary.

**More Doctors Smoke CAMELS than any other cigarette!**

In addition, a retailer in Massachusetts may have no means of communicating to passersby on the street that it sells tobacco products because alternative forms of advertisement, like newspapers, do not allow that retailer to propose an instant transaction in the way that onsite advertising does. The ban on any indoor advertising that is visible from the outside also presents problems in establishments like convenience stores, which have unique security concerns that counsel in favor of full visibility of the store from the outside. It is these sorts of considerations that the Attorney General failed to incorporate into the regulatory scheme.

We conclude that the Attorney General has failed to show that the outdoor advertising regulations for smokeless tobacco and cigars are not more extensive than necessary to advance the State's substantial interest in preventing underage tobacco use. Justice Stevens urges that the Court remand the case for further development of the factual record. Post, at 12-14. We believe that a remand is inappropriate in this case because the State had ample opportunity to develop a record with respect to tailoring (as it had to justify its decision to regulate advertising), and additional evidence would not alter the nature of the scheme before the Court. See Greater New Orleans, 527 U. S., at 189, n. 6.

A careful calculation of the costs of a speech regulation does not mean that a State must demonstrate that there is no incursion on legitimate speech interests, but a speech regulation cannot unduly impinge on the speaker's ability to propose a commercial transaction and the adult listener's opportunity to obtain information about products. After reviewing the outdoor advertising regulations, we find the calculation in this case insufficient for purposes of the First Amendment.

C

Massachusetts has also restricted indoor, point-of-sale advertising for smokeless tobacco and cigars. Advertising cannot be "placed lower than five feet from the floor of any retail establishment which is located within a one thousand foot radius of" any school or playground. 940 Code of Mass. Regs. §§21.04(5)(b), 22.06(5)(b) (2000). The District Court invalidated these provisions, concluding that the Attorney General had not provided a sufficient basis for regulating indoor advertising. 84 F. Supp. 2d, at 192-193, 195. The Court of Appeals reversed. 218 F. 3d, at 50-51. The court explained: "We do have some misgivings about the effectiveness of a restriction that is based on the assumption that minors under five feet tall will not, or will less frequently, raise their view above eye-level, but we find that such [a] determination falls within that range of reasonableness in which the Attorney General is best suited to pass judgment." Id., at 51.

We conclude that the point-of-sale advertising regulations fail both the third and fourth steps of the Central Hudson analysis. A regulation cannot be sustained if it " `provides only ineffective or remote support for the government's purpose,' " Edenfield, 507 U. S., at 770 (quoting Central Hudson, 447 U. S., at 564), or if there is "little chance" that the restriction will advance the State's goal, Greater New Orleans, supra, at 193 (internal quotation marks omitted). As outlined above, the State's goal is to prevent minors from using tobacco products and to curb demand for that activity by limiting youth exposure to advertising. The 5 foot rule does not seem to advance that goal. Not all children are less than 5 feet tall, and those who are certainly have the ability to look up and take in their surroundings.

By contrast to Justice Stevens, post, at 16-17, we do not believe this regulation can be construed as a mere regulation of conduct under United States v. O'Brien, 391 U. S. 367 (1968). To qualify as a regulation of communicative action governed by the scrutiny outlined in O'Brien, the State's regulation must be unrelated to expression. Texas v. Johnson, 491 U. S. 397, 403 (1989). See also Erie v. Pap's A. M., 529 U. S. 277, 289-296 (2000) (plurality opinion). Here, Massachusetts' height restriction is an attempt to regulate directly the communicative impact of indoor advertising.

Massachusetts may wish to target tobacco advertisements and displays that entice children, much like floor-level candy displays in a convenience store, but the blanket height restriction does not constitute a reasonable fit with that goal. The Court of Appeals recognized that the efficacy of the regulation was questionable, but decided that "[i]n any event, the burden on speech imposed by the provision is very limited." 218 F. 3d, at 51. There is no de minimis exception for a speech restriction that lacks sufficient tailoring or justification. We conclude that the restriction on the height of indoor advertising is invalid under Central Hudson's third and fourth prongs.

D

The Attorney General also promulgated a number of regulations that restrict sales practices by cigarette, smokeless tobacco, and cigar manufacturers and retailers. Among other restrictions, the regulations bar the use of self-service displays and require that tobacco products be placed out of the reach of all consumers in a location accessible only to salespersons. 940 Code of Mass. Regs. §§21.04(2)(c)-(d), 22.06(2)(c)-(d) (2000). The cigarette petitioners do not challenge the sales practices regulations on pre-emption grounds. Brief for Petitioners Lorillard Tobacco Co. et al. in No. 00-596, at 5, n. 2. Two of the cigarette petitioners (Brown & Williamson Tobacco Corporation and Lorillard Tobacco Company), petitioner U. S. Smokeless Tobacco Company, and the cigar petitioners challenge the sales practices regulations on First Amendment grounds. The cigar petitioners additionally challenge a provision that prohibits sampling or promotional giveaways of cigars or little cigars. 940 Code of Mass. Regs. §22.06(1)(a).

The District Court concluded that these restrictions implicate no cognizable speech interest, 84 F. Supp. 2d, at 195-196, but the Court of Appeals did not fully adopt that reasoning. The Court of Appeals recognized that self-service displays "often do have some communicative commercial function," but noted that the restriction in the regulations "is not on speech, but rather on the physical location of actual tobacco products." 218 F. 3d, at 53. The court reasoned that nothing in the regulations would prevent the display of empty tobacco product containers, so long as no actual tobacco product was displayed, much like movie jackets at a video store. Ibid. With respect to cigar products, the court observed that retailers traditionally allow access to those products, so that the consumer may make a selection on the basis of a number of objective and subjective factors including the aroma and feel of the cigars. Ibid. Even assuming a speech interest, however, the court concluded that the regulations were narrowly tailored to serve the State's substantial interest in preventing access to tobacco products by minors. Id., at 54. The court also noted that the restrictions do not apply to adult-only establishments. Ibid.

Petitioners devoted little of their briefing to the sales practices regulations, and our understanding of the regulations is accordingly limited by the parties' submissions. As we read the regulations, they basically require tobacco retailers to place tobacco products behind counters and require customers to have contact with a salesperson before they are able to handle a tobacco product.

The cigarette and smokeless tobacco petitioners contend that "the same First Amendment principles that require invalidation of the out-door and indoor advertising restrictions require invalidation of the display regulations at issue in this case." Brief for Petitioners Lorillard Tobacco Co. et al. in No. 00-596, at 46, n. 7. See also Reply Brief for Petitioner U. S. Smokeless Tobacco Co. in Nos. 00-596 and 00-597, at 12, n. 7. The cigar petitioners contend that self-service displays for cigars cannot be prohibited because each brand of cigar is unique and customers traditionally have sought to handle and compare cigars at the time of purchase. Brief for Petitioners Altadis U. S. A. Inc. et al. in No. 00-597, at 23, n. 9; Reply Brief for Petitioners Altadis U. S. A. Inc. et al. in No. 00-597, p. 10, n. 7.

We reject these contentions. Assuming that petitioners have a cognizable speech interest in a particular means of displaying their products, cf. Cincinnati v. Discovery Network, Inc., 507 U. S. 410 (1993) (distribution of a magazine through newsracks), these regulations withstand First Amendment scrutiny.

Massachusetts' sales practices provisions regulate conduct that may have a communicative component, but Massachusetts seeks to regulate the placement of tobacco products for reasons unrelated to the communication of ideas. See O'Brien, supra, at 382. See also Pap's A. M., 529 U. S., at 289 (plurality opinion); id., at 310 (Souter, J., concurring in part and dissenting in part); Johnson, 491 U. S., at 403. We conclude that the State has demonstrated a substantial interest in preventing access to tobacco products by minors and has adopted an appropriately narrow means of advancing that interest. See O'Brien, supra, at 382.

CANCER CURES SMOKING.

CANCER PATIENTS AID ASSOCIATION

Unattended displays of tobacco products present an opportunity for access without the proper age verification required by law. Thus, the State prohibits self-service and other displays that would allow an individual to obtain tobacco products without direct contact with a salesperson. It is clear that the regulations leave open ample channels of communication. The regulations do not significantly impede adult access to tobacco products. Moreover, retailers have other means of exercising any cognizable speech interest in the presentation of their products. We presume that vendors may place empty tobacco packaging on open display, and display actual tobacco products so long as that display is only accessible to sales personnel. As for cigars, there is no indication in the regulations that a customer is unable to examine a cigar prior to purchase, so long as that examination takes place through a salesperson.

The cigar petitioners also list Massachusetts' prohibition on sampling and free giveaways among the regulations they challenge on First Amendment grounds. See 940 Code of Mass. Regs. §22.06(1)(a) (2000); Brief for Petitioners Altadis U. S. A. Inc. et al. in No. 00-597, at 2. At no point in their briefs or at oral argument, however, did the cigar petitioners argue the merits of their First Amendment claim with respect to the sampling and giveaway regulation. We decline to address an issue that was not sufficiently briefed and argued before this Court. See Northwest Airlines, Inc. v. County of Kent, 510 U. S. 355, 366, n. 10 (1994); Williams v. United States, 503 U. S. 193, 206 (1992); Granfinanciera, S. A. v. Nordberg, 492 U. S. 33, 38-40 (1989).

We conclude that the sales practices regulations withstand First Amendment scrutiny. The means chosen by the State are narrowly tailored to prevent access to tobacco products by minors, are unrelated to expression, and leave open alternative avenues for vendors to convey information about products and for would-be customers to inspect products before purchase.

IV

We have observed that "tobacco use, particularly among children and adolescents, poses perhaps the single most significant threat to public health in the United States." FDA v. Brown & Williamson Tobacco Corp., 529 U. S., at 161. From a policy perspective, it is understandable for the States to attempt to prevent minors from using tobacco products before they reach an age where they are capable of weighing for themselves the risks and potential benefits of tobacco use, and other adult activities. Federal law, however, places limits on policy choices available to the States.

In this case, Congress enacted a comprehensive scheme to address cigarette smoking and health in advertising and pre-empted state regulation of cigarette advertising that attempts to address that same concern, even with respect to youth. The First Amendment also constrains state efforts to limit advertising of tobacco products, because so long as the sale and use of tobacco is lawful for adults, the tobacco industry has a protected interest in communicating information about its products and adult customers have an interest in receiving that information.

To the extent that federal law and the First Amendment do not prohibit state action, States and localities remain free to combat the problem of underage tobacco use by appropriate means. The judgment of the United States Court of Appeals for the First Circuit is therefore affirmed in part and reversed in part, and the cases are remanded for further proceedings consistent with this opinion.

It is so ordered.

**Justice Kennedy, with whom Justice Scalia joins, concurring in part and concurring in the judgment.**

The obvious overbreadth of the outdoor advertising restrictions suffices to invalidate them under the fourth part of the test in Central Hudson Gas & Elec. Corp. v. Public Serv. Comm'n of N. Y., 447 U. S. 557

(1980). As a result, in my view, there is no need to consider whether the restrictions satisfy the third part of the test, a proposition about which there is considerable doubt. Cf. post, at 13-14 (Thomas, J., concurring in part and concurring in judgment). Neither are we required to consider whether Central Hudson should be retained in the face of the substantial objections that can be made to it. See post, at 4-11 (opinion of Thomas, J.). My continuing concerns that the test gives insufficient protection to truthful, nonmisleading commercial speech require me to refrain from expressing agreement with the Court's application of the third part of Central Hudson. See, e.g., 44 Liquormart, Inc. v. Rhode Island, 517 U. S. 484, 501-504 (1996) (opinion of Stevens, J., joined by Kennedy and Ginsburg, JJ.). With the exception of Part III-B-1, then, I join the opinion of the Court.

**Justice Thomas, concurring in part and concurring in the judgment.**

I join the opinion of the Court (with the exception of Part III-B-1) because I agree that the Massachusetts cigarette advertising regulations are preempted by the Federal Cigarette Labeling and Advertising Act, 15 U. S. C. §1331 et seq. I also agree with the Court's disposition of the First Amendment challenges to the other regulations at issue here, and I share the Court's view that the regulations fail even the intermediate scrutiny of Central Hudson Gas & Elec. Corp. v. Public Serv. Comm'n of N. Y., 447 U. S. 557 (1980). At the same time, I continue to believe that when the government seeks to restrict truthful speech in order to suppress the ideas it conveys, strict scrutiny is appropriate, whether or not the speech in question may be characterized as "commercial." See 44 Liquormart, Inc. v. Rhode Island, 517 U. S. 484, 518 (1996) (Thomas, J., concurring in part and concurring in judgment). I would subject all of the advertising restrictions to strict scrutiny and would hold that they violate the First Amendment.

....

Respondents suggest that tobacco advertising is misleading because "its youthful imagery and ... sheer ubiquity" leads children to believe "that tobacco use is desirable and pervasive." Brief for Respondents 33; see also Brief for United States as Amicus Curiae 7 ("[S]o many children lack the maturity in judgment to resist the tobacco industry's appeals to excitement, glamour, and independence"). This justification is belied, however, by the sweeping overinclusivity of the regulations. Massachusetts has done nothing to target its prohibition to advertisements appealing to "excitement, glamour, and independence"; the ban applies with equal force to appeals to torpor, homeliness, and servility. It has not focused on "youthful imagery"; smokers depicted on the sides of buildings may no more play shuffleboard than they may ride skateboards.

. . .

Respondents have identified no principle of law or logic that would preclude the imposition of restrictions on fast food and alcohol advertising similar to those they seek to impose on tobacco advertising. Cf. Tr. of Oral Arg. 56-57. In effect, they seek a "vice" exception to the First Amendment. No such exception exists. See 44 Liquormart, 517 U. S., at 513-514 (opinion of Stevens, J., joined by Kennedy, Thomas, and Ginsburg, JJ.). If it did, it would have almost no limit, for "any product that poses some threat to public health or public morals might reasonably be characterized by a state legislature as relating to `vice activity.' " Id., at 514. That is why "a `vice' label that is unaccompanied by a corresponding prohibition against the commercial behavior at issue fails to provide a principled justification for the regulation of commercial speech about that activity." Ibid.

No legislature has ever sought to restrict speech about an activity it regarded as harmless and inoffensive. Calls for limits on expression always are made when the specter of some threatened harm is looming. The identity of the harm may vary. People will be inspired by totalitarian dogmas and subvert the Republic. They will be inflamed by racial demagoguery and embrace hatred and bigotry. Or they will be enticed by cigarette advertisements and choose to smoke, risking disease. It is therefore no answer for the State to say that the makers of cigarettes are doing harm: perhaps they are. But in that respect they are no different from the purveyors of other harmful products, or the advocates of harmful ideas. When the State seeks to silence them, they are all entitled to the protection of the First Amendment.

**Justice Souter, concurring in part and dissenting in part.**

I join Parts I, II-C, II-D, III-A, III-B-1, III-C, and III-D of the Court's opinion. I join Part I of the opinion of Justice Stevens concurring in the judgment in part and dissenting in part. I respectfully dissent from Part III-B-2 of the opinion of the Court, and like Justice Stevens would remand for trial on the constitutionality of the 1,000-foot limit.

**Justice Stevens, with whom Justice Ginsburg and Justice Breyer join, and with whom Justice Souter joins as to Part I, concurring in part, concurring in the judgment in part, and dissenting in part.**

This suit presents two separate sets of issues. The first--involving preemption--is straightforward. The second--involving the First Amendment--is more complex. Because I strongly disagree with the Court's conclusion that the Federal Cigarette Labeling and Advertising Act of 1965 (FCLAA or Act), 15 U. S. C. §1331 et seq. as amended, precludes States and localities from regulating the location of cigarette advertising, I dissent from Parts II-A and II-B of the Court's opinion. On the First Amendment questions, I agree with the Court both that the outdoor advertising restrictions imposed by Massachusetts serve legitimate and important state interests and that the record does not indicate that the measures were properly tailored to serve those interests.

Because the present record does not enable us to adjudicate the merits of those claims on summary judgment, I would vacate the decision upholding those restrictions and remand for trial on the constitutionality of the outdoor advertising regulations. Finally, because I do not believe that either the point-of-sale advertising restrictions or the sales practice restrictions implicate significant First Amendment concerns, I would uphold them in their entirety.

I am firmly convinced that, when Congress amended the preemption provision in 1969, it did not intend to expand the application of the provision beyond content regulations.6 I, therefore, find the conclusion inescapable that the zoning regulation at issue in this suit is not a "requirement or prohibition ... with respect to ... advertising" within the meaning of the 1969 Act.7 Even if I were not so convinced, however, I would still dissent from the Court's conclusion with regard to preemption, because the provision is, at the very least, ambiguous. The historical record simply does not reflect that it was Congress' " `clear and manifest purpose,' " Id., at 516, to preempt attempts by States to utilize their traditional zoning authority to protect the health and welfare of minors. Absent such a manifest purpose, Massachusetts and its sister States retain their traditional police powers.

II

On the First Amendment issues raised by petitioners, my disagreements with the majority are less significant. I would, however, reach different dispositions as to the 1,000-foot rule and the height restrictions for indoor advertising, and my evaluation of the sales practice restrictions differs from the Court's.

The 1,000-Foot Rule

I am in complete accord with the Court's analysis of the importance of the interests served by the advertising restrictions. As the Court lucidly explains, few interests are more "compelling," ante, at 34, than ensuring that minors do not become addicted to a dangerous drug before they are able to make a mature and informed decision as to the health risks associated with that substance. Unlike other products sold for human consumption, tobacco products are addictive and ultimately lethal for many long-term users. When that interest is combined with the State's concomitant concern for the effective enforcement of its laws regarding the sale of tobacco to minors, it becomes clear that Massachusetts' regulations serve interests of the highest order and are, therefore, immune from any ends-based challenge, whatever level of scrutiny one chooses to employ.

Nevertheless, noble ends do not save a speech-restricting statute whose means are poorly tailored. Such statutes may be invalid for two different reasons. First, the means chosen may be insufficiently related to the ends they purportedly serve. See, e.g., Rubin v. Coors Brewing Co., 514 U. S. 476 (1995) (striking a statute prohibiting beer labels from displaying alcohol content because the provision did not significantly forward the government's interest in the health, safety, and welfare of its citizens). Alternatively, the statute may be so broadly drawn that, while effectively achieving its ends, it unduly restricts communications that are unrelated to its policy aims. See, e.g., United States v. Playboy Entertainment Group, Inc., 529 U. S. 803, 812 (2000) (striking a statute intended to protect children from indecent television broadcasts, in part because it constituted "a significant restriction of communication between speakers and willing adult listeners"). The second difficulty is most frequently encountered when government adopts measures for the protection of children that impose substantial restrictions on the ability of adults to communicate with one another. See, e.g., Playboy Entertainment Group, Inc., supra;

Reno v. American Civil Liberties Union, 521 U. S. 844 (1997); Sable Communications of Cal., Inc. v. FCC, 492 U. S. 115 (1989).

To my mind, the 1,000-foot rule does not present a tailoring problem of the first type. For reasons cogently explained in our prior opinions and in the opinion of the Court, we may fairly assume that advertising stimulates consumption and, therefore, that regulations limiting advertising will facilitate efforts to stem consumption.9 See, e.g., Rubin, 514 U. S., at 487; United States v. Edge Broadcasting Co., 509 U. S. 418, 434 (1993); ante, at 27. Furthermore, if the government's intention is to limit consumption by a particular segment of the community--in this case, minors--it is appropriate, indeed necessary, to tailor advertising restrictions to the areas where that segment of the community congregates--in this case, the area surrounding schools and playgrounds.

However, I share the majority's concern as to whether the 1,000-foot rule unduly restricts the ability of cigarette manufacturers to convey lawful information to adult consumers. This, of course, is a question of line-drawing. While a ban on all communications about a given subject would be the most effective way to prevent children from exposure to such material, the state cannot by fiat reduce the level of discourse to that which is "fit for children." Butler v. Michigan, 352 U. S. 380, 383 (1957); cf. Bolger v. Youngs Drug Products Corp., 463 U. S. 60, 74 (1983) ("The level of discourse reaching a mailbox simply cannot be limited to that which would be suitable for a sandbox"). On the other hand, efforts to protect children from exposure to harmful material will undoubtedly have some spillover effect on the free speech rights of adults. See, e.g., FCC v. Pacifica Foundation, 438 U. S. 726, 749-750, and n. 28 (1978).

Finding the appropriate balance is no easy matter. Though many factors plausibly enter the equation when calculating whether a child-directed location restriction goes too far in regulating adult speech, one crucial question is whether the regulatory scheme leaves available sufficient "alternative avenues of communication." Renton v. Playtime Theatres, Inc., 475 U. S. 41, 50 (1986); Members of City Council of Los Angeles v. Taxpayers for Vincent, 466 U. S. 789, 819 (1984) (Brennan, J., dissenting); accord ante, at 33. Because I do not think the record contains sufficient information to enable us to answer that question, I would vacate the award of summary judgment upholding the 1,000-foot rule and remand for trial on that issue. Therefore, while I agree with the majority that the Court of Appeals did not sufficiently consider the implications of the 1,000-foot rule for the lawful communication of adults, see ante, at 31-36, I dissent from the disposition reflected in Part III-B-2 of the Court's opinion.

There is no doubt that the 1,000-foot rule prohibits cigarette advertising in a substantial portion of Massachusetts' largest cities. Even on that question, however, the parties remain in dispute as to the percentage of these urban areas that is actually off limits to tobacco advertising. See ante, at 32. Moreover, the record is entirely silent on the impact of the regulation in other portions of the Commonwealth. The dearth of reliable statistical information as to the scope of the ban is problematic.

More importantly, the Court lacks sufficient qualitative information as to the areas where cigarette advertising is prohibited and those where it is permitted. The fact that 80% or 90% of an urban area is unavailable to tobacco advertisements may be constitutionally irrelevant if the available areas are so heavily trafficked or so central to the city's cultural life that they provide a sufficient forum for the propagation of a manufacturer's message. One electric sign in Times Square or at the foot of the Golden Gate Bridge may be seen by more potential customers than a hundred signs dispersed in residential neighborhoods.

Finally, the Court lacks information as to other avenues of communication available to cigarette manufacturers and retailers. For example, depending on the answers to empirical questions on which we lack data, the ubiquity of print advertisements hawking particular brands of cigarettes might suffice to inform adult consumers of the special advantages of the respective brands. Similarly, print advertisements, circulars mailed to people's homes, word of mouth, and general information may or may not be sufficient to imbue the adult population with the knowledge that particular stores, chains of stores, or types of stores sell tobacco products.10

In granting summary judgment for the respondents, the District Judge treated the First Amendment issues in this suit as pure questions of law and stated that "there are no material facts in dispute concerning these issues." 84 F. Supp. 2d, at 183. With due respect, I disagree. While the ultimate question before us is one of law, the answer to that question turns on complicated factual questions relating to the practical effects of the regulations. As the record does not reveal the answer to these disputed questions of fact, the court should have denied summary judgment to both parties and allowed the parties to present further evidence.

. . .

I note, moreover, that the alleged "overinclusivity" of the advertising regulations, ante, at 8, (Thomas, J., concurring in part and concurring in judgment), while relevant to whether the regulations are narrowly tailored, does not "beli[e]" the claim that tobacco advertising imagery misleads children into believing that smoking is healthy, glamorous, or sophisticated, ibid. See Brief of Amicus Curiae American Legacy Foundation in Support of Respondent 4-5 and nn. 9, 10; Brief of Amicus Curiae City of Los Angeles in Support of Respondent 4 (documenting charge that advertisements for cigarettes and smokeless tobacco target underage smokers). For purposes of summary judgment, the State conceded that the tobacco companies' advertising concerns lawful activity and is not misleading. Under the Court's disposition of the case today, the State remains free to proffer evidence that the advertising is in fact misleading. See Virginia Bd. of Pharmacy v. Virginia Citizens Consumer Council, Inc., 425 U. S. 748, 771 (1976) ("[M]uch commercial speech is not provably false, or even wholly false, but only deceptive or misleading. We foresee no obstacle to a State's dealing effectively with this problem"). I would vacate the grant of summary judgment to respondents on this issue and remand for further proceedings.

# CHAPTER 8

# Free press and fair trial

# Sheppard v. Maxwell (1966)

U.S Supreme Court

384 U.S. 333 (1966)

Decided June 6, 1966

Warren  Douglas  **Clark**  Harlan  Brennan  Stewart  White  Fortas  Black

Decision: 8 votes for Sheppard, 1 vote(s) against

**MR. JUSTICE CLARK delivered the opinion of the Court.**

This federal habeas corpus application involves the question whether Sheppard was deprived of a fair trial in his state conviction for the second-degree murder of his wife because of the trial judge's failure to protect Sheppard sufficiently from the massive, pervasive and prejudicial publicity that attended his prosecution. The United States District Court held that he was not afforded a fair trial, and granted the writ subject to the State's right to put Sheppard to trial again, 231 F.Supp. 37 (D.C.S.D. Ohio 1964). The Court of Appeals for the Sixth Circuit re-versed by a divided vote, 346 F.2d 707 (1965). We granted certiorari, 382 U.S. 916 (1965). We have concluded that Sheppard did not receive a fair trial consistent with the Due Process Clause of the Fourteenth Amendment and, therefore, reverse the judgment.

I

Marilyn Sheppard, petitioner's pregnant wife, was bludgeoned to death in the upstairs bed-room of their lakeshore home in Bay Village, Ohio, a suburb of Cleveland. On the day of the tragedy, July 4, 1954, Shep-pard pieced together for sev-eral local officials the following story: he and his wife had enter-tained neighborhood friends, the Aherns, on the previous evening at their home. After dinner, they watched television in the living room. Sheppard became drowsy and dozed off to sleep on a couch. Later, Mar-ilyn partially awoke him saying that she was going to bed. The next thing he remembered, was hearing his wife cry out in the early morning hours. He hurried upstairs and, in the dim light from the hall, saw a "form" stand-ing next to his wife's bed. A s he struggled with the "form," he was struck on the back of the neck and rendered unconscious. On regaining his senses, he found himself on the floor next to his wife's bed. He rose, looked at her, took her pulse and "felt that she was gone." He then went to his son's room and found him unmolested. Hearing a noise, he

hurried downstairs. He saw a "form" running out the door and pursued it to the lake shore. He grappled with it on the beach, and again lost consciousness. Upon his recovery, he was lying face down with the lower portion of his body in the water. He returned to his home, checked the pulse on his wife's neck, and "determined or thought that she was gone." He then went downstairs and called a neighbor, Mayor Houk of Bay Village. The Mayor and his wife came over at once, found Sheppard slumped in an easy chair downstairs and asked, "What happened?" Sheppard replied: "I don't know, but somebody ought to try to do something for Marilyn." Mrs. Houk immediately went up to the bedroom. The Mayor told Sheppard, "Get hold of yourself. Can you tell me what happened?"

Sheppard then related the above-outlined events. After Mrs. Houk discovered the body, the Mayor called the local police, Dr. Richard Sheppard, petitioner's brother, and the Aherns. The local police were the first to arrive. They, in turn, notified the Coroner and Cleveland police. Richard Sheppard then arrived, determined that Marilyn was dead, examined his brother's injuries, and removed him to the nearby clinic operated by the Sheppard family. When the Coroner, the Cleveland police and other officials arrived, the house and surrounding area were thoroughly searched, the rooms of the house were photographed, and many persons, including the Houks and the Aherns, were interrogated. The Sheppard home and premises were taken into "protective custody," and remained so until after the trial.

From the outset, officials focused suspicion on Sheppard. After a search of the house and premises on the morning of the tragedy, Dr. Gerber, the Coroner, is reported -- and it is undenied -- to have told his men, "Well, it is evident the doctor did this, so let's go get the confession out of him." He proceeded to interrogate and examine Sheppard while the latter was under sedation in his hospital room. On the same occasion, the Coroner was given the clothes Sheppard wore at the time of the tragedy, together with the personal items in them. Later that, afternoon Chief Eaton and two Cleveland police officers interrogated

Sheppard at some length, confronting him with evidence, and demanding explanations. Asked by Officer Shotke to take a lie detector test, Sheppard said he would if it were reliable. Shotke replied that it was "infallible," and "you might as well tell us all about it now." At the end of the interrogation, Shotke told Sheppard: "I think you killed your wife." Still later in the same afternoon, a physician sent by the Coroner was permitted to make a detailed examination of Sheppard. Until the Coroner's inquest on July 22, at which time he was subpoenaed, Sheppard made himself available for frequent and extended questioning without the presence of an attorney.

On July 7, the day of Marilyn Sheppard's funeral, a newspaper story appeared in which Assistant County Attorney Mahon -- later the chief prosecutor of Sheppard -- sharply criticized the refusal of the Sheppard family to permit his immediate questioning. From there on, headline stories repeatedly stressed Sheppard's lack of cooperation with the police and other officials. Under the headline "Testify Now In Death, Bay Doctor Is Ordered," one story described a visit by Coroner Gerber and four police officers to the hospital on July 8. When Sheppard insisted that his lawyer be present, the Coroner wrote out a subpoena and served it on him. Sheppard then agreed to submit to questioning without counsel, and the subpoena was torn up. The officers questioned him for several hours. On July 9, Sheppard, at the request of the Coroner, reenacted the tragedy at his home before the Coroner, police officers, and a group of newsmen, who apparently were invited by the Coroner. The home was locked, so that Sheppard was obliged to wait outside until the Coroner arrived. Sheppard's performance was reported in detail by the news media, along with photographs. The newspapers also played up Sheppard's refusal to take a lie detector test and "the protective ring" thrown up by his family. Front-page newspaper headlines announced on the same day that "Doctor Balks At Lie Test; Retells Story." A column opposite that story contained an "exclusive" interview with Sheppard headlined: "Loved My Wife, She Loved Me,' Sheppard Tells News Reporter." The next day, another headline story disclosed that Sheppard had "again late yesterday refused to take a lie

144

detector test," and quoted an Assistant County Attorney as saying that, "at the end of a nine-hour questioning of Dr. Sheppard, I felt he was now ruling [a test] out completely." But subsequent newspaper articles reported that the Coroner was still pushing Sheppard for a lie detector test. More stories appeared when Sheppard would not allow authorities to inject him with "truth serum."

On the 20th, the "editorial artillery" opened fire with a front-page charge that somebody is "getting away with murder." The editorial attributed the ineptness of the investigation to

"friendships, relationships, hired lawyers, a husband who ought to have been subjected instantly to the same third-degree to which any other person under similar circumstances is subjected. . . ."

The following day, July 21, another page-one editorial was headed: "Why No Inquest? Do It Now, Dr. Gerber." The Coroner called an inquest the same day, and subpoenaed Sheppard. It was staged the next day in a school gymnasium; the Coroner presided with the County Prosecutor as his advisor and two detectives as bailiffs. In the front of the room was a long table occupied by reporters, television and radio personnel, and broadcasting equipment. The hearing was broadcast with live microphones placed at the Coroner's seat and the witness stand. A swarm of reporters and photographers attended. Sheppard was brought into the room by police who searched him in full view of several hundred spectators. Sheppard's counsel were present during the three-day inquest, but were not permitted to participate.

When Sheppard's chief counsel attempted to place some documents in the record, he was forcibly ejected from the room by the Coroner, who received cheers, hugs, and kisses from ladies in the audience. Sheppard was questioned for five and one-half hours about his actions on the night of the murder, his married life, and a love affair with Susan Hayes. At the end of the hearing, the Coroner announced that he "could" order Sheppard held for the grand jury, but did not do so.

Throughout this period, the newspapers emphasized evidence that tended to incriminate Sheppard and pointed out discrepancies in his statements to authorities. At the same time, Sheppard made many public statements to the press, and wrote feature articles asserting his innocence. During the inquest on July 26, a headline in large type stated: "Kerr [Captain of the Cleveland Police] Urges Sheppard's Arrest." In the story, Detective McArthur

"disclosed that scientific tests at the Sheppard home have definitely established that the killer washed off a trail of blood from the murder bedroom to the downstairs section,"

a circumstance casting doubt on Sheppard's accounts of the murder. No such evidence was produced at trial. The newspapers also delved into Sheppard's personal life. Articles stressed his extramarital love affairs as a motive for the crime. The newspapers portrayed Sheppard as a Lothario, fully explored his relationship with Susan Hayes, and named a number of other women who were allegedly involved with him. The testimony at trial never showed that Sheppard had any illicit relationships besides the one with Susan Hayes.

On July 28, an editorial entitled "Why Don't Police Quiz Top Suspect" demanded that Sheppard be taken to police headquarters. It described him in the following language:

"Now proved under oath to be a liar, still free to go about his business, shielded by his family, protected by a smart lawyer who has made monkeys of the police and authorities, carrying a gun part of the time, left free to do whatever he pleases. . . ."

A front-page editorial on July 30 asked: "Why Isn't Sam Sheppard in Jail?" It was later titled "Quit Stalling -- Bring Him In." After calling Sheppard "the most unusual murder suspect ever seen around these parts," the article said that, "[e]xcept for some superficial questioning during Coroner Sam Gerber's inquest, he has been scot-free of any official grilling. . . ." It asserted that he was "surrounded by an iron curtain of protection [and] concealment."

That night, at 10 o'clock, Sheppard was arrested at his father's home on a charge of murder. He was taken to the Bay Village City Hall, where hundreds of people, newscasters, photographers and reporters were awaiting his arrival. He was immediately arraigned -- having been denied a temporary delay to secure the presence of counsel -- and bound over to the grand jury.

The publicity then grew in intensity until his indictment on August 17. Typical of the coverage during this period is a front-page interview entitled: "DR. SAM:

I

Wish There Was Something I Could Get Off My Chest -- but There Isn't.'" Unfavorable publicity included items such as a cartoon of the body of a sphinx with Sheppard's head and the legend below: "

I Will Do Everything In My Power to Help Solve This Terrible Murder.' -- Dr. Sam Sheppard." Headlines announced, inter alia, that: "Doctor Evidence is Ready for Jury," "Corrigan Tactics Stall Quizzing," "Sheppard Gay Set' Is Revealed By Houk," "Blood Is Found In Garage," "New Murder Evidence Is Found, Police Claim," "Dr. Sam Faces Quiz At Jail On Marilyn's Fear Of Him." On August 18, an article appeared under the headline "Dr. Sam Writes His Own Story." And reproduced across the entire front page was a portion of the typed statement signed by Sheppard:

"I am not guilty of the murder of my wife, Marilyn. How could I, who have been trained to help people and devoted my life to saving life, commit such a terrible and revolting crime?"

We do not detail the coverage further. There are five volumes filled with similar clippings from each of the three Cleveland newspapers covering the period from the murder until Sheppard's conviction in December, 1954. The record includes no excerpts from newscasts on radio and television, but, since space was reserved in the courtroom for these media, we assume that their coverage was equally large.

II

With this background, the case came on for trial two weeks before the November general election at which the chief prosecutor was a candidate for common pleas judge and the trial judge, Judge Blythin, was a candidate to succeed himself. Twenty-five days before the case was set, 75 veniremen were called as prospective jurors. All three Cleveland newspapers published the names and addresses of the veniremen. As a consequence, anonymous letters and telephone calls, as well as calls from friends, regarding the impending prosecution were received by all of the prospective jurors. The selection of the jury began on October 18, 1954.

The courtroom in which the trial was held measured 26 by 48 feet. A long temporary table was set up inside the bar, in back of the single counsel table. It ran the width of the courtroom, parallel to the bar railing, with one end less than three feet from the jury box. Approximately 20 representatives of newspapers and wire services were assigned seats at this table by the court. Behind the bar railing there were four rows of benches. These seats were likewise assigned by the court for the entire trial. The first row was occupied by representatives of television and radio stations, and the second and third rows by reporters from out-of-town newspapers and magazines. One side of the last row, which accommodated 14 people, was assigned to Sheppard's family, and the other to Marilyn's. The public was permitted to fill vacancies in this row on special passes only. Representatives of the news media also used all the rooms on the courtroom floor, including the room where cases were ordinarily called and assigned for trial. Private telephone lines and telegraphic equipment were installed in these rooms so that reports from the trial could be speeded to the papers. Station WSRS was permitted to set up broadcasting facilities on the third floor of the courthouse next door to the jury room, where the jury rested during recesses in the trial and deliberated. Newscasts were made from this room throughout the trial, and while the jury reached its verdict.

On the sidewalk and steps in front of the courthouse, television and newsreel cameras were occasionally used to take motion pictures of the participants in the trial, including the jury and the judge. Indeed, one television broadcast carried a staged interview of the judge as he entered the courthouse. In the corridors outside the courtroom, there was a host of photographers and television personnel with flash cameras, portable lights and motion picture cameras. This group photographed the prospective jurors during selection of the jury. After the trial opened, the witnesses, counsel, and jurors were photographed and televised whenever they entered or left the courtroom. Sheppard was brought to the courtroom about 10 minutes before each session began; he was surrounded by reporters and extensively photographed for the newspapers and television. A rule of court prohibited picture-taking in the courtroom during the actual sessions of the court, but no restraints were put on photographers during recesses, which were taken once each morning and afternoon, with a longer period for lunch.

All of these arrangements with the news media and their massive coverage of the trial continued during the entire nine weeks of the trial. The courtroom remained crowded to capacity with representatives of news media. Their movement in and out of the courtroom often caused so much confusion that, despite the loudspeaker system installed in the courtroom, it was difficult for the witnesses and counsel to be heard. Furthermore, the reporters clustered within the bar of the small courtroom made confidential talk among Sheppard and his counsel almost impossible during the proceedings. They frequently had to leave the courtroom to obtain privacy. And many times when counsel wished to raise a point with the judge out of the hearing of the jury, it was necessary to move to the judge's chambers. Even then, news media representatives so packed the judge's anteroom that counsel could hardly return from the chambers to the courtroom. The reporters vied with each other to find out what counsel and the judge had discussed, and often these matters later appeared in newspapers accessible to the jury.

The daily record of the proceedings was made available to the newspapers, and the testimony of each witness was printed verbatim in the local editions, along with objections of counsel, and rulings by the judge. Pictures of Sheppard, the judge, counsel, pertinent witnesses, and the jury often accompanied the daily newspaper and television accounts. At times, the newspapers published photographs of exhibits introduced at the trial, and the rooms of Sheppard's house were featured, along with relevant testimony.

The jurors themselves were constantly exposed to the news media. Every juror except one testified at *voir dire* to reading about the case in the Cleveland papers or to having heard broadcasts about it. Seven of the 12 jurors who rendered the verdict had one or more Cleveland papers delivered in their home; the remaining jurors were not interrogated on the point. Nor were there questions as to radios or television sets in the jurors' homes, but we must assume that most of them owned such conveniences. As the selection of the jury progressed, individual pictures of prospective members appeared daily. During the trial, pictures of the jury appeared over 40 times in the Cleveland papers alone. The court permitted photographers to take pictures of the jury in the box, and individual pictures of the members in the jury room. One newspaper ran pictures of the jurors at the Sheppard home when they went there to view the scene of the murder. Another paper featured the home life of an alternate juror. The day before the verdict

was rendered -- while the jurors were at lunch and sequestered by two bailiffs -- the jury was separated into two groups to pose for photographs which appeared in the newspapers.

III

We now reach the conduct of the trial. While the intense publicity continued unabated, it is sufficient to relate only the more flagrant episodes:

1. On October 9, 1954, nine days before the case went to trial, an editorial in one of the newspapers criticized defense counsel's random poll of people on the streets as to their opinion of Sheppard's guilt or innocence in an effort to use the resulting statistics to show the necessity for change of venue. The article said the survey "smacks of mass jury tampering," called on defense counsel to drop it, and stated that the bar association should do something about it. It characterized the poll as "nonjudicial, nonlegal, and nonsense." The article was called to the attention of the court, but no action was taken.

2. On the second day of *voir dire* examination, a debate was staged and broadcast live over WHK radio. The participants, newspaper reporters, accused Sheppard's counsel of throwing roadblocks in the way of the prosecution and asserted that Sheppard conceded his guilt by hiring a prominent criminal lawyer. Sheppard's counsel objected to this broadcast and requested a continuance, but the judge denied the motion. When counsel asked the court to give some protection from such events, the judge replied that "WHK doesn't have much coverage," and that

"[a]fter all, we are not trying this case by radio or in newspapers or any other means. We confine ourselves seriously to it in this courtroom, and do the very best we can."

3. While the jury was being selected, a two-inch headline asked: "But Who Will Speak for Marilyn?" The front-page story spoke of the "perfect face" of the accused. "Study that face as long as you want. Never will you get from it a hint of what might be the answer. . . ." The two brothers of the accused were described as

"Prosperous, poised. His two sisters-in law. Smart, chic, well groomed. His elderly father. Courtly, reserved. A perfect type for the patriarch of a staunch clan."

The author then noted Marilyn Sheppard was "still off-stage," and that she was an only child whose mother died when she was very young and whose father had no interest in the case. But the author -- through quotes from Detective Chief James McArthur -- assured readers that the prosecution's exhibits would speak for Marilyn. "Her story," McArthur stated, "will come into this courtroom through our witnesses." The article ends:

"Then you realize how what and who is missing from the perfect setting will be supplied."

" How in the Big Case justice will be done."

" Justice to Sam Sheppard."

" And to Marilyn Sheppard."

4. As has been mentioned, the jury viewed the scene of the murder on the first day of the trial. Hundreds of reporters, cameramen and onlookers were there, and one representative of the news media was permitted to accompany the jury while it inspected the Sheppard home. The time of the jury's visit was revealed so far in advance that one of the newspapers was able to rent a helicopter and fly over the house taking pictures of the jurors on their tour.

5. On November 19, a Cleveland police officer gave testimony that tended to contradict details in the written statement Sheppard made to the Cleveland police. Two days later, in a broadcast heard over Station WHK in Cleveland, Robert Considine likened Sheppard to a perjurer and compared the episode to Alger Hiss' confrontation with Whittaker Chambers. Though defense counsel asked the judge to question the jury to ascertain how many heard the broadcast, the court refused to do so. The judge also overruled the motion for continuance based on the same ground, saying:

"Well, I don't know, we can't stop people, in any event, listening to it. It is a matter of free speech, and the court can't control everybody. . . . We are not going to harass the jury every morning. . . . I t is getting to the point where if we do it every morning, we are suspecting the jury. I have confidence in this jury. . . . "

6. On November 24, a story appeared under an eight-column headline: "Sam Called A Jekyll-Hyde' By Marilyn, Cousin To Testify." It related that Marilyn had recently told friends that Sheppard was a "Dr. Jekyll and Mr. Hyde" character. No such testimony was ever produced at the trial. The story went on to announce:

"The prosecution has a 'bombshell witness' on tap who will testify to Dr. Sam's display of fiery temper -- countering the defense claim that the defendant is a gentle physician with an even disposition."

Defense counsel made motions for change of venue, continuance and mistrial, but they were denied. No action was taken by the court.

7. When the trial was in its seventh week, Walter Winchell broadcast over WXEL television and WJW radio that Carole Beasley, who was under arrest in New York City for robbery, had stated that, as Sheppard's mistress, she had borne him a child. The defense asked that the jury be queried on the broadcast. Two jurors admitted in open court that they had heard it. The judge asked each: "Would that have any effect upon your judgment?" Both replied, "No." This was accepted by the judge as sufficient; he merely asked the jury to "pay no attention whatever to that type of scavenging. . . . Let's confine ourselves to this courtroom, if you please." In answer to the motion for mistrial, the judge said:

"Well, even, so, Mr. Corrigan, how are you ever going to prevent those things, in any event? I don't justify them at all. I think it is outrageous, but in a sense, it is outrageous even if there were no trial here. The trial has nothing to do with it in the Court's mind, as far as its outrage is concerned, but -- "

"Mr. CORRIGAN: I don't know what effect it had on the mind of any of these jurors, and I can't find out unless inquiry is made."

"The COURT: How would you ever, in any jury, avoid that kind of a thing?"

8. On December 9, while Sheppard was on the witness stand, he testified that he had been mistreated by Cleveland detectives after his arrest. Although he was not at the trial, Captain Kerr of the Homicide Bureau issued a press statement denying Sheppard's allegations which appeared under the headline: *"Bare-faced Liar,' Kerr Says of Sam." Captain Kerr never appeared as a witness at the trial.*

9. After the case was submitted to the jury, it was sequestered for its deliberations, which took five days and four nights. After the verdict, defense counsel ascertained that the jurors had been allowed to make telephone calls to their homes every day while they were sequestered at the hotel. Although the telephones had been removed from the jurors' rooms, the jurors were permitted to use the phones in the bailiffs' rooms. The calls were placed by the jurors themselves; no record was kept of the jurors who made calls, the telephone numbers or the parties called. The bailiffs sat in the room where they could hear only the jurors' end of the conversation. The court had not instructed the bailiffs to prevent such calls. By a subsequent motion, defense counsel urged that this ground alone warranted a new trial, but the motion was overruled, and no evidence was taken on the question.

The principle that justice cannot survive behind walls of silence has long been reflected in the "Anglo-American distrust for secret trials." *In re Oliver,*333 U. S. 257,

333 U. S. 268 (1948). A responsible press has always been regarded as the handmaiden of effective judicial administration, especially in the criminal field. Its function in this regard is documented by an impressive record of service over several centuries. The press does not simply publish information about trials, but guards against the miscarriage of justice by subjecting the police, prosecutors, and judicial processes to extensive public scrutiny and criticism. This Court has, therefore, been unwilling to place any direct limitations on the freedom traditionally exercised by the news media for "[w]hat transpires in the courtroom is public property." *Craig v. Harney,*331 U. S. 367, 331 U. S. 374 (1947). The

"unqualified prohibitions laid down by the framers were intended to give to liberty of the press . . . the broadest scope that could be countenanced in an orderly society."

*Bridges v. California,*314 U. S. 252, 314 U. S. 265 (1941). And where there was "no threat or menace to the integrity of the trial," *Craig v. Harney, supra,* at 331 U. S. 377, we have consistently required that the press have a free hand, even though we sometimes deplored its sensationalism.

But the Court has also pointed out that "[l]egal trials are not like elections, to be won through the use of the meeting-hall, the radio, and the newspaper." *Bridges v. California, supra,* at 314 U. S. 271. And the Court has insisted that no one be punished for a crime without "a charge fairly made and fairly tried in a public tribunal free of prejudice, passion, excitement, and tyrannical power." *Chambers v. Florida,*309 U. S. 227, 309 U. S. 236-237 (1940).

"Freedom of discussion should be given the widest range compatible with the essential requirement of the fair and orderly administration of justice."

*Pennekamp v. Florida,*328 U. S. 331, 328 U. S. 347 (1946). But it must not be allowed to divert the trial from the

"very purpose of a court system . . . to adjudicate controversies, both criminal and civil, in the calmness and solemnity of the courtroom according to legal procedures."

*Cox v. Louisiana,*379 U. S. 559, 379 U. S. 583 (1965) (BLACK, J., dissenting). Among these "legal procedures" is the requirement that the jury's verdict be based on evidence received in open court, not from outside sources. Thus, in *Marshall v. United States,*360 U. S. 310 (1959), we set aside a federal conviction where the jurors were exposed, "through news accounts," to information that was not admitted at trial. We held that the prejudice from such material "may indeed be greater" than when it is part of the prosecution's evidence, "for it is then not tempered by protective procedures." At 360 U. S. 313. At the same time, we did not consider dispositive the statement of each juror

"that he would not be influenced by the news articles, that he could decide the case only on the evidence of record, and that he felt no prejudice against petitioner as a result of the articles."

At 360 U. S. 312. Likewise, in *Irvin v. Dowd,*366 U. S. 717 (1961), even though each juror indicated that he could render an impartial verdict despite exposure to prejudicial newspaper articles, we set aside the conviction, holding:

"With his life at stake, it is not requiring too much that petitioner be tried in an atmosphere undisturbed by so huge a wave of public passion. . . ."

The undeviating rule of this Court was expressed by Mr. Justice Holmes over half a century ago in *Patterson v. Colorado,*205 U. S. 454, 205 U. S. 462 (1907):

"The theory of our system is that the conclusions to be reached in a case will be induced only by evidence and argument in open court, and not by any outside influence, whether of private talk or public print."

Moreover, "the burden of showing essential unfairness . . . as a demonstrable reality," *Adams v. United*

*States ex rel. McCann,*317 U. S. 269, 317 U. S. 281 (1942), need not be undertaken when television has exposed the community "repeatedly and in depth to the spectacle of [the accused] personally confessing in detail to the crimes with which he was later to be charged." *Rideau v. Louisiana,*373 U. S. 723, 373 U. S. 726 (1963). In *Turner v. Louisiana,*379 U. S. 466 (1965), two key witnesses were deputy sheriffs who doubled as jury shepherds during the trial. The deputies swore that they had not talked to the jurors about the case, but the Court nonetheless held that,

"even if it could be assumed that the deputies never did discuss the case directly with any members of the jury, it would be blinking reality not to recognize the extreme prejudice inherent in this continual association. . . ."

Only last Term, in *Estes v. Texas,*381 U. S. 532 (1965), we set aside a conviction despite the absence of any showing of prejudice. We said there:

"It is true that, in most cases involving claims of due process deprivations, we require a showing of identifiable prejudice to the accused. Nevertheless, at times, a procedure employed by the State involves such a probability that prejudice will result that it is deemed inherently lacking in due process."

At 381 U. S. 542-543. And we cited with approval the language of MR. JUSTICE BLACK for the Court in *In re Murchison,*349 U. S. 133, 349 U. S. 136 (1955), that "our system of law has always endeavored to prevent even the probability of unfairness."

V

It is clear that the totality of circumstances in this case also warrants such an approach. Unlike Estes, Sheppard was not granted a change of venue to a locale away from where the publicity originated; nor was his jury sequestered. The Estes jury saw none of the television broadcasts from the courtroom. On the contrary, the Sheppard jurors were subjected to newspaper, radio, and television coverage of the trial while not taking part in the proceedings. They were allowed to go their separate ways outside of the courtroom, without adequate directions not to read or listen to anything concerning the case. The judge's "admonitions" at the beginning of the trial are representative:

"I would suggest to you and caution you that you do not read any newspapers during the progress of this trial, that you do not listen to radio comments, nor watch or listen to television comments, insofar as this case is concerned. You will feel very much better as the trial proceeds. . . . I am sure that we shall all feel very much better if we do not indulge in any newspaper reading or listening to any comments whatever about the matter while the case is in progress. After it is all over, you can read it all to your heart's content. . . ."

At intervals during the trial, the judge simply repeated his "suggestions" and "requests" that the jurors not expose themselves to comment upon the case. Moreover, the jurors were thrust into the role of celebrities by the judge's failure to insulate them from reporters and photographers. *See Estes v. Texas, supra,* at 381 U. S. 545-546. The numerous pictures of the jurors, with their addresses, which appeared in the newspapers before and during the trial itself exposed them to expressions of opinion from both cranks and friends. The fact that anonymous letters had been received by prospective jurors should have made the judge aware that this publicity seriously threatened the jurors' privacy.

The press coverage of the Estes trial was not nearly as massive and pervasive as the attention given by the

Cleveland newspapers and broadcasting stations to Sheppard's prosecution. Sheppard stood indicted for the murder of his wife; the State was demanding the death penalty. For months, the virulent publicity about Sheppard and the murder had made the case notorious. Charges and countercharges were aired in the news media besides those for which Sheppard was called to trial. In addition, only three months before trial, Sheppard was examined for more than five hours without counsel during a three-day inquest which ended in a public brawl. The inquest was televised live from a high school gymnasium seating hundreds of people. Furthermore, the trial began two weeks before a hotly contested election at which both Chief Prosecutor Mahon and Judge Blythin were candidates for judgeships.

While we cannot say that Sheppard was denied due process by the judge's refusal to take precautions against the influence of pretrial publicity alone, the court's later rulings must be considered against the setting in which

the trial was held. In light of this background, we believe that the arrangements made by the judge with the news media caused Sheppard to be deprived of that "judicial serenity and calm to which [he] was entitled." *Estes v. Texas, supra,* at 381 U. S. 536. The fact is that bedlam reigned at the courthouse during the trial, and newsmen took over practically the entire courtroom, hounding most of the participants in the trial, especially Sheppard. At a temporary table within a few feet of the jury box and counsel table sat some 20 reporters, staring at Sheppard and taking notes. The erection of a press table for reporters inside the bar is unprecedented. The bar of the court is reserved for counsel, providing them a safe place in which to keep papers and exhibits and to confer privately with client and co-counsel. It is designed to protect the witness and the jury from any distractions, intrusions or influences, and to permit bench discussions of the judge's rulings away from the hearing of the public and the jury. Having assigned almost all of the available seats in the courtroom to the news media, the judge lost his ability to supervise that environment. The movement of the reporters in and out of the courtroom caused frequent confusion and disruption of the trial. And the record reveals constant commotion within the bar. Moreover, the judge gave the throng of newsmen gathered in the corridors of the courthouse absolute free rein. Participants in the trial, including the jury, were forced to run a gauntlet of reporters and photographers each time they entered or left the courtroom. The total lack of consideration for the privacy of the jury was demonstrated by the assignment to a broadcasting station of space next to the jury room on the floor above the courtroom, as well as the fact that jurors were allowed to make telephone calls during their five-day deliberation.

## VI

There can be no question about the nature of the publicity which surrounded Sheppard's trial. We agree, as did the Court of Appeals, with the findings in Judge Bell's opinion for the Ohio Supreme Court:

"Murder and mystery, society, sex and suspense were combined in this case in such a manner as to intrigue and captivate the public fancy to a degree perhaps unparalleled in recent annals. Throughout the pre-indictment investigation, the subsequent legal skirmishes, and the nine-week trial, circulation-conscious editors catered to the insatiable interest of the American public in the bizarre. . . . In this atmosphere of a 'Roman holiday' for the news media, Sam Sheppard stood trial for his life."

165 Ohio St. at 294, 135 N.E.2d at 342. Indeed, every court that has considered this case, save the court that tried it, has deplored the manner in which the news media inflamed and prejudiced the public. Much of the material printed or broadcast during the trial was never heard from the witness stand, such as the charges that Sheppard had purposely impeded the murder investigation, and must be guilty, since he had hired a prominent criminal lawyer; that Sheppard was a perjurer; that he had sexual relations with numerous women; that his slain wife had characterized him as a "Jekyll-Hyde"; that he was "a bare-faced liar" because of his testimony as to police treatment; and, finally, that a woman convict claimed Sheppard to be the father of her illegitimate child. As the trial progressed, the newspapers summarized and interpreted the evidence, devoting particular attention to the material that incriminated Sheppard, and often drew unwarranted inferences from testimony. At one point, a front-page picture of Mrs. Sheppard's blood-stained pillow was published after being "doctored" to show more clearly an alleged imprint of a surgical instrument.

Nor is there doubt that this deluge of publicity reached at least some of the jury. On the only occasion that the jury was queried, two jurors admitted in open court to hearing the highly inflammatory charge that a prison inmate claimed Sheppard as the father of her illegitimate child. Despite the extent and nature of the publicity to which the jury was exposed during trial, the judge refused defense counsel's other requests that the jurors be asked whether they had read or heard specific prejudicial comment about the case, including the incidents we have previously summarized. In these circumstances, we can assume that some of this material reached members of the jury. *See Commonwealth v. Crehan,* 345 Mass. 609, 188 N.E.2d 923 (1963).

VII

The court's fundamental error is compounded by the holding that it lacked power to control the publicity about the trial. From the very inception of the proceedings, the judge announced that neither he nor anyone else could restrict prejudicial news accounts. And he reiterated this view on numerous occasions. Since he viewed the news media as his target, the judge never considered other means that are often utilized to reduce the appearance of prejudicial material and to protect the jury from outside influence. We conclude that these procedures would have been sufficient to guarantee Sheppard a fair trial, and so do not consider what sanctions might be available against a recalcitrant press, nor the charges of bias now made against the state trial judge.

The carnival atmosphere at trial could easily have been avoided, since the courtroom and courthouse premises are subject to the control of the court. As we stressed in *Estes,* the presence of the press at judicial proceedings must be limited when it is apparent that the accused might otherwise be prejudiced or disadvantaged. Bearing in mind the massive pretrial publicity, the judge should have adopted stricter rules governing the use of the courtroom by newsmen, as Sheppard's counsel requested. The number of reporters in the courtroom itself could have been limited at the first sign that their presence would disrupt the trial. They certainly should not have been placed inside the bar. Furthermore, the judge should have more closely regulated the conduct of newsmen in the courtroom. For instance, the judge belatedly asked them not to handle and photograph trial exhibits lying on the counsel table during recesses.

Secondly, the court should have insulated the witnesses. All of the newspapers and radio stations apparently interviewed prospective witnesses at will, and in many instances disclosed their testimony. A typical example was the publication of numerous statements by Susan Hayes, before her appearance in court, regarding her love affair with Sheppard. Although the witnesses were barred from the courtroom dur-

ing the trial, the full verbatim testimony was available to them in the press. This completely nullified the judge's imposition of the rule. *See Estes v. Texas, supra,* at 381 U. S. 547.

Thirdly, the court should have made some effort to control the release of leads, information, and gossip to the press by police officers, witnesses, and the counsel for both sides. Much of the information thus disclosed was inaccurate, leading to groundless rumors and confusion. That the judge was aware of his responsibility in this respect may be seen from his warning to Steve Sheppard, the accused's brother, who had apparently made public statements in an attempt to discredit testimony for the prosecution. The judge made this statement in the presence of the jury:

"Now, the Court wants to say a word. That he was told -- he has not read anything about it at all -- but he was informed that Dr. Steve Sheppard, who has been granted the privilege of remaining in the courtroom during the trial, has been trying the case in the newspapers and making rather uncomplimentary comments about the testimony of the witnesses for the State."

"Let it be now understood that, if Dr. Steve Sheppard wishes to use the newspapers to try his case while we are trying it here, he will be barred from remaining in the courtroom during the progress of the trial if he is to be a witness in the case."

"The Court appreciates he cannot deny Steve Sheppard the right of free speech, but he can deny him the . . . privilege of being in the courtroom if he wants to avail himself of that method during the progress of the trial."

Defense counsel immediately brought to the court's attention the tremendous amount of publicity in the Cleveland press that "misrepresented entirely the testimony" in the case. Under such circumstances, the judge should have at least warned the newspapers to check the accuracy of their accounts. And it is obvious that the judge should have further sought to alleviate this problem by imposing control over the statements made to the news media by counsel, witnesses, and especially the Coroner and police officers. The prosecution repeatedly made evidence available to the news media which was never offered in the trial. Much of the "evidence" disseminated in this fashion was clearly inadmissible. The exclusion of such evidence in court is rendered meaningless when news media make it available to the public. For example, the publicity about Sheppard's refusal to take a lie detector test came directly from police officers and the Coroner. The story that Sheppard had been called a "Jekyll-Hyde" personality by his wife was attributed to a prosecution witness. No such testimony was given. The further report that there was "a bombshell witness' on tap" who would testify as to Sheppard's "fiery temper" could only have emanated from the prosecution. Moreover, the newspapers described in detail clues that had been found by the police, but not put into the record.

The fact that many of the prejudicial news items can be traced to the prosecution as well as the defense aggravates the judge's failure to take any action. *See Stroble v. California*, 343 U. S. 181, 343 U. S. 201 (1952) (Frankfurter, J., dissenting). Effective control of these sources -- concededly within the court's power -- might well have prevented the divulgence of inaccurate information, rumors, and accusations that made up much of the inflammatory publicity, at least after Sheppard's indictment.

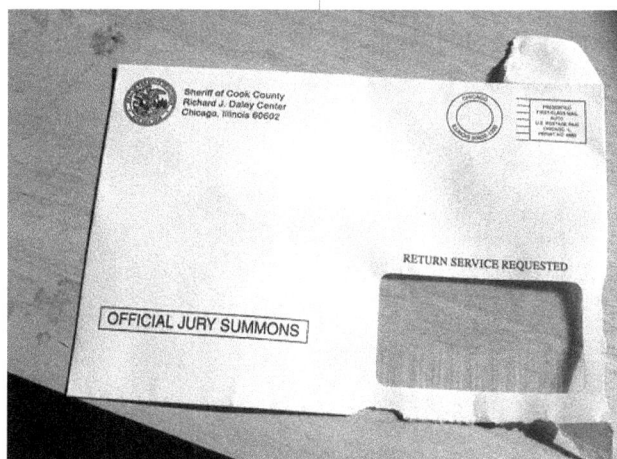

More specifically, the trial court might well have proscribed extrajudicial statements by any lawyer, party, witness, or court official which divulged prejudicial matters, such as the refusal of Sheppard to submit to interrogation or take any lie detector tests; any statement made by Sheppard to officials; the identity of prospective witnesses or their probable testimony; any belief in guilt or innocence; or like statements concerning the merits of the case. *See State v. Van Duyne,* 43 N.J. 369, 389, 204 A.2d 841, 852 (1964), in which the court interpreted Canon 20 of the American Bar Association's Canons of Professional Ethics to prohibit such statements.

Being advised of the great public interest in the case, the mass coverage of the press, and the potential prejudicial impact of publicity, the court could also have requested the appropriate city and county officials to promulgate a regulation with respect to dissemination of information about the case by their employees. In addition, reporters who wrote or broadcast prejudicial stories could have been warned as to the impropriety of publishing material not introduced in the proceedings. The judge was put on notice of such events by defense counsel's complaint about the WHK broadcast on the second day of trial. *See* p. 384 U. S. 346 *supra*. In this manner, Sheppard's right to a trial free from outside interference would have been given added protection without corresponding curtailment of the news media. Had the judge, the other officers of the court, and the police placed the interest of justice first, the news media would have soon learned to be content with the task of reporting the case as it unfolded in the courtroom -- not pieced together from extrajudicial statements.

From the cases coming here, we note that unfair and prejudicial news comment on pending trials has become increasingly prevalent. Due process requires that the accused receive a trial by an impartial jury free from outside influences. Given the pervasiveness of modern communications and the difficulty of effacing prejudicial publicity from the minds of the jurors, the trial courts must take strong measures to ensure that the balance is never weighed against the accused. And appellate tribunals have the duty to make an independent evaluation of the circumstances. Of course, there is nothing

that proscribes the press from reporting events that transpire in the courtroom. But where there is a reasonable likelihood that prejudicial news prior to trial will prevent a fair trial, the judge should continue the case until the threat abates, or transfer it to another county not so permeated with publicity. In addition, sequestration of the jury was something the judge should have raised *sua sponte* with counsel. If publicity during the proceedings threatens the fairness of the trial, a new trial should be ordered. But we must remember that reversals are but palliatives; the cure lies in those remedial measures that will prevent the prejudice at its inception. The courts must take such steps by rule and regulation that will protect their processes from prejudicial outside interferences. Neither prosecutors, counsel for defense, the accused, witnesses, court staff nor enforcement officers coming under the jurisdiction of the court should be permitted to frustrate its function. Collaboration between counsel and the press as to information affecting the fairness of a criminal trial is not only subject to regulation, but is highly censurable, and worthy of disciplinary measures.

Since the state trial judge did not fulfill his duty to protect Sheppard from the inherently prejudicial publicity which saturated the community and to control disruptive influences in the courtroom, we must reverse the denial of the habeas petition. The case is remanded to the District Court with instructions to issue the writ and order that Sheppard be released from custody unless the State puts him to its charges again within a reasonable time.

It is so ordered.

# Nebraska Press Association v. Stuart (1976)

U.S. Supreme Court

427 U.S. 539 (1976)

Decided June 30, 1976

Burger  Brennan  Stewart  White  Marshall  Blackmun  Powell  Rehnquist  Stevens

Decision: 9 votes for Nebraska Press Assoc., 0 vote(s) against

**MR. CHIEF JUSTICE BURGER delivered the opinion of the Court.**

The respondent State District Judge entered an order restraining the petitioners from publishing or broadcasting accounts of confessions or admissions made by the accused or facts "strongly implicative" of the accused in a widely reported murder of six persons. We granted certiorari to decide whether the entry of such an order on the showing made before the state court violated the constitutional guarantee of freedom of the press. [427 U.S. 539, 542]

I

On the evening of October 18, 1975, local police found the six members of the Henry Kellie family murdered in their home in Sutherland, Neb., a town of about 850 people. Police released the description of a suspect, Erwin Charles Simants, to the reporters who had hastened to the scene of the crime. Simants was arrested and arraigned in Lincoln County Court the following morning, ending a tense night for this small rural community.

The crime immediately attracted widespread news coverage, by local, regional, and national newspapers, radio and television stations. Three days after the crime, the County Attorney and Simants' attorney joined in asking the County Court to enter a restrictive order relating to "matters that may or may not be publicly reported or disclosed to the public," because of the "mass coverage by news media" and the "reasonable likelihood of prejudicial news which would make difficult, if not impossible, the impaneling of an impartial jury and tend to prevent a fair trial." The County Court heard oral argument but took no evidence; no attorney for members of the press appeared at this stage. The County Court granted the prosecutor's motion for a restrictive order and entered it the next day, October 22. The order prohibited everyone in attendance from "releas[ing] or authoriz[ing] the release for public dissemination in any form or manner whatsoever any testimony given or evidence adduced"; the order also required members of the press to observe the Nebraska Bar-Press Guidelines. 1 [427 U.S. 539, 543]

Simants' preliminary hearing was held the same day, open to the public but subject to the order. The County Court bound over the defendant for trial to the State District Court. The charges, as amended to reflect the autopsy findings, were that Simants had committed the murders in the course of a sexual assault.

Petitioners - several press and broadcast associations, publishers, and individual reporters - moved on October 23 for leave to intervene in the District Court, asking that the restrictive order imposed by the County Court be vacated. The District Court conducted a hearing, at which the County Judge testified and newspaper articles about the Simants case were admitted in evidence. The District Judge granted petitioners' motion to intervene and, on October 27, entered his own restrictive order. The judge found "because of the nature of the crimes charged in the complaint that there is a clear and present danger that pre-trial publicity could impinge upon the defendant's right to a fair trial." The order applied only until the jury was impaneled, and specifically prohibited petitioners from reporting five subjects: (1) the existence or contents of a confession Simants had made to law enforcement officers, which had been introduced in open court at arraignment; (2) the fact or nature of statements Simants had made to other persons; (3) the contents of a note he had written the night of the crime; (4) certain aspects of the medical testimony at the preliminary hearing; and (5) the identity of the [427 U.S. 539, 544]  victims of the alleged sexual assault and the nature of the assault. It also prohibited reporting the exact nature of the restrictive order itself. Like the County Court's order, this order incorporated the Nebraska Bar-Press Guidelines. Finally, the order set out a plan for attendance, seating, and courthouse traffic control during the trial.

Four days later, on October 31, petitioners asked the District Court to stay its order. At the same time, they applied to the Nebraska Supreme Court for a writ of mandamus, a stay, and an expedited appeal from the order. The State of Nebraska and the defendant Simants intervened in these actions. The Nebraska Supreme Court heard oral argument on November 25, and issued its per curiam opinion December 1. State v. Simants, 194 Neb. 783, 236 N. W. 2d 794 (1975). 2  [427 U.S. 539, 545]

The Nebraska Supreme Court balanced the "heavy presumption against . . . constitutional validity" that an order restraining publication bears, New York Times Co. v. United States, 403 U.S. 713, 714 (1971), against the importance of the defendant's right to trial by an impartial jury. Both society and the individual defendant, the court held, had a vital interest in assuring that Simants be tried by an impartial jury. Because of the publicity surrounding the crime, the court determined that this right was in jeopardy. The court noted that Nebraska statutes required the District Court to try Simants within six months of his arrest, and that a change of venue could move the trial only to adjoining counties, which had been subject to essentially the same publicity as Lincoln County. The Nebraska Supreme Court held that "[u]nless the absolutist position of the relators was constitutionally correct, it would appear that the District Court acted properly." 194 Neb., at 797, 236 N. W. 2d, at 803.

The Nebraska Supreme Court rejected that "absolutist position," but modified the District Court's order to accommodate the defendant's right to a fair trial and the petitioners' interest in reporting pretrial events. The order as modified prohibited reporting of only three matters: (a) the existence and nature of any confessions or admissions made by the defendant to law enforcement officers, (b) any confessions or admissions made to any third parties, except members of the press, and (c) other facts "strongly implicative" of the accused. The Nebraska Supreme Court did not rely on the Nebraska Bar-Press Guidelines. See n. 1, supra. After construing Nebraska law to permit closure in certain circumstances, the court remanded the case to the District Judge for reconsideration of the issue whether pretrial hearings should be closed to the press and public. [427 U.S. 539, 546]

We granted certiorari to address the important issues raised by the District Court order as modified by the Nebraska Supreme Court, but we denied the motion to expedite review or to stay entirely the order of the State District Court pending Simants' trial. 423 U.S. 1027 (1975). We are informed by the parties that since we granted certiorari, Simants has been convicted of murder and sentenced to death. His appeal is pending in the Nebraska Supreme Court.

The Nebraska Bar-Press Guidelines are voluntary standards adopted by members of the state bar and news media to deal with the reporting of crimes and criminal trials. They outline the matters of fact that may appropriately be reported, and also list what items are not generally appropriate for reporting, including confessions, opinions on guilt or innocence, statements that would influence the outcome of a trial, the results of tests or examinations, comments on the credibility of witnesses, and evidence presented in the jury's absence.

II

...

We therefore conclude that this case is not moot, and proceed to the merits.

III

The problems presented by this case are almost as old as the Republic. Neither in the Constitution nor in contemporaneous writings do we find that the conflict between these two important rights was anticipated, yet it is inconceivable that the authors of the Constitution were unaware of the potential conflicts between the right to an unbiased jury and the guarantee of freedom of the press. The unusually able lawyers who helped write the Constitution and later drafted the Bill of Rights were familiar with the historic episode in which John Adams defended British soldiers charged with homicide for firing into a crowd of Boston demonstrators; they were intimately familiar with the clash of the adversary system and the part that passions of the populace sometimes play in influencing potential jurors. They did not address themselves directly to the situation presented by this case; their chief concern was the need for freedom of expression in the political arena and the dialogue in ideas. But they recognized that there were risks to private rights from an unfettered press. Jefferson, for example, [427 U.S. 539, 548] writing from Paris in 1786 concerning press attacks on John Jay, stated:

"In truth it is afflicting that a man who has past his life in serving the public . . . should yet be liable to have his peace of mind so much disturbed by any individual who shall think proper to arraign him in a newspaper. It is however an evil for which there is no remedy. Our liberty depends on the freedom of the press, and that cannot be limited without being lost. . . ." 9 Papers of Thomas Jefferson 239 (J. Boyd ed. 1954).

See also F. Mott, Jefferson and the Press 21, 38-46 (1943).

The trial of Aaron Burr in 1807 presented Mr. Chief Justice Marshall, presiding as a trial judge, with acute problems in selecting an unbiased jury. Few people in the area of Virginia from which jurors were drawn had not formed some opinions concerning Mr. Burr or the case, from newspaper accounts and heightened discussion both private and public. The Chief Justice conducted a searching voir dire of the two panels eventually called, and rendered a substantial opinion on the purposes of voir dire and the standards to be applied. See 1 Causes Celebres, Trial of Aaron Burr for Treason 404-427, 473-481 (1879); United States v. Burr, 25 F. Cas. 49 (No. 14,692g) (CC Va. 1807). Burr was acquitted, so there was no occasion for appellate review to examine the problem of prejudicial pretrial publicity. Mr. Chief Justice Marshall's careful voir dire inquiry into the matter of possible bias makes clear that the problem is not a new one.

The speed of communication and the pervasiveness of the modern news media have exacerbated these problems, however, as numerous appeals demonstrate. The trial of Bruno Hauptmann in a small New Jersey community for [427 U.S. 539, 549] the abduction and murder of the Charles Lindberghs' infant child probably was the most widely covered trial up to that time, and the nature of the coverage produced widespread public reaction. Criticism was directed at the "carnival" atmosphere that pervaded the community and the courtroom itself. Responsible leaders of press and the legal profession - including other judges - pointed out that much of this sorry performance could have been controlled by a vigilant trial judge and by other public officers subject to the control of the court. See generally Hudon, Freedom of the Press Versus Fair Trial: The Remedy Lies With the Courts, 1 Val. U. L. Rev. 8, 12-14 (1966); Hallam, Some Object Lessons on Publicity in Criminal Trials, 24 Minn. L. Rev. 453 (1940); Lippmann, The Lindbergh Case in Its Relation to American Newspapers, in Problems of Journalism 154-156 (1936).

The excesses of press and radio and lack of responsibility of those in authority in the Hauptmann case and others of that era led to efforts to develop voluntary guidelines for courts, lawyers, press, and broadcasters. See generally J. Lofton, Justice and the Press 117-130 (1966). 3 The effort was renewed in 1965 when the American Bar Association embarked on a project to develop standards for all aspects of criminal justice, including guidelines to accommodate the right to a fair trial and the rights of a free press. See Powell, The Right to a [427 U.S. 539, 550] Fair Trial, 51 A. B. A. J. 534 (1965). The resulting standards, approved by the Association in 1968, received support from most of the legal profession. American Bar Association Project on Standards for Criminal Justice, Fair Trial and Free Press (Approved Draft 1968). Other groups have undertaken similar studies. See Report of the Judicial Conference Committee on the Operation of the Jury System, "Free Press-Fair Trial" Issue, 45 F. R. D. 391 (1968); Special Committee on Radio, Television, and the Administration of Justice of the Association of the Bar of the City of New York, Freedom of the Press and Fair Trial (1967). In the wake of these efforts, the cooperation between bar associations and members of the press led to the adoption of voluntary guidelines like Nebraska's. See n. 1, supra; American Bar Association Legal Advisory Committee on Fair Trial and Free Press, The Rights of Fair Trial and Free Press 1-6 (1969).

In practice, of course, even the most ideal guidelines are subjected to powerful strains when a case such as Simants' arises, with reporters from many parts of the country on the scene. Reporters from distant places are unlikely to consider themselves bound by local standards. They report to editors outside the area covered by the guidelines, and their editors are likely to be guided only by their own standards. To contemplate how a state court can control acts of a newspaper or broadcaster outside its jurisdiction, even though the newspapers and broadcasts reach the very community from which jurors are to be selected, suggests something of the practical difficulties of managing such guidelines.

160

The problems presented in this case have a substantial history outside the reported decisions of courts, in the efforts of many responsible people to accommodate the competing interests. We cannot resolve all of them, for [427 U.S. 539, 551] it is not the function of this Court to write a code. We look instead to this particular case and the legal context in which it arises.

IV

The Sixth Amendment in terms guarantees "trial, by an impartial jury . . ." in federal criminal prosecutions. Because "trial by jury in criminal cases is fundamental to the American scheme of justice," the Due Process Clause of the Fourteenth Amendment guarantees the same right in state criminal prosecutions. Duncan v. Louisiana, 391 U.S. 145, 149 (1968).

"In essence, the right to jury trial guarantees to the criminally accused a fair trial by a panel of impartial, `indifferent' jurors. . . . `A fair trial in a fair tribunal is a basic requirement of due process.' In re Murchison, 349 U.S. 133, 136 . In the ultimate analysis, only the jury can strip a man of his liberty or his life. In the language of Lord Coke, a juror must be as `indifferent as he stands unsworne.' Co. Litt. 155b. His verdict must be based upon the evidence developed at the trial." Irvin v. Dowd, 366 U.S. 717, 722 (1961).

In the overwhelming majority of criminal trials, pretrial publicity presents few unmanageable threats to this important right. But when the case is a "sensational" one tensions develop between the right of the accused to trial by an impartial jury and the rights guaranteed others by the First Amendment. The relevant decisions of this Court, even if not dispositive, are instructive by way of background.

In Irvin v. Dowd, supra, for example, the defendant was convicted of murder following intensive and hostile news coverage. The trial judge had granted a defense motion for a change of venue, but only to an [427 U.S. 539, 552] adjacent county, which had been exposed to essen-

tially the same news coverage. At trial, 430 persons were called for jury service; 268 were excused because they had fixed opinions as to guilt. Eight of the 12 who served as jurors thought the defendant guilty, but said they could nevertheless render an impartial verdict. On review the Court vacated the conviction and death sentence and remanded to allow a new trial for, "[w]ith his life at stake, it is not requiring too much that petitioner be tried in an atmosphere undisturbed by so huge a wave of public passion . . . ." 366 U.S., at 728 .

Similarly, in Rideau v. Louisiana, 373 U.S. 723 (1963), the Court reversed the conviction of a defendant whose staged, highly emotional confession had been filmed with the cooperation of local police and later broadcast on television for three days while he was awaiting trial, saying "[a]ny subsequent court proceedings in a community so pervasively exposed to such a spectacle could be but a hollow formality." Id., at 726. And in Estes v. Texas, 381 U.S. 532 (1965), the Court held that the defendant had not been afforded due process where the volume of trial publicity, the judge's failure to control the proceedings, and the telecast of a hearing and of the trial itself "inherently prevented a sober search for the truth." Id., at 551. See also Marshall v. United States, 360 U.S. 310 (1959).

In Sheppard v. Maxwell, 384 U.S. 333 (1966), the Court focused sharply on the impact of pretrial publicity and a trial court's duty to protect the defendant's constitutional right to a fair trial. With only Mr. Justice Black dissenting, and he without opinion, the Court ordered a new trial for the petitioner, even though the first trial had occurred 12 years before. Beyond doubt the press had shown no responsible concern for the constitutional guarantee of a fair trial; the community [427 U.S. 539, 553] from which the jury was drawn had been inundated by publicity hostile to the defendant. But the trial judge "did not fulfill his duty to protect [the defendant] from the inherently prejudicial publicity which saturated the community and to control disruptive influences in the courtroom." Id., at 363. The Court noted that "unfair and prejudicial news comment on pending trials has become increasingly prevalent," id., at 362, and issued a strong warning:

"Due process requires that the accused receive a trial by an impartial jury free from outside influences. Given the pervasiveness of modern communications and the difficulty of effacing prejudicial publicity from the minds of the jurors, the trial courts must take strong measures to ensure that the balance is never weighed against the accused. . . . Of course, there is nothing that proscribes the press from reporting events that transpire in the courtroom. But where there is a reasonable likelihood that prejudicial news prior to trial will prevent a fair trial, the judge should continue the case until the threat abates, or transfer it to another county not so permeated with publicity. In addition, sequestration of the jury was something the judge should have raised sua sponte with counsel. If publicity during the proceedings threatens the fairness of the trial, a new trial should be ordered. But we must remember that reversals are but palliatives; the cure lies in those remedial measures that will prevent the prejudice at its inception. The courts must take such steps by rule and regulation that will protect their processes from prejudicial outside interferences. Neither prosecutors, counsel for defense, the accused, witnesses, court staff nor enforcement officers coming under the jurisdiction of the [427 U.S. 539, 554] court should be permitted to frustrate its function. Collaboration between counsel and the press as to information affecting the fairness of a criminal trial is not only subject to regulation, but is highly censurable and worthy of disciplinary measures." Id., at 362-363 (emphasis added).

Because the trial court had failed to use even minimal efforts to insulate the trial and the jurors from the "deluge of publicity," id., at 357, the Court vacated the judgment of conviction and a new trial followed, in which the accused was acquitted.

Cases such as these are relatively rare, and we have held in other cases that trials have been fair in spite of widespread publicity. In Stroble v. California, 343 U.S. 181 (1952), for example, the Court affirmed a con-

viction and death sentence challenged on the ground that pretrial news accounts, including the prosecutor's release of the defendant's recorded confession, were allegedly so inflammatory as to amount to a denial of due process. The Court disapproved of the prosecutor's conduct, but noted that the publicity had receded some six weeks before trial, that the defendant had not moved for a change of venue, and that the confession had been found voluntary and admitted in evidence at trial. The Court also noted the thorough examination of jurors on void dire and the careful review of the facts by the state courts, and held that petitioner had failed to demonstrate a denial of due process. See also Murphy v. Florida, 421 U.S. 794 (1975); Beck v. Washington, 369 U.S. 541 (1962).

Taken together, these cases demonstrate that pretrial publicity - even pervasive, adverse publicity - does not inevitably lead to an unfair trial. The capacity of the jury eventually impaneled to decide the case fairly is influenced by the tone and extent of the publicity, [427 U.S. 539, 555] which is in part, and often in large part, shaped by what attorneys, police, and other officials do to precipitate news coverage. The trial judge has a major responsibility. What the judge says about a case, in or out of the courtroom, is likely to appear in newspapers and broadcasts. More important, the measures a judge takes or fails to take to mitigate the effects of pretrial publicity - the measures described in Sheppard - may well determine whether the defendant receives a trial consistent with the requirements of due process. That this responsibility has not always been properly discharged is apparent from the decisions just reviewed.

The costs of failure to afford a fair trial are high. In the most extreme cases, like Sheppard and Estes, the risk of injustice was avoided when the convictions were reversed. But a reversal means that justice has been delayed for both the defendant and the State; in some cases, because of lapse of time retrial is impossible or further prosecution is gravely handicapped. Moreover, in borderline cases in which the conviction is not reversed, there is some possibility of an injustice unredressed. The "strong measures" outlined in Sheppard v. Maxwell are means by which a trial judge can try to avoid exacting these costs from society or from the accused.

The state trial judge in the case before us acted responsibility, out of a legitimate concern, in an effort to protect the defendant's right to a fair trial. 4 What we must decided is not simply whether the Nebraska courts erred [427 U.S. 539, 556] in seeing the possibility of real danger to the defendant's rights, but whether in the circumstances of this case the means employed were foreclosed by another provision of the Constitution.

V

The First Amendment provides that "Congress shall make no law . . . abridging the freedom . . . of the press," and it is "no longer open to doubt that the liberty of the press, and of speech, is within the liberty safeguarded by the due process clause of the Fourteenth Amendment from invasion by state action." Near v. Minnesota ex rel. Olson, 283 U.S. 697, 707 (1931). See also Grosjean v. American Press Co., 297 U.S. 233, 244 (1936). The Court has interpreted these guarantees to afford special protection against orders that prohibit the publication or broadcast of particular information or commentary - orders that impose a "previous" or "prior" restraint on speech. None of our decided cases on prior restraint involved restrictive orders entered to protect a defendant's right to a fair and impartial jury, but the opinions on prior restraint have a common thread relevant to this case.

In Near v. Minnesota ex rel. Olson, supra, the Court held invalid a Minnesota statute providing for the abatement as a public nuisance of any "malicious, scandalous and defamatory newspaper, magazine or other periodical." Near had published an occasional weekly newspaper described by the County Attorney's complaint as "largely devoted to malicious, scandalous and defamatory articles" concerning political and

other public figures. 283 U.S., at 703 . Publication was enjoined pursuant to the statute. Excerpts from Near's paper, set out in the dissenting opinion of Mr. Justice Butler, show beyond question that one of its principal characteristics was blatant anti-Semitism. See id., at 723, 724-727, n. 1. [427 U.S. 539, 557]

Mr. Chief Justice Hughes, writing for the Court, noted that freedom of the press is not an absolute right, and the State may punish its abuses. He observed that the statute was "not aimed at the redress of individual or private wrongs." Id., at 708, 709. He then focused on the statute:

"[T]he operation and effect of the statute in substance is that public authorities may bring the owner or publisher of a newspaper or periodical before a judge upon a charge of conducting a business of publishing scandalous and defamatory matter . . . and unless the owner or publisher is able . . . to satisfy the judge that the [matter is] true and . . . published with good motives . . . his newspaper or periodical is suppressed . . . . This is of the essence of censorship." Id., at 713.

The Court relied on Patterson v. Colorado ex rel. Attorney General, 205 U.S. 454, 462 (1907): "[T]he main purpose of [the First Amendment] is `to prevent all such previous restraints upon publications as had been practiced by other governments.'" 5 Reversed.

MR. JUSTICE POWELL, concurring.

Although I join the opinion of the Court, in view of the importance of the case I write to emphasize the unique burden that rests upon the party, whether it be the State or a defendant, who undertakes to show the necessity for prior restraint on pretrial publicity. *

In my judgment a prior restraint properly may issue only when it is shown to be necessary to prevent the dissemination of prejudicial publicity that otherwise poses a high likelihood of preventing, directly and irreparably, the impaneling of a jury meeting the Sixth Amendment requirement of impartiality. This requires a showing that (i) there is a clear threat to the fairness of trial, (ii) such a threat is posed by the actual publicity to be restrained, and (iii) no less restrictive alternatives are available. Notwithstanding such a showing, a restraint may not issue unless it also is shown that previous publicity or publicity from unrestrained sources will not render the restraint inefficacious. The threat to the fairness [427 U.S. 539, 572] of the trial is to be evaluated in the context of Sixth Amendment law on impartiality, and any restraint must comply with the standards of specificity always required in the First Amendment context.

I believe these factors are sufficiently addressed in the Court's opinion to demonstrate beyond question that the prior restraint here was impermissible.

**MR. JUSTICE BRENNAN, with whom MR. JUSTICE STEWART and MR. JUSTICE MARSHALL join, concurring in the judgment.**

The question presented in this case is whether, consistently with the First Amendment, a court may enjoin the press, in advance of publication, 1 from reporting or commenting on information acquired from public court proceedings, public court records, or other sources about pending judicial proceedings. The Nebraska Supreme Court upheld such a direct prior restraint on the press, issued by the judge presiding over a sensational state murder trial, on the ground that there existed a "clear and present danger that pretrial publicity could substantially impair the right of the defendant [in the murder trial] to a trial by an impartial jury unless restraints were imposed." State v. Simants, 194 Neb. 783, 794, 236 N. W. 2d 794, 802 (1975). The right to a fair trial by a jury of one's peers is unquestionably one of the most precious and sacred safeguards enshrined in the Bill of Rights. I would hold, however, that resort to prior restraints on the freedom of the press is a constitutionally impermissible method for enforcing that right; judges have at their disposal a broad spectrum of devices for ensuring that fundamental fairness is accorded the [427 U.S. 539, 573] accused without neces-

sitating so drastic an incursion on the equally fundamental and salutary constitutional mandate that discussion of public affairs in a free society cannot depend on the preliminary grace of judicial censors.

The principles enunciated in Near were so universally accepted that the precise issue did not come before us again until Organization for a Better Austin v. Keefe, [427 U.S. 539, 558] 402 U.S. 415 (1971). There the state courts had enjoined the petitioners from picketing or passing out literature of any kind in a specified area. Noting the similarity to Near v. Minnesota, a unanimous Court held:

Here, as in that case, the injunction operates, not to redress alleged private wrongs, but to suppress, on the basis of previous publications, distribution of literature `of any kind' in a city of 18,000.

Any prior restraint on expression comes to this Court with a `heavy presumption' against its constitutional validity. Carroll v. Princess Anne, 393 U.S. 175, 181 (1968); Bantam Books, Inc. v. Sullivan, 372 U.S. 58, 70 (1963). Respondent thus carries a heavy burden of showing justification for the imposition of such a restraint. He has not met that burden. . . . Designating the conduct as an invasion of privacy, the apparent basis for the injunction here, is not sufficient to support an injunction against peaceful distribution of informational literature of the nature revealed by this record." 402 U.S., at 418-420.

More recently in New York Times Co. v. United States, 403 U.S. 713 (1971), the Government sought to enjoin the publication of excerpts from a massive, classified study of this Nation's involvement in the Vietnam conflict, going back to the end of the Second World War. The dispositive opinion of the Court simply concluded that the Government had not met its heavy burden of showing justification for the prior restraint. Each of the six concurring Justices and the three dissenting Justices expressed his views separately, but "every member of the Court, tacitly or explicitly, accepted the Near and Keefe condemnation of prior restraint as presumptively unconstitutional." Pittsburgh Press Co. v. Human Rel. [427 U.S. 539, 559]   Comm'n, 413 U.S. 376, 396 (1973) (BURGER, C. J., dissenting). The Court's conclusion in New York Times suggests that the burden on the Government is not reduced by the temporary nature of a restraint; in that case the Government asked for a temporary restraint solely to permit it to study and assess the impact on national security of the lengthy documents at issue.

The thread running through all these cases is that prior restraints on speech and publication are the most serious and the least tolerable infringement on First Amendment rights. A criminal penalty or a judgment in a defamation case is subject to the whole panoply of protections afforded by deferring the impact of the judgment until all avenues of appellate review have been exhausted. Only after judgment has become final, correct or otherwise, does the law's sanction become fully operative.

A prior restraint, by contrast and by definition, has an immediate and irreversible sanction. If it can be said that a threat of criminal or civil sanctions after publication "chills" speech, prior restraint "freezes" it at least for the time. 6

The damage can be particularly great when the prior restraint falls upon the communication of news and commentary on current events. Truthful reports of public judicial proceedings have been afforded special protection against subsequent punishment. See Cox Broadcasting Corp v. Cohn, 420 U.S. 469, 492 -493 (1975); see also, Craig v. Harney, 331 U.S. 367, 374 (1947). For the same reasons the protection against prior restraint should have particular force as applied to reporting of criminal proceedings, whether the crime in question is a single isolated act or a pattern of criminal conduct.

"A responsible press has always been regarded as [427 U.S. 539, 560] the handmaiden of effective judicial administration, especially in the criminal field. Its function in this regard is documented by an impressive record of service over several centuries. The press does not simply publish information about trials but guards against the miscarriage of justice by subjecting the police, prosecutors, and judicial processes to extensive public scrutiny and criticism." Sheppard v. Maxwell, 384 U.S., at 350 .

The extraordinary protections afforded by the First Amendment carry with them something in the nature of a fiduciary duty to exercise the protected rights responsibly - a duty widely acknowledged but not always observed by editors and publishers. It is not asking too much to suggest that those who exercise First Amendment rights in newspapers or broadcasting enterprises direct some effort to protect the rights of an accused to a fair trial by unbiased jurors.

Of course, the order at issue - like the order requested in New York Times - does not prohibit but only postpones publication. Some news can be delayed and most commentary can even more readily be delayed without serious injury, and there often is a self-imposed delay when responsible editors call for verification of information. But such delays are normally slight and they are self-imposed. Delays imposed by governmental authority are a different matter.

"We have learned, and continue to learn, from what we view as the unhappy experiences of other nations where government has been allowed to meddle in the internal editorial affairs of newspapers. Regardless of how beneficent-sounding the purposes of controlling the press might be, we . . . remain intensely skeptical about those measures that would allow government to insinuate itself into the editorial [427 U.S. 539, 561]   rooms of this Nation's press." Miami Herald Publishing Co. v. Tornillo, 418 U.S. 241, 259 (1974) (WHITE, J., concurring).

See also Columbia Broadcasting v. Democratic Comm., 412 U.S. 94 (1973). As a practical matter, moreover, the element of time is not unimportant if press coverage is to fulfill its traditional function of bringing news to the public promptly.

The authors of the Bill of Rights did not undertake to assign priorities as between First Amendment and Sixth Amendment rights, ranking one as superior to the other. In this case, the petitioners would have us declare the right of an accused subordinate to their right to publish in all circumstances. But if the authors of these guarantees, fully aware of the potential conflicts between them, were unwilling or unable to resolve the issue by assigning to one priority over the other, it is not for us to rewrite the Constitution by undertaking what they declined to do. It is unnecessary, after nearly two centuries, to establish a priority applicable in all circumstances. Yet it is nonetheless clear that the barriers to prior restraint remain high unless we are to abandon what the Court has said for nearly a quarter of our national existence and implied throughout all of it. The history of even wartime suspension of categorical guarantees, such as habeas corpus or the right to trial by civilian courts, see Ex parte Milligan, 4 Wall. 2 (1867), cautions against suspending explicit guarantees.

The Nebraska courts in this case enjoined the publication of certain kinds of information about the Simants case. There are, as we suggested earlier, marked differences in setting and purpose between the order entered here and the orders in Near, Keefe, and New York Times, but as to the underlying issue - the right of the press to be free from prior restraints on publication - those [427 U.S. 539, 562] cases form the backdrop against which we must decide this case.

VI

We turn now to the record in this case to determine whether, as Learned Hand put it, "the gravity of the `evil,' discounted by its improbability, justifies such invasion of free speech as is necessary to avoid the danger." United States v. Dennis, 183 F.2d 201, 212 (CA2 1950), aff'd, 341 U.S. 494 (1951); see also L. Hand, The Bill of Rights 58-61 (1958). To do so, we must examine the evidence before the trial judge when the order was entered to determine (a) the nature and extent of pretrial news coverage; (b) whether other measures would be likely to mitigate the effects of unrestrained pretrial publicity; and (c) how effectively a restraining order would operate to prevent the threatened danger. The precise terms of the restraining order are also important. We must then consider whether the record supports the entry of a prior restraint on publication, one of the most extraordinary remedies known to our jurisprudence.

A

In assessing the probable extent of publicity, the trial judge had before him newspapers demonstrating that the crime had already drawn intensive news coverage, and the testimony of the County Judge, who had entered the initial restraining order based on the local and national attention the case had attracted. The District Judge was required to assess the probable publicity that would be given these shocking crimes prior to the time a jury was selected and sequestered. He then had to examine the probable nature of the publicity and determine how it would affect prospective jurors.

Our review of the pretrial record persuades us that the trial judge was justified in concluding that there would [427 U.S. 539, 563] be intense and pervasive pretrial publicity concerning this case. He could also reasonably conclude, based on common human experience, that publicity might impair the defendant's right to a fair trial. He did not purport to say more, for he found only "a clear and present danger that pre-trial publicity could impinge upon the defendant's right to a fair trial." (Emphasis added.) His conclusion as to the impact of such publicity on prospective jurors was of necessity speculative, dealing as he was with factors unknown and unknowable.

B

We find little in the record that goes to another aspect of our task, determining whether measures short of an order restraining all publication would have insured the defendant a fair trial. Although the entry of the order might be read as a judicial determination that other measures would not suffice, the trial court made no express findings to that effect; the Nebraska Supreme Court referred to the issue only by implication. See 194 Neb., at 797-798, 236 N. W. 2d, at 803.

Most of the alternatives to prior restraint of publication in these circumstances were discussed with obvious approval in Sheppard v. Maxwell, 384 U.S., at 357 -362: (a) change of trial venue to a place less exposed to the intense publicity that seemed imminent in Lincoln County; 7 (b) postponement of the trial to allow [427 U.S. 539, 564]   public attention to subside; (c) searching questioning of prospective jurors, as Mr. Chief Justice Marshall used in the Burr case, to screen out those with fixed opinions as to guilt or innocence; (d) the use of emphatic and clear instructions on the sworn duty of each juror to decide the issues only on evidence presented in open court. Sequestration of jurors is, of course, always available. Although that measure insulates jurors only after they are sworn, it also enhances the likelihood of dissipating the impact of pretrial publicity and emphasizes the elements of the jurors' oaths.

This Court has outlined other measures short of prior restraints on publication tending to blunt the impact of pretrial publicity. See Sheppard v. Maxwell, supra, at 361-362. Professional studies have filled out these suggestions, recommending that trial courts in appropriate cases limit what the contending lawyers, the police, and witnesses may say to anyone. See American Bar Association Project on Standards for Criminal Justice, Fair Trial and Free Press 2-15 (App. Draft 1968). 8  [427 U.S. 539, 565]

We have noted earlier that pretrial publicity, even if pervasive and concentrated, cannot be regarded as leading automatically and in every kind of criminal case to an unfair trial. The decided cases "cannot be made to stand for the proposition that juror exposure to information about a state defendant's prior convictions or to news accounts of the crime with which he is charged alone presumptively deprives the defendant of due process." Murphy v. Florida, 421 U.S., at 799 . Appellate evaluations as to the impact of publicity take into account what other measures were used to mitigate the adverse effects of publicity. The more difficult prospective or predictive assessment that a trial judge must make also calls for a judgment as to whether other precautionary steps will suffice.

We have therefore examined this record to determine the probable efficacy of the measures short of prior restraint on the press and speech. There is no finding that alternative measures would not have protected Simants' rights, and the Nebraska Supreme Court did no more than imply that such measures might not be adequate. Moreover, the record is lacking in evidence to support such a finding.

C

We must also assess the probable efficacy of prior restraint on publication as a workable method of protecting Simants' right to a fair trial, and we cannot ignore the reality of the problems of managing and enforcing pretrial restraining orders. The territorial jurisdiction of the issuing court is limited by concepts of sovereignty, see, e. g., Hanson v. Denckla, 357 U.S. 235 (1958); Pennoyer v. Neff, 95 U.S. 714 (1878). The need for in [427 U.S. 539, 566]   personam jurisdiction also presents an obstacle to a restraining order that applies to publication at large as distinguished from restraining publication within a given jurisdiction. 9 See generally American Bar Association, Legal Advisory Committee on Fair Trial and Free Press, Recommended Court Procedure to Accommodate Rights of Fair Trial and Free Press (Rev. Draft, Nov. 1975); Rendleman, Free Press-Fair Trial: Review of Silence Orders, 52 N.C. L. Rev. 127, 149-155 (1973). 10

The Nebraska Supreme Court narrowed the scope of the restrictive order, and its opinion reflects awareness of the tensions between the need to protect the accused as fully as possible and the need to restrict publication as little as possible. The dilemma posed underscores how [427 U.S. 539, 567] difficult it is for trial judges to predict what information will in fact undermine the impartiality of jurors, and the difficulty of drafting an order that will effectively keep prejudicial information from prospective jurors. When a restrictive order is sought, a court can anticipate only part of what will develop that may injure the accused. But information not so obviously prejudicial may emerge, and what may properly be published in these "gray zone" circumstances may not violate the restrictive order and yet be prejudicial.

Finally, we note that the events disclosed by the record took place in a community of 850 people. It is reasonable to assume that, without any news accounts being printed or broadcast, rumors would travel swiftly by word of mouth. One can only speculate on the accuracy of such reports, given the generative propensities of rumors; they could well be more damaging than reasonably accurate news accounts. But plainly a whole community cannot be restrained from discussing a subject intimately affecting life within it.

Given these practical problems, it is far from clear that prior restraint on publication would have protected Simants' rights.

D

Finally, another feature of this case leads us to conclude that the restrictive order entered here is not supportable. At the outset the County Court entered a very broad restrictive order, the terms of which are not before us; it then held a preliminary hearing open to the public and the press. There was testimony concerning at least two incriminating statements made by Simants to private persons; the statement - evidently a confession - that he gave to law enforcement officials was also introduced. The State District Court's later order was entered after this public hearing and, as modified by the [427 U.S. 539, 568] Nebraska Su-

preme Court, enjoined reporting of (1) "[c]onfessions or admissions against interest made by the accused to law enforcement officials"; (2) "[c]onfessions or admissions against interest, oral or written, if any, made by the accused to third parties, excepting any statements, if any, made by the accused to representatives of the news media"; and (3) all "[o]ther information strongly implicative of the accused as the perpetrator of the slayings." 194 Neb., at 801, 236 N. W. 2d, at 805.

To the extent that this order prohibited the reporting of evidence adduced at the open preliminary hearing, it plainly violated settled principles: "[T]here is nothing that proscribes the press from reporting events that transpire in the courtroom." Sheppard v. Maxwell, 384 U.S., at 362 -363. See also Cox Broadcasting Corp. v. Cohn, 420 U.S. 469 (1975); Craig v. Harney, 331 U.S. 367 (1947). The County Court could not know that closure of the preliminary hearing was an alternative open to it until the Nebraska Supreme Court so construed state law; but once a public hearing had been held, what transpired there could not be subject to prior restraint.

The third prohibition of the order was defective in another respect as well. As part of a final order, entered after plenary review, this prohibition regarding "implicative" information is too vague and too broad to survive the scrutiny we have given to restraints on First Amendment rights. See, e. g., Hynes v. Mayor of Oradell, 425 U.S. 610 (1976); Buckley v. Valeo, 424 U.S. 1, 76 -82 (1976); NAACP v. Button, 371 U.S. 415 (1963). The third phase of the order entered falls outside permissible limits.


E

The record demonstrates, as the Nebraska courts held, that there was indeed a risk that pretrial news accounts, [427 U.S. 539, 569] true or false, would have some adverse impact on the attitudes of those who might be called as jurors. But on the record now before us it is not clear that further publicity, unchecked, would so distort the views of potential jurors that 12 could not be found who would, under proper instructions, fulfill their sworn duty to render a just verdict exclusively on the evidence presented in open court. We cannot say on this record that alternatives to a prior restraint on petitioners would not have sufficiently mitigated the adverse effects of pretrial publicity so as to make prior restraint unnecessary. Nor can we conclude that the restraining order actually entered would serve its intended purpose. Reasonable minds can have few doubts about the gravity of the evil pretrial publicity can work, but the probability that it would do so here was not demonstrated with the degree of certainty our cases on prior restraint require.

Of necessity our holding is confined to the record before us. But our conclusion is not simply a result of assessing the adequacy of the showing made in this case; it results in part from the problems inherent in meeting the heavy burden of demonstrating, in advance of trial, that without prior restraint a fair trial will be denied. The practical problems of managing and enforcing restrictive orders will always be present. In this sense, the record now before us is illustrative rather than exceptional. It is significant that when this Court has reversed a state conviction because of prejudicial publicity, it has carefully noted that some course of action short of prior restraint would have made a critical difference. See Sheppard v. Maxwell, supra, at 363; Estes v. Texas, 381 U.S., at 550 -551; Rideau v. Louisiana, 373 U.S., at 726 ; Irvin v. Dowd, 366 U.S., at 728 . However difficult it may be, we need not rule out the possibility of showing the kind of threat to fair trial rights that would possess [427 U.S. 539, 570]   the requisite degree of certainty to justify restraint. This Court has frequently denied that First Amendment rights are absolute and has consistently rejected the proposition that a prior restraint can never be employed. See New York Times Co. v. United States, 403 U.S. 713 (1971); Organization for a Better Austin v. Keefe, 402 U.S. 415 (1971); Near v. Minnesota ex rel. Olson, 283 U.S. 697 (1931).

Our analysis ends as it began, with a confrontation between prior restraint imposed to protect one vital constitutional guarantee and the explicit command of another that the freedom to speak and publish shall not be abridged. We reaffirm that the guarantees of freedom of expression are not an absolute prohibition under all circumstances, but the barriers to prior restraint remain high and the presumption against its use continues intact. We hold that, with respect to the order entered in this case prohibiting reporting or commentary on judicial proceedings held in public, the barriers have not been overcome; to the extent that this order restrained publication of such material, it is clearly invalid. To the extent that it prohibited publication based on information gained from other sources, we conclude that the heavy burden imposed as a condition to securing a prior restraint was not met and the judgment of the Nebraska Supreme Court is therefore

*Re-*                                                                                              *versed.*

CHAPTER 9

# Political speech

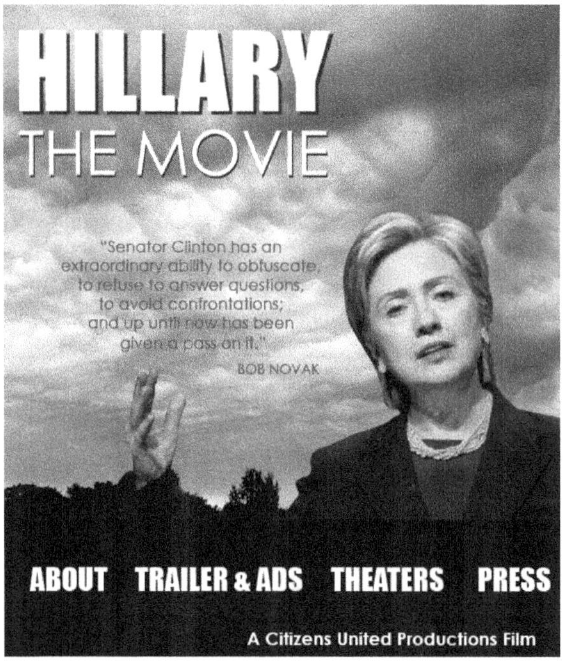

# Red Lion Broadcasting Co., Inc. v. Federal Communications Commission (1969)

US Supreme Court

395 U.S. 367 (1969)

Decided June 9, 1969

Warren   White   Black   Harlan   Stewart   Marshall   Brennan

Decision: 7 votes for , 0 vote(s) against

**MR. JUSTICE WHITE delivered the opinion of the Court**

The Federal Communications Commission has for many years imposed on radio and television broadcasters the requirement that discussion of public issues be presented on broadcast stations, and that each side of those issues must be given fair coverage. This is known as the fairness doctrine, which originated very early in the history of broadcasting and has maintained its present outlines for some time. It is an obligation whose content has been defined in a long series of FCC rulings in particular cases, and which is distinct from the statutory requirement of § 315 of the Communications Act that equal time be allotted all qualified candidates for public office. Two aspects of the fairness doctrine, relating to personal attacks in the context of controversial public issues and to political editorializing, were codified more precisely in the form of FCC regulations in 1967.

. . .

I

A

The Red Lion Broadcasting Company is licensed to operate a Pennsylvania radio station, WGCB. On November 27, 1964, WGCB carried a 15-minute broadcast by the Reverend Billy James Hargis as part of a "Christian Crusade" series. A book by Fred J. Cook entitled "Goldwater -- Extremist on the Right" was discussed by Hargis, who said that Cook had been fired by a newspaper for making false charges against city officials; that Cook had then worked for a Communist-affiliated publication; that he had defended Alger Hiss and attacked J. Edgar Hoover and the Central Intelligence Agency, and that he had now written a "book to smear and destroy Barry Goldwater." When Cook heard of the broadcast, he concluded that he had been personally attacked and demanded free reply time, which the station refused. After an exchange of letters among Cook, Red Lion, and the FCC, the FCC declared that the Hargis broadcast constituted a personal attack on Cook; that Red Lion had failed to meet its obligation under the fairness doctrine ....

C

Believing that the specific application of the fairness doctrine in *Red Lion,* and the promulgation of the regulations in *RTNDA,* are both

authorized by Congress and enhance, rather than abridge, the freedoms of speech and press protected by the First Amendment, we hold
them valid and constitutional, reversing the judgment below in
*RTNDA* and affirming the judgment below in *Red Lion.*

II

The history of the emergence of the fairness doctrine and of the related
legislation shows that the Commission's action in the
*Red Lion* case did not exceed its authority, and that,
in adopting the new regulations, the Commission
was implementing congressional policy, rather than
embarking on a frolic of its own.

A

Before 1927, the allocation of frequencies was left entirely to the private sector, and the result was chaos.

It quickly became apparent that broadcast frequencies constituted a scarce resource whose use could be
regulated and rationalized only by the Government.
Without government control, the medium would be
of little use because of the cacaphony of competing
voices, none of which could be clearly and predicta-
bly heard. Consequently, the Federal Radio Commission was established to allocate frequencies among
competing applicants in a manner responsive to the
public "convenience, interest, or necessity."

Very shortly thereafter, the Commission expressed
its view that the

"public interest requires ample play for the free and fair competition of
opposing views, and the commission believes that the principle applies
. . . to all discussions of issues of importance to the public."

which fall short of abridgment of the freedom of speech and press, and
of the censorship proscribed by § 326 of the Act.

. . .

III

The broadcasters challenge the fairness doctrine
and its specific manifestations in the personal attack and political editorial rules on conventional
First Amendment grounds, alleging that the rules
abridge their freedom of speech and press. Their
contention is that the First Amendment protects
their desire to use their allotted frequencies continuously to broadcast whatever they choose, and
to exclude whomever they choose from ever using
that frequency.

. . . .

A

Although broadcasting is clearly a medium affected by a First Amendment interest, *United
States v. Paramount Pictures, Inc.,*334 U. S. 131,
334 U. S. 166 (1948), differences in the characteristics of new media justify differences in the First
Amendment standards applied to them.  For ex-
ample, the ability of new technology to produce sounds more raucous
than those of the human voice justifies restrictions on the sound level,
and on the hours and places of use, of sound trucks so long as the re-

strictions are reasonable and applied without discrimination. *Kovacs v. Cooper,*336 U. S. 77 (1949).

Just as the Government may limit the use of sound-amplifying equipment potentially so noisy that it drowns out civilized private speech, so may the Government limit the use of broadcast equipment. The right of free speech of a broadcaster, the user of a sound truck, or any other individual does not embrace a right to snuff out the free speech of others. *Associated Press v. United States,*326 U. S. 1, 326 U. S. 20 (1945).

. . . .

Where there are substantially more individuals who want to broadcast than there are frequencies to allocate, it is idle to posit an unabridgeable First Amendment right to broadcast comparable to the right of every individual to speak, write, or publish. If 100 persons want broadcast licenses, but there are only 10 frequencies to allocate, all of them may have the same "right" to a license, but, if there is to be any effective communication by radio, only a few can be licensed, and the rest must be barred from the airwaves.

. . . .

By the same token, as far as the First Amendment is concerned, those who are licensed stand no better than those to whom licenses are refused. A license permits broadcasting, but the licensee has no constitutional right to be the one who holds the license or to monopolize a radio frequency to the exclusion of his fellow citizens. There is nothing in the First Amendment which prevents the Government from requiring a licensee to share his frequency with others and to conduct himself as a proxy or fiduciary with obligations to present those views and voices which are representative of his community and which would otherwise, by necessity, be barred from the airwaves.

. . . .

It is the right of the viewers and listeners, not the right of the broadcasters, which is paramount. See FCC v. Sanders Bros. Radio Station,309 U. S. 470, 309 U. S. 475 (1940)

. . . .

In view of the scarcity of broadcast frequencies, the Government's role in allocating those frequencies, and the legitimate claims of those unable without governmental assistance to gain access to those frequencies for expression of their views, we hold the regulations and ruling at issue here are both authorized by statute and constitutional. The judgment of the Court of Appeals in *Red Lion* is affirmed ... and the causes remanded for proceedings consistent with this opinion.

It is so ordered.

# Miami Herald Pub. Co. v. Tornillo (1974)

U.S. Supreme Court

418 U.S. 241 (1974)

Decided June 25, 1974

Burger  Douglas  Brennan  Stewart  White  Marshall  Blackmun  Powell  Rehnquist

Decision: 9 votes for Miami Herald Publishing Co., 0 vote(s) against

**MR. CHIEF JUSTICE BURGER delivered the opinion of the Court.**

The issue in this case is whether a state statute granting a political candidate a right to equal space to reply to criticism and attacks on his record by a newspaper violates the guarantees of a free press.

I

In the fall of 1972, appellee, Executive Director of the Classroom Teachers Association, apparently a teachers' collective bargaining agent, was a candidate for the Florida House of Representatives. On September 20, 1972, and again on September 29, 1972, appellant printed editorials critical of appellee's candidacy. In response to these editorials, appellee demanded that appellant print verbatim his replies, defending the role of the Classroom Teachers Association and the organization's accomplishments for the citizens of Dade County. Appellant declined to print the appellee's replies, and appellee brought suit in Circuit Court, Dade County, seeking declaratory and injunctive relief and actual and punitive damages in excess of $5,000. The action was premised on Florida Statute § 104.38 (1973), a "right of reply" statute which provides that, if a candidate for nomination or election is assailed regarding his personal character or official record by any newspaper, the candidate has the right to demand that the newspaper print, free of cost to the candidate, any reply the candidate may make to the newspaper's charges. The reply must appear in as conspicuous a place and in the same kind of type as the charges which prompted the reply, provided it does not take up more space than the charges. Failure to comply with the statute constitutes a first-degree misdemeanor.

Appellant sought a declaration that § 104.38 was unconstitutional. After an emergency hearing requested by appellee, the Circuit Court denied injunctive relief because, absent special circumstances, no injunction could properly issue against the commission of a crime, and held that § 104.38 was unconstitutional as an infringement on the freedom of the press under the First and Fourteenth Amendments to the Constitution. 38 Fla.Supp. 80 (1972). The Circuit Court concluded that dictating what a newspaper must print was no different from dictating what it must not print. The Circuit Judge viewed the statute's vagueness as serving "to restrict and stifle protected expression." Id. at 83. Appellee's cause was dismissed with prejudice.

On direct appeal, the Florida Supreme Court reversed, holding that § 104.38 did not violate constitutional guarantees. 287 So.2d 78 (1973). [Footnote 3] It held that free speech was enhanced, and not abridged, by the Florida right-of-reply statute, which, in that court's view, furthered the "broad societal interest in the free flow of information to the public." Id. at 82. It also held that the statute is

Page 418 U. S. 246

not impermissibly vague; the statute informs "those who are subject to it as to what conduct on their part will render them liable to its penalties." Id. at 85. [Footnote 4] Civil remedies, including damages, were held to be available under this statute; the case was remanded to the trial court for further proceedings not inconsistent with the Florida Supreme Court's opinion.

We postponed consideration of the question of jurisdiction to the hearing of the case on the merits. 414 U.S. 1142 (1974).

II

Although both parties contend that this Court has jurisdiction to review the judgment of the Florida Supreme Court, a suggestion was initially made that the judgment of the Florida Supreme Court might not be "final" under 28 U.S.C. § 1257. [Footnote 5] In North Dakota State Pharmacy Bd. v. Snyder's Stores,414 U. S. 156 (1973), we reviewed a judgment of the North Dakota Supreme Court, under which the case had been remanded so that further state proceedings could be conducted respecting Snyder's application for a permit to operate a drug store. We held that to be a final judgment for purposes of our jurisdiction. Under the principles of finality enunciated in Snyder's Stores, the judgment of

(1973), we reviewed a judgment of the North Dakota Supreme Court, under which the case had been remanded so that further state proceedings could be conducted respecting Snyder's application for a permit to operate a drug store. We held that to be a final judgment for purposes of our jurisdiction. Under the principles of finality enunciated in *Snyder's Stores,* the judgment of the Florida Supreme Court in this case is ripe for review by this Court.

III

A

The challenged statute creates a right to reply to press criticism of a candidate for nomination or election. The statute was enacted in 1913, and this is only the second recorded case decided under its provisions.

Appellant contends the statute is void on its face because it purports to regulate the content of a newspaper in violation of the First Amendment. Alternatively it is urged that the statute is void for vagueness, since no editor could know exactly what words would call the statute into operation. It is also contended that the statute fails to distinguish between critical comment which is, and which is not, defamatory.

B

The appellee and supporting advocates of an enforceable right of access to the press vigorously argue that government has an obligation to ensure that a wide variety of views reach the public. The contentions of access proponents will be set out in some detail. It is urged that, at the time the First Amendment to the Constitution was ratified in 1791 as part of our Bill of Rights, the press was broadly representative of the people it was serving. While many of the newspapers were intensely

175

partisan and narrow in their views, the press collectively presented a broad range of opinions to readers. Entry into publishing was inexpensive; pamphlets and books provided meaningful alternatives to the organized press for the expression of unpopular ideas, and often treated events and expressed views not covered by conventional newspapers. A true marketplace of ideas existed in which there was relatively easy access to the channels of communication.

Access advocates submit that, although newspapers of the present are superficially similar to those of 1791, the press of today is in reality very different from that known in the early years of our national existence. In the past half century, a communications revolution has seen the introduction of radio and television into our lives, the promise of a global community through the use of communications satellites, and the specter of a "wired" nation by means of an expanding cable television network with two-way capabilities. The printed press, it is said, has not escaped the effects of this revolution. Newspapers have become big business, and there are far fewer of them to serve a larger literate population. Chains of newspapers, national newspapers, national wire and news services, and one-newspaper towns are the dominant features of a press that has become noncompetitive and enormously powerful and influential in its capacity to manipulate popular opinion and change the course of events. Major metropolitan newspapers have collaborated to establish news services national in scope. Such national news organizations provide syndicated "interpretive reporting" as well as syndicated features and commentary, all of which can serve as part of the new school of "advocacy journalism."

The elimination of competing newspapers in most of our large cities, and the concentration of control of media that results from the only newspaper's being owned by the same interests which own a television station and a radio station, are important components of this trend toward concentration of control of outlets to inform the public. The result of these vast changes has been to place in a few hands the power to inform the American people and shape public opinion. Much of the editorial opinion and commentary that is printed is that of syndicated columnists distributed nationwide and, as a result, we are told, on national and world issues there tends to be a homogeneity of editorial opinion, commentary, and interpretive analysis. The abuses of bias and manipulative reportage are, likewise, said to be the result of the vast accumulations of unreviewable power in the modern media empires. In effect, it is claimed, the public has lost any ability to respond or to contribute in a meaningful way to the debate on issues. The monopoly of the means of communication allows for little or no critical analysis of the media except in professional journals of very limited readership.

**104.38 *Newspaper assailing candidate in an election; space for reply*** -- If any newspaper in its columns assails the personal character of any candidate for nomination or for election in any election, or charges said candidate with malfeasance or misfeasance in office, or otherwise attacks his official record, or gives to another free space for such purpose, such newspaper shall upon request of such candidate immediately publish free of cost any reply he may make thereto in as conspicuous a place and in the same kind of type as the matter that calls for such reply, provided such reply does not take up more space than the matter replied to. Any person or firm failing to comply with the provisions of this section shall be guilty of a misdemeanor of the first degree, punishable as provided in § 775.082 or § 775.083.

"This concentration of nationwide news organizations -- like other large institutions -- has grown increasingly remote from and unresponsive to the popular constituencies on which they depend and which depend on them."

Report of the Task Force in Twentieth Century Fund Task Force Report for a National News Council, A Free and Responsive Press 4 (1973). Appellee cites the report of the Commission on Freedom of the Press, chaired by Robert M. Hutchins, in which it was stated, as long ago as 1947, that "[t]he right of free

public expression has . . . lost its earlier reality." Commission on Freedom of the Press, A Free and Responsible Press 15 (1947).

The obvious solution, which was available to dissidents at an earlier time when entry into publishing was relatively inexpensive, today would be to have additional newspapers. But the same economic factors which have caused the disappearance of vast numbers of metropolitan newspapers, have made entry into the marketplace of ideas served by the print media almost impossible. It is urged that the claim of newspapers to be "surrogates for the public" carries with it a concomitant fiduciary obligation to account for that stewardship. From this premise, it is reasoned that the only effective way to insure fairness and accuracy and to provide for some accountability is for government to take affirmative action. The First Amendment interest

The text of the September 20, 1972, editorial:

**"The State's Laws And Pat Tornillo"**

"LOOK who's upholding the law!"

"Pat Tornillo, boss of the Classroom Teachers Association and candidate for the State Legislature in the Oct. 3 runoff election, has denounced his opponent as lacking 'the knowledge to be a legislator, as evidenced by his failure to file a list of contribution to and expenditures of his campaign as required by law.'"

"Czar Tornillo calls 'violation of this law inexcusable.'"

"This is the same Pat Tornillo who led the CTA strike from February 19 to March 11, 1968, against the school children and taxpayers of Dade County. Call it whatever you will, it was an illegal act against the public interest, and clearly prohibited by the statutes."

"We cannot say it would be illegal, but certainly it would be inexcusable of the voters if they sent Pat Tornillo to Tallahassee to occupy the seat for District 103 in the House of Representatives."

of the public in being informed is said to be in peril because the "marketplace of ideas" is today a monopoly controlled by the owners of the market.

Proponents of enforced access to the press take comfort from language in several of this Court's decisions which suggests that the First Amendment acts as a sword as well as a shield, that it imposes obligations on the owners of the press in addition to protecting the press from government regulation. In *Associated Press v. United States,*326 U. S. 1, 326 U. S. 20 (1945), the Court, in rejecting the argument that the press is immune from the antitrust laws by virtue of the First Amendment, stated:

"The First Amendment, far from providing an argument against application of the Sherman Act, here provides powerful reasons to the contrary. That Amendment rests on the assumption that the widest possible dissemination of information from diverse and antagonistic sources is essential to the welfare of the public, that a free press is a condition of a free society. Surely a command that the government itself shall not impede the free flow of ideas does not afford nongovernmental combinations a refuge if they impose restraints upon that constitutionally guaranteed freedom. Freedom to publish means freedom for all and not for some. Free-

177

dom to publish is guaranteed by the Constitution, but freedom to combine to keep others from publishing is not. Freedom of the press from governmental interference under the First Amendment does not sanction repression of that freedom by private interests."

(Footnote omitted.)

In *New York Times Co. v. Sullivan,*376 U. S. 254, 376 U. S. 270 (1964), the Court spoke of "a profound national commitment to the principle that debate on public issues should be uninhibited, robust, and wide-open." It is argued that the "uninhibited, robust" debate is not "wide-open," but open only to a monopoly in control of the press. Appellee cites the plurality opinion in *Rosenbloom v. Metromedia, Inc.,*403 U. S. 29, 403 U. S. 47, and n. 15 (1971), which he suggests seemed to invite experimentation by the States in right-to-access regulation of the press.

Access advocates note that MR. JUSTICE DOUGLAS a decade ago expressed his deep concern regarding the effects of newspaper monopolies:

"Where one paper has a monopoly in an area, it seldom presents two sides of an issue. It too often hammers away on one ideological or political line, using its monopoly position not to educate people, not to promote debate, but to inculcate in its readers one philosophy, one attitude -- and to make money."

"The newspapers that give a variety of views and news that is not slanted or contrived are few indeed. And the problem promises to get worse. . . ."

### The text of the September 29, 1972 editorial:

"FROM the people who brought you this -- the teacher strike of '68 -- come now instructions on how to vote for responsible government, *i.e.,* against Crutcher Harrison and Ethel Beckham, for Pat Tornillo. The tracts and blurbs and bumper stickers pile up daily in teachers' school mailboxes amidst continuing pouts that the School Board should be delivering all this at your expense. The screeds say the strike is not an issue. We say maybe it wouldn't be were it not a part of a continuation of disregard of any and all laws the CTA might find aggravating. Whether in defiance of zoning laws at CTA Towers, contracts and laws during the strike, or, more recently, state prohibitions against soliciting campaign funds amongst teachers, CTA says fie and try and sue us -- what's good for CTA is good for CTA, and that is natural law. Tornillo's law, maybe. For years now, he has been kicking the public shin to call attention to his shakedown statesmanship. He and whichever acerbic prexy is in alleged office have always felt their private ventures so chock-full of public weal that we should leap at the chance to nab the tab, be it half the glorious Leader's salary or the dues check-off or anything else except perhaps mileage on the staff hydrofoil. Give him public office, says Pat, and he will no doubt live by the Golden Rule. Our translation reads that as more gold and more rule."

The Great Rights 12125, 127 (E. Cahn ed.1963). They also claim the qualified support of Professor Thomas I. Emerson, who has written that "[a] limited right of access to the press can be safely enforced," although he believes that "[g]overnment measures to encourage a multiplicity of outlets, rather than compelling a few outlets to represent everybody, seems a preferable course of action."

T. Emerson, The System of Freedom of Expression 671 (1970).

IV

However much validity may be found in these arguments, at each point the implementation of a remedy such as an enforceable right of access necessarily calls for some mechanism, either governmental or consensual. If it is governmental coercion, this at once brings about a confrontation with the express provisions of the First Amendment and the judicial gloss on that Amendment developed over the years.

The Court foresaw the problems relating to government-enforced access as early as its decision in *Associated Press v. United States, supra.* There, it carefully contrasted the private "compulsion to print" called for by the Association's bylaws with the provisions of the District Court decree against appellants which "does not compel AP or its members to permit publication of anything which their *reason' tells them should not be published." 326 U.S. at 326 U. S. 20 n. 18. In Branzburg v. Hayes,408 U. S. 665, 408 U. S. 681 (1972), we emphasized that the cases then* before us

"involve no intrusions upon speech or assembly, no prior restraint or restriction on what the press may publish, and no express or implied. command that the press publish what it prefers to withhold."

In *Columbia Broadcasting System, Inc. v. Democratic National Committee,*412 U. S. 94, 412 U. S. 117 (1973), the plurality opinion as to Part III noted:

"The power of a privately owned newspaper to advance its own political, social, and economic views is bounded by only two factors: first, the acceptance of a sufficient number of readers -- and hence advertisers -- to assure financial success, and second, the journalistic integrity of its editors and publishers."

**WHY ARE WE ASKING THAT THE LEGISLATURE INCREASE TEACHER SALARIES?**

An attitude strongly adverse to any attempt to extend a right of access to newspapers was echoed by other Members of this Court in their separate opinions in that case. *Id*. at 412 U. S. 145 (STEWART, J., concurring); *id*. at 412 U. S. 182 n. 12 (BRENNAN, J., joined by MARSHALL, J., dissenting). Recently, while approving a bar against employment advertising specifying "male" or "female" preference, the Court's opinion in *Pittsburgh Press Co. v. Human Relations Comm'n,*413 U. S. 376, 413 U. S. 391 (1973), took pains to limit its holding within narrow bounds:

"Nor, *a fortiori,* does our decision authorize any restriction whatever, whether of content or layout, on stories or commentary originated by Pittsburgh Press, its columnists, or its contributors. On the contrary, we reaffirm unequivocally the protection afforded to editorial judgment and to the free expression of views on these and other issues, however controversial."

Dissenting in *Pittsburgh Press,* MR. JUSTICE STEWART, joined by MR. JUSTICE DOUGLAS, expressed the view that no "government agency -- local, state, or federal can tell a newspaper in advance what it can print and what it cannot." *Id*. at 413 U. S. 400. *See Associates & Aldrich Co. v. Times Mirror Co.,* 440 F.2d 133, 135 (CA9 1971).

We see that, beginning with *Associated Press, supra,* the Court has expressed sensitivity as to whether a restriction or requirement constituted the compulsion exerted by government on a newspaper to print that which it would not otherwise print. The clear implication has been that any such a compulsion to publish that which "*reason' tells them should not be published*" is unconstitutional. *A responsible press is an undoubtedly desirable goal, but press responsibility is not mandated by the Constitution, and, like many other virtues, it cannot be legislated.*

Appellee's argument that the Florida statute does not amount to a restriction of appellant's right to speak, because "the statute in question here has not prevented the Miami Herald from saying anything it wished," [Footnote 21] begs the core question. Compelling editors or publishers to publish that which "reason' tells them should not be published" is what is at issue in this case. The Florida statute operates as a command in the same sense as a statute or regulation forbidding appellant to publish specified matter. Governmental restraint on publishing need not fall into familiar or traditional patterns to be subject to constitutional limitations on governmental powers. Grosjean v. American Press Co.,297 U. S. 233, 297 U. S. 244-245 (1936). The Florida statute exacts a penalty on the basis of the content of a newspaper. The first phase of the penalty resulting from the compelled printing of a reply is exacted in terms of the cost in printing and composing time and materials and in taking up space that could be devoted to other material the newspaper may have preferred to print. It is correct, as appellee contends, that a newspaper is not subject to the finite technological limitations of time that confront a broadcaster, but it is not correct to say that, as an economic reality, a newspaper can proceed to infinite expansion of its column space to accommodate the replies that a government agency determines or a statute commands the readers should have available. [Footnote 22]

Faced with the penalties that would accrue to any newspaper that published news or commentary arguably within the reach of the right-of-access statute, editors might well conclude that the safe course is to avoid controversy. Therefore, under the operation of the Florida statute, political and electoral coverage would be blunted or reduced. [Footnote 23] Government-enforced right of access inescapably "dampens the vigor and limits the variety of public debate," *New York Times Co. v. Sullivan,* 376 U.S. at 376 U. S. 279. The Court, in *Mills v. Alabama,*384 U. S. 214, 384 U. S. 218 (1966), stated:

"[T]here is practically universal agreement that a major purpose of [the First] Amendment was to protect the free discussion of governmental affairs. This of course includes discussions of candidates. . . . "

Even if a newspaper would face no additional costs to comply with a compulsory access law and would not be forced to forgo publication of news or opinion by the inclusion of a reply, the Florida statute fails to clear the barriers of the First Amendment because of its intrusion into the function of editors. A newspaper is more than a passive receptacle or conduit for news, comment, and advertising. [Footnote 24] The choice of material to go into a new paper, and the decisions made as to limitations on the size and content of the paper, and treatment of public issues and public official -- whether fair or unfair -- constitute the exercise of editorial control and judgment. It has yet to be demonstrated how governmental regulation of this crucial process can be exercised consistent with First Amendment guarantees of a free press as they have evolved to this time. Accordingly, the judgment of the Supreme Court of Florida is reversed.

It is so ordered.

# Campaign Finance and the First Amendment

*In the United States, at the federal level, campaign finance law is enacted by Congress and enforced by the Federal Election Commission (FEC), an independent federal agency. Campaign finance law in the United States changed drastically in the wake of the recent Supreme Court's decisions in Citizens United v. FEC and McCutcheon v. Federal Election Commission.*

Roberts  Scalia  **Kennedy**  Thomas  **Alito**  Stevens  Ginsburg  Breyer  Sotomayor

Decision: 5 votes for Citizens United, 4 vote(s) against

### Summary: Citizens United v. Federal Election Commission (2010)

> "Government may not suppress political speech on the basis of the speaker's corporate identity. No sufficient governmental interest justifies limits on the political speech of nonprofit or for-profit corporations."

> - Justice Kennedy, writing for the Court in *Citizens United*

**Background of the Case**: Citizens United sought an injunction against the Federal Election Commission in the United States District Court for the District of Columbia to prevent the application of the Bipartisan Campaign Reform Act (BCRA) to its film *Hillary: The Movie*.

*The Movie* expressed opinions about whether Senator Hillary Rodham Clinton would make a good president.

In an attempt to regulate "big money" campaign contributions, the BCRA applies a variety of restrictions to "electioneering communications." Section 203 of the BCRA prevents corporations or labor unions from funding such communication from their general treasuries. Sections 201 and 311 require the disclosure of donors to such communication and a disclaimer when the communication is not authorized by the candidate it intends to support.

Citizens United argued that: 1) Section 203 violates the First Amendment on its face and when applied to *The Movie* and its related advertisements, and that 2) Sections 201 and 203 are also unconstitutional as applied to the circumstances.

The United States District Court denied the injunction. Section 203 on its face was not unconstitutional because the Supreme Court in *McConnell v. FEC* had already reached that determination. The District Court also held that *The Movie* was the functional equivalent of express advocacy, as it attempted to inform voters that Senator Clinton was unfit for office, and thus Section 203 was not unconstitutionally applied. Lastly, it held that Sections 201 and 203 were not unconstitutional as applied to the *The Movie* or its advertisements. The court reasoned that the *McConnell* decision recognized that disclosure of donors "might be unconstitutional if it imposed an unconstitutional burden on the freedom to associate in support of a particular cause," but those circumstances did not exist in Citizen United's claim.

**The decision**: The majority held that under the First Amendment corporate funding of independent political broadcasts in candidate elections cannot be limited because political speech is indispensable to a democracy, which is no less true because the speech comes from a corporation.

The majority also held that the BCRA's disclosure requirements as applied to *The Movie* were constitutional, reasoning that disclosure is justified by a "governmental interest" in providing the "electorate with information" about election-related spending resources.

Source: http://www.oyez.org/cases/2000-2009/2008/2008_08_205

Beginning in 2010, *Citizens United* dramatically altered campaign finance. The Court ruled that corporations and unions are entitled to the protection of the First Amendment for political speech and that restrictions on the ability of corporations to speak directly, rather than through separate PACs, are unconstitutional. Finding that the restrictions must survive strict scrutiny – that is, must be narrowly tailored to achieve a compelling interest – the Court rejected the argument that the law was essential to prevent corruption in the political process.

And in a 2013 decision, a majority of Court continued to reject the reasoning and experience of Congress, and substituted their own judgment about what democratic practice requires.

### Summary: McCutcheon v. Federal Election Commission (2013)

"The government may no more restrict how many candidates or causes a donor may support than it may tell a newspaper how many candidates it may endorse."

Chief Justice John G. Roberts

**Background of the Case:** In 2002, Congress passed the Bipartisan Campaign Reform Act (BCRA), which established two sets of limits to campaign contributions. The base limit placed restrictions on how much money a contributor—defined broadly as individuals, partnerships, and other organizations—may give to specified categories of recipients. The aggregate limit restricted how much money an individual may donate in a two-year election cycle.

Shaun McCutcheon sued the Federal Election Commission, arguing that the aggregate limit violated the First Amendment by failing to serve a "cognizable government interest."

**The decision:** Chief Justice John G. Roberts, Jr. delivered the opinion for the four-justice plurality, and held the two-year aggregate campaign contribution limit was unconstitutional under the First Amendment because the aggregate limit did little to address the concerns that the Bipartisan Campaign Reform Act was meant to address, and at the same time limited participation in the democratic process.

The Court held that since the aggregate limit fails to meet the stated objective of preventing corruption, it does not survive the "rigorous" standard of review laid out by previous precedent dealing with campaign contributions from a First Amendment perspective and is therefore unconstitutional.

The aggregate limit also prevents a donor from contributing beyond a specific amount to more than a certain number of candidates, which may force him to choose which interests he can seek to advance in a given election.

The plurality held that the collective interest in combating corruption can only be pursued as long as it does not unnecessarily curtail an individual's freedom of speech, and in this case the aggregate limit is not sufficiently closely tailored to accomplish this goal.

In a strongly-worded dissent, Justice Stephen G. Breyer wrote that the plurality's opinion causes great harm to the democratic process because it misconstrued the nature of competing constitutional issues and destroys campaign finance laws.

Thus Court's decision McCutcheon reflected sharply different visions of the meaning of the First Amendment and the role of government in regulating elections, with the majority deeply skeptical of government efforts to control participation in politics, and the minority saying that such oversight was needed to ensure a functioning democracy.

## Before and After the Supreme Court's Ruling

How Wednesday's decision in *McCutcheon v. Federal Election Commission* changes the total amount individual donors can contribute to federal candidates, national parties and political committees. Changes are highlighted in yellow. APRIL 2 2014

| | To candidates | To national parties and other political groups | Combined |
|---|---|---|---|
| Before Wednesday's Ruling | $2,600 to each candidate per election, limited to **$48,600** in total for all candidates, every two years. | $32,400 to each national party committee, $10,000 to a party's state, district and local committees, and $5,000 to any other political committee per year; limited to **$74,600** in total, every two years. | Limited to **$123,200** contributed to candidates, parties, and political committees every two years. |
| After Wednesday's Ruling | $2,600 to each candidate per election. **No limit** on total amount contributed directly to candidates. | $32,400 to each national party committee, $10,000 to a party's state, district, and local committees, and $5,000 to any other political committee per year. **No limit** on total amount contributed to parties and other political groups. | **No limit** on total amount contributed to candidates, parties and political committees in an election. |

Source:

http://www.nytimes.com/2014/04/03/us/politics/supreme-court-ruling-on-campaign-contributions.html

# National security

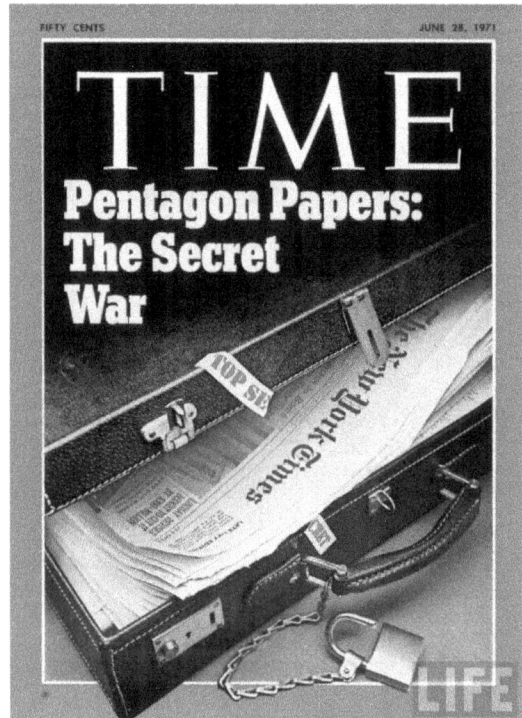

# New York Times Co. v. United States (1971)

U.S. Supreme Court

403 U.S. 713 (1971)

Decided: June 30, 1971  (Argued: June 26, 1971)

Black  Douglas  Brennan  Stewart  White  Marshall  Burger  Harlan  Blackmun

Decision: 6 votes for New York Times, 3 vote(s) against

## PER CURIAM

We granted certiorari in these cases in which the United States seeks to enjoin the New York Times and the Washington Post from publishing the contents of a classified study entitled "History of U.S. Decision-Making Process on Viet Nam Policy." Post, pp. 942, 943.

"Any system of prior restraints of expression comes to this Court bearing a heavy presumption against its constitutional validity." Bantam Books, Inc. v. Sullivan, 372 U.S. 58, 70 (1963); see also Near v. Minnesota, 283 U.S. 697 (1931). The Government "thus carries a heavy burden of showing justification for the imposition of such a restraint." Organization for a Better Austin v. Keefe, 402 U.S. 415, 419 (1971). The District Court for the Southern District of New York, in the New York Times case, and the District Court for the District of Columbia and the Court of Appeals for the District of Columbia Circuit, in the Washington Post case, held that the Government had not met that burden. We agree.

The judgment of the Court of Appeals for the District of Columbia Circuit is therefore affirmed. The order of the Court of Appeals for the Second Circuit is reversed, and the case is remanded with directions to enter a judgment affirming the judgment of the District Court for the Southern District of New York. The stays entered June 25, 1971, by the Court are vacated. The judgments shall issue forthwith.

So ordered.

* Together with No. 1885, United States v. Washington Post Co. et al., on certiorari to the United States Court of Appeals for the District of Columbia Circuit.

## MR. JUSTICE BLACK, with whom MR. JUSTICE DOUGLAS joins, concurring.

I adhere to the view that the Government's case against the Washington Post should have been dismissed, and that the injunction against the New York Times should have been vacated without oral argument when the cases were first presented to this Court. I believe [p715] that every moment's continuance of the injunctions against these newspapers amounts to a flagrant, indefensible, and continuing violation of the First Amendment. Furthermore, after oral argument, I agree completely that we must affirm the judgment of the Court of Appeals for the District of Columbia Circuit and reverse the judgment of the Court of Appeals for the Second Circuit for the reasons stated by my Brothers DOUGLAS and BRENNAN. In my view, it is unfortunate that some of my Brethren are apparently willing to hold that the publication of news may sometimes be enjoined. Such a holding would make a shambles of the First Amendment.

Our Government was launched in 1789 with the adoption of the Constitution. The Bill of Rights, including the First Amendment, followed in 1791. Now, for the first time in the 182 years since the founding of the Republic, the federal courts are asked to hold that the First Amendment does not mean what it says, but rather means that the Government can halt the publication of current news of vital importance to the people of this country.

In seeking injunctions against these newspapers, and in its presentation to the Court, the Executive Branch seems to have forgotten the essential purpose and history of the First Amendment. When the Constitution was adopted, many people strongly opposed it because the document contained no Bill of Rights to safeguard certain basic freedoms. [n1] They especially feared that the [p716] new powers granted to a central government might be interpreted to permit the government to curtail freedom of religion, press, assembly, and speech. In response to an overwhelming public clamor, James Madison offered a series of amendments to satisfy citizens that these great liberties would remain safe and beyond the power of government to abridge. Madison proposed what later became the First Amendment in three parts, two of which are set out below, and one of which proclaimed:

The people shall not be deprived or abridged of their right to speak, to write, or to publish their sentiments, and the freedom of the press, as one of the great bulwarks of liberty, shall be inviolable. [n2]

(Emphasis added.) The amendments were offered to curtail and restrict the general powers granted to the Executive, Legislative, and Judicial Branches two years before in the original Constitution. The Bill of Rights changed the original Constitution into a new charter under which no branch of government could abridge the people's freedoms of press, speech, religion, and assembly. Yet the Solicitor General argues and some members of the Court appear to agree that the general powers of the Government adopted in the original Constitution should be interpreted to limit and restrict the specific and emphatic guarantees of the Bill of Rights adopted later. I can imagine no greater perversion of history. Madison and the other Framers of the First Amendment, able men [p717] that they were, wrote in language they earnestly believed could never be misunderstood: "Congress shall make no law . . . abridging the freedom . . . of the press. . . ." Both the history and language of the First Amendment support the view that the press must be left free to publish news, whatever the source, without censorship, injunctions, or prior restraints.

In the First Amendment, the Founding Fathers gave the free press the protection it must have to fulfill its essential role in our democracy. The press was to serve the governed, not the governors. The Government's power to censor the press was abolished so that the press would remain forever free to censure the Government. The press was protected so that it could bare the secrets of government and inform the people. Only a free and unrestrained press can effectively expose deception in government. And paramount among the responsibilities of a free press is the duty to prevent any part of the government from deceiving the people and sending them off to distant lands to die of foreign fevers and foreign shot and shell. In my view, far from deserving condemnation for their courageous reporting, the New York Times, the Washington Post, and other newspapers should be commended for serving the purpose that the Founding Fathers saw so clearly. In revealing the workings of government that led to the Vietnam war, the newspapers nobly did precisely that which the Founders hoped and trusted they would do.

The Government's case here is based on premises entirely different from those that guided the Framers of the First Amendment. The Solicitor General has carefully and emphatically stated:

Now, Mr. Justice [BLACK], your construction of . . . [the First Amendment] is well known, and I certainly respect it. You say that no law means no law, and that should be obvious. I can only [p718] say, Mr. Justice, that to me it is equally obvious that "no law" does not mean "no law," and I would seek to persuade the Court that that is true. . . . [T]here are other parts of the Constitution that grant powers and responsibilities to the Executive, and . . . the First Amendment was not intended to make it impossible for the Executive to function or to protect the security of the United States.

And the Government argues in its brief that, in spite of the First Amendment,

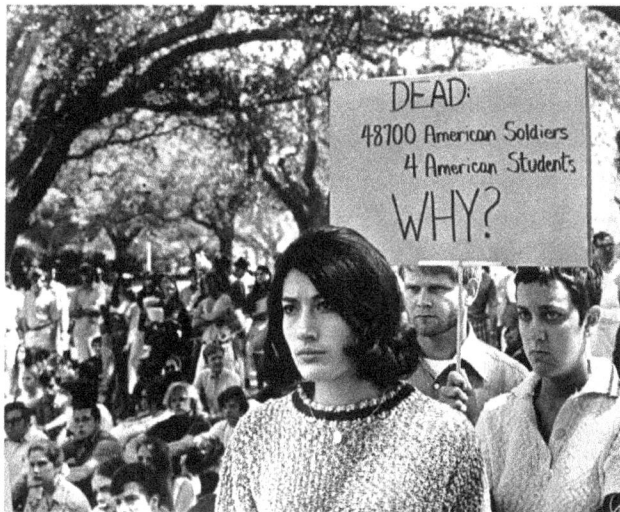

[t]he authority of the Executive Department to protect the nation against publication of information whose disclosure would endanger the national security stems from two interrelated sources: the constitutional power of the President over the conduct of foreign affairs and his authority as Commander-in-Chief.

In other words, we are asked to hold that, despite the First Amendment's emphatic command, the Executive Branch, the Congress, and the Judiciary can make laws enjoining publication of current news and abridging freedom of the press in the name of "national security." The Government does not even attempt to rely on any act of Congress. Instead, it makes the bold and dangerously far-reaching contention that the courts should take it upon themselves to "make" a law abridging freedom of the press in the name of equity, presidential power and national security, even when the representatives of the people in Congress have adhered to the command of the First Amendment and refused to make such a law. See concurring opinion of MR. JUSTICE DOUGLAS. To find that the President has "inherent power" to halt the publication of news by resort to the courts would wipe out the First Amendment and destroy the fundamental liberty and security of the very people the Government hopes to make "secure." No one can read the history of the adoption of the First Amendment without being convinced beyond any doubt that it was injunctions like those sought here that Madison and his collaborators intended to outlaw in this Nation for all time.

The word "security" is a broad, vague generality whose contours should not be invoked to abrogate the fundamental law embodied in the First Amendment. The guarding of military and diplomatic secrets at the expense of informed representative government provides no real security for our Republic. The Framers of the First Amendment, fully aware of both the need to defend a new nation and the abuses of the English and Colonial governments, sought to give this new society strength and security by providing that freedom of speech, press, religion, and assembly should not be abridged. This thought was eloquently expressed in 1937 by Mr. Chief Justice Hughes -- great man and great Chief Justice that he was -- when the Court held a man could not be punished for attending a meeting run by Communists.

The greater the importance of safeguarding the community from incitements to the overthrow of our institutions by force and violence, the more imperative is the need to preserve inviolate the constitutional rights of free speech, free press and free [p720] assembly in order to maintain the opportunity for free political discussion, to the end that government may be responsive to the will of the people and that changes, if desired, may be obtained by peaceful means. Therein lies the security of the Republic, the very foundation of constitutional government.

**MR. JUSTICE DOUGLAS, with whom MR. JUSTICE BLACK joins, concurring.**

While I join the opinion of the Court, I believe it necessary to express my views more fully.

It should be noted at the outset that the First Amendment provides that "Congress shall male no law . . . abridging the freedom of speech, or of the press." That leaves, in my view, no room for governmental restraint on the press. [n1]

There is, moreover, no statute barring the publication by the press of the material which the Times and the Post seek to use. Title 18 U.S.C. § 793(e) provides that

[w]hoever having unauthorized possession of, access to, or control over any document, writing . . . or information relating to the national defense which information the possessor has reason to believe could be used to the injury of the United States or to the advantage of any foreign nation, willfully communicates . . . the same to any person not entitled to receive it . . . [s]hall be fined [p721] not more than $10,000 or imprisoned not more than ten years, or both.

The Government suggests that the word "communicates" is broad enough to encompass publication.

There are eight sections in the chapter on espionage and censorship, §§ 792-799. In three of those eight, "publish" is specifically mentioned: § 794(b) applies to

Whoever, in time of war, with intent that the same shall be communicated to the enemy, collects, records, publishes, or communicates . . . [the disposition of armed forces].

Section 797 applies to whoever "reproduces, publishes, sells, or gives away" photographs of defense installations.

Section 798, relating to cryptography, applies to whoever: "communicates, furnishes, transmits, or otherwise makes available . . . or publishes" the described material. [n2] (Emphasis added.)

Thus, it is apparent that Congress was capable of, and did, distinguish between publishing and communication in the various sections of the Espionage Act.

The other evidence that § 793 does not apply to the press is a rejected version of § 793. That version read:

During any national emergency resulting from a war to which the United States is a party, or from threat of such a war, the President may, by proclamation, declare the existence of such emergency and, by proclamation, prohibit the publishing or communicating of, or the at-

188

tempting to publish or communicate any information relating to the national defense which, in his judgment, is of such character that it is or might be useful to the [p722] enemy.

55 Cong.Rec. 1763. During the debates in the Senate, the First Amendment was specifically cited, and that provision was defeated. 55 Cong.Rec. 2167.

Judge Gurfein's holding in the Times case that this Act does not apply to this case was therefore preeminently sound. Moreover, the Act of September 23, 1950, in amending 18 U.S.C. § 793 states in § 1(b) that:

Nothing in this Act shall be construed to authorize, require, or establish military or civilian censorship or in any way to limit or infringe upon freedom of the press or of speech as guaranteed by the Constitution of the United States and no regulation shall be promulgated hereunder having that effect.

64 Stat. 987. Thus, Congress has been faithful to the command of the First Amendment in this area.

So any power that the Government possesses must come from its "inherent power."

The power to wage war is "the power to wage war successfully." See Hirabayashi v. United States, 320 U.S. 81, 93. But the war power stems from a declaration of war. The Constitution by Art. I, § 8, gives Congress, not the President, power "[t]o declare War." Nowhere are presidential wars authorized. We need not de-

cide, therefore, what leveling effect the war power of Congress might have.

These disclosures [n3] may have a serious impact. But that is no basis for sanctioning a previous restraint on [p723] the press. As stated by Chief Justice Hughes in Near v. Minnesota, 283 U.S. 697, 719-720:

While reckless assaults upon public men, and efforts to bring obloquy upon those who are endeavoring faithfully to discharge official duties, exert a baleful influence and deserve the severest condemnation in public opinion, it cannot be said that this abuse is greater, and it is believed to be less, than that which characterized the period in which our institutions took shape. Meanwhile, the administration of government has become more complex, the opportunities for malfeasance and corruption have multiplied, crime has grown to most serious proportions, and the danger of its protection by unfaithful officials and of the impairment of the fundamental security of life and property by criminal alliances and official neglect, emphasizes the primary need of a vigilant and courageous press, especially in great cities. The fact that the liberty of the press may be abused by miscreant purveyors of scandal does not make any the less necessary the immunity of the press from previous restraint in dealing with official misconduct.

As we stated only the other day in Organization for a Better Austin v. Keefe, 402 U.S. 415, 419, "[a]ny prior restraint on expression comes to this Court with a "heavy presumption" against its constitutional validity."

The Government says that it has inherent powers to go into court and obtain an injunction to protect the national interest, which, in this case, is alleged to be national security.

Near v. Minnesota, 283 U.S. 697, repudiated that expansive doctrine in no uncertain terms.

The dominant purpose of the First Amendment was to prohibit the widespread practice of governmental suppression [p724] of embarrassing information. It is common knowledge that the First Amendment was adopted against the widespread use of the common law of seditious libel to punish the dissemination of material that is embarrassing to the powers-that-be. See T. Emerson, The System of Freedom of Expression, c. V (1970); Z. Chafee, Free Speech in the United States, c. XIII (1941). The present cases will, I think, go down in history as the most dramatic illustration of that principle. A debate of large proportions goes on in the Nation over our posture in Vietnam. That debate antedated the disclosure of the contents of the present documents. The latter are highly relevant to the debate in progress.

Secrecy in government is fundamentally anti-democratic, perpetuating bureaucratic errors. Open debate and discussion of public issues are vital to our national health. On public questions, there should be "uninhibited, robust, and wide-open" debate. New York Times Co. v. Sullivan, 376 U.S. 254, 269-270.

I would affirm the judgment of the Court of Appeals in the Post case, vacate the stay of the Court of Appeals in the Times case, and direct that it affirm the District Court.

The stays in these cases that have been in effect for more than a week constitute a flouting of the principles of the First Amendment as interpreted in Near v. Minnesota.

**MR. JUSTICE BRENNAN, concurring.**

I

I write separately in these cases only to emphasize what should be apparent: that our judgments in the present cases may not be taken to indicate the propriety, in the future, of issuing temporary stays and restraining [p725] orders to block the publication of material sought to be suppressed by the Government. So far as I can determine, never before has the United States sought to enjoin a newspaper from publishing information in its possession. The relative novelty of the questions presented, the necessary haste with which decisions were reached, the magnitude of the interests asserted, and the fact that all the parties have concentrated their arguments upon the question whether permanent restraints were proper may have justified at least some of the restraints heretofore imposed in these cases. Certainly it is difficult to fault the several courts below for seeking to assure that the issues here involved were preserved for ultimate review by this Court. But even if it be assumed that some of the interim restraints were proper in the two cases before us, that assumption has no bearing upon the propriety of similar judicial action in the future. To begin with, there has now been ample time for reflection and judgment; whatever values there may be in the preservation of novel questions for appellate review may not support any restraints in the future. More important, the First Amendment stands as an absolute bar to the imposition of judicial restraints in circumstances of the kind presented by these cases.

II

The error that has pervaded these cases from the outset was the granting of any injunctive relief whatsoever, interim or otherwise. The entire thrust of the Government's claim throughout these cases has been that publication of the material sought to be enjoined "could," or "might," or "may" prejudice the national interest in various ways. But the First Amendment tolerates absolutely no prior judicial restraints of the press predicated upon surmise or conjecture that untoward consequences [p726] may result. [*] Our cases, it is true, have indicated that there is a single, extremely narrow class of cases in which the First Amendment's ban on prior judicial restraint may be overridden. Our cases have thus far indicated that such cases may arise only when the Nation "is at war," Schenck v. United States, 249 U.S. 47, 52 (1919), during which times

[n]o one would question but that a government might prevent actual obstruction to its recruiting service or the publication of the sailing dates of transports or the number and location of troops.

Near v. Minnesota, 283 U.S. 697, 716 (1931). Even if the present world situation were assumed to be tantamount to a time of war, or if the power of presently available armaments would justify even in peace-time the suppression of information that would set in motion a nuclear holocaust, in neither of these actions has the Government presented or even alleged that publication of items from or based upon the material at issue would cause the happening of an event of that nature. "[T]he chief purpose of [the First Amendment's] guaranty [is] to prevent previous restraints upon publication." Near v. Minnesota, supra, at 713. Thus, only governmental allegation and proof that publication must inevitably, directly, [p727] and immediately cause the occurrence of an event kindred to imperiling the safety of a transport already at sea can support even the issuance of an interim restraining order. In no event may mere conclusions be sufficient, for if the Executive Branch seeks judicial aid in preventing publication, it must inevitably submit the basis upon which that aid is sought to scrutiny by the judiciary. And, therefore, every restraint issued in this case, whatever its form, has violated the First Amendment -- and not less so because that restraint was justified as necessary to afford the courts an opportunity to examine the claim more thoroughly. Unless and until the Government has clearly made out its case, the First Amendment commands that no injunction may issue.

*

Freedman v. Maryland, 380 U.S. 51 (1965), and similar cases regarding temporary restraints of allegedly obscene materials are not in point. For those cases rest upon the proposition that "obscenity is not protected by the freedoms of speech and press." Roth v. United States, 354 U.S. 476, 481 (1957). Here there is no question but that the material sought to be suppressed is within the protection of the First Amendment; the only question is whether, notwithstanding that fact, its publication may be enjoined for a time because of the presence of an overwhelming national interest. Similarly, copyright cases have no pertinence here: the Government is not asserting an interest in the particular form of words chosen in the documents, but is seeking to suppress the ideas expressed therein. And the copyright laws, of course, protect only the form of expression, and not the ideas expressed.

**MR. JUSTICE STEWART, with whom MR. JUSTICE WHITE joins, concurring.**

In the governmental structure created by our Constitution, the Executive is endowed with enormous power in the two related areas of national defense and international relations. This power, largely unchecked by the Legislative [n1] and Judicial [n2] branches, has been pressed to the very hilt since the advent of the nuclear missile age. For better or for worse, the simple fact is that a [p728] President of the United States possesses vastly greater constitutional independence in these two vital areas of power than does, say, a prime minister of a country with a parliamentary form of government.

In the absence of the governmental checks and balances present in other areas of our national life, the only effective restraint upon executive policy and power in the areas of national defense and international affairs may lie in an enlightened citizenry -- in an informed and critical public opinion which alone can here protect the values of democratic government. For this reason, it is perhaps here that a press that is alert, aware, and free most vitally serves the basic purpose of the First

Amendment. For, without an informed and free press, there cannot be an enlightened people.

Yet it is elementary that the successful conduct of international diplomacy and the maintenance of an effective national defense require both confidentiality and secrecy. Other nations can hardly deal with this Nation in an atmosphere of mutual trust unless they can be assured that their confidences will be kept. And, within our own executive departments, the development of considered and intelligent international policies would be impossible if those charged with their formulation could not communicate with each other freely, frankly, and in confidence. In the area of basic national defense, the frequent need for absolute secrecy is, of course, self-evident.

I think there can be but one answer to this dilemma, if dilemma it be. The responsibility must be where the power is. [n3] If the Constitution gives the Executive [p729] a large degree of unshared power in the conduct of foreign affairs and the maintenance of our national defense, then, under the Constitution, the Executive must have the largely unshared duty to determine and preserve the degree of internal security necessary to exercise that power successfully. It is an awesome responsibility, requiring judgment and wisdom of a high order. I should suppose that moral, political, and practical considerations would dictate that a very first principle of that wisdom would be an insistence upon avoiding secrecy for its own sake. For when everything is classified, then nothing is classified, and the system becomes one to be disregarded by the cynical or the careless, and to be manipulated by those intent on self-protection or self-promotion. I should suppose, in short, that the hallmark of a truly effective internal security system would be the maximum possible disclosure, recognizing that secrecy can best be preserved only when credibility is truly maintained. But, be that as it may, it is clear to me that it is the constitutional duty of the Executive -- as a matter of sovereign prerogative, and not as a matter of law as the courts know law -- through the promulgation and enforcement of executive regulations, to protect [p730] the confidentiality necessary to carry out its responsibilities in the fields of international relations and national defense.

This is not to say that Congress and the courts have no role to play. Undoubtedly, Congress has the power to enact specific and appropriate criminal laws to protect government property and preserve government secrets. Congress has passed such laws, and several of them are of very colorable relevance to the apparent circumstances of these cases. And if a criminal prosecution is instituted, it will be the responsibility of the courts to decide the applicability of the criminal law under which the charge is brought. Moreover, if Congress should pass a specific law authorizing civil proceedings in this field, the courts would likewise have the duty to decide the constitutionality of such a law, as well as its applicability to the facts proved.

But in the cases before us, we are asked neither to construe specific regulations nor to apply specific laws. We are asked, instead, to perform a function that the Constitution gave to the Executive, not the Judiciary. We are asked, quite simply, to prevent the publication by two newspapers of material that the Executive Branch insists should not, in the national interest, be published. I am convinced that the Executive is correct with respect to some of the documents involved. But I cannot say that disclosure of any of them will surely result in direct, immediate, and irreparable damage to our Nation or its people. That being so, there can under the First Amendment be but one judicial resolution of the issues before us. I join the judgments of the Court.

## MR. CHIEF JUSTICE BURGER, dissenting.

So clear are the constitutional limitations on prior restraint against expression that, from the time of Near v. Minnesota, 283 U.S. 697 (1931), until recently in Organization for a Better Austin v. Keefe, 402 U.S. 415 (1971), we have had little occasion to be concerned with cases involving prior restraints against news reporting on matters of public interest.

There is, therefore, little variation among the members of the Court in terms of resistance to prior restraints against publication. Adherence to this basic constitutional principle, however, does not make these cases simple. In these cases, the imperative of a free and unfettered press comes into collision with another imperative, the effective functioning of a complex modern government, and, specifically, the effective exercise of certain constitutional powers of the Executive. Only those who view the First Amendment as an absolute in all circumstances -- a view I respect, but reject -- can find such cases as these to be simple or easy.

These cases are not simple for another and more immediate reason. We do not know the facts of the cases. No District Judge knew all the facts. No Court of Appeals judge knew all the facts. No member of this Court knows all the facts.

Why are we in this posture, in which only those judges to whom the First Amendment is absolute and permits of no restraint in any circumstances or for any reason, are really in a position to act?

I suggest we are in this posture because these cases have been conducted in unseemly haste. MR. JUSTICE HARLAN covers the chronology of events demonstrating the hectic pressures under which these cases have been processed, and I need not restate them. The prompt [p749] setting of these cases reflects our universal abhorrence of prior restraint. But prompt judicial action does not mean unjudicial haste.

Here, moreover, the frenetic haste is due in large part to the manner in which the Times proceeded from the date it obtained the purloined documents. It seems reasonably clear now that the haste precluded reasonable and deliberate judicial treatment of these cases, and was not warranted. The precipitate action of this Court aborting trials not yet completed is not the kind of judicial conduct that ought to attend the disposition of a great issue.

The newspapers make a derivative claim under the First Amendment; they denominate this right as the public "right to know"; by implication, the Times asserts a sole trusteeship of that right by virtue of its journalistic "scoop." The right is asserted as an absolute. Of course, the First Amendment right itself is not an absolute, as Justice Holmes so long ago pointed out in his aphorism concerning the right to shout "fire" in a crowded theater if there was no fire. There are other exceptions, some of which Chief Justice Hughes mentioned by way of example in Near v. Minnesota. There are no doubt other exceptions no one has had occasion to describe or discuss. Conceivably, such exceptions may be lurking in these cases and, would have been flushed had they been properly considered in the trial courts, free from unwarranted deadlines and frenetic pressures. An issue of this importance should be tried and heard in a judicial atmosphere conducive to thoughtful, reflective deliberation, especially when haste, in terms of hours, is unwarranted in light of the long period the Times, by its own choice, deferred publication.

It is not disputed that the Times has had unauthorized possession of the documents for three to four months, during which it has had its expert analysts studying them, presumably digesting them and preparing the material for publication. During all of this time, the Times, presumably in its capacity as trustee of the public's "right to know," has held up publication for purposes it considered proper, and thus public knowledge was delayed. No doubt this was for a good reason; the analysis of 7,000 pages of complex material drawn from a vastly greater volume of material would inevitably take time, and the writing of good news stories takes time. But why should the United States Government, from whom this information was illegally acquired by someone, along with all the counsel, trial judges, and appellate judges be placed under needless pressure? After these months of deferral, the alleged "right to know" has somehow and suddenly become a right that must be vindicated instanter.

Would it have been unreasonable, since the newspaper could anticipate the Government's objections to release of secret material, to give the Government an opportunity to review the entire collection and determine whether agreement could be reached on publication? Stolen or not, if security was not, in fact, jeopardized, much of the material could no doubt have been declassified, since it spans a period ending in 1968. With such an approach -- one that great newspapers have in the past practiced and stated editorially to be the duty of an honorable press -- the newspapers and Government might well have narrowed [p751] the area of disagreement as to what was and was not publishable, leaving the remainder to be resolved in orderly litigation, if necessary. To me, it is hardly believable that a newspaper long regarded as a great institution in American life would fail to perform one of the basic and simple duties of every citizen with respect to the discovery or possession of stolen property or secret government documents. That duty, I had thought -- perhaps naively -- was to report forthwith, to responsible public officers. This duty rests on taxi drivers, Justices, and the New York Times. The course followed by the Times, whether so calculated or not, removed any possibility of orderly litigation of the issue. If the action of the judges up to now has been correct, that result is sheer happenstance.

Our grant of the writ of certiorari before final judgment in the Times case aborted the trial in the District Court before it had made a complete record pursuant to the mandate of the Court of Appeals for the Second Circuit.

The consequence of all this melancholy series of events is that we literally do not know what we are acting on. As I see it, we have been forced to deal with litigation concerning rights of great magnitude without an adequate record, and surely without time for adequate treatment either in the prior proceedings or in this Court. It is interesting to note that counsel on both sides, in oral argument before this Court, were frequently unable to respond to questions on factual points. Not surprisingly, they pointed out that they had been working literally "around the

clock," and simply were unable to review the documents that give rise to these cases and [p752] were not familiar with them. This Court is in no better posture. I agree generally with MR. JUSTICE HARLAN and MR. JUSTICE BLACKMUN, but I am not prepared to reach the merits.

I would affirm the Court of Appeals for the Second Circuit and allow the District Court to complete the trial aborted by our grant of certiorari, meanwhile preserving the status quo in the Post case. I would direct that the District Court, on remand, give priority to the Times case to the exclusion of all other business of that court, but I would not set arbitrary deadlines.

I should add that I am in general agreement with much of what MR. JUSTICE WHITE has expressed with respect to penal sanctions concerning communication or retention of documents or information relating to the national defense.

We all crave speedier judicial processes, but, when judges are pressured, as in these cases, the result is a parody of the judicial function.

1. As noted elsewhere, the Times conducted its analysis of the 47 volumes of Government documents over a period of several months, and did so with a degree of security that a government might envy. Such security was essential, of course, to protect the enterprise from others. Meanwhile, the Times has copyrighted its material, and there were strong intimations in the oral argument that the Times contemplated enjoining its use by any other publisher in violation of its copyright. Paradoxically, this would afford it a protection, analogous to prior restraint, against all others -- a protection the Times denies the Government of the United States.

2. Interestingly, the Times explained its refusal to allow the Government to examine its own purloined documents by saying in substance this might compromise its sources and informants! The Times thus asserts a right to guard the secrecy of its sources while denying that the Government of the United States has that power.

194

3. With respect to the question of inherent power of the Executive to classify papers, records, and documents as secret, or otherwise unavailable for public exposure, and to secure aid of the courts for enforcement, there may be an analogy with respect to this Court. No statute gives this Court express power to establish and enforce the utmost security measures for the secrecy of our deliberations and records. Yet I have little doubt as to the inherent power of the Court to protect the confidentiality of its internal operations by whatever judicial measures may be required.

**MR. JUSTICE HARLAN, with whom THE CHIEF JUSTICE and MR. JUSTICE BLACKMUN join, dissenting.**

These cases forcefully call to mind the wise admonition of Mr. Justice Holmes, dissenting in Northern Securities Co. v. United States, 193 U.S. 197, 400-401 (1904):

Great cases, like hard cases, make bad law. For great cases are called great not by reason of their real importance in shaping the law of the future, but because of some accident of immediate overwhelming interest which appeals to the feelings and distorts the judgment. These immediate interests exercise a kind of hydraulic pressure which makes what previously was clear seem doubtful, and before which even well settled principles of law will bend.

With all respect, I consider that the Court has been almost irresponsibly feverish in dealing with these cases.

Both the Court of Appeals for the Second Circuit and the Court of Appeals for the District of Columbia Circuit rendered judgment on June 23. [*] The New York Times' petition for certiorari, its motion for accelerated consideration thereof, and its application for interim relief were filed in this Court on June 24 at about 11 a.m. The application of the United States for interim relief in the Post case was also filed here on June 24 at about 7:15 p.m. This Court's order setting a hearing before us on June 26 at 11 a.m., a course which I joined only to avoid the possibility of even more peremptory action by the Court, was issued less than 24 hours before. The record in the Post case was filed with the Clerk shortly before 1 p.m. on June 25; the record in the Times case did not arrive until 7 or 8 o'clock that same night. The briefs of the parties were received less than two hours before argument on June 26.

This frenzied train of events took place in the name of the presumption against prior restraints created by the First Amendment. Due regard for the extraordinarily important and difficult questions involved in these litigations should have led the Court to shun such a precipitate timetable. In order to decide the merits of these cases properly, some or all of the following questions should have been faced:

1. Whether the Attorney General is authorized to bring these suits in the name of the United States. Compare In re Debs, 158 U.S. 564 (1895), with Youngstown Sheet & Tube Co. v. Sawyer, 343 U.S. 579 (1952). This question involves as well the construction and validity of a singularly opaque statute -- the Espionage Act, 18 U.S.C. § 793(e).

2. Whether the First Amendment permits the federal courts to enjoin publication of stories which would present a serious threat to national security. See Near v. Minnesota, 283 U.S. 697, 716 (1931) (dictum).

3. Whether the threat to publish highly secret documents is of itself a sufficient implication of national security to justify an injunction on the theory that, regardless of the contents of the documents, harm enough results simply from the demonstration of such a breach of secrecy.

4. Whether the unauthorized disclosure of any of these particular documents would seriously impair the national security.

5. What weight should be given to the opinion of high officers in the Executive Branch of the Government with respect to questions 3 and 4.

6. Whether the newspapers are entitled to retain and use the documents notwithstanding the seemingly uncontested facts that the documents, or the originals of which they are duplicates, were purloined from the Government's possession, and that the newspapers received them with knowledge that they had been feloniously acquired. Cf. Liberty Lobby, Inc. v. Pearson, 129 U.S.App.D.C. 74, 390 F.2d 489 (1967, amended 1968).

7. Whether the threatened harm to the national security or the Government's possessory interest in the documents justifies the issuance of an injunction against publication in light of --

a. The strong First Amendment policy against prior restraints on publication; [p755]

b. The doctrine against enjoining conduct in violation of criminal statutes; and

c. The extent to which the materials at issue have apparently already been otherwise disseminated.

These are difficult questions of fact, of law, and of judgment; the potential consequences of erroneous decision are enormous. The time which has been available to us, to the lower courts, and to the parties has been wholly inadequate for giving these cases the kind of consideration they deserve. It is a reflection on the stability of the judicial process that these great issues -- as important as any that have arisen during my time on the Court -- should have been decided under the pressures engendered by the torrent of publicity that has attended these litigations from their inception.

Forced as I am to reach the merits of these cases, I dissent from the opinion and judgments of the Court. Within the severe limitations imposed by the time constraints under which I have been required to operate, I can only state my reasons in telescoped form, even though, in dif-

ferent circumstances, I would have felt constrained to deal with the cases in the fuller sweep indicated above.

It is a sufficient basis for affirming the Court of Appeals for the Second Circuit in the Times litigation to observe that its order must rest on the conclusion that, because of the time elements the Government had not been given an adequate opportunity to present its case [p756] to the District Court. At the least this conclusion was not an abuse of discretion.

In the Post litigation, the Government had more time to prepare; this was apparently the basis for the refusal of the Court of Appeals for the District of Columbia Circuit on rehearing to conform its judgment to that of the Second Circuit. But I think there is another and more fundamental reason why this judgment cannot stand -- a reason which also furnishes an additional ground for not reinstating the judgment of the District Court in the Times litigation, set aside by the Court of Appeals. It is plain to me that the scope of the judicial function in passing upon the activities of the Executive Branch of the Government in the field of foreign affairs is very narrowly restricted. This view is, I think, dictated by the concept of separation of powers upon which our constitutional system rests.

In a speech on the floor of the House of Representatives, Chief Justice John Marshall, then a member of that body, stated:

The President is the sole organ of the nation in its external relations, and its sole representative with foreign nations.

10 Annals of Cong. 613 (1800). From that time, shortly after the founding of the Nation, to this, there has been no substantial challenge to this description of the scope of executive power. See United States v. Curtiss-Wright Corp., 299 U.S. 304, 319-321 (1936), collecting authorities.

From this constitutional primacy in the field of foreign affairs, it seems to me that certain conclusions necessarily follow. Some of these were stated concisely by President Washington, declining the request of the House of Representatives for the papers leading up to the negotiation of the Jay Treaty:

The nature of foreign negotiations requires caution, and their success must often depend on secrecy; [p757] and even when brought to a conclusion, a full disclosure of all the measures, demands, or eventual concessions which may have been proposed or contemplated would be extremely impolitic; for this might have a pernicious influence on future negotiations, or produce immediate inconveniences, perhaps danger and mischief, in relation to other powers.

1 J. Richardson, Messages and Papers of the Presidents 194-195 (1896).

The power to evaluate the "pernicious influence" of premature disclosure is not, however, lodged in the Executive alone. I agree that, in performance of its duty to protect the values of the First Amendment against political pressures, the judiciary must review the initial Executive determination to the point of satisfying itself that the subject matter of the dispute does lie within the proper compass of the President's foreign relations power. Constitutional considerations forbid "a complete abandonment of judicial control." Cf. United States v. Reynolds, 345 U.S. 1, 8 (1953). Moreover, the judiciary may properly insist that the determination that disclosure of the subject matter would irreparably impair the national security be made by the head of the Executive Department concerned -- here, the Secretary of State or the Secretary of Defense -- after actual personal consideration by that officer. This safeguard is required in the analogous area of executive claims of privilege for secrets of state. See id. at 8 and n. 20; Duncan v. Cammell, Laird Co., [1942] A.C. 624, 638 (House of Lords).

But, in my judgment, the judiciary may not properly go beyond these two inquiries and redetermine for itself the probable impact of disclosure on the national security.

[T]he very nature of executive decisions as to foreign policy is political, not judicial. Such decisions [p758] are wholly confided by our Constitution to the political departments of the government, Executive and Legislative. They are delicate, complex, and involve large elements of prophecy. They are and should be undertaken only by those directly responsible to the people whose welfare they advance or imperil. They are decisions of a kind for which the Judiciary has neither aptitude, facilities nor responsibility, and which has long been held to belong in the domain of political power not subject to judicial intrusion or inquiry.

Chicago & Southern Air Lines v. Waterman Steamship Corp., 333 U.S. 103, 111 (1948) (Jackson, J.).

Even if there is some room for the judiciary to override the executive determination, it is plain that the scope of review must be exceedingly narrow. I can see no indication in the opinions of either the District Court or the Court of Appeals in the Post litigation that the conclusions of the Executive were given even the deference owing to an administrative agency, much less that owing to a co-equal branch of the Government operating within the field of its constitutional prerogative.

Accordingly, I would vacate the judgment of the Court of Appeals for the District of Columbia Circuit on this ground, and remand the case for further proceedings in the District Court. Before the commencement of such further proceedings, due opportunity should be afforded the Government for procuring from the Secretary of State or the Secretary of Defense or both an expression of their views on the issue of national security. The ensuing review by the District Court should be in accordance with the views expressed in this opinion. And, for the reasons stated above, I would affirm the judgment of the Court of Appeals for the Second Circuit.

Pending further hearings in each case conducted under the appropriate ground rules, I would continue the [p759] restraints on publication. I cannot believe that the doctrine prohibiting prior restraints reaches to the point of preventing courts from maintaining the status quo long enough to act responsibly in matters of such national importance as those involved here.

* The hearing in the Post case before Judge Gesell began at 8 a.m. on June 21, and his decision was rendered, under the hammer of a deadline imposed by the Court of Appeals, shortly before 5 p.m. on the same day. The hearing in the Times case before Judge Gurfein was held on June 18, and his decision was rendered on June 19. The Government's appeals in the two cases were heard by the Courts of Appeals for the District of Columbia and Second Circuits, each court sitting en banc, on June 22. Each court rendered its decision on the following afternoon.

**MR. JUSTICE BLACKMUN, dissenting.**

I join MR. JUSTICE HARLAN in his dissent. I also am in substantial accord with much that MR. JUSTICE WHITE says, by way of admonition, in the latter part of his opinion.

At this point, the focus is on only the comparatively few documents specified by the Government as critical. So far as the other material -- vast in amount -- is concerned, let it be published and published forthwith if the newspapers, once the strain is gone and the sensationalism is eased, still feel the urge so to do.

But we are concerned here with the few documents specified from the 47 volumes. Almost 70 years ago, Mr. Justice Holmes, dissenting in a celebrated case, observed:

Great cases, like hard cases, make bad law. For great cases are called great not by reason of their real importance in shaping the law of the future, but because of some accident of immediate overwhelming interest which appeals to the feelings and distorts the judgment. These immediate interests exercise a kind of hydraulic pressure. . . .

Northen Securities Co. v. United States, 193 U.S. 197, 400-401 (1904). The present cases, if not great, are at least unusual in their posture and implications, and the Holmes observation certainly has pertinent application.

The New York Times clandestinely devoted a period of three months to examining the 47 volumes that came into its unauthorized possession. Once it had begun publication [p760] of material from those volumes, the New York case now before us emerged. It immediately assumed, and ever since has maintained, a frenetic pace and character. Seemingly, once publication started, the material could not be made public fast enough. Seemingly, from then on, every deferral or delay, by restraint or otherwise, was abhorrent, and was to be deemed violative of the First Amendment and of the public's "right immediately to know." Yet that newspaper stood before us at oral argument and professed criticism of the Government for not lodging its protest earlier than by a Monday telegram following the initial Sunday publication.

The District of Columbia case is much the same.

Two federal district courts, two United States courts of appeals, and this Court -- within a period of less than three weeks from inception until today -- have been pressed into hurried decision of profound constitutional issues on inadequately developed and largely assumed facts without the careful deliberation that, one would hope, should characterize the American judicial process. There has been much writing about the law and little knowledge and less digestion of the facts. In the New York case, the judges, both trial and appellate, had not yet examined the basic material when the case was brought here. In the District of Columbia case, little more was done, and what was accomplished in this respect was only on required remand, with the Washington Post, on the excuse that it was trying to protect its source of information, initially refusing to reveal what material it actually possessed, and with the District Court forced to make assumptions as to that possession.

With such respect as may be due to the contrary view, this, in my opinion, is not the way to try a lawsuit of this magnitude and asserted importance. It is not the way for federal courts to adjudicate, and to be required to adjudicate, issues that allegedly concern the Nation's [p761] vital welfare. The country would be none the worse off were the cases tried quickly, to be sure, but in the customary and properly deliberative manner. The most recent of the material, it is said, dates no later than 1968, already about three years ago, and the Times itself took three months to formulate its plan of procedure and, thus, deprived its public for that period.

The First Amendment, after all, is only one part of an entire Constitution. Article II of the great document vests in the Executive Branch primary power over the conduct of foreign affairs, and places in that branch the responsibility for the Nation's safety. Each provision of the Constitution is important, and I cannot subscribe to a doctrine of unlimited absolutism for the First Amendment at the cost of downgrading other provisions. First Amendment absolutism has never commanded a majority of this Court. See, for example, Near v. Minnesota, 283 U.S. 697, 708 (1931), and Schenck v. United States, 249 U.S. 47, 52 (1919). What is needed here is a weighing, upon properly developed standards, of the broad right of the press to print and of the very narrow right of the Govern-

ment to prevent. Such standards are not yet developed. The parties here are in disagreement as to what those standards should be. But even the newspapers concede that there are situations where restraint is in order and is constitutional. Mr. Justice Holmes gave us a suggestion when he said in Schenck,

It is a question of proximity and degree. When a nation is at war, many things that might be said in time of peace are such a hindrance to its effort that their utterance will not be endured so long as men fight and that no Court could regard them as protected by any constitutional right.

I therefore would remand these cases to be developed expeditiously, of course, but on a schedule permitting the [p762] orderly presentation of evidence from both sides, with the use of discovery, if necessary, as authorized by the rules, and with the preparation of briefs, oral argument, and court opinions of a quality better than has been seen to this point. In making this last statement, I criticize no lawyer or judge. I know from past personal experience the agony of time pressure in the preparation of litigation. But these cases and the issues involved and the courts, including this one, deserve better than has been produced thus far.

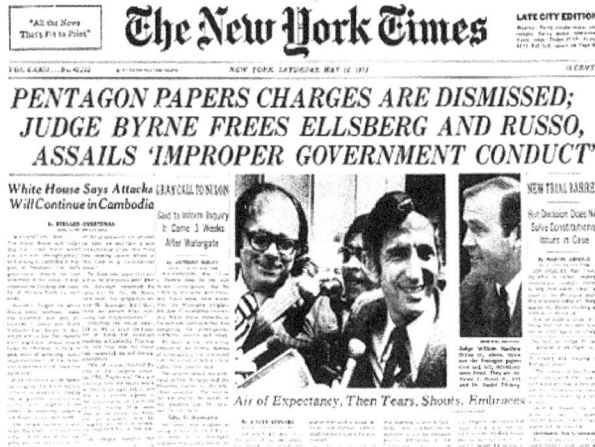

The New York Times

PENTAGON PAPERS CHARGES ARE DISMISSED; JUDGE BYRNE FREES ELLSBERG AND RUSSO, ASSAILS 'IMPROPER GOVERNMENT CONDUCT'

It may well be that, if these cases were allowed to develop as they should be developed, and to be tried as lawyers should try them and as courts should hear them, free of pressure and panic and sensationalism, other light would be shed on the situation, and contrary considerations, for me, might prevail. But that is not the present posture of the litigation.

The Court, however, decides the cases today the other way. I therefore add one final comment.

I strongly urge, and sincerely hope, that these two newspapers will be fully aware of their ultimate responsibilities to the United States of America. Judge Wilkey, dissenting in the District of Columbia case, after a review of only the affidavits before his court (the basic papers had not then been made available by either party), concluded that there were a number of examples of documents that, if in the possession of the Post and if published, "could clearly result in great harm to the nation," and he defined "harm" to mean

the death of soldiers, the destruction of alliances, the greatly increased difficulty of negotiation with our enemies, the inability of our diplomats to negotiate. . . .

I, for one, have now been able to give at least some cursory study not only to the affidavits, but to the material itself. I regret to say that, from this examination, I fear that Judge Wilkey's statements have possible foundation. I therefore share [p763] his concern. I hope that damage has not already been done. If, however, damage has been done, and if, with the Court's action today, these newspapers proceed to publish the critical documents and there results therefrom

the death of soldiers, the destruction of alliances, the greatly increased difficulty of negotiation with our enemies, the inability of our diplomats to negotiate,

to which list I might add the factors of prolongation of the war and of further delay in the freeing of United States prisoners, then the Nation's people will know where the responsibility for these sad consequences rests.

# Branzburg v. Hayes (1972)

US Supreme Court

408 U.S. 665 (1972)

Decided: June 29, 1972

Burger · White · Blackmun · Powell · Rehnquist · Douglas · Brennan · Stewart · Marshall

Decision: 5 votes for Hayes, 4 vote(s) against

**Opinion of the Court by MR. JUSTICE WHITE, announced by THE CHIEF JUSTICE.**

The issue in these cases is whether requiring newsmen to appear and testify before state or federal grand juries abridges the freedom of speech and press guaranteed by the First Amendment. We hold that it does not.

I

The writ of certiorari in No. 70-85, Branzburg v. Hayes and Meigs, brings before us two judgments of the Kentucky Court of Appeals, both involving petitioner Branzburg, a staff reporter for the Courier-Journal, a daily newspaper published in Louisville, Kentucky.

On November 15, 1969, the Courier-Journal carried a story under petitioner's by-line describing in detail his observations of two young residents of Jefferson County synthesizing hashish from marihuana, an activity which, they asserted, earned them about $5,000 in three weeks. The article included a photograph of a pair of hands working above a laboratory table on which was a substance identified by the caption as hashish. The article stated that petitioner had promised not to reveal the identity of the two hashish makers. Petitioner was shortly subpoenaed by the Jefferson County grand jury; he appeared, but refused to identify the individuals he had seen possessing marihuana or the persons he had seen making hashish from marihuana. A state trial court judge [n3] ordered petitioner to answer these questions and rejected his contention that the Kentucky reporters' privilege statute, Ky.Rev.Stat. § 421.100 (1962) the First Amendment of the United States Constitution, or §§ 1, 2, and 8 of the Kentucky Constitution authorized his refusal to answer. Petitioner then sought prohibition and mandamus in the Kentucky Court of Appeals on the same ground, but the Court of Appeals denied the petition. Branzburg v. Pound, 461 S.W.2d 345 (1970), as modified on denial of rehearing, Jan. 22, 1971. It held that petitioner had abandoned his First Amendment argument in a supplemental memorandum he had filed and tacitly rejected his argument based on the Kentucky Constitution. It also construed Ky.Rev.Stat. § 421.100 as affording a newsman the privilege of refusing to divulge the identity of an informant who supplied him with information, but held that the statute did not permit a reporter to refuse to testify about events he had observed personally, including the identities of those persons he had observed.

The second case involving petitioner Branzburg arose out of his later story published on January 10, 1971, which described in detail the use of drugs in Frankfort, Kentucky. The article reported that, in order to provide a comprehensive survey of the "drug scene" in Frankfort, petitioner had "spent two weeks interviewing several dozen drug users in the capital city," and had seen some of them smoking marihuana. A number of conversations with and observations of several unnamed drug users were recounted. Subpoenaed to appear before a Franklin County grand jury "to testify in the matter of violation of statutes concerning use and sale of drugs," petitioner Branzburg moved to quash the summons; the motion was denied, although an order was issued protecting Branzburg from revealing "confidential associations, sources or information" but requiring that he "answer any questions which concern or pertain to any criminal act, the commission of which was actually observed by [him]." Prior to the time he was slated to appear before the grand jury, petitioner sought mandamus and prohibition from the Kentucky Court of Appeals, arguing that, if he were forced to go before the grand jury or to answer questions regarding the identity of informants or disclose information given to him in confidence, his effectiveness as a reporter would be greatly damaged. The Court of Appeals once again denied the requested writs, reaffirming its construction of Ky.Rev.Stat. § 421.100, and rejecting petitioner's claim of a First Amendment privilege. It distinguished Caldwell v. United States, 434 F.2d 1081 (CA9

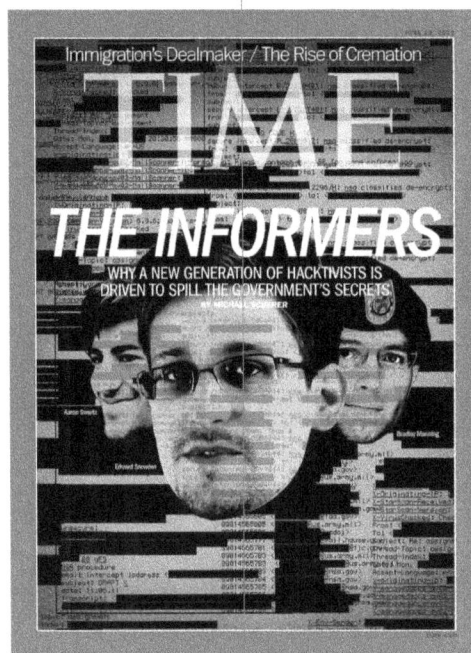

1970), and it also announced its "misgivings" about that decision, asserting that it represented "a drastic departure from the generally recognized rule that the sources of information of a newspaper reporter are not privileged under the First Amendment." It characterized petitioner's fear that his ability to obtain news would be destroyed as

so tenuous that it does not, in the opinion of this court, present an issue of abridgement of the freedom of the press within the meaning of that term as used in the Constitution of the United States.

Petitioner sought a writ of certiorari to review both judgments of the Kentucky Court of Appeals, and we granted the writ. 402 U.S. 942 (1971).

In re Pappas, No. 70-94, originated when petitioner Pappas, a television newsman-photographer working out of the Providence, Rhode Island, office of a New Bedford, Massachusetts, television station, was called to New Bedford on July 30, 1970, to report on civil disorders there which involved fires and other turmoil. He intended to cover a Black Panther news conference at that group's headquarters in a boarded-up store. Petitioner found the streets around the store barricaded, but he ultimately gained entrance to the area and recorded and photographed a prepared statement read by one of the Black Panther leaders at about 3 p.m. He then asked for and received permission to reenter the area. Returning at about 9 o'clock, he was allowed to enter and remain inside Panther headquarters. As a condition of entry, Pappas agreed not to disclose anything he saw or heard inside the store except an anticipated police raid, which Pappas, "on his own," was free to photograph and report as he wished. Pappas stayed inside the headquarters for about three hours, but there was no police raid, and petitioner wrote no story and did not otherwise reveal what had occurred in the store while he was there. Two months later, petitioner was summoned before the Bristol County Grand Jury and appeared, answered questions as to his name, address, employment, and what he had seen and heard outside Panther headquarters, but refused to answer any questions about what had taken place inside headquarters while he was there, claiming that the First Amendment afforded him a privilege to protect confidential informants and their information. A second summons was then served upon him, again directing him to appear before the grand jury and "to give such evidence as he knows relating to any matters which may be inquired of on behalf of the Commonwealth before . . . the Grand Jury." His motion to quash on First Amendment and other grounds was denied by the trial judge who, noting the absence of a statutory newsman's privilege in Massachusetts, ruled that petitioner had no constitutional privilege to refuse to divulge to the grand jury what he had seen and heard, including the identity of persons he had observed. The case was reported for decision to the Supreme Judicial Court of Massachusetts. The record there did not include a transcript of the hearing on the motion to quash, nor did it reveal the specific questions petitioner had refused to answer, the expected nature of his testimony, the nature of the grand jury investigation, or the likelihood of the grand jury's securing the information it sought from petitioner by other means. The Supreme Judicial Court, however, took

judicial notice that, in July, 1970, there were serious civil disorders in New Bedford, which involved street barricades, exclusion of the public from certain streets, fires, and similar turmoil. We were told at the arguments that there was gunfire in certain streets. We assume that the grand jury investigation was an appropriate effort to discover and indict those responsible for criminal acts.

358 Mass. 604, 607, 266 N.E.2d 297, 299 (1971). The court then reaffirmed prior Massachusetts holdings that testimonial privileges were "exceptional" and "limited," stating that "[t]he principle that the public 'has a right to every man's evidence'" had usually been preferred, in the Commonwealth, to countervailing interests. Ibid. The court rejected the holding of the Ninth Circuit in Caldwell v. United States, supra, and

adhere[d] to the view that there exists no constitutional newsman's privilege, either qualified or absolute, to refuse to appear and testify before a court or grand jury.

358 Mass. at 612, 266 N.E.2d at 302-303. Any adverse effect upon the free dissemination of news by virtue of petitioner's being called to testify was deemed to be only "indirect, theoretical, and uncertain." Id. at 612, 266 N.E.2d at 302. The court concluded that

[t]he obligation of newsmen . . . is that of every citizen . . . to appear when summoned, with relevant written or other material when required, and to answer relevant and reasonable inquiries.

Id. at 612, 266 N.E.2d at 303. The court nevertheless noted that grand juries were subject to supervision by the presiding judge, who had the duty "to prevent oppressive, unnecessary, irrelevant, and other improper inquiry and investigation," ibid., to insure that a witness' Fifth Amendment rights were not infringed, and to assess the propriety, necessity, and pertinence of the probable testimony to the investigation in progress. The burden was deemed to be on the witness to establish the impropriety of the summons or the questions asked. The denial of the motion to quash was affirmed, and we granted a writ of certiorari to petitioner Pappas. 402 U.S. 942 (1971).

United States v. Caldwell, No. 70-57, arose from subpoenas issued by a federal grand jury in the Northern District of California to respondent Earl Caldwell, a reporter for the New York Times assigned to cover the Black Panther Party and other black militant groups. A subpoena duces tecum was served on respondent on February 2, 1970, ordering him to appear before the grand jury to testify and to bring with him notes and tape recordings of interviews given him for publication by officers and spokesmen of the Black Panther Party concerning the aims, purposes, and activities of that organization. Respondent objected to the scope of this subpoena, and an agreement between his counsel and the Government attorneys resulted in a continuance. A second subpoena, served on March 16, omitted the documentary requirement and simply ordered Caldwell "to appear . . . to testify before the Grand Jury." Respondent and his employer, the New York Times, moved to quash on the ground that the unlimited breadth of the subpoenas and the fact that Caldwell would have to appear in secret before the grand jury would destroy his working relationship with the Black Panther Party and "suppress vital First Amendment freedoms . . . by driving a wedge of distrust and silence between the news media and the militants." App. 7. Respondent argued that "so drastic an incursion upon First Amendment freedoms" should not be permitted "in the absence of a compelling governmental interest -- not shown here -- in requiring Mr. Caldwell's appearance before the grand jury." Ibid. The motion was supported by amicus curiae memoranda from other publishing concerns and by affidavits from newsmen asserting the unfavorable impact on news sources of requiring reporters to appear before grand juries. The Government filed three memoranda in opposition to the motion to quash, each supported by affidavits. These documents stated that the grand jury was investigating, among other things, possible violations of a number of criminal statutes, including 18 U.S.C. § 871 (threats against the President), 18 U.S.C. § 1751 (assassination, attempts to assassinate, conspiracy to assassinate the President), 18 U.S.C. § 231 (civil disorders), 18 U.S.C. § 2101 (interstate travel to incite a riot), and 18 U.S.C. § 1341 (mail frauds and swindles). It was recited that, on November 15, 1969, an officer of the Black Panther Party made a publicly televised speech in which he had declared that "[w]e will kill Richard Nixon" and that this threat had been repeated in three subsequent issues of the Party newspaper. App. 66, 77. Also referred to were various writings by Caldwell about the Black Panther Party, including an arti-

cle published in the New York Times on December 14, 1969, stating that "[i]n their role as the vanguard in a revolutionary struggle, the Panthers have picked up guns," and quoting the Chief of Staff of the Party as declaring:

We advocate the very direct overthrow of the Government by way of force and violence. By picking up guns and moving against it because we recognize it as being oppressive and, in recognizing that, we know that the only solution to it is armed struggle [sic].

App. 62. The Government also stated that the Chief of Staff of the Party had been indicted by the grand jury on December 3, 1969, for uttering threats against the life of the President in violation of 18 U.S.C. § 871 and that various efforts had been made to secure evidence of crimes under investigation through the immunization of persons allegedly associated with the Black Panther Party.

On April 6, the District Court denied the motion to quash, Application of Caldwell, 311 F.Supp. 358 (ND Cal.1970), on the ground that "every person within the jurisdiction of the government" is bound to testify upon being properly summoned. Id. at 360 (emphasis in original). Nevertheless, the court accepted respondent's First Amendment arguments to the extent of issuing a protective order providing that, although respondent had to divulge whatever information had been given to him for publication, he

shall not be required to reveal confidential associations, sources or information received, developed or maintained by him as a professional journalist in the course of his efforts to gather news for dissemination to the public through the press or other news media.

The court held that the First Amendment afforded respondent a privilege to refuse disclosure of such confidential information until there had been a showing by the Government of a compelling and overriding national interest in requiring Mr. Caldwell's testimony which cannot be served by any alternative means.

Id. at 362.

Subsequently, the term of the grand jury expired, a new grand jury was convened, and a new subpoena ad testificandum was issued and served on May 22, 1970. A new motion to quash by respondent and memorandum in opposition by the Government were filed, and, by stipulation of the parties, the motion was submitted on the prior record. The court denied the motion to quash, repeating the protective provisions in its prior order but this time directing Caldwell to appear before the grand jury pursuant to the May 22 subpoena. Respondent refused to appear before the grand jury, and the court issued an order to show cause why he should not be held in contempt. Upon his further refusal to go before the grand jury, respondent was ordered committed for contempt until such time as he complied with the court's order or until the expiration of the term of the grand jury.

Respondent Caldwell appealed the contempt order, and the Court of Appeals reversed. Caldwell v. United States, 434 F.2d 1081 (CA9 1970). Viewing the issue before it as whether Caldwell was required to appear before the grand jury at all, rather than the scope of permissible interrogation, the court first determined that the First Amendment provided a qualified testimonial privilege to newsmen; in its view, requiring a reporter like Caldwell to testify would deter his informants from communicating with him in the future and would cause him to censor his writings in an effort to avoid being subpoenaed. Absent compelling reasons for requiring his testimony, he was held privileged to withhold it. The court also held, for similar First Amendment reasons, that, absent some special showing of necessity by the Government, attendance by Caldwell at a secret meeting of the grand jury was something he was privileged to refuse because of the potential impact of such an appearance on the flow of news to the public. We granted the United States' petition for certiorari. 402 U.S. 942 (1971).

II

Petitioners Branzburg and Pappas and respondent Caldwell press First Amendment claims that may be simply put: that, to gather news, it is often necessary to agree either not to identify the source of information published or to publish only part of the facts revealed, or both; that, if the reporter is nevertheless [p680] forced to reveal these confidences to a grand jury, the source so identified and other confidential sources of other reporters will be measurably deterred from furnishing publishable information, all to the detriment of the free flow of information protected by the First Amendment. Although the newsmen in these cases do not claim an absolute privilege against official interrogation in all circumstances, they assert that the reporter should not be forced either to appear or to testify before a grand jury or at trial until and unless sufficient grounds are shown for believing that the reporter possesses information relevant to a crime the grand jury is investigating, that the information the reporter has is unavailable from other sources, and that the need for the information is sufficiently compelling to override the claimed invasion of First Amendment interests occasioned by the disclosure. Principally relied upon are prior cases emphasizing the importance of the First Amendment guarantees to individual development and to our system of representative government, decisions requiring that official action with adverse impact on First Amendment rights be justified by a public interest that is "compelling" or "paramount," and those precedents establishing the principle that justifiable governmental goals may not be achieved by unduly broad means having an unnecessary impact on protected rights of speech, press, or association. The heart of the claim is that the burden on news gathering resulting from compelling reporters to disclose confidential information outweighs any public interest in obtaining the information.

We do not question the significance of free speech, press, or assembly to the country's welfare. Nor is it suggested that news gathering does not qualify for First Amendment protection; without some protection for seeking out the news, freedom of the press could be eviscerated. But these cases involve no intrusions upon speech or assembly, no prior restraint or restriction on what the press may publish, and no express or implied command that the press publish what it prefers to withhold. No exaction or tax for the privilege of publishing, and no penalty, civil or criminal, related to the content of published material is at issue here. The use of confidential sources by the press is not forbidden or restricted; reporters remain free to seek news from any source by means within the law. No attempt is made to require the press to publish its sources of information or indiscriminately to disclose them on request.

The sole issue before us is the obligation of reporters to respond to grand jury subpoenas as other citizens do, and to answer questions relevant to an investigation into the commission of crime. Citizens generally are not constitutionally immune from grand jury subpoenas, and neither the First Amendment nor any other constitutional provision protects the average citizen from disclosing to a grand jury information that he has received in confidence. The claim is, however, that reporters are exempt from these obligations because, if forced to respond to subpoenas and identify their sources or disclose other confidences, their informants will refuse or be reluctant to furnish newsworthy information in the future. This asserted burden on news gathering is said to make compelled testimony from newsmen constitutionally suspect, and to require a privileged position for them.

It is clear that the First Amendment does not invalidate every incidental burdening of the press that may result from the enforcement of civil or criminal statutes of general applicability. Under prior cases, otherwise valid laws serving substantial public interests may be enforced against the press as against others, despite the possible burden that may be imposed. The Court has emphasized that

[t]he publisher of a newspaper has no special immunity from the application of general laws. He has no special privilege to invade the rights and liberties of others.

Associated Press v. NLRB, 301 U.S. 103, 132-133 (1937). It was there held that the Associated Press, a news-gathering and disseminating organization, was not exempt from the requirements of the National Labor Relations Act. The holding was reaffirmed in Oklahoma Press Publishing Co. v. Walling, 327 U.S. 186, 192-193 (1946), where the Court rejected the claim that applying the Fair Labor Standards Act to a newspaper publishing business would abridge the freedom of press guaranteed by the First Amendment. See also Mabee v. White Plains Publishing Co., 327 U.S. 178 (1946). Associated Press v. United States, 326 U.S. 1 (1945), similarly overruled assertions that the First Amendment precluded application of the Sherman Act to a newsgathering and disseminating organization. Cf. Indiana Farmer's Guide Publishing Co. v. Prairie Farmer Publishing Co., 293 U.S. 268, 276 (1934); Citizen Publish in Co. v. United States, 394 U.S. 131, 139 (1969); Lorain Journal Co. v. United States, 342 U.S. 143, 155-156 (1951). Likewise, a newspaper may be subjected to nondiscriminatory forms of general taxation. Grosjean v. American Press Co., 297 U.S. 233, 250 (1936); Murdock v. Pennsylvania, 319 U.S. 105, 112 (1943).

The prevailing view is that the press is not free to publish with impunity everything and anything it desires to publish. Although it may deter or regulate what is said or published, the press may not circulate knowing or reckless falsehoods damaging to private reputation without subjecting itself to liability for damages, including punitive damages, or even criminal prosecution. See New York Times Co. v. Sullivan, 376 U.S. 254, 279-280 (1964); Garrison v. Louisiana, 379 U.S. 64, 74 (1964); Curtis Publishing Co. v. Butts, 388 U.S. 130, 147 (1967) (opinion of Harlan, J.,); Monitor Patriot Co. v. Roy, 401 U.S. 265, 277 (1971). A newspaper or a journalist may also be punished for contempt of court, in appropriate circumstances. Craig v. Harney, 331 U.S. 367, 377-378 (1947).

It has generally been held that the First Amendment does not guarantee the press a constitutional right of special access to information not available to the public generally. Zemel v. Rusk, 381 U.S. 1"] 381 U.S. 1, 16-17 (1965); 381 U.S. 1, 16-17 (1965); New York Times Co. v. United States, 403 U.S. 713, 728-730 (1971), (STEWART, J., concurring); Tribune Review Publishing Co. v. Thomas, 254 F.2d 883, 885 (CA3 1958); In the Matter of United Press Assns. v. Valente, 308 N.Y. 71, 77, 123 N.E.2d 777, 778 (1954). In Zemel v. Rusk, supra, for example, the Court sustained the Government's refusal to validate passports to Cuba even though that restriction "render[ed] less than wholly free the flow of information concerning that country." Id. at 16. The ban on travel was held constitutional, for "[t]he right to speak and publish does not carry with it the unrestrained right to gather information." Id. at 17.

Despite the fact that news gathering may be hampered, the press is regularly excluded from grand jury proceedings, our own conferences, the meetings of other official bodies gathered in executive session, and the meetings of private organizations. Newsmen have no constitutional right of access to the scenes of crime or disaster when the general public is excluded, and they may be prohibited from attending or publishing information about trials if such restrictions re necessary to assure a defendant a fair trial before an impartial tribunal. In Sheppard v. Maxwell, 384 U.S. 333 (1966), for example, the Court reversed a state court conviction where the trial court failed to adopt "stricter rules governing the use of the courtroom by newsmen, as Sheppard's counsel requested," neglected to insulate witnesses from the press, and made no "effort to control the release of leads, information, and gossip to the press by police officers, witnesses, and the counsel for both sides." Id. at 358, 359.

[T]he trial court might well have proscribed extrajudicial statements by any lawyer, party, witness, or court official which divulged prejudicial matters.

Id. at 361. See also Estes v. Texas, 381 U.S. 532, 539-540 (1965); Rideau v. Louisiana, 373 U.S. 723, 726 (1963).

It is thus not surprising that the great weight of authority is that newsmen are not exempt from the normal duty of appearing before a grand jury and answering questions relevant to a criminal investigation. At common law, courts consistently refused to recognize the existence of any privilege authorizing a newsman to refuse to reveal confidential information to a grand jury. See, e.g., Ex Parte Lawrence, 116 Cal. 298, 48 P. 124 (1897); Plunkett v. Hamilton, 136 Ga. 72, 70 S.E. 781 (1911); Clein v. State, 52 So.2d 117 (Fla.1950); In re Grunow, 84 N.J.L. 235, 85 A. 1011 (1913); People ex rel. Mooney v. Sheriff, 269 N.Y. 291, 199 N.E. 415 (1936); Joslyn v. People, 67 Colo. 297, 184 P. 375 (1919); Adams v. Associated Press, 46 F.R.D. 439 (SD Tex.1969); Brewster v. Boston Herald-Traveler Corp., 20 F.R.D. 416 (Mass.1957). See generally Annot., 7 A.L.R.3d 591 (1966). In 1958, a news gatherer asserted for the first time that the First Amendment exempted confidential information from public disclosure pursuant to a subpoena issued in a civil suit, Garland v. Torre, 259 F.2d 545 (CA2), cert. denied, 358 U.S. 910 (1958), but the claim was denied, and this argument has been almost uniformly rejected since then, although there are occasional dicta that, in circumstances not presented here, a newsman might be excused. In re Goodfader, 45 Haw. 317, 367 P.2d 472 (1961); In re Taylor, 412 Pa. 32, 193 A.2d 181 (1963); State v. Buchanan, 250 Ore. 244, 436 P.2d 729, cert. denied, 392 U.S. 905 (1968); Murphy v. Colorado (No.19604, Sup.Ct.Colo.), cert. denied, 365 U.S. 843 (1961) (unreported, discussed in In re Goodfader, supra, at 366, 367 P.2d at 498 (Mizuha, J., dissenting)). These courts have applied the presumption against the existence of an asserted testimonial privilege, United States v. Bryan, 339 U.S. 323, 331 (1950), and have concluded that the First Amendment interest asserted by the newsman was outweighed by the general obligation of a citizen to appear before a grand jury or at trial, pursuant to a subpoena, and give what information he possesses. The opinions of the state courts in Branzburg and Pappas are typical of the prevailing view, although a few recent cases, such as Caldwell, have recognized and given effect to some form of constitutional newsman's privilege. See State v. Knops, 49 Wis.2d 647, 183 N.W.2d 93 (1971) (dictum); Alioto v. Cowles Communications, Inc., C.A. No. 52150 (ND Cal.1969); In re Grand Jury Witnesses, 322 F.Supp. 573 (ND Cal.1970); People v. Dohrn, Crim. No. 69-3808 (Cook County, Ill., Cir. Ct.1970).

The prevailing constitutional view of the newsman's privilege is very much rooted in the ancient role of the grand jury that has the dual function of determining if there is probable cause to believe that a crime has been committed and of protecting citizens against unfounded [p687] criminal prosecutions. Grand jury proceedings are constitutionally mandated for the institution of federal criminal prosecutions for capital or other serious crimes, and "its constitutional prerogatives are rooted in long centuries of Anglo-American history." Hannah v. Larche, 363 U.S. 420, 489-490 (1960) (Frankfurter, J., concurring in result). The Fifth Amendment provides that "[n]o person shall be held to answer for a capital, or otherwise infamous crime, unless on a presentment or indictment of a Grand Jury." The adoption of the grand jury "in our Constitution as the sole method for preferring charges in serious criminal cases shows the high place it held as an instrument of justice." Costello v. United States, 350 U.S. 359, 362 (1956). Although state systems of criminal procedure differ greatly among themselves, the grand jury is similarly guaranteed by many state constitutions and plays an important role in fair and effective law enforcement in the overwhelming majority of the States. Because its task is to inquire into the existence of possible criminal conduct and to return only well founded indictments, its investigative powers are necessarily broad.

It is a grand inquest, a body with powers of investigation and inquisition, the scope of whose inquiries is not to be limited narrowly by questions of propriety or forecasts of the probable result of the investigation, or by doubts whether any particular individual will be found properly subject to an accusation of crime.

Blair v. United States, 250 U.S. 273, 282 (1919). Hence, the grand jury's authority to subpoena witnesses is not only historic, id. at 279-281, but essential to its task. Although the powers of the grand jury are not unlimited and are subject to the supervision of a judge, the long-standing principle that "the public . . . has a right to every man's evidence," except for those persons protected by a constitutional, common law, or statutory privilege, United States v. Bryan, 339 U.S. at 331; Blackmer v. United States, 284 U.S. 421, 438 (1932); 8 J. Wigmore, Evidence § 2192 (McNaughton rev.1961), is particularly applicable to grand jury proceedings.

A number of States have provided newsmen a statutory privilege of varying breadth, but the majority have not done so, and none has been provided by federal statute. [n28] Until now, the only testimonial privilege for unofficial witnesses that is rooted in the Federal Constitution is the Fifth Amendment privilege against compelled self-incrimination. We are asked to create another by interpreting the First Amendment to grant newsmen a testimonial privilege that other citizens do not enjoy. This we decline to do. Fair and effective law enforcement aimed at providing security for the person and property of the individual is a fundamental function of government, and the grand jury plays an important, constitutionally mandated role in this process. On the records now before us, we perceive no basis for holding hat the public interest in law enforcement and in ensuring effective grand jury proceedings if insufficient to override the consequential, but uncertain, burden on news gathering that is said to result from insisting that reporters, like other citizens, respond to relevant questions put to them in the course of a valid grand jury investigation or criminal trial.

This conclusion itself involves no restraint on what newspapers may publish or on the type or quality of information reporters may seek to acquire, nor does it threaten the vast bulk of confidential relationships between reporters and their sources. Grand juries address themselves to the issues of whether crimes have been committed and who committed them. Only where news sources themselves are implicated in crime or possess information relevant to the grand jury's task need they or the reporter be concerned about grand jury subpoenas. Nothing before us indicates that a large number or percentage of all confidential news sources falls into either category and would in any way be deterred by our holding that the Constitution does not, as it never has, exempt the newsman from performing the citizen's normal duty of appearing and furnishing information relevant to the grand jury's task.

The preference for anonymity of those confidential informants involved in actual criminal conduct is presumably a product of their desire to escape criminal prosecution, and this preference, while understandable, is hardly deserving of constitutional protection. It would be frivolous to assert -- and no one does in these cases -- that the First Amendment, in the interest of securing news or otherwise, confers a license on either the reporter or his news sources to violate valid criminal laws. Although stealing documents or private wiretapping could provide newsworthy information, neither reporter nor source is immune from conviction for such conduct, whatever the impact on the flow of news. Neither is immune, on First Amendment grounds, from testifying against the other, before the grand jury or at a criminal trial. The Amendment does not reach so far as to override the interest of the public in ensuring that neither reporter nor source is invading the rights of other citizens through reprehensible conduct forbidden to all other persons. To assert the contrary proposition

is to answer it, since it involves in its very statement the contention that the freedom of the press is the freedom to do wrong with impunity and implies the right to frustrate and defeat the discharge of those governmental duties upon the performance of which the freedom of all, in-

cluding that of the press, depends. . . . It suffices to say that, however complete is the right of the press to state public things and discuss them, that right, as every other right enjoyed in human society, is subject to the restraints which separate right from wrongdoing.

Toledo Newspaper Co. v. United States, 247 U.S. 402, 419-420 (1918).

Thus, we cannot seriously entertain the notion that the First Amendment protects a newsman's agreement to conceal the criminal conduct of his source, or evidence thereof, on the theory that it is better to write about crime than to do something about it. Insofar as any reporter in these cases undertook not to reveal or testify about the crime he witnessed, his claim of privilege under the First Amendment presents no substantial question. The crimes of news sources are no less reprehensible and threatening to the public interest when witnessed by a reporter than when they are not.

There remain those situations where a source is not engaged in criminal conduct but has information suggesting illegal conduct by others. Newsmen frequently receive information from such sources pursuant to a tacit or express agreement to withhold the source's name and suppress any information that the source wishes not published. Such informants presumably desire anonymity in order to avoid being entangled as a witness in a criminal trial or grand jury investigation. They may fear that disclosure will threaten their job security or personal safety, or that it will simply result in dishonor or embarrassment.

The argument that the flow of news will be diminished by compelling reporters to aid the grand jury in a criminal investigation is not irrational, nor are the records before us silent on the matter. But we remain unclear how often and to what extent informers are actually deterred from furnishing information when newsmen are forced to testify before a grand jury. The available data indicate that some newsmen rely a great deal on confidential sources, and that some informants are particularly sensitive to the threat of exposure, and may be silenced if it is held by this Court that, ordinarily, newsmen must testify pursuant to subpoenas, but the evidence fails to demonstrate that there would be a significant constriction of the flow of news to the public if this Court reaffirms the prior common law and constitutional rule regarding the testimonial obligations of newsmen. Estimates of the inhibiting effect of such subpoenas on the willingness of informants to make disclosures to newsmen are widely divergent and to a great extent speculative. It would be difficult to canvass the views of the informants themselves; surveys of reporters on this topic are chiefly opinions of predicted informant behavior and must be viewed in the light of the professional self-interest of the interviewees. Reliance by the press on confidential informants does not mean that all such sources will, in fact, dry up because of the later possible appearance of the newsman before a grand jury. The reporter may never be called, and, if he objects to testifying, the prosecution may not insist. Also, the relationship of many informants to the press is a symbiotic one which is unlikely to be greatly inhibited by the threat of subpoena: quite often, such informants are members of a minority political or cultural group that relies heavily on the media to propagate its views, publicize its aims, and magnify its exposure to the public. Moreover, grand juries characteristically conduct secret proceedings, and law enforcement officers are themselves experienced in dealing with informers, and have their own methods for protecting them without interference with the effective administration of justice. There is little before us indicating that informants whose interest in avoiding exposure is that it may threaten job security, personal safety, or peace of mind, would in fact, be in a worse position, or would think they would be, if they risked placing their trust in public officials as well as reporters. We doubt if the informer who prefers anonymity but is sincerely interested in furnishing evidence of crime will always or very often be deterred by the prospect of dealing with those public authorities characteristically charged with the duty to protect the public interest as well as his.

Accepting the fact, however, that an undetermined number of informants not themselves implicated in crime will nevertheless, for whatever reason, refuse to talk to newsmen if they fear identification by a reporter in an official investigation, we cannot accept the argument that the public interest in possible future news about crime from undisclosed, unverified sources must take precedence over the public interest in pursuing and prosecuting those crimes reported to the press by informants and in thus deterring the commission of such crimes in the future.

We note first that the privilege claimed is that of the reporter, not the informant, and that, if the authorities independently identify the informant, neither his own reluctance to testify nor the objection of the newsman would shield him from grand jury inquiry, whatever the impact on the flow of news or on his future usefulness as a secret source of information. More important, it is obvious that agreements to conceal information relevant to commission of crime have very little to recommend them from the standpoint of public policy. Historically, the common law recognized a duty to raise the "hue and cry" and report felonies to the authorities. Misprision of a felony -- that is, the concealment of a felony "which a man knows, but never assented to . . . [so as to become] either principal or accessory," 4 W. Blackstone, Commentaries *121, was often said to be a common law crime. The first Congress passed a statute, 1 Stat. 113, § 6, as amended, 35 Stat. 1114, § 146, 62 Stat. 884, which is still in effect, defining a federal crime of misprision:

Whoever, having knowledge of the actual commission of a felony cognizable by a court of the United States, conceals and does not as soon as possible make known the same to some judge or other person in civil or military authority under the United States, shall be [guilty of misprision].

18 U.S.C. § 4. It is apparent from this statute, as well as from our history and that of England, that concealment of crime and agreements to do so are not looked upon with favor. Such conduct deserves no encomium, and we decline now to afford it First Amendment protection by denigrating the duty of a citizen, whether reporter or informer, to re-

spond to grand jury subpoena and answer relevant questions put to him.

Of course, the press has the right to abide by its agreement not to publish all the information it has, but the right to withhold news is not equivalent to a First Amendment exemption from the ordinary duty of all other citizens to furnish relevant information to a grand jury performing an important public function. Private restraints on the flow of information are not so favored by the First Amendment that they override all other public interests. As Mr. Justice Black declared in another context,

[f]reedom of the press from governmental interference under the First Amendment does not sanction repression of that freedom by private interests.

Associated Press v. United States, 326 U.S. at 20.

Neither are we now convinced that a virtually impenetrable constitutional shield, beyond legislative or judicial control, should be forged to protect a private system of informers operated by the press to report on criminal conduct, a system that would be unaccountable to the public, would pose a threat to the citizen's justifiable expectations of privacy, and would equally protect well intentioned informants and those who for pay or otherwise betray their trust to their employer or associates. The public, through its elected and appointed law enforcement officers regularly utilizes informers, and in proper circumstances may assert a privilege against disclosing the identity of these informers. But

[t]he purpose of the privilege is the furtherance and protection of the public interest in effective law enforcement. The privilege recognizes the obligation of citizens to communicate their knowledge of the commission of crimes to law enforcement officials and, by preserving their anonymity, encourages them to perform that obligation.

Roviaro v. United States, 353 U.S. 53, 59 (1957). Such informers enjoy no constitutional protection. Their testimony is available to the public when desired by grand juries or at criminal trials; their identity cannot be concealed from the defendant when it is critical to his case. Id. at 60-61, 62; McCray v. Illinois, 386 U.S. 300, 310 (1967); Smith v. Illinois, 390 U.S. 129, 131 (1968); Alford v. United States, 282 U.S. 687, 693 (1931). Clearly, this system is not impervious to control by the judiciary and the decision whether to unmask an informer or to continue to profit by his anonymity is in public, not private, hands. We think that it should remain there and that public authorities should retain the options of either insisting on the informer's testimony relevant to the prosecution of crime or of seeking the benefit of further information that his exposure might prevent.

We are admonished that refusal to provide a First Amendment reporter's privilege will undermine the freedom of the press to collect and disseminate news. But this is not the lesson history teaches us. As noted previously, the common law recognized no such privilege, and the constitutional argument was not even asserted until 1958. From the beginning of our country the press has operated without constitutional protection for press informants, and the press has flourished. The existing constitutional rules have not been a serious obstacle to either the development or retention of confidential news sources by the press.

It is said that currently press subpoenas have multiplied, that mutual distrust and tension between press and officialdom have increased, that reporting styles have changed, and that there is now more need for confidential sources, particularly where the press seeks news about minority cultural and political groups or dissident organizations suspicious of the law and public officials. These developments, even if true, are treacherous grounds for a far-reaching interpretation of the First Amendment fastening a nationwide rule on courts, grand juries, and prosecuting officials everywhere. The obligation to testify in response to grand jury subpoenas will not threaten these sources not involved with criminal conduct and without information relevant to grand jury investigations, and we cannot hold that the Constitution places the sources in these two categories either above the law or beyond its reach.

The argument for such a constitutional privilege rests heavily on those cases holding that the infringement of protected First Amendment rights must be no broader than necessary to achieve a permissible governmental purpose, see cases cited at 408 U.S. 665 n19"]n.19, supra. We do not deal, however, with a governmental institution that has abused its proper function, as a legislative committee does when it "expose[s] for the sake of exposure." n.19, supra. We do not deal, however, with a governmental institution that has abused its proper function, as a legislative committee does when it "expose[s] for the sake of exposure." Watkins v. United States, 354 U.S. 178"] 354 U.S. 178, 200 (157). Nothing in the record indicates that these grand juries were "prob[ing] at will and without relation to existing need." DeGregory v. Attorney General of New Hampshire, 383 U.S. 825, 829 (1966). Nor did the grand juries attempt to invade protected First Amendment rights by forcing wholesale disclosure of names and organizational affiliations for a purpose that was not germane to the determination of whether crime has been committed, cf. NAACP v. Alabama, 357 U.S. 449 (1958); 354 U.S. 178, 200 (157). Nothing in the record indicates that these grand juries were "prob[ing] at will and without relation to existing need." DeGregory v. Attorney General of New Hampshire, 383 U.S. 825, 829 (1966). Nor did the grand juries attempt

The three minimal tests we contend must be met before testimony divulging confidences may be compelled from a reporter are these:

1. The government must clearly show that there is probable cause to believe that the reporter possesses information which is specifically relevant to a specific probable violation of law.

2. The government must clearly show that the information it seeks cannot be obtained by alternative means, which is to say, from sources other than the reporter.

3. The government must clearly demonstrate a compelling and overriding interest in the information.

Brief for New York Times as Amicus Curiae 29.

to invade protected First Amendment rights by forcing wholesale disclosure of names and organizational affiliations for a purpose that was not germane to the determination of whether crime has been committed, cf. NAACP v. Alabama, 357 U.S. 449 (1958); NAACP v. Button, 371 U.S. 415 (1963); Bates v. Little Rock, 361 U.S. 516 (1960), and the characteristic secrecy of grand jury proceedings is a further protection against the undue invasion of such rights. See Fed.Rule Crim.Proc. 6(e). The investigative power of the grand jury is necessarily broad if its public responsibility is to be adequately discharged. Costello v. United States, 350 U.S. at 364.

The requirements of those cases, see n. 18, supra, which hold that a State's interest must be "compelling" or "paramount" to justify even an indirect burden on First Amendment rights, are also met here. As we have indicated, the investigation of crime by the grand jury implements a fundamental governmental role of securing the safety of the person and property of the citizen, and it appears to us that calling reporters to give testimony in the manner and for the reasons that other citizens are called "bears a reasonable relationship to the achievement of the governmental purpose asserted as its justification." Bates v. Little Rock, supra, at 525. If the test is that the government "convincingly show a substantial relation between the information sought and a subject of overriding and compelling state interest," Gibson v. Florida Legislative Investigation Committee, 372 U.S. 539, 546 (1963), it is quite apparent (1) that the State has the necessary interest in extirpating the traffic in illegal drugs, in forestalling assassination attempts on the President, and in preventing the community from being disrupted by violent disorders endangering both persons and property; and (2) that, based on the stories Branzburg and Caldwell wrote and Pappas' admitted conduct, the grand jury called these reporters as they would others -- because it was likely that they could supply information to help the government determine whether illegal conduct had occurred and, if it had, whether there was sufficient evidence to return an indictment.

Similar considerations dispose of the reporters' claims that preliminary to requiring their grand jury appearance, the State must show that a crime has been committed and that they possess relevant information not available from other sources, for only the grand jury itself can make this determination. The role of the grand jury as an important instrument of effective law enforcement necessarily includes an investigatory function with respect to determining whether a crime has been committed and who committed it. To this end it must call witnesses, in the manner best suited to perform its task.

When the grand jury is performing its investigatory function into a general problem area . . . society's interest is best served by a thorough and extensive investigation.

Wood v. Georgia, 370 U.S. 375, 392 (1962). A grand jury investigation

is not fully carried out until every available clue has been run down and all witnesses examined in every proper way to find if a crime has been committed.

United States v. Stone, 429 F.2d 138, 140 (CA2 1970). Such an investigation may be triggered by tips, rumors, evidence proffered by the prosecutor, or the personal knowledge of the grand jurors. Costello v. United States, 350 U.S. at 362. It is only after the grand jury has examined the evidence that a determination of whether the proceeding will result in an indictment can be made.

It is impossible to conceive that in such cases the examination of witnesses must be stopped until a basis is laid by an indictment formally preferred, when the very object of the examination is to ascertain who shall be indicted.

Hale v. Henkel, 201 U.S. 43, 65 (1906). See also Hendricks v. United States, 223 U.S. 178 (1912); Blair v. United States, 250 U.S. at 282-283. We see no reason to hold that these reporters, any more than other citizens, should be excused from furnishing information that may help the grand jury in arriving at its initial determinations.

The privilege claimed here is conditional, not absolute; given the suggested preliminary showings and compelling need, the reporter would be required to testify. Presumably, such a rule would reduce the instances in which reporters could be required to appear, but predicting in advance when and in what circumstances they could be compelled to do so would be difficult. Such a rule would also have implications for the issuance of compulsory process to reporters at civil and criminal trials and at legislative hearings. If newsmen's confidential sources are as sensitive as they are claimed to be, the prospect of being unmasked whenever a judge determines the situation justifies it is hardly a satisfactory solution to the problem. For them, it would appear that only an absolute privilege would suffice.

We are unwilling to embark the judiciary on a long and difficult journey to such an uncertain destination. The administration of a constitutional newsman's privilege would present practical and conceptual difficulties of a high order. Sooner or later, it would be necessary to define those categories of newsmen who qualified for the privilege, a questionable procedure in light of the traditional doctrine that liberty of the press is the right of the lonely pamphleteer who uses carbon paper or a mimeograph just as much as of the large metropolitan publisher who utilizes the latest photocomposition methods. Cf. In re Grand Jury Witnesses, 322 F.Supp. 573, 574 (ND Cal.1970). Freedom of the press is a "fundamental personal right" which is not confined to newspapers and periodicals. It necessarily embraces pamphlets and leaflets. . . . The press in its historic connotation comprehends every sort of publication which affords a vehicle of information and opinion.

Lovell v. Griffin, 303 U.S. 444, 450, 452 (138). See also Mills v. Alabama, 34 U.S. 214, 219 (1966); Murdock v. Pennsylvania, 319 U.S. 105, 111 (1943). The informative function asserted by representatives of the organized press in the present cases is also performed by lecturers, political pollsters, novelists, academic researchers, and dramatists. Almost any author may quite accurately assert that he is contributing to the flow of information to the public, that he relies on confidential sources of information, and that these sources will be silenced if he is forced to make disclosures before a grand jury.

In each instance where a reporter is subpoenaed to testify, the courts would also be embroiled in preliminary factual and legal determinations with respect to whether the proper predicate had been laid for the reporter's appearance: Is there probable cause to believe a crime has been committed? Is it likely that the reporter has useful information gained in confidence? Could the grand jury obtain the information elsewhere? Is the official interest sufficient to outweigh the claimed privilege?

Thus, in the end, by considering whether enforcement of a particular law served a "compelling" governmental interest, the courts would be inextricably involved in distinguishing between the value of enforcing different criminal laws. By requiring testimony from a reporter in investigations involving some crimes but not in others, they would be making a value judgment that a legislature had declined to make, since, in each case, the criminal law involved would represent a considered legislative judgment, not constitutionally suspect, of what conduct is liable to criminal prosecution. The task of judges, like other officials outside the legislative branch, is not to make the law, but to uphold it in accordance with their oaths.

At the federal level, Congress has freedom to determine whether a statutory newsman's privilege is necessary and desirable and to fashion standards and rules as narrow or broad as deemed necessary to deal with the evil discerned and, equally important, to refashion those rules as experience from time to time may dictate. There is also merit in leaving state legislatures free, within First Amendment limits, to fashion their own standards in light of the conditions and problems with respect to the relations between law enforcement officials and press in their own areas. It goes without saying, of course, that we are powerless to bar state courts from responding in their own way and construing their own constitutions so as to recognize a newsman's privilege, either qualified or absolute.

In addition, there is much force in the pragmatic view that the press has at its disposal powerful mechanisms of communication, and is far from helpless to protect itself from harassment or substantial harm. Furthermore, if what the newsmen urged in these cases is true -- that law enforcement cannot hope to gain, and may suffer from subpoenaing newsmen before grand juries -- prosecutors will be loath to risk so much for so little. Thus, at the federal level, the Attorney General has already fashioned a set of rules for federal officials in connection with subpoenaing members of the press to testify before grand juries or at criminal trials. These rules are a major step in the direction the reporters herein desire to move. They may prove wholly sufficient to resolve the bulk of disagreements and controversies between press and federal officials.

Finally, as we have earlier indicated, news gathering is not without its First Amendment protections, and grand jury investigations, if instituted or conducted other than in good faith, would pose wholly different issues for resolution under the First Amendment. Official harassment of the press undertaken not for purposes of law enforcement, but to disrupt a reporter's relationship with his news sources would have no justification. Grand juries are subject to judicial control and subpoenas to motions to quash. We do not expect courts will forget that grand juries must operate within the limits of the First Amendment as well as the Fifth.

## III

We turn, therefore, to the disposition of the cases before us. From what we have said, it necessarily follows that the decision in United States v. Caldwell, No. 70-57, must be reversed. If there is no First Amendment privilege to refuse to answer the relevant and material questions asked during a good faith grand jury investigation, then it is a fortiori true that there is no privilege to refuse to appear before such a grand jury until the Government demonstrates some "compelling need" for a newsman's testimony. Other issues were urged upon us, but since they were not passed upon by the Court of Appeals, we decline to address them in the first instance.

The decisions in No. 70-85, Branzburg v. Hayes and Branzburg v. Meigs, must be affirmed. Here, petitioner refused to answer question that directly related to criminal conduct that he had observed and written about. The Kentucky Court of Appeals noted that marihuana is defined as a narcotic drug by statute, Ky.Rev.Stat. § 218.010(14) (1962), and that unlicensed possession or compounding of it is a felony punishable by both fine and imprisonment. Ky.Rev.Stat. § 218.210 (1962). It held that petitioner "saw the commission of the statutory felonies of unlawful possession of marijuana and the unlawful conversion of it into hashish," in Branzburg v. Pound, 461 S.W.2d at 346. Petitioner may be presumed to have observed similar violations of the state narcotics laws during the research he did for the story that forms the basis of the subpoena in Branzburg v. Meigs. In both cases, if what petitioner wrote was true, he had direct information to provide the grand jury concerning the commission of serious crimes.

The only question presented at the present time in In re Pappas, No. 70-94, is whether petitioner Pappas must appear before the grand jury to testify pursuant to subpoena. The Massachusetts Supreme Judicial Court characterized the record in this case as "meager," and it is not clear what petitioner will be asked by the grand jury. It is not even clear that he will be asked to divulge information received in confidence. We affirm the decision of the Massachusetts Supreme Judicial Court and hold that petitioner must appear before the grand jury to answer the questions put to him, subject, of course, to the supervision of the presiding judge as to "the propriety, purposes, and scope of the grand jury inquiry and the pertinence of the probable testimony." 358 Mass. at 614, 266 N.E.2d at 303-304.

So ordered.

MR. JUSTICE POWELL, concurring.

I add this brief statement to emphasize what seems to me to be the limited nature of the Court's holding. The Court does not hold that newsmen, subpoenaed to testify before a grand jury, are without constitutional rights with respect to the gathering of news or in safeguarding their sources. Certainly, we do not hold, as suggested in MR. JUSTICE STEWART's dissenting opinion, that state and federal authorities are free to "annex" the news media as "an investigative arm of government." ....

In short, the courts will be available to newsmen under circumstances where legitimate First Amendment interests require protection.

## MR. JUSTICE DOUGLAS, dissenting in No. 757, United States v. Caldwell.

Caldwell, a black, is a reporter for the New York Times and was assigned to San Francisco with the hope that he could report on the activities and attitudes of the Black Panther Party. Caldwell in time gained the complete confidence of its members, and wrote in-depth articles about them.

He was subpoenaed to appear and testify before a federal grand jury and to bring with him notes and tapes covering interviews with its members. A hearing on a motion to quash was held. The District Court ruled that, while Caldwell had to appear before the grand jury, he did not have to reveal confidential communications unless the court was satisfied that there was a "compelling and overriding national interest." See 311 F.Supp. 358, 362. Caldwell filed a notice of appeal and the Court of Appeals dismissed the appeal without opinion.

Shortly thereafter, a new grand jury was impaneled and it issued a new subpoena for Caldwell to testify. On a motion to quash, the District Court issued an order substantially identical to its earlier one.

Caldwell refused to appear, and was held in contempt. On appeal, the Court of Appeals vacated the judgment of contempt. It said that the revealing of confidential sources of information jeopardized a First Amendment freedom and that Caldwell did not have to appear before the grand jury absent a showing that there was a "compelling and overriding national interest" in pursuing such an interrogation.

The District Court had found that Caldwell's knowledge of the activities of the Black Panthers "derived in substantial part" from information obtained "within the scope of a relationship of trust and confidence." Id. at 361. It also found that confidential relationships of this sort are commonly developed and maintained by [p712] professional journalists, and are indispensable to their work of gathering, analyzing, and publishing the news.

The District Court further had found that compelled disclosure of information received by a journalist within the scope of such confidential relationships jeopardized those relationships, and thereby impaired the journalist's ability to gather, analyze, and publish the news.

....

The Court of Appeals agreed with the findings of the District Court, but held that Caldwell did not have to appear at all before the grand jury absent a "compelling need" shown by the Government. 434 F.2d 1081.

....

II

Today's decision will impede the wide-open and robust dissemination of ideas and counterthought which a free press both fosters and protects and which is essential to the success of intelligent self-government. Forcing a reporter before a grand jury will have two retarding effects upon the ear and the pen of the press. Fear of exposure will cause dissidents to communicate less openly to trusted reporters. And fear of accountability will cause editors and critics to write with more restrained pens.

....

I would also reverse the judgments in No. 785, Branzburg v. Hayes, and No. 794, In re Pappas, for the reasons stated in the above dissent in No. 757, United States v. Caldwell.

**MR. JUSTICE STEWART, with whom MR. JUSTICE BRENNAN and MR. JUSTICE MARSHALL join, dissenting.**

The Court's crabbed view of the First Amendment reflect a disturbing insensitivity to the critical role of an independent press in our society. The question whether a reporter has a constitutional right to a confidential relationship with his source is of first impression here, but the principles that should guide our decision are as basic as any to be found in the Constitution. While MR. JUSTICE POWELL's enigmatic concurring opinion gives some hope of a more flexible view in the future, the Court in these cases holds that a newsman has no First Amendment right to protect his sources when called before a grand jury. The Court thus invites state and federal authorities to undermine the historic independence of the press by attempting to annex the journalistic profession as an investigative arm of government. Not only will this decision impair performance of the press' constitutionally protected functions, but it will, I am convinced, in the long run harm, rather than help, the administration of justice.

I respectfully dissent.

# CHAPTER 11

# Indeceny and obscenity

# Federal Communications Commission v. Pacifica Foundation (1978)

U.S. Supreme Court

38 U.S. 726 (1978)

Decided July 3, 1978

Burger  Blackmun  Powell  Rehnquist  **Stevens**  Brennan  Stewart  White  Marshall

Decision: 5 votes for FCC, 4 vote(s) against

**MR. JUSTICE STEVENS delivered the opinion of the Court (Parts I, II, III, and IV-C) and an opinion in which THE CHIEF JUSTICE and MR. JUSTICE REHNQUIST joined (Parts IV-A and IV-B).**

This case requires that we decide whether the Federal Communications Commission has any power to regulate a radio broadcast that is indecent but not obscene.

A satiric humorist named George Carlin recorded a 12-minute monologue entitled "Filthy Words" before a live audience in a California theater. He began by referring to his thoughts about "the words you couldn't say on the public, ah, airwaves, um, the ones you definitely wouldn't say, ever." He proceeded to list those words and repeat them over and over again in a variety of colloquialisms. The transcript of the recording, which is appended to this opinion, indicates frequent laughter from the audience.

At about 2 o'clock in the afternoon on Tuesday, October 30, 1973, a New York radio station, owned by respondent Pacifica Foundation, broadcast the "Filthy Words" monologue. A few weeks later a man, who stated that he had heard the broadcast while driving with his young son, wrote a letter complaining to the Commission. He stated that, although he could perhaps understand the "record's being sold for private use, I certainly cannot understand the broadcast of same over the air that, supposedly, you control."

The complaint was forwarded to the station for comment. I n its response, Pacifica explained that the monologue had been played during a program about contemporary society's attitude toward language, and that, immediately before its broadcast, listeners had been advised that it included "sensitive language which might be regarded as offensive to some." Pacifica characterized George Carlin as "a significant social satirist" who,

"like Twain and Sahl before him, examines the language of ordinary people. . . . Carlin is not mouthing obscenities, he is merely using words to satirize as harmless and essentially silly our attitudes towards those words."

Pacifica stated that it was not aware of any other complaints about the broadcast.

On February 21, 1975, the Commission issued a declaratory order granting the complaint and holding that Pacifica "could have been the subject of administrative sanctions." 56 F.C.C.2d 94, 99. The Commission did not impose formal sanctions, but it did state that the order would be

"associated with the station's license file, and, in the event that subsequent complaints are received, the Commission will then decide whether it should utilize any of the available sanctions it has been granted by Congress. "

In its memorandum opinion, the Commission stated that it intended to "clarify the standards which will be utilized in considering" the growing number of complaints about indecent speech on the airwaves. Id. at 94. Advancing several reasons for treating broadcast speech differently from other forms of expression, the Commission found a power to regulate indecent broadcasting in two statutes: 18 U.S.C. § 1464 (1976 ed.), which forbids the use of "any obscene, indecent, or profane language by means of radio communications," and 47 U.S.C. § 303(g), which requires the Commission to "encourage the larger and more effective use of radio in the public interest."

The Commission characterized the language used in the Carlin monologue as "patently offensive," though not necessarily obscene, and expressed the opinion that it should be regulated by principles analogous to those found in the law of nuisance, where the

"law generally speaks to channeling behavior more than actually prohibiting it. . . . [T]he concept of 'indecent' is intimately connected with the exposure of children to language that describes, in terms patently offensive as measured by contemporary community standards for the broadcast medium, sexual or excretory activities and organs, at times

of the day when there is a reasonable risk that children may be in the audience."

56 F.C.C.2d at 98.

Applying these considerations to the language used in the monologue as broadcast by respondent, the Commission concluded that certain words depicted sexual and excretory activities in a patently offensive manner, noted that they "were broadcast at a time when children were undoubtedly in the audience (i.e., in the early afternoon)," and that the prerecorded language, with these offensive words "repeated over and over," was "deliberately broadcast." Id. at 99. In summary, the Commission stated: "We therefore hold that the language as broadcast was indecent and prohibited by 18 U.S.C. [§] 1464. " Ibid.

After the order issued, the Commission was asked to clarify its opinion by ruling that the broadcast of indecent words as part of a live newscast would not be prohibited. The Commission issued another opinion in which it pointed out that it

"never intended to place an absolute prohibition on the broadcast of this type of language, but rather sought to channel it to times of day when children most likely would not be exposed to it."

59 F.C.C.2d 892 (1976). The Commission noted that its "declaratory order was issued in a specific factual context," and declined to comment on various hypothetical situations presented by the petition. Id. at 893. It relied on its

"long-standing policy of refusing to issue interpretive rulings or advisory opinions when the critical facts are not explicitly stated or there is a possibility that subsequent events will alter them."

Ibid.

The United States Court of Appeals for the District of Columbia Circuit reversed, with each of the three judges on the panel writing separately.

181 U.S.App.D.C. 132, 556 F.2d 9. Judge Tamm concluded that the order represented censorship and was expressly prohibited by § 326 of the Communications Act. Alternatively, Judge Tamm read the Commission opinion as the functional equivalent of a rule, and concluded that it was "overbroad." 181 U.S.App.D.C. at 141, 556 F.2d at 18. Chief Judge Bazelon's concurrence rested on the Constitution. He was persuaded that § 326's prohibition against censorship is inapplicable to broadcasts forbidden by § 1464. However, he concluded that § 1464 must be narrowly construed to cover only language that is obscene or otherwise unprotected by the First Amendment. 181 U.S.App.D.C. at 140-153, 556 F.2d at 24-30. Judge Leventhal, in dissent, stated that the only issue was whether the Commission could regulate the language "as broadcast." Id. at 154, 556 F.2d at 31. Emphasizing the interest in protecting children not only from exposure to indecent language, but also from exposure to the idea that such language has official approval, id. at 160, and n. 18, 556 F.2d at 37, and n. 18, he concluded that the Commission had correctly condemned the daytime broadcast as indecent.

Having granted the Commission's petition for certiorari, 434 U.S. 1008, we must decide: (1) whether the scope of judicial review encompasses more than the Commission's determination that the monologue was indecent "as broadcast"; (2) whether the Commission's order was a form of censorship forbidden by § 326; (3) whether the broadcast was indecent within the meaning of § 1464; and (4) whether the order violates the First Amendment of the United States Constitution.

## I

The general statements in the Commission's memorandum opinion do not change the character of its order. Its action was an adjudication under 5 U.S.C. § 554(e) (1976 ed.); it did not purport to engage in formal rulemaking or in the promulgation of any regulations. The order "was issued in a specific factual context"; questions concerning possible ac-

tion in other contexts were expressly reserved for the future. The specific holding was carefully confined to the monologue "as broadcast."

"This Court . . . reviews judgments, not statements in opinions." Black v. Cutter Laboratories, 351 U. S. 292, 351 U. S. 297. That admonition has special force when the statements raise constitutional questions, for it is our settled practice to avoid the unnecessary decision of such issues. Rescue Army v. Municipal Court, 331 U. S. 549, 331 U. S. 568 569. However appropriate it may be for an administrative agency to write broadly in an adjudicatory proceeding, federal courts have never been empowered to issue advisory opinions. See Herb v. Pitcairn, 324 U. S. 117, 324 U. S. 126. Accordingly, the focus of our review must be on the Commission's determination that the Carlin monologue was indecent as broadcast.

## II

The relevant statutory questions are whether the Commission's action is forbidden "censorship" within the meaning of 47 U.S.C. § 326 and whether speech that concededly is not obscene may be restricted as "indecent" under the authority of 18 U.S.C. § 1464 (1976 ed.). The questions are not unrelated, for the two statutory provisions have a common origin. Nevertheless, we analyze them separately.

Section 29 of the Radio Act of 1927 provided:

"Nothing in this Act shall be understood or construed to give the licensing authority the power of censorship over the radio communications or signals transmitted by any radio station, and no regulation or condition shall be promulgated or fixed by the licensing authority which shall interfere with the right of free speech by means of radio communications. No person within the jurisdiction of the United States shall utter any obscene, indecent, or profane language by means of radio communication."

44 Stat. 1172.

The prohibition against censorship unequivocally denies the Commission any power to edit proposed broadcasts in advance and to excise material considered inappropriate for the airwaves. The prohibition, however, has never been construed to deny the Commission the power to review the content of completed broadcasts in the performance of its regulatory duties. During the period between the original enactment of the provision in 1927 and its reenactment in the Communications Act of 1934, the courts and the Federal Radio Commission held that the section deprived the Commission of the power to subject "broadcasting matter to scrutiny prior to its release," but they concluded that the Commission's "undoubted right" to take note of past program content when considering a licensee's renewal application "is not censorship."

Not only did the Federal Radio Commission so construe the statute prior to 1934; its successor, the Federal Communications Commission, has consistently interpreted the provision in the same way ever since. See Note, Regulation of Program Content by the FCC, 77 Harv.L.Rev. 701 (1964). And, until this case, the Court of Appeals for the District of Columbia Circuit has consistently agreed with this construction. Thus, for example, in his opinion in Anti-Defamation League of B'nai B'rith v. FCC, 131 U.S.App.D.C. 146, 403 F.2d 169 (1968), cert. denied, 394 U.S. 930, Judge Wright forcefully pointed out that the Commission is not prevented from canceling the license of a broadcaster who persists in a course of improper programming. He explained:

"This would not be prohibited 'censorship' . . . any more than would the Commission's considering on a license renewal application whether a broadcaster allowed 'coarse, vulgar, suggestive, double-meaning' programming; programs containing such material are grounds for denial of a license renewal."

131 U.S.App.D.C. at 150-151, n. 3, 403 F.2d at 173-174, n. 3. See also Office of Communication of United Church of Christ v. FCC, 123 U.S.App.D.C. 328, 359 F.2d 994 (1966).

Entirely apart from the fact that the subsequent review of program content is not the sort of censorship at which the statute was directed, its history makes it perfectly clear that it was not intended to limit the Commission's power to regulate the broadcast of obscene, indecent, or profane language. A single section of the 1927 Act is the source of both the anti-censorship provision and the Commission's authority to impose sanctions for the broadcast of indecent or obscene language. Quite plainly, Congress intended to give meaning to both provisions. Respect for that intent requires that the censorship language be read as inapplicable to the prohibition on broadcasting obscene, indecent, or profane language.

There is nothing in the legislative history to contradict this conclusion. The provision was discussed only in generalities when it was first enacted. In 1934, the anti-censorship provision and the prohibition against indecent broadcasts were reenacted in the same section, just as in the 1927 Act. In 1948, when the Criminal Code was revised to include provisions that had previously been located in other Titles of the United States Code, the prohibition against obscene, indecent, and profane broadcasts was removed from the Communications Act and reenacted as § 1464 of Title 18. 62 Stat. 769 and 866. That rearrangement of the Code cannot reasonably be interpreted as having been intended to change the meaning of the anti-censorship provision. H.R.Rep. No. 304, 80th Cong., 1st Sess., A106 (1947). Cf. Tidewater Oil Co. v. United States, 409 U. S. 151, 409 U. S. 162.

We conclude, therefore, that § 326 does not limit the Commission's authority to impose sanctions on licensees who engage in obscene, indecent, or profane broadcasting.

III

The only other statutory question presented by this case is whether the afternoon broadcast of the "Filthy Words" monologue was indecent within the meaning of § 1464. Even that question is narrowly confined by the arguments of the parties.

The Commission identified several words that referred to excretory or sexual activities or organs, stated that the repetitive, deliberate use of those words in an afternoon broadcast when children are in the audience was patently offensive, and held that the broadcast was indecent. Pacifica takes issue with the Commission's definition of indecency, but does not dispute the Commission's preliminary determination that each of the components of its definition was present. Specifically, Pacifica does not quarrel with the conclusion that this afternoon broadcast was patently offensive. Pacifica's claim that the broadcast was not indecent within the meaning of the statute rests entirely on the absence of prurient appeal.

The plain language of the statute does not support Pacifica's argument. The words "obscene, indecent, or profane" are written in the disjunctive, implying that each has a separate meaning. Prurient appeal is an element of the obscene, but the normal definition of "indecent" merely refers to nonconformance with accepted standards of morality.

Pacifica argues, however, that this Court has construed the term "indecent" in related statutes to mean "obscene," as that term was defined in Miller v. California, 413 U. S. 15. Pacifica relies most heavily on the construction this Court gave to 18 U.S.C. § 1461 in Hamling v. United States, 418 U. S. 87. See also United States v. 12 200-ft. Reels of Film, 413 U. S. 123, 413 U. S. 130 n. 7 (18 U.S.C. § 1462) (dicta). Hamling rejected a vagueness attack on § 1461, which forbids the mailing of "obscene, lewd, lascivious, indecent, filthy or vile" material. In holding that the statute's coverage is limited to obscenity, the Court followed the lead of Mr. Justice Harlan in Manual Enterprises, Inc. v. Day, 370 U. S. 478. In that case, Mr. Justice Harlan recognized that § 1461 contained a variety of words with many shades of meaning. Nonetheless, he thought that the phrase "obscene, lewd, lascivious, indecent, filthy or vile," taken as a whole, was clearly limited to the obscene, a reading

well grounded in prior judicial constructions: "[T]he statute, since its inception, has always been taken as aimed at obnoxiously debasing portrayals of sex." 370 U.S. at 370 U. S. 483. In Hamling, the Court agreed with Mr. Justice Harlan that § 1461 was meant only to regulate obscenity in the mails; by reading into it the limits set by Miller v. California, supra, the Court adopted a construction which assured the statute's constitutionality.

The reasons supporting Hamling's construction of § 1461 do not apply to § 1464. Although the history of the former revealed primary concern with the prurient, the Commission has long interpreted § 1464 as encompassing more than the obscene. The former statute deals primarily with printed matter enclosed in sealed envelopes mailed from one individual to another; the latter deals with the content of public broadcasts. It is unrealistic to assume that Congress intended to impose precisely the same limitations on the dissemination of patently offensive matter by such different means. Because neither our prior decisions nor the language or history of § 1464 supports the conclusion that prurient appeal is an essential component of indecent language, we reject Pacifica's construction of the statute. When that construction is put to one side, there is no basis for disagreeing with the Commission's conclusion that indecent language was used in this broadcast.


IV

Pacifica makes two constitutional attacks on the Commission's order. First, it argues that the Commission's construction of the statutory language broadly encompasses so much constitutionally protected speech that reversal is required even if Pacifica's broadcast of the "Filthy Words" monologue is not itself protected by the First Amendment. Second, Pacifica argues that, inasmuch as the recording is not obscene, the Constitution forbids any abridgment of the right to broadcast it on the radio.

A

The first argument fails because our review is limited to the question whether the Commission has the authority to proscribe this particular broadcast. As the Commission itself emphasized, its order was "issued in a specific factual context." 59 F.C.C.2d at 893. That approach is appropriate for courts as well as the Commission when regulation of indecency is at stake, for indecency is largely a function of context -- it cannot be adequately judged in the abstract.

The approach is also consistent with Red Lion Broadcasting Co. v. FCC, 395 U. S. 367. In that case, the Court rejected an argument that the Commission's regulations defining the fairness doctrine were so vague that they would inevitably abridge the broadcasters' freedom of speech. The Court of Appeals had invalidated the regulations because their vagueness might lead to self-censorship of controversial program content. Radio Television News Directors Assn. v. United States, 400 F.2d 1002, 1016 (CA7 1968). This Court reversed. After noting that the Commission had indicated, as it has in this case, that it would not impose sanctions without warning in cases in which the applicability of the law was unclear, the Court stated:

"We need not approve every aspect of the fairness doctrine to decide these cases, and we will not now pass upon the constitutionality of these regulations by envisioning the most extreme applications conceivable, United States v. Sullivan, 332 U. S. 689, 332 U. S. 694 (1948), but will deal with those problems if and when they arise."

It is true that the Commission's order may lead some broadcasters to censor themselves. At most, however, the Commission's definition of indecency will deter only the broadcasting of patently offensive references to excretory and sexual organs and activities. While some of these references may be protected, they surely lie at the periphery of First Amendment concern. Cf. Bates v. State Bar of Arizona, 433 U. S. 350, 433 U. S. 380-381. Young v. American Mini Theatres, Inc., 427 U. S. 50, 427 U. S. 61. The danger dismissed so summarily in Red Lion, in

contrast, was that broadcasters would respond to the vagueness of the regulations by refusing to present programs dealing with important social and political controversies. Invalidating any rule on the basis of its hypothetical application to situations not before the Court is "strong medicine," to be applied "sparingly and only as a last resort." Broadrick v. Oklahoma, 413 U. S. 601, 413 U. S. 613. We decline to administer that medicine to preserve the vigor of patently offensive sexual and excretory speech.

B

When the issue is narrowed to the facts of this case, the question is whether the First Amendment denies government any power to restrict the public broadcast of indecent language in any circumstances.] For if the government has any such power, this was an appropriate occasion for its exercise.

The words of the Carlin monologue are unquestionably "speech" within the meaning of the First Amendment. It is equally clear that the Commission's objections to the broadcast were based in part on its content. The order must therefore fall if, as Pacifica argues, the First Amendment prohibits all governmental regulation that depends on the content of speech. Our past cases demonstrate, however, that no such absolute rule is mandated by the Constitution.

The classic exposition of the proposition that both the content and the context of speech are critical elements of First Amendment analysis is Mr. Justice Holmes' statement for the Court in Schenck v. United States, 249 U. S. 47, 249 U. S. 52:

"We admit that, in many places and in ordinary times, the defendants, in saying all that was said in the circular, would have been within their constitutional rights. But the character of every act depends upon the circumstances in which it is done. . . . The most stringent protection of free speech would not protect a man in falsely shouting fire in a theatre and causing a panic. It does not even protect a man from an injunction against uttering words that may have all the effect of force. . . . The question in every case is whether the words used are used in such circumstances and are of such a nature as to create a clear and present danger that they will bring about the substantive evils that Congress has a right to prevent."

Other distinctions based on content have been approved in the years since Schenck. The government may forbid speech calculated to provoke a fight. See Chaplinsky v. New Hampshire, 315 U. S. 568. It may pay heed to the "common sense differences' between commercial speech and other varieties." Bates v. State Bar of Arizona, supra at 433 U. S. 381. It may treat libels against private citizens more severely than libels against public officials. See Gertz v. Robert Welch, Inc., 418 U. S. 323. Obscenity may be wholly prohibited. Miller v. California, 413 U. S. 15. And, only two Terms ago, we refused to hold that a "statutory classification is unconstitutional because it is based on the content of communication protected by the First Amendment." Young v. American Mini Theatres, Inc., supra, at 427 U. S. 52.

The question in this case is whether a broadcast of patently offensive words dealing with sex and excretion may be regulated because of its content. Obscene materials have been denied the protection of the First Amendment because their content is so offensive to contemporary moral standards. Roth v. United States, 354 U. S. 476. But the fact that society may find speech offensive is not a sufficient reason for suppressing it. Indeed, if it is the speaker's opinion that gives offense, that consequence is a reason for according it constitutional protection. For it is a central tenet of the First Amendment that the government must remain neutral in the marketplace of ideas. If there were any reason to believe that the Commission's characterization of the Carlin monologue as offensive could be traced to its political content -- or even to the fact that it satirized contemporary attitudes about four-letter words -- First Amendment protection might be required. But that is simply not this case. These words offend for the same reasons that obscenity offends. Their place in the hierarchy of First Amendment values was aptly sketched by Mr. Justice Murphy when he said:

"[S]uch utterances are no essential part of any exposition of ideas, and are of such slight social value as a step to truth that any benefit that may be derived from them is clearly outweighed by the social interest in order and morality."

Chaplinski v. New Hampshire, 315 U.S. at 315 U. S. 572.

Although these words ordinarily lack literary, political, or scientific value, they are not entirely outside the protection of the First Amendment. Some uses of even the most offensive words are unquestionably protected. See, e.g., Hess v. Indiana, 414 U. S. 105. Indeed, we may assume, arguendo, that this monologue would be protected in other contexts. Nonetheless, the constitutional protection accorded to a communication containing such patently offensive sexual and excretory language need not be the same in every context. It is a characteristic of speech such as this that both its capacity to offend and its "social value," to use Mr. Justice Murphy's term, vary with the circumstances. Words that are commonplace in one setting are shocking in another. To paraphrase Mr. Justice Harlan, one occasion's lyric is another's vulgarity. Cf. Cohen v. California, 403 U. S. 15, 403 U. S. 25.

In this case, it is undisputed that the content of Pacifica's broadcast was "vulgar," "offensive," and "shocking." Because content of that character is not entitled to absolute constitutional protection under all circumstances, we must consider its context in order to determine whether the Commission's action was constitutionally permissible.

C

We have long recognized that each medium of expression presents special First Amendment problems. Joseph Burstyn, Inc. v. Wilson, 343 U. S. 495, 343 U. S. 502-503. And of all forms of communication, it is broadcasting that has received the most limited First Amendment protection. Thus, although other speakers cannot be licensed except under laws that carefully define and narrow official discretion, a broadcaster may be deprived of his license and his forum if the Commission decides that such an action would serve "the public interest, convenience, and necessity." Similarly, although the First Amendment protects newspaper publishers from being required to print the replies of those whom they criticize, Miami Herald Publishing Co. v. Tornillo, 418 U. S. 241, it affords no such protection to broadcasters; on the contrary, they must give free time to the victims of their criticism. Red Lion Broadcasting Co. v. FCC, 395 U. S. 367.

The reasons for these distinctions are complex, but two have relevance to the present case. First, the broadcast media have established a uniquely pervasive presence in the lives of all Americans. Patently offensive, indecent material presented over the airwaves confronts the citizen not only in public, but also in the privacy of the home, where the individual's right to be left alone plainly outweighs the First Amendment rights of an intruder. Rowan v. Post Office Dept., 397 U. S. 72. Because the broadcast audience is constantly tuning in and out, prior warnings cannot completely protect the listener or viewer from unexpected program content. To say that one may avoid further offense by turning off the radio when he hears indecent language is like saying that the remedy for an assault is to run away after the first blow. One may hang up on an indecent phone call, but that option does not give the caller a constitutional immunity or avoid a harm that has already taken place.

Second, broadcasting is uniquely accessible to children, even those too young to read. Although Cohen's written message might have been incomprehensible to a first grader, Pacifica's broadcast could have enlarged a child's vocabulary in an instant. Other forms of offensive expression may be withheld from the young without restricting the expression at its source. Bookstores and motion picture theaters, for example, may be prohibited from making indecent material available to children. We held in Ginsberg v. New York, 390 U. S. 629, that the gov-

ernment's interest in the "wellbeing of its youth" and in supporting "parents' claim to authority in their own household" justified the regulation of otherwise protected expression. Id. at 390 U. S. 640 and 390 U. S. 639. The ease with which children may obtain access to broadcast material, coupled with the concerns recognized in Ginsberg, amply justify special treatment of indecent broadcasting.

It is appropriate, in conclusion, to emphasize the narrowness of our holding. This case does not involve a two-way radio conversation between a cab driver and a dispatcher, or a telecast of an Elizabethan comedy. We have not decided that an occasional expletive in either setting would justify any sanction or, indeed, that this broadcast would justify a criminal prosecution. The Commission's decision rested entirely on a nuisance rationale under which context is all-important. The concept requires consideration of a host of variables. The time of day was emphasized by the Commission. The content of the program in which the language is used will also affect the composition of the audience, and differences between radio, television, and perhaps closed-circuit transmissions, may also be relevant. As Mr. Justice Sutherland wrote, a "nuisance may be merely a right thing in the wrong place, -- like a pig in the parlor instead of the barnyard." Euclid v. Ambler Realty Co., 272 U. S. 365, 272 U. S. 383. We simply hold that, when the Commission finds that a pig has entered the parlor, the exercise of its regulatory power does not depend on proof that the pig is obscene.

The judgment of the Court of Appeals is reversed.

It is so ordered.

## APPENDIX TO OPINION OF THE COURT

The following is a verbatim transcript of "Filthy Words" prepared by the Federal Communications Commission.

*Aruba-du, ruba-tu, ruba-tu. I was thinking about the curse words and the swear words, the cuss words and the words that you can't say, that you're not supposed to say all the time, [']cause words or people into words want to hear your words. Some guys like to record your words and sell them back to you if they can, (laughter) listen in on the telephone, write down what words you say. A guy who used to be in Washington knew that his phone was tapped, used to answer, Fuck Hoover, yes, go ahead. (laughter) Okay, I was thinking one night about the words you couldn't say on the public, ah, airwaves, um, the ones you definitely wouldn't say, ever, [']cause I heard a lady say bitch one night on television, and it was cool like she was talking about, you know, ah, well, the bitch is the first one to notice that in the litter Johnie right. (murmur) Right. And, uh, bastard you can say, and hell and damn, so I have to figure out which ones you couldn't and ever and it came down to seven but the list is open to amendment, and in fact, has been changed, uh, by now, ha, a lot of people pointed things out to me, and I noticed some myself. The original seven words were shit, piss, fuck, cunt, cock-sucker, motherfucker, and tits. Those are the ones that will curve your spine, grow hair on your hands and (laughter) maybe, even bring us, God help us, peace without honor (laughter) um, and a bourbon. (laughter) And now the first thing that we noticed was that word fuck was really repeated in there because the word motherfucker is a compound word and it's another form of the word fuck. (laughter) You want to be a purist it doesn't really, it can't be on the list of basic words. Also, cock sucker is a compound word and neither half of that is really dirty. The word -- the half sucker that's merely suggestive (laughter) and the word cock is a half-way dirty word, 50% dirty -- dirty half the time, depending on what you mean by it. (laughter) Uh, remember when you first heard it, like in 6th grade, you used to giggle. And the cock crowed three times, heh (laughter) the cock -- three times. It's in the Bible, cock in the Bi-*

*ble. (laughter) And the first time you heard about a cock-fight, remember -- What? Huh? naw. It ain't that, are you stupid? man. (laughter, clapping) It's chickens, you know, (laughter) Then you have the four letter words from the old Anglo-Saxon fame. Uh, shit and fuck. The word shit, uh, is an interesting kind of word in that the middle class has never really accepted it and approved it. They use it like, crazy but it's not really okay. It's still a rude, dirty, old kind of gushy word. (laughter) They don't like that, but they say it, like, they say it like, a lady now in a middle-class home, you'll hear most of the time she says it as an expletive, you know, it's out of her mouth before she knows. She says, Oh shit oh shit, (laughter) oh shit. If she drops something, Oh, the shit hurt the broccoli. Shit. Thank you. (footsteps fading away) (papers ruffling)*

*Read it! (from audience)*

*Shit! (laughter) I won the Grammy, man, for the comedy album. Isn't that groovy? (clapping, whistling) (murmur) That's true. Thank you. Thank you man. Yeah. (murmur) (continuous clapping) Thank you man. Thank you. Thank you very much, man. Thank, no, (end of continuous clapping) for that and for the Grammy, man, [']cause (laughter) that's based on people liking it man, yeh, that's ah, that's okay man. (laughter) Let's let that go, man. I got my Grammy. I can let my hair hang down now, shit. (laughter) Ha! So! Now the word shit is okay for the man. At work you can say it like crazy. Mostly figuratively, Get that shit out of here,*

*will ya? I don't want to see that shit anymore. I can't colt that shit, buddy. I've had that shit up to here. I think you're full of shit myself (laughter) He don't know shit from Shinola. (laughter) you know that? (laughter) Always wondered how the Shi-nola people felt about that (laughter) Hi, I'm the new man from Shinola. (laughter) Hi, how are ya? Nice to see ya. (laughter)*

*How are ya? (laughter) Boy, I don't know whether to shit or wind my watch. (laughter) Guess, I'll shit on my watch. (laughter) Oh, the shit is going to hit de fan. (laughter) Built like a brick shit-house. (laughter) Up, he's up shit's creek. (laughter) He's had it. (laughter) He hit me, I'm sorry. (laughter) Hot shit, holy shit, tough shit, eat shit, (laughter) shit-eating grin. Uh, whoever thought of that was ill. (murmur laughter) He had a shit-eating grin! He had a what? (laughter) Shit on a stick. (laughter) Shit in a handbag. I always like that. He ain't worth shit in a handbag. (laughter) Shitty. He acted real shitty. (laughter) You know what I mean? (laughter) I got the money back, but a real shitty attitude. Heh, he had a shit-fit. (laughter) Wow! Shit-fit. Whew! Glad I wasn't there. (murmur, laughter) All the animals -- Bull shit, horse shit, cow shit, rat shit, bat shit. (laughter) First time I heard bat shit, I really came apart. A guy in Oklahoma, Boggs, said it, man. Aw! Bat shit. (laughter) Vera reminded me of that last night, ah (murmur). Snake shit, slicker than owl shit. (laughter) Get your shit together. Shit or get off the pot. (laughter) I got a shit-load full of them. (laughter) I got a shit-pot full, all right. Shit-head, shit-heel, shit in your heart, shit for brains, (laughter) shit-face, heh (laughter) I always try to think how that could have originated; the first guy that said that. Somebody got drunk and fell in some shit, you know. (laughter) Hey, I'm shit-face. (laughter) Shitface, today. (laughter) Anyway, enough of that shit. (laughter) The big one, the word fuck that's the one that hangs them up the most. [']Cause in a lot of cases that's the very act that hangs them up the most. So, it's natural that the word would, uh, have the same effect. It's a great word, fuck, nice word, easy word, cute word, kind of. Easy word to say. One syllable, short u. (laughter) Fuck. (Murmur) You know, it's easy. Starts with a nice soft sound -- fuh -- ends with a kh. Right? (laughter) A little something for everyone. Fuck (laughter) Good word. Kind of a proud word, too. Who are you? I am FUCK. (laughter) FUCK OF THE MOUN-*

*TAIN. (laughter) Tune in again next week to FUCK OF THE MOUNTAIN. (laughter) It's an interesting word too, [']cause it's got a double kind of a life -- personality -- dual, you know, whatever the right phrase is. It leads a double life, the word fuck. First of all, it means, sometimes, most of the time, fuck. What does it mean? It means to make love. Right? We're going to make love, yeh, we're going to fuck, yeh, we're going to fuck, yeh, we're going to make love. (laughter) we're really going to fuck, yeh, we're going to make love. Right? And it also means the beginning of life, it's the act that begins life, so there's the word hanging around with words like love, and life, and yet, on the other hand, it's also a word that we really use to hurt each other with, man. It's a heavy. It's one that you have toward the end of the argument. (laughter) Right? (laughter) You finally can't make out. Oh, fuck you man. I said, fuck you. (laughter, murmur) Stupid fuck. (laughter) Fuck you and everybody that looks like you, (laughter) man. It would be nice to change the movies that we already have and substitute the word fuck for the word kill, wherever we could, and some of those movie cliches would change a little bit. Madfuckers still on the loose. Stop me before I fuck again. Fuck the ump, fuck the ump, fuck the ump, fuck the ump, fuck the ump. Easy on the clutch Bill, you'll fuck that engine again. (laughter) The other shit one was, I don't give a shit. Like it's worth something, you know? (laughter) I don't give a shit. Hey, well, I don't take no shit, (laughter) you know what I mean? You know why I don't take no shit? (laughter)*

*[']Cause I don't give a shit. (laughter) If I give a shit, I would have to pack shit. (laughter) But I don't pack no shit cause I don't give a shit. (laughter) You wouldn't shit me, would you? (laughter) That's a joke when you're a kid with a worm looking out the bird's ass. You wouldn't shit me, would you? (laughter) It's an eight-year-old joke but a good one. (laughter) The additions to the list. I found three more words that had to be put on*

228

*the list of words you could never say on television, and they were fart, turd and twat, those three. (laughter) Fart, we talked about, it's harmless. It's like tits, it's a cutie word, no problem. Turd, you can't say, but who wants to, you know? (laughter) The subject never comes up on the panel, so I'm not worried about that one. Now the word twat is an interesting word. Twat! Yeh, right in the twat. (laughter) Twat is an interesting word because it's the only one I know of, the only slang word applying to the, a part of the sexual anatomy that doesn't have another meaning to it. Like, ah, snatch, box and pussy all have other meanings, man. Even in a Walt Disney movie, you can say, We're going to snatch that pussy and put him in a box and bring him on the airplane. (murmur, laughter) Everybody loves it. The twat stands alone, man, as it should. And two-way words. Ah, ass is okay providing you're riding into town on a religious feast day. (laughter) You can't say, up your ass. (laughter) You can say, stuff it! (murmur) There are certain things you can say -- its weird, but you can just come so close. Before I cut, I, uh, want to, ah, thank you for listening to my words, man, fellow, uh space travelers. Thank you man for tonight and thank you also. (clapping whistling)*

**MR. JUSTICE POWELL, with whom MR. JUSTICE BLACKMUN joins, concurring in part and concurring in the judgment.**

I join Parts I, II, III, and IV-C of MR. JUSTICE STEVENS' opinion. The Court today reviews only the Commission's holding that Carlin's monologue was indecent "as broadcast" at two o'clock in the afternoon, and not the broad sweep of the Commission's opinion. A....

The issue, however, is whether the Commission may impose civil sanctions on a licensee radio station for broadcasting the monologue at two o'clock in the afternoon. The Commission's primary concern was to prevent the broadcast from reaching the ears of unsupervised children who were likely to be in the audience at that hour. In essence, the Commission sought to "channel" the monologue to hours when the fewest unsupervised children would be exposed to it. ....

Making the sensitive judgments required in these cases is not easy. But this responsibility has been reposed initially in the Commission, and its judgment is entitled to respect.

It is argued that, despite society's right to protect its children from this kind of speech, and despite everyone's interest in not being assaulted by offensive speech in the home, the Commission's holding in this case is impermissible because it prevents willing adults from listening to Carlin's monologue over the radio in the early afternoon hours. It is said that this ruling will have the effect of "reduc[ing] the adult population . . . to [hearing] only what is fit for children." Butler v. Michigan, 352 U. S. 380, 352 U. S. 383 (1957).

...

The Commission's holding does not prevent willing adults from purchasing Carlin's record, from attending his performances, or, indeed, from reading the transcript reprinted as an appendix to the Court's opinion. On its face, it does not prevent respondent Pacifica Foundation from broadcasting the monologue during late evening hours, when fewer children are likely to be in the audience, nor from broadcasting discussions of the contemporary use of language at any time during the day. The Commission's holding, and certainly the Court's holding today, does not speak to cases involving the isolated use of a potentially offensive word in the course of a radio broadcast, as distinguished from the verbal shock treatment administered by respondent here. In short, I agree that, on the facts of this case, the Commission's order did not violate respondent's First Amendment rights.

....

# Miller v. California (1972)

US Supreme Court

Miller v. California, 413 U.S. 15 (1972)

Decided: June 21, 1973

Burger   White   Blackmun   Powell   Rehnquist   Douglas   Brennan   Stewart   Marshall

Decision: 5 votes for Miller, 4 vote(s) against

**MR. CHIEF JUSTICE BURGER delivered the opinion of the Court.**

This is one of a group of "obscenity-pornography" cases being reviewed by the Court in a reexamination of standards enunciated in earlier cases involving what Mr. Justice Harlan called "the intractable obscenity problem." Interstate Circuit, Inc. v. Dallas, 390 U.S. 676, 704 (1968) (concurring and dissenting).

Appellant conducted a mass mailing campaign to advertise the sale of illustrated books, euphemistically called "adult" material. After a jury trial, he was convicted of violating California Penal Code § 311.2(a), a misdemeanor, by knowingly distributing obscene matter, [n1] [p17] and the Appellate Department, Superior Court of California, County of Orange, summarily affirmed the judgment without opinion. Appellant's conviction was specifically [p18] based on his conduct in causing five unsolicited advertising brochures to be sent through the mail in an envelope addressed to a restaurant in Newport Beach, California. The envelope was opened by the manager of the restaurant and his mother. They had not requested the brochures; they complained to the police.

The brochures advertise four books entitled "Intercourse," "Man-Woman," "Sex Orgies Illustrated," and "An Illustrated History of Pornography," and a film entitled "Marital Intercourse." While the brochures contain some descriptive printed material, primarily they consist of pictures and drawings very explicitly depicting men and women in groups of two or more engaging in a variety of sexual activities, with genitals often prominently displayed.

I

This case involves the application of a State's criminal obscenity statute to a situation in which sexually explicit materials have been thrust by aggressive sales action upon unwilling recipients who had in no way indicated any desire to receive such materials. This Court has recognized that the States have a legitimate interest in prohibiting dissemination or exhibition of obscene material [n2] [p19] when the mode of dissemination carries with it a significant danger of offending the sensibilities of unwilling recipients or of exposure to juveniles. Stanley v. Georgia, 394 U.S. 557, 567 (1969); Ginsberg v. New York, 390 U.S. 629, 637-643 (1968); Interstate Circuit, Inc. v. Dallas, supra, at 690; Redrup v. New York, 386 U.S. 767, 769 (1967); Jacobellis v. Ohio, 378 U.S. 184, 195 (1964). See Rabe v. Washington, 405 U.S. 313, 317 (1972) (BURGER, C.J., concurring); United States v. Reidel, 402 U.S. 351, 360-362 (1971) (opinion of MARSHALL, J.); Joseph Burstyn, Inc. v. Wilson, 343 U.S. 495, 502 (1952); Breard v. Alexandria, 341 U.S. 622, 644 645 (1951); Kovacs v. Cooper, 336 U.S. 77, 88-89 (1949); Prince v. Massachusetts, 321 U.S. 158, 169-170 (1944). Cf. Butler v. Michigan, 32 U.S. 380, 382-383 (1957); Public Utilities Comm'n v. Pollak, 343 U.S. 451, 464-465 (1952) It is in this context that we are called [p20] on to define the standards which must be used to identify obscene material that a State may regulate without infringing on the First Amendment as applicable to the States through the Fourteenth Amendment.

The dissent of MR. JUSTICE BRENNAN reviews the background of the obscenity problem, but since the Court now undertakes to formulate standards more concrete than those in the past, it is useful for us to focus on two of the landmark cases in the somewhat tortured history of the Court's obscenity decisions. In Roth v. United States, 354 U.S. 476 (1957), the Court sustained a conviction under a federal statute punishing the mailing of "obscene, lewd, lascivious or filthy . . ." materials. The key to that holding was the Court's rejection of the claim that obscene materials were protected by the First Amendment. Five Justices joined in the opinion stating:

All ideas having even the slightest redeeming social importance -- unorthodox ideas, controversial ideas, even ideas hateful to the prevailing climate of opinion -- have the full protection of the [First Amendment]

At the time of the commission of the alleged offense, the California Penal Code read in relevant part:

§ 311.2 Sending or bringing into state for sale or distribution; printing, exhibiting, distributing or possessing within state

(a) Every person who knowingly: sends or causes to be sent, or brings or causes to be brought, into this state for sale or distribution, or in this state prepares, publishes, prints, exhibits, distributes, or offers to distribute, or has in his possession with intent to distribute or to exhibit or offer to distribute, any obscene matter is guilty of a misdemeanor. . . .

§ 311. Definitions

As used in this chapter:

(a) "Obscene" means that to the average person, applying contemporary standards, the predominant appeal of the matter, taken as a whole, is to prurient interest, i.e., a shameful or morbid interest in nudity, sex, or excretion, which goes substantially beyond customary limits of candor in description or representation of such matters and is matter which is utterly without redeeming social importance.

354 U.S. at 48 85 (footnotes omitted).

Nine years later, in Memoirs v. Massachusetts, 383 U.S. 413 (1966), the Court veered sharply away from the Roth concept and, with only three Justices in the plurality opinion, articulated a new test of obscenity. The plurality held that, under the Roth definition,

guaranties, unless excludable because they encroach upon the limited area of more important interests. But implicit in the history of the First Amendment is the rejection of obscenity as utterly without redeeming social importance. . . . This is the same judgment expressed by this Court in Chaplinsky v. New Hampshire, 315 U.S. 568, 571-572:

. . . There are certain well defined and narrowly limited classes of speech, the prevention and punishment of which have never been thought to raise any Constitutional problem. These include the lewd and obscene. . . . It has been well observed that such utterances are no essential part of any exposition of ideas, and are of such slight social [p21] value as a step to truth that any benefit that may be derived from them is clearly outweighed by the social interest in order and morality. . . .

[Emphasis by Court in Roth opinion.]

We hold that obscenity is not within the area of constitutionally protected speech or press.

as elaborated in subsequent cases, three elements must coalesce: it must be established that (a) the dominant theme of the material, taken as a whole, appeals to a prurient interest in sex; (b) the material is patently offensive because it affronts contemporary community standards relating to the description or representation of sexual matters; and (c) the material is utterly without redeeming social value.

Id. at 418. The sharpness of the break with Roth, represented by the third element of the Memoirs test and emphasized by MR. JUSTICE WHITE's dissent, id. at 460-462, was further underscored when the Memoirs plurality went on to state:

The Supreme Judicial Court erred in holding that a book need not be "unqualifiedly worthless before it can be deemed obscene." A book cannot be proscribed unless it is found to be utterly without redeeming social value.

Id. at 419 (emphasis in original).

While Roth presumed "obscenity" to be "utterly without redeeming social importance," Memoirs required [p22] that to prove obscenity it must be affirmatively established that the material is "utterly without redeeming social value." Thus, even as they repeated the words of Roth, the Memoirs plurality produced a drastically altered test that called on the prosecution to prove a negative, i.e., that the material was "utterly without redeeming social value" -- a burden virtually impossible to discharge under our criminal standards of proof. Such considerations caused Mr. Justice Harlan to wonder if the "utterly without redeeming social value" test had any meaning at all. See Memoirs v. Massachusetts, id. at 459 (Harlan, J., dissenting). See also id. at 461 (WHITE, J., dissenting); United States v. Groner, 479 F.2d 577, 579581 (CA5 1973).

Apart from the initial formulation in the Roth case, no majority of the Court has at any given time been able to agree on a standard to determine what constitutes obscene, pornographic material subject to regu-

lation under the States' police power. See, e.g., Redrup v. New York, 386 U.S. at 770-771. We have seen "a variety of views among the members of the Court unmatched in any other course of constitutional adjudication." Interstate Circuit, Inc. v. Dallas, 390 U.S. at 704-705 (Harlan, J., concurring and dissenting) (footnote omitted). [n3] This is not remarkable, for in the area [p23] of freedom of speech and press the courts must always remain sensitive to any infringement on genuinely serious literary, artistic, political, or scientific expression. This is an area in which there are few eternal verities.

The case we now review was tried on the theory that the California Penal Code § 311 approximately incorporates the three-stage Memoirs test, supra. But now the Memoirs test has been abandoned as unworkable by its author, [n4] and no Member of the Court today supports the Memoirs formulation.

II

This much has been categorically settled by the Court, that obscene material is unprotected by the First Amendment. Kois v. Wisconsin, 408 U.S. 229 (1972); United States v. Reidel, 402 U.S. at 354; Roth v. United States, supra, at 485. [n5] "The First and Fourteenth Amendments have never been treated as absolutes [footnote omitted]." Breard v. Alexandria, 341 U.S. at 642, and cases cited. See Times Film Corp. v. Chicago, 365 U.S. 43, 47-50 (1961); Joseph Burstyn, Inc. v. Wilson, 343 U.S. at 502. We acknowledge, however, the inherent dangers of undertaking to regulate any form of expression. State statutes designed to regulate obscene materials must be [p24] carefully limited. See Interstate Circuit, Inc. v. Dallas, supra, at 682-685. As a result, we now confine the permissible scope of such regulation to works which depict or describe sexual conduct. That conduct must be specifically defined by the applicable state law, as written or authoritatively construed. [n6] A state offense must also be limited to works which, taken as a whole, appeal to the prurient interest in sex, which portray sexual conduct in a patently offensive way, and which, taken as a whole, do not have serious literary, artistic, political, or scientific value.

The basic guidelines for the trier of fact must be: (a) whether "the average person, applying contemporary community standards" would find that the work, taken as a whole, appeals to the prurient interest, Kois v. Wisconsin, supra, at 230, quoting Roth v. United States, supra, at 489; (b) whether the work depicts or describes, in a patently offensive way, sexual conduct specifically defined by the applicable state law; and (c) whether the work, taken as a whole, lacks serious literary, artistic, political, or scientific value. We do not adopt as a constitutional standard the "utterly without redeeming social value" test of Memoirs v. Massachusetts, [p25] 383 U.S. at 419; that concept has never commanded the adherence of more than three Justices at one time. [n7] See supra at 21. If a state law that regulates obscene material is thus limited, as written or construed, the First Amendment values applicable to the States through the Fourteenth Amendment are adequately protected by the ultimate power of appellate courts to conduct an independent review of constitutional claims when necessary. See Kois v. Wisconsin, supra, at 232; Memoirs v. Massachusetts, supra, at 459-460 (Harlan, J., dissenting); Jacobellis v. Ohio, 378 U.S. at 204 (Harlan, J., dissenting); New York Times Co. v. Sullivan, 376 U.S. 254, 284-285 (1964); Roth v. United States, supra, at 497-498 (Harlan, J., concurring and dissenting).

We emphasize that it is not our function to propose regulatory schemes for the States. That must await their concrete legislative efforts. It is possible, however, to give a few plain examples of what a state statute could define for regulation under part (b) of the standard announced in this opinion, supra:

(a) Patently offensive representations or descriptions of ultimate sexual acts, normal or perverted, actual or simulated.

(b) Patently offensive representations or descriptions of masturbation, excretory functions, and lewd exhibition of the genitals.

Sex and nudity may not be exploited without limit by films or pictures exhibited or sold in places of public accommodation any more than live sex and nudity can [p26] be exhibited or sold without limit in such public places. [n8] At a minimum, prurient, patently offensive depiction or description of sexual conduct must have serious literary, artistic, political, or scientific value to merit First Amendment protection. See Kois v. Wisconsin, supra, at 230-232; Roth v. United States, supra, at 487; Thornhill v. Alabama, 310 U.S. 88, 101-102 (1940). For example, medical books for the education of physicians and related personnel necessarily use graphic illustrations and descriptions of human anatomy. In resolving the inevitably sensitive questions of fact and law, we must continue to rely on the jury system, accompanied by the safeguards that judges, rules of evidence, presumption of innocence, and other protective features provide, as we do with rape, murder, and a host of other offenses against society and its individual members.

MR. JUSTICE BRENNAN, author of the opinions of the Court, or the plurality opinions, in Roth v. United States, supra; Jacobellis v. Ohio, supra; Ginzburg v. United [p27] States, 383 U.S. 463 (1966), Mishkin v. New York, 383 U.S. 502 (1966); and Memoirs v. Massachusetts, supra, has abandoned his former position and now maintains that no formulation of this Court, the Congress, or the States can adequately distinguish obscene material unprotected by the First Amendment from protected expression, Paris Adult Theatre I v. Slaton, post, p. 73 (BRENNAN, J., dissenting). Paradoxically, MR. JUSTICE BRENNAN indicates that suppression of unprotected obscene material is permissible to avoid exposure to unconsenting adults, as in this case, and to juveniles, although he gives no indication of how the division between protected and nonprotected materials may be drawn with greater precision for these purposes than for regulation of commercial exposure to consenting adults only. Nor does he indicate where in the Constitution he finds the authority to distinguish between a willing "adult" one month past the state law age of majority and a willing "juvenile" one month younger.

Under the holdings announced today, no one will be subject to prosecution for the sale or exposure of obscene materials unless these materials depict or describe patently offensive "hard core" sexual conduct specifically defined by the regulating state law, as written or construed. We are satisfied that these specific prerequisites will provide fair notice to a dealer in such materials that his public and commercial activities may bring prosecution. See Roth v. United States, supra, at 491-492. Cf. Ginsberg v. New York, 390 U.S. at 643. [n10] If [p28] the inability to define regulated materials with ultimate, god-like precision altogether removes the power of the States or the Congress to regulate, then "hard core" pornography may be exposed without limit to the juvenile, the passerby, and the consenting adult alike, as, indeed, MR. JUSTICE DOUGLAS contends. As to MR. JUSTICE DOUGLAS' position, see United States v. Thirty-seven Photographs, 402 U.S. 363, 379-380 (1971) (Black, J., joined by DOUGLAS, J., dissenting); Ginzburg v. United States, supra, at 476, 491-492 (Black, J., and DOUGLAS, J., dissenting); Jacobellis v. Ohio, supra, at 196 (Black, J., joined by DOUGLAS, J., concurring); Roth, supra, at 508-514 (DOUGLAS, J., dissenting). In this belief, however, MR. JUSTICE DOUGLAS now stands alone.

MR. JUSTICE BRENNAN also emphasizes "institutional stress" in justification of his change of view. Noting that "[t]he number of obscenity cases on our docket gives ample testimony to the burden that has been placed upon this Court," he quite rightly remarks that the examination of contested materials "is hardly a source of edification to the members of this Court." Paris Adult [p29] Theatre I v. Slaton, post, at 92, 93. He also notes, and we agree, that "uncertainty of the standards creates a continuing source of tension between state and federal courts. . . ."

The problem is . . . that one cannot say with certainty that material is obscene until at least five members of this Court, applying inevitably obscure standards, have pronounced it so.

Id. at 93, 92.

It is certainly true that the absence, since Roth, of a single majority view of this Court as to proper standards for testing obscenity has placed a strain on both state and federal courts. But today, for the first time since Roth was decided in 1957, a majority of this Court has agreed on concrete guidelines to isolate "hard core" pornography from expression protected by the First Amendment. Now we may abandon the casual practice of Redrup v. New York, 386 U.S. 767 (1967), and attempt to provide positive guidance to federal and state courts alike.

This may not be an easy road, free from difficulty. But no amount of "fatigue" should lead us to adopt a convenient "institutional" rationale -- an absolutist, "anything goes" view of the First Amendment -- because it will lighten our burdens. [n11] "Such an abnegation of judicial supervision in this field would be inconsistent with our duty to uphold the constitutional guarantees." Jacobellis v. Ohio, supra, at 187-188 (opinion of BRENNAN, J.). Nor should we remedy "tension between state and federal courts" by arbitrarily depriving the States of a power reserved to them under the Constitution, a power which they have enjoyed and exercised continuously from before the adoption of the First Amendment to this day. See Roth v. United States, supra, at 482-485.

Our duty admits of no "substitute for facing up [p30] to the tough individual problems of constitutional judgment involved in every obscenity case." [Roth v. United States, supra, at 498]; see Manual Enterprises, Inc. v. Day, 370 U.S. 478, 488 (opinion of Harlan, J.) [footnote omitted].

Jacobellis v. Ohio, supra, at 188 (opinion of BRENNAN, J.).

III

Under a National Constitution, fundamental First Amendment limitations on the powers of the States do not vary from community to community, but this does not mean that there are, or should or can be, fixed, uniform national standards of precisely what appeals to the "prurient interest" or is "patently offensive." These are essentially questions of fact, and our Nation is simply too big and too diverse for this Court to reasonably expect that such standards could be articulated for all 50 States in a single formulation, even assuming the prerequisite consensus exists. When triers of fact are asked to decide whether "the average person, applying contemporary community standards" would consider certain materials "prurient," it would be unrealistic to require that the answer be based on some abstract formulation. The adversary system, with lay jurors as the usual ultimate factfinders in criminal prosecutions, has historically permitted triers of fact to draw on the standards of their community, guided always by limiting instructions on the law. To require a State to structure obscenity proceedings around evidence of a national "community standard" would be an exercise in futility.

As noted before, this case was tried on the theory that the California obscenity statute sought to incorporate the tripartite test of Memoirs. This, a "national" standard of First Amendment protection enumerated by a plurality of this Court, was correctly regarded at the time of trial as limiting state prosecution under the controlling case [p31] law. The jury, however, was explicitly instructed that, in determining whether the "dominant theme of the material as a whole . . . appeals to the prurient interest," and, in determining whether the material "goes substantially beyond customary limits of candor and affronts contemporary community standards of decency," it was to apply "contemporary community standards of the State of California."

During the trial, both the prosecution and the defense assumed that the relevant "community standards" in making the factual determination of obscenity were those of the State of California, not some hypothetical standard of the entire United States of America. Defense counsel at trial never objected to the testimony of the State's expert on community standards [n12] or to the instructions of the trial judge on "state-wide" standards. On appeal to the Appellate Department, Superior Court of California, County of Orange, appellant for the first time contended that application of state, rather than national, standards violated the First and Fourteenth Amendments.

We conclude that neither the State's alleged failure to offer evidence of "national standards," nor the trial court's charge that the jury consider state community standards, were constitutional errors. Nothing in the First Amendment requires that a jury must consider hypothetical and unascertainable "national standards" when attempting to determine whether certain materials are obscene as a matter [p32] of fact. Mr. Chief Justice Warren pointedly commented in his dissent in Jacobellis v. Ohio, supra, at 200:

It is my belief that, when the Court said in Roth that obscenity is to be defined by reference to "community standards," it meant community standards -- not a national standard, as is sometimes argued. I believe that there is no provable "national standard." . . . At all events, this Court has not been able to enunciate one, and it would be unreasonable to expect local courts to divine one.

It is neither realistic nor constitutionally sound to read the First Amendment as requiring that the people of Maine or Mississippi accept public depiction of conduct found tolerable in Las Vegas, or New York City. [n13] [p33] See Hoyt v. Minnesota, 399 U.S. at 524-525 (1970) (BLACKMUN, J., dissenting); Walker v. Ohio, 398 U.S. at 434 (1970) (BURGER, C.J., dissenting); id. at 434-435 (Harlan, J., dissenting); Cain v. Kentucky, 397 U.S. 319 (1970) (BURGER, C.J., dissenting); id. at 319-320 (Harlan, J., dissenting); United States v. Groner, 479 F.2d at 581-583; O'Meara & Shaffer, Obscenity in The Supreme Court: A Note on Jacobellis v. Ohio, 40 Notre Dame Law. 1, 6-7 (1964).

See also Memoirs v. Massachusetts, 383 U.S. at 458 (Harlan, J., dissenting); Jacobellis v. Ohio, supra, at 203-204 (Harlan, J., dissenting); Roth v. United States, supra, at 505-506 (Harlan, J., concurring and dissenting). People in different States vary in their tastes and attitudes, and this diversity is not to be strangled by the absolutism of imposed uniformity. As the Court made clear in Mishkin v. New York, 383 U.S. at 508-509, the primary concern with requiring a jury to apply the standard of "the average person, applying contemporary community standards" is to be certain that, so far as material is not aimed at a deviant group, it will be judged by its impact on an average person, rather than a particularly susceptible or sensitive person -- or indeed a totally insensitive one. See Roth v. United States, supra, at 489. Cf. the now discredited test in Regina v. Hicklin, [1868] L.R. 3 Q.B. 360. We hold that the requirement that the jury evaluate the materials with reference to "contemporary [p34] standards of the State of California" serves this protective purpose and is constitutionally adequate. [n14]

IV

The dissenting Justices sound the alarm of repression. But, in our view, to equate the free and robust exchange of ideas and political debate with commercial exploitation of obscene material demeans the grand conception of the First Amendment and its high purposes in the historic struggle for freedom. It is a "misuse of the great guarantees of free speech and free press. . . ." Breard v. Alexandria, 341 U.S. at 645. The First Amendment protects works which, taken as a whole, have serious literary, artistic, political, or scientific value, regardless of whether the government or a majority of the people approve of the ideas these works represent.

The protection given speech and press was fashioned to assure unfettered interchange of ideas for the bringing about of [p35] political and social changes desired by the people,

Roth v. United States, supra, at 484 (emphasis added). See Kois v. Wisconsin, 408 U.S. at 230-232; Thornhill v. Alabama, 310 U.S. at 101-102. But the public portrayal of hard-core sexual conduct for its own sake, and for the ensuing commercial gain, is a different matter. [n15]

There is no evidence, empirical or historical, that the stern 19th century American censorship of public distribution and display of material relating to sex, see Roth v. United States, supra, at 482-485, in any way limited or affected expression of serious literary, artistic, political, or scientific ideas. On the contrary, it is beyond any question that the era following Thomas Jefferson to Theodore Roosevelt was an "extraordinarily vigorous period" not just in economics and politics, but in belles lettres and in "the outlying fields of social and political philosophies." [n16] We do not see the harsh hand [p36] of censorship of ideas -- good or bad, sound or unsound -- and "repression" of political liberty lurking in every state regulation of commercial exploitation of human interest in sex.

MR. JUSTICE BRENNAN finds "it is hard to see how state-ordered regimentation of our minds can ever be forestalled." Paris Adult Theatre I v. Slaton, post, at 110 (BRENNAN, J., dissenting). These doleful anticipations assume that courts cannot distinguish commerce in ideas, protected by the First Amendment, from commercial exploitation of obscene material. Moreover, state regulation of hard-core pornography so as to make it unavailable to nonadults, a regulation which

236

MR. JUSTICE BRENNAN finds constitutionally permissible, has all the elements of "censorship" for adults; indeed even more rigid enforcement techniques may be called for with such dichotomy of regulation. See Interstate Circuit, Inc. v. Dallas, 390 U.S. at 690. [n17] One can concede that the "sexual revolution" of recent years may have had useful byproducts in striking layers of prudery from a subject long irrationally kept from needed ventilation. But it does not follow that no regulation of patently offensive "hard core" materials is needed or permissible; civilized people do not allow unregulated access to heroin because it is a derivative of medicinal morphlne.

In sum, we (a) reaffirm the Roth holding that obscene material is not protected by the First Amendment; (b) hold that such material can be regulated by the States, subject to the specific safeguards enunciated [p37] above, without a showing that the material is "utterly without redeeming social value"; and (c) hold that obscenity is to be determined by applying "contemporary community standards," see Kois v. Wisconsin, supra, at 230, and Roth v. United States, supra, at 489, not "national standards." The judgment of the Appellate Department of the Superior Court, Orange County, California, is vacated and the case remanded to that court for further proceedings not inconsistent with the First Amendment standards established by this opinion. See United States v. 12 200-ft. Reels of Film, post at 130 n. 7.

Vacated and remanded.

## MR. JUSTICE DOUGLAS, dissenting.

I

Today we leave open the way for California [n1] to send a man to prison for distributing brochures that advertise books and a movie under freshly written standards defining obscenity which until today is decision were never the part of any law.

The Court has worked hard to define obscenity and concededly has failed. ....

It has indeed been said of that definition, "I could never succeed in [defining it] intelligibly," but "I know it when I see it." [n4]

Today we would add a new three-pronged test:

(a) whether "the average person, applying contemporary community standards," would find that the work, taken as a whole, appeals to the prurient interest, . . . (b) whether the work depicts or describes, in a patently offensive way, sexual conduct specifically defined by the applicable state law, and (c) whether the work, taken as a whole, lacks serious literary, artistic, political, or scientific value.

Those are the standards we ourselves have written into the Constitution. [n5] Yet how under these vague tests can [p40] we sustain convictions for the sale of an article prior to the time when some court has declared it to be obscene?

....

My contention is that, until a civil proceeding has placed a tract beyond the pale, no criminal prosecution should be sustained. For no more vivid illustration of vague and uncertain laws could be designed than those we have fashioned. As Mr. Justice Harlan has said:

....

I do not think we, the judges, were ever given the constitutional power to make definitions of obscenity. If it is to be defined, let the people debate and decide by a constitutional amendment what they want to ban as obscene and what standards they want the legislatures and the courts to apply. Perhaps the people will decide that the path towards a mature, integrated society requires [p47] that all ideas competing for acceptance must have no censor. Perhaps they will decide otherwise.

Whatever the choice, the courts will have some guidelines. Now we have none except our own predilections.

**MR. JUSTICE BRENNAN, with whom MR. JUSTICE STEWART and MR. JUSTICE MARSHALL join, dissenting.**

....

For it is clear that, under my dissent in Paris Adult Theatre I, the statute under which the prosecution was brought is unconstitutionally overbroad, and therefore invalid on its face. [*]

....

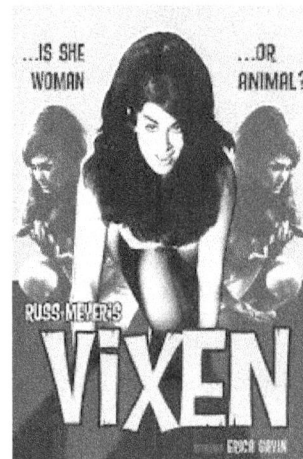

## SECTION 3

# Federal obscenity law

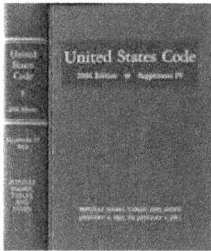

**A Citizen's Guide to U.S. Federal Law on Obscenity**

The U.S. Supreme Court established the test that judges and juries use to determine whether matter is obscene in three major cases: *Miller v. California*, 413 U.S. 15, 24-25 (1973); *Smith v. United States*, 431 U.S. 291, 300-02, 309 (1977); and *Pope v. Illinois*, 481 U.S. 497, 500-01 (1987). The three-pronged *Miller* test is as follows:

1.    Whether the average person, applying contemporary adult community standards, finds that the matter, taken as a whole, appeals to prurient interests (*i.e.*, an erotic, lascivious, abnormal, unhealthy, degrading, shameful, or morbid interest in nudity, sex, or excretion);

2.    Whether the average person, applying contemporary adult community standards, finds that the matter depicts or describes sexual conduct in a patently offensive way (*i.e.*, ultimate sexual acts, normal or perverted, actual or simulated, masturbation, excretory functions, lewd exhibition of the genitals, or sado-masochistic sexual abuse); and

3.    Whether a reasonable person finds that the matter, taken as a whole, lacks serious literary, artistic, political, or scientific value.

Any material that satisfies this three-pronged test may be found obscene.

Federal law prohibits the possession with intent to sell or distribute obscenity, to send, ship, or receive obscenity, to import obscenity, and to transport obscenity across state boarders for purposes of distribution. Although the law does not criminalize the private possession of obscene matter, the act of receiving such matter could violate the statutes prohibiting the use of the U.S. Mails, common carriers, or interactive computer services for the purpose of transportation (See 18 U.S.C. § 1460; 18 U.S.C. § 1461; 18 U.S.C. § 1462; 18 U.S.C. § 1463). Convicted offenders face fines and imprisonment. It is also illegal to aid or abet in the commission of these crimes, and individuals who commit such acts are also punishable under federal obscenity laws.

In addition, federal law prohibits both the production of obscene matter with intent to sell or distribute, and engaging in a business of selling or transferring obscene matter using or affecting means or facility of interstate or foreign commerce, including the use of interactive computer services. (See 18 U.S.C. § 1465; 18 U.S.C. § 1466). For example, it is illegal to sell and distribute obscene material on the Internet. Convicted offenders face fines and up to 5 years in prison.

Moreover, Sections 1464 and 1468 of Title 18, United States Code, specifically prohibit the broadcast or distribution of obscene matter by radio communication or by cable or subscription television respectively. Convicted offenders under these statutes face fines and up to 2 years in prison.

Obscenity Involving Minors

Federal statues specifically prohibit obscenity involving minors, and convicted offenders generally face harsher statutory penalties than if the offense involved only adults.

Section 1470 of Title 18, United States Code, prohibits any individual from knowingly transferring or attempting to transfer obscene matter using the U.S. mail or any means or facility of interstate or foreign commerce to a minor under 16 years of age. Convicted offenders face fines and imprisonment for up to 10 years.

Section 1466A of Title 18, United State Code, makes it illegal for any person to knowingly produce, distribute, receive, or possess with intent to transfer or distribute visual representations, such as drawings, cartoons, or paintings that appear to depict minors engaged in sexually explicit conduct and are deemed obscene.

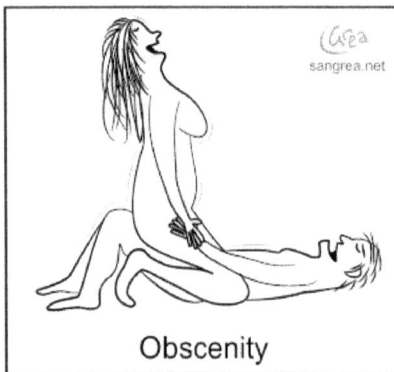

Obscenity

This statute offers an alternative 2-pronged test for obscenity with a lower threshold than the *Miller* test. The matter involving minors can be deemed obscene if it (i) depicts an image that is, or appears to be a minor engaged in graphic bestiality, sadistic or masochistic abuse, or sexual intercourse and (ii) if the image lacks serious literary, artistic, political, or scientific value. A first time offender convicted under this statute faces fines and at least 5 years to a maximum of 20 years in prison.

There are also laws to protect children from obscene or harmful material on the Internet. For one, federal law prohibits the use of misleading domain names, words, or digital images on the Internet with intent to deceive a minor into viewing harmful or obscene material (See 18 U.S.C. §§ 2252B, 2252C). It is illegal for an individual to know-ingly use interactive computer services to display obscenity in a manner that makes it available to a minor less than 18 years of age (See 47 U.S.C. § 223(d) –Communications Decency Act of 1996, as amended by the PROTECT Act of 2003). It is also illegal to knowingly make a commercial communication via the Internet that includes obscenity and is available to any minor less than 17 years of age (See 47 U.S.C. § 231 –Child Online Protection Act of 1998).

Family entertainment

The standard of what is harmful to minors may differ from the standard applied to adults. Harmful materials for minors include any communication consisting of nudity, sex or excretion that (i) appeals to the prurient interest of minors, (ii) is patently offensive to prevailing standards in the adult community with respect to what is suitable material for minors, (iii) and lacks serious literary, artistic, political, or scientific value for minors.

In addition to facing imprisonment and fines, convicted offenders of federal obscenity laws involving minors may also be required to register as sex offenders. Furthermore, in some circumstances, obscenity violations involving minors may also be subject to prosecution under federal child pornography laws, which yield serve statutory penalties

Source:
http://www.justice.gov/criminal/ceos/citizensguide/citizensguide_obscenity.html

# California Penal Code Section 311

311. As used in this chapter, the following definitions apply:

(a) "Obscene matter" means matter, taken as a whole, that to the average person, applying contemporary statewide standards, appeals to
the prurient interest, that, taken as a whole, depicts or describes sexual conduct in a patently offensive way, and that, taken as a whole, lacks serious literary, artistic, political, or scientific value.

(1) If it appears from the nature of the matter or the circumstances of its dissemination, distribution, or exhibition that it is designed for clearly defined deviant sexual groups, the appeal of the matter shall be judged with reference to its intended recipient group.

(2) In prosecutions under this chapter, if circumstances of production, presentation, sale, dissemination, distribution, or publicity indicate that matter is being commercially exploited by the defendant for the sake of its prurient appeal, this evidence is probative with respect to the nature of the matter and may justify the conclusion that the matter lacks serious literary, artistic, political, or scientific value.

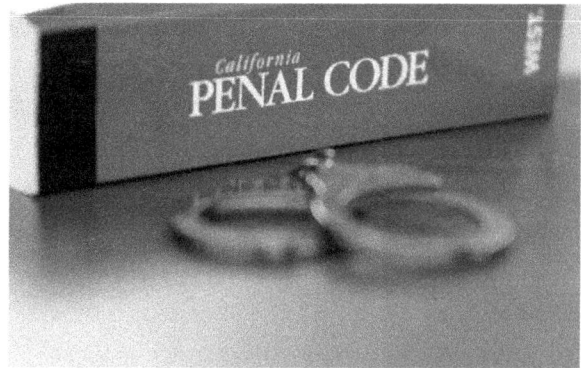

(3) In determining whether the matter taken as a whole lacks serious literary, artistic, political, or scientific value in description or representation of those matters, the fact that the defendant knew that the matter depicts persons under the age of 16 years engaged in sexual conduct, as defined in subdivision (c) of Section 311.4, is a factor that may be considered in making that

determination.

(b) "Matter" means any book, magazine, newspaper, or other printed or written material, or any picture, drawing, photograph, motion picture, or other pictorial representation, or any statue or other figure, or any recording, transcription, or mechanical, chemical, or electrical reproduction, or any other article, equipment, machine, or material. "Matter" also means live or recorded telephone messages if transmitted, disseminated, or distributed as part of a commercial transaction.

(c) "Person" means any individual, partnership, firm, association, corporation, limited liability company, or other legal entity.

(d) "Distribute" means transfer possession of, whether with or without consideration.

(e) "Knowingly" means being aware of the character of the matter or live conduct.

(f) "Exhibit" means show.

(g) "Obscene live conduct" means any physical human body activity, whether performed or engaged in alone or with other persons, including but not limited to singing, speaking, dancing, acting, simulating, or pantomiming, taken as a whole, that to the average person, applying contemporary statewide standards, appeals to the prurient interest and is conduct that, taken as a whole, depicts or describes sexual conduct in a patently offensive way and that, taken as a whole, lacks serious literary, artistic, political, or scientific value.

(1) If it appears from the nature of the conduct or the circumstances of its production, presentation, or exhibition that it is designed for clearly defined deviant sexual groups, the appeal of the conduct shall be judged with reference to its intended recipient group.

(2) In prosecutions under this chapter, if circumstances of production, presentation, advertising, or exhibition indicate that live conduct is being commercially exploited by the defendant for the sake of its prurient appeal, that evidence is probative with respect to the nature of the conduct and may justify the conclusion that the conduct lacks serious literary, artistic, political, or scientific value.

(3) In determining whether the live conduct taken as a whole lacks serious literary, artistic, political, or scientific value in description or representation of those matters, the fact that the defendant knew that the live conduct depicts persons under the age of 16 years engaged in sexual conduct, as defined in subdivision (c) of Section 311.4, is a factor that may be considered in making that determination.

(h) The Legislature expresses its approval of the holding of People v. Cantrell, 7 Cal. App. 4th 523, that, for the purposes of this chapter, matter that "depicts a person under the age of 18 years personally engaging in or personally simulating sexual conduct" is limited to visual works that depict that conduct.

311.2.  (a) Every person who knowingly sends or causes to be sent, or brings or causes to be brought, into this state for sale or distribution, or in this state possesses, prepares, publishes, produces, or prints, with intent to distribute or to exhibit to others, or who offers to distribute, distributes, or exhibits to others, any obscene matter is for a first offense, guilty of a misdemeanor. If the person has previously been convicted of any violation of this section, the court may, in addition to the punishment authorized in Section 311.9, impose a fine not exceeding fifty thousand dollars ($50,000).

  (b) Every person who knowingly sends or causes to be sent, or brings or causes to be brought, into this state for sale or distribution, or in this state possesses, prepares, publishes, produces, develops, duplicates, or prints any representation of information, data, or image, including, but not limited to, any film, filmstrip, photograph, negative, slide, photocopy, videotape, video laser disc, computer hardware, computer software, computer floppy disc, data storage media, CD-ROM, or computer-generated equipment or any other computer-generated image that contains or incorporates in any manner, any film or filmstrip, with intent to distribute or to exhibit to, or to exchange with, others for commercial consideration, or who offers to distribute, distributes, or exhibits to, or exchanges with, others for commercial consideration, any obscene matter, knowing that the matter depicts a person under the age of 18 years personally engaging in or personally simulating sexual conduct, as defined in Section 311.4, is guilty of a felony and shall be punished by imprisonment in the state prison for two, three, or six years, or by a fine not exceeding one hundred thousand dollars ($100,000), in the absence of a finding that the defendant would be incapable of paying that fine, or by both that fine and imprisonment.

* * *

(g) It does not constitute a violation of this section for a telephone corporation, as defined by Section 234 of the Public Utilities Code, to carry or transmit messages described in this chapter or to perform related activities in providing telephone services.

311.6.  Every person who knowingly engages or participates in, manages, produces, sponsors, presents or exhibits obscene live conduct to or before an assembly or audience consisting of at least one person or spectator in any public place or in any place exposed to public view, or in any place open to the public or to a segment thereof, whether or not an admission fee is charged, or whether or not attendance is conditioned upon the presentation of a membership card or other token, is guilty of a misdemeanor.

312.1.  In any prosecution for a violation of the provisions of this chapter or of Chapter 7.6 (commencing with Section 313), neither the prosecution nor the defense shall be required to introduce expert witness testimony concerning the obscene or harmful character of the matter or live conduct which is the subject of the prosecution. Any evidence which tends to establish contemporary community standards appeal to prurient interest or of customary limits of candor in the of description or representation of nudity, sex, or excretion, or which bears upon the question of significant literary, artistic, political, educational, or scientific value shall, subject to the provisions of the Evidence Code, be admissible when offered by either the prosecution or by the defense.

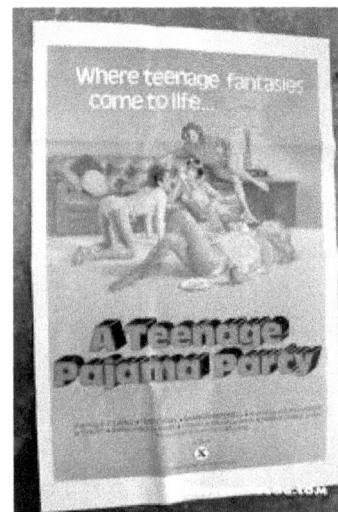

# CHAPTER 12

# Copyright and fair use

COPYRIGHT

COPYLEFT

# Harper & Row v. Nation Enterprises (1985)

U.S. Supreme Court

471 U.S. 539 (1985)

Decided May 20, 1985

Burger  Blackmun  Powell  Rehnquist  Stevens  O'Connor  Brennan  White  Marshall

Decision: 6 votes for Harper & Row, Publishers, Inc., 3 vote(s) against

**JUSTICE O'CONNOR delivered the opinion of the Court.**

This case requires us to consider to what extent the "fair use" provision of the Copyright Revision Act of 1976 (hereinafter the Copyright Act), 17 U.S.C. § 107, sanctions the unauthorized use of quotations from a public figure's unpublished manuscript. In March, 1979, an undisclosed source provided The Nation Magazine with the unpublished manuscript of "A Time to Heal: The Autobiography of Gerald R. Ford." Working directly from the purloined manuscript, an editor of The Nation produced a short piece entitled "The Ford Memoirs -- Behind the Nixon Pardon." The piece was timed to "scoop" an article scheduled shortly to appear in Time Magazine. Time had agreed to purchase the exclusive right to print prepublication excerpts from the copyright holders, Harper & Row Publishers, Inc. (hereinafter Harper & Row), and Reader's Digest Association, Inc. (hereinafter Reader's Digest). As a result of The Nation article, Time canceled its agreement. Petitioners brought a successful copyright action against The Nation. On appeal, the Second Circuit reversed the lower court's finding of infringement, holding that The Nation's act was sanctioned as a "fair use" of the copyrighted material. We granted certiorari, 467 U.S. 1214 (1984), and we now reverse.

I

In February, 1977, shortly after leaving the White House, former President Gerald R. Ford contracted with petitioners Harper & Row and Reader's Digest, to publish his as yet unwritten memoirs. The memoirs were to contain "significant hitherto unpublished material" concerning the Watergate crisis, Mr. Ford's pardon of former President Nixon, and "Mr. Ford's reflections on this period of history, and the morality and personalities involved." App. to Pet. for Cert. C-14 - C-15. In addition to the right to publish the Ford memoirs in book form, the agreement gave petitioners the exclusive right to license prepublication excerpts, known in the trade as "first serial rights." Two years later, as the memoirs were nearing completion, petitioners negotiated a prepublication licensing agreement with Time, a weekly news magazine. Time agreed to pay $25,000, $12,500 in advance and an additional $12,500 at publication, in exchange for the right to excerpt 7,500 words from Mr. Ford's account of the Nixon pardon. The issue featuring the excerpts was timed to appear approximately one week before shipment of the full-length book version to bookstores. Exclusivity was an important consideration; Harper & Row instituted procedures designed to maintain the confidentiality of the manuscript, and Time retained the right to renegotiate the second payment should the material appear in print prior to its release of the excerpts.

Two to three weeks before the Time article's scheduled release, an unidentified person secretly brought a copy of the Ford manuscript to Victor Navasky, editor of The Nation, a political commentary magazine. Mr. Navasky knew that his possession of the manuscript was not authorized, and that the manuscript must be returned quickly to his "source" to avoid discovery. 557 F.Supp. 1067, 1069 (SDNY 1983). He hastily put together what he believed was "a real hot news story" composed of quotes, paraphrases, and facts drawn exclusively from the manuscript. Ibid. Mr. Navasky attempted no independent commentary, research or criticism, in part because of the need for speed if he was to "make news" by "publish[ing] in advance of publication of the Ford book." App. 416-417. The 2,250-word article, reprinted in the Appendix to this opinion, appeared on April 3, 1979. As a result of The Nation's article, Time canceled its piece and refused to pay the remaining $12,500.

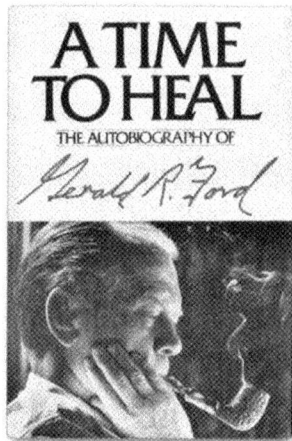

Petitioners brought suit in the District Court for the Southern District of New York, alleging conversion, tortious interference with contract, and violations of the Copyright Act. After a 6-day bench trial, the District Judge found that "A Time to Heal" was protected by copyright at the time of The Nation publication and that respondents' use of the copyrighted material constituted an infringement under the Copyright Act, §§ 106(1), (2), and (3), protecting respectively the right to reproduce the work, the right to license preparation of derivative works, and the right of first distribution of the copyrighted work to the public. App. to Pet. for Cert. C-29 - C-30. The District Court rejected respondents' argument that The Nation's piece was a "fair use" sanctioned by § 107 of the Act. Though billed as "hot news," the article contained no new facts. The magazine had "published its article for profit," taking "the heart" of "a soon-to-be published" work. This unauthorized use "caused the Time agreement to be aborted, and thus diminished the value of the copyright." 557 F.Supp. at 1072. Although certain elements of the Ford memoirs, such as historical facts and memoranda, were not per se copyrightable, the District Court held that it was

"the totality of these facts and memoranda collected, together with Ford's reflections, that made them of value to The Nation, [and] this . . . totality . . . is protected by the copyright laws."

Id. at 1072-1073. The court awarded actual damages of $12,500.

A divided panel of the Court of Appeals for the Second Circuit reversed. The majority recognized that Mr. Ford's verbatim "reflections" were original "expression" protected by copyright. But it held that the District Court had erred in assuming the "coupling [of these reflections] with uncopyrightable fact transformed that information into a copyrighted totality.'" 723 F.2d 195, 205 (1983). The majority noted that copyright attaches to expression, not facts or ideas. It concluded that, to avoid granting a copyright monopoly over the facts underlying history and news, "`expression' [in such works must be confined] to its barest elements -- the ordering and choice of the words themselves." Id. at 204. Thus similarities between the original and the challenged work traceable to the copying or paraphrasing of uncopyrightable material, such as historical facts, memoranda and other public documents, and quoted remarks of third parties, must be disregarded in evaluating whether the second author's use was fair or infringing.

"When the uncopyrighted material is stripped away, the article in The Nation contains, at most, approximately 300 words that are copyrighted. These remaining paragraphs and scattered phrases are all verbatim quotations from the memoirs which had not appeared previously in other publications. They include a short segment of Ford's conversations with Henry Kissinger and several other individuals. Ford's impressionistic depictions of Nixon, ill with phlebitis after the resignation and pardon, and of Nixon's character, constitute the major portion of this material. It is these parts of the magazine piece on which [the court] must focus in [its] examination of the question whether there was a 'fair use' of copyrighted matter."

Id. at 206. Examining the four factors enumerated in § 107, see infra at 471 U. S. 547, n. 2, the majority found the purpose of the article was "news reporting," the original work was essentially factual in nature, the 300 words appropriated were insubstantial in relation to the 2,250-word piece, and the impact on the market for the original was minimal, as "the evidence [did] not support a finding that it was the very limited use of expression per se which led to Time's decision not to print the excerpt." The Nation's borrowing of verbatim quotations merely "len[t] authenticity to this politically significant material . . . complementing the reporting of the facts." 723 F.2d at 208. The Court of Appeals was especially influenced by the "politically significant" nature of the subject matter and its conviction that it is not "the purpose of the Copyright Act to impede that harvest of knowledge so necessary to a democratic state" or "chill the activities of the press by forbidding a circumscribed use of copyrighted words." Id. at 197, 209.

II

We agree with the Court of Appeals that copyright is intended to increase, and not to impede, the harvest of knowledge. But we believe the Second Circuit gave insufficient deference to the scheme established by the Copyright Act for fostering the original works that provide the seed and substance of this harvest. The rights conferred by copyright are designed to assure contributors to the store of knowledge a fair return for their labors. Twentieth Century Music Corp. v. Aiken, 422 U. S. 151, 422 U. S. 156 (1975).

Article I, § 8, of the Constitution provides:

"The Congress shall have Power . . . to Promote the Progress of Science and useful Arts, by securing for limited Times to Authors and Inventors the exclusive Right to their respective Writings and Discoveries."

As we noted last Term:

"[This] limited grant is a means by which an important public purpose may be achieved. It is intended to motivate the creative activity of authors and inventors by the provision of a special reward, and to allow the public access to the products of their genius after the limited period of exclusive control has expired."

Sony Corp. of America v. Universal City Studios, Inc., 464 U. S. 417, 464 U. S. 429 (1984). "The monopoly created by copyright thus rewards the individual author in order to benefit the public." Id. at 464 U. S. 477 (dissenting opinion). This principle applies equally to works of fiction and nonfiction. The book at issue here, for example, was two years in the making, and began with a contract giving the author's copyright to the publishers in exchange for their services in producing and marketing the work. In preparing the book, Mr. Ford drafted essays and word portraits of public figures and participated in hundreds of taped interviews that were later distilled to chronicle his personal viewpoint. It is evident that the monopoly granted by copyright actively served its intended purpose of inducing the creation of new material of potential historical value.

Section 106 of the Copyright Act confers a bundle of exclusive rights to the owner of the copyright. [Footnote 1] Under the Copyright Act, these rights -- to publish, copy, and distribute the author's work -- vest in the author of an original work from the time of its creation. § 106. In practice, the author commonly sells his rights to publishers who offer royalties in exchange for their services in producing and marketing the author's work. The copyright owner's rights, however, are subject to certain statutory exceptions. §§ 107-118. Among these is § 107, which codifies the traditional privilege of other authors to make "fair use" of an earlier writer's work. [Footnote 2] In addition, no author may copyright facts or ideas. § 102. The copyright is limited to those aspects of the work -- termed "expression" -- that display the stamp of the author's originality.

Creation of a nonfiction work, even a compilation of pure fact, entails originality. See, e.g., Schroeder v. William Morrow & Co., 566 F.2d 3 (CA7 1977) (copyright in gardening directory); cf. Burrow-Giles Lithographic Co. v. Sarony, 111 U. S. 53, 111 U. S. 58 (1884) (originator of a photograph may claim copyright in his work). The copyright holders of "A Time to Heal" complied with the relevant statutory notice and registration procedures. See §§ 106, 401, 408; App. to Pet. for Cert. C-20. Thus there is no dispute that the unpublished manuscript of "A Time to Heal," as a whole, was protected by § 106 from unauthorized reproduction. Nor do respondents dispute that verbatim copying of excerpts of the manuscript's original form of expression would constitute infringement unless excused as fair use. See 1 M. Nimmer, Copyright § 2.11[B], p. 2-159 (1984) (hereinafter Nimmer). Yet copyright does not prevent subsequent users from copying from a prior author's work those constituent elements that are not original -- for example, quotations borrowed under the rubric of fair use from other copyrighted works, facts, or materials in the public domain -- as long as such use does not unfairly appropriate the author's original contributions. Ibid.; A. Latman, Fair Use of Copyrighted Works (1958), reprinted as Study No. 14 in Copyright Law Revision Studies Nos. 1416, prepared for the Senate Committee on the Judiciary, 86th Cong., 2d Sess., 7 (1960) (hereinafter Latman). Perhaps the controversy between the lower courts in this case over copyrightability is more aptly styled a dispute over whether The Nation's appropriation of unoriginal and uncopyrightable elements encroached on the originality embodied in the work as a whole. Especially in the realm of factual narrative, the law is currently unsettled regarding the ways in which uncopyrightable elements combine with the author's original contributions to form protected expression. Compare Wainwright Securities Inc. v. Wall Street Transcript Corp., 558 F.2d 91 (CA2 1977) (protection accorded author's analysis, structuring of material and marshaling of facts), with Hoehling v. Universal City Studios, Inc., 618 F.2d 972 (CA2 1980) (limiting protection to ordering and choice of words). See, e.g., 1 Nimmer § 2.11[D], at 2-164 - 2-165.

We need not reach these issues, however, as The Nation has admitted to lifting verbatim quotes of the author's original language totaling between 300 and 400 words and constituting some 13% of The Nation article. In using generous verbatim excerpts of Mr. Ford's unpublished manuscript to lend authenticity to its account of the forthcoming memoirs, The Nation effectively arrogated to itself the right of first publication, an important marketable subsidiary right. For the reasons set forth below, we find that this use of the copyrighted manuscript, even stripped to the verbatim quotes conceded by The Nation to be copyrightable expression, was not a fair use within the meaning of the Copyright Act.

## III

### A

Fair use was traditionally defined as "a privilege in others than the owner of the copyright to use the copyrighted material in a reasonable manner without his consent." H. Ball, Law of Copyright and Literary Property 260 (1944) (hereinafter Ball). The statutory formulation of the defense of fair use in the Copyright Act reflects the intent of Congress to codify the common law doctrine. 3 Nimmer § 13.05. Section 107 requires a case-by-case determination whether a particular use is fair, and the statute notes four nonexclusive factors to be considered. This approach was "intended to restate the [preexisting] judicial doctrine of fair use, not to change, narrow, or enlarge it in any way." H.R.Rep. No. 94-1476, p. 66 (1976) (hereinafter House Report).

"[T]he author's consent to a reasonable use of his copyrighted works ha[d] always been implied by the courts as a necessary incident of the constitutional policy of promoting the progress of science and the useful arts, since a prohibition of such use would inhibit subsequent writers from attempting to improve upon prior works, and thus . . . frustrate the very ends sought to be attained."

Ball 260. Professor Latman, in a study of the doctrine of fair use commissioned by Congress for the revision effort, see Sony Corp. of America v. Universal City Studios, Inc., 464 U.S. at 464 U. S. 462-463, n. 9 (dissenting opinion), summarized prior law as turning on the

"importance of the material copied or performed from the point of view of the reasonable copyright owner. In other words, would the reasonable copyright owner have consented to the use?"

Latman 15. [Footnote 3]

As early as 1841, Justice Story gave judicial recognition to the doctrine in a case that concerned the letters of another former President, George Washington.

"[A] reviewer may fairly cite largely from the original work, if his design be really and truly to use the passages for the purposes of fair and reasonable criticism. On the other hand, it is as clear that, if he thus cites the most important parts of the work, with a view not to criticise, but to supersede the use of the original work, and substitute the review for it, such a use will be deemed in law a piracy."

Folsom v. Marsh, 9 F.Cas. 342, 344-345 (No. 4,901) (CC Mass.) As Justice Story's hypothetical illustrates, the fair use doctrine has always precluded a use that "supersede[s] the use of the original." Ibid. Accord, S.Rep. No. 94-473, p. 65 (1975) (hereinafter Senate Report).

Perhaps because the fair use doctrine was predicated on the author's implied consent to "reasonable and customary" use when he released his work for public consumption, fair use traditionally was not recognized as a defense to charges of copying from an author's as yet unpublished works. [Footnote 4] Under common law copyright, "the property of the author . . . in his intellectual creation [was] absolute until he voluntarily part[ed] with the same." American Tobacco Co. v. Werckmeister, 207 U. S. 284, 207 U. S. 299 (1907); 2 Nimmer § 8.23, at 8-273. This absolute rule, however, was tempered in practice by the equitable nature of the fair use doctrine. In a given case, factors such as implied consent through de facto publication on performance or dissemination of a work may tip the balance of equities in favor of prepublication use. See Copyright Law Revision -- Part 2: Discussion and Comments on Report of the Register of Copyrights on General Revision of the U.S. Copyright Law, 88th Cong., 1st Sess., 27 (H.R. Comm. Print 1963) (discussion suggesting works disseminated to the public in a form not constituting a technical "publication" should nevertheless be subject to fair use); 3 Nimmer § 13.05, at 13-62, n. 2. But it has never been seriously disputed that "the fact that the plaintiff's work is unpublished . . . is a factor tending to negate the defense of fair use." Ibid. Publication of an author's expression before he has authorized its dissemination seriously infringes the author's right to decide when and whether it will be made public, a factor not present in fair use of published works.

Respondents contend, however, that Congress, in including first publication among the rights enumerated in § 106, which are expressly subject to fair use under § 107, intended that fair use would apply in pari materia to published and unpublished works. The Copyright Act does not support this proposition.

The Copyright Act represents the culmination of a major legislative reexamination of copyright doctrine. See Mills Music, Inc. v. Snyder, 469 U. S. 153, 469 U. S. 159-160 (1985); Sony Corp. of America v. Universal City Studios, Inc., 464 U.S. at 464 U. S. 462-463, n. 9 (dissenting opinion). Among its other innovations, it eliminated publication "as a dividing line between common law and statutory protection," House Report at 129, extending statutory protection to all works from the time of their creation. It also recognized for the first time a distinct statutory right of first publication, which had previously been an element of the common law protections afforded unpublished works. The Report of the House Committee on the Judiciary confirms that

"Clause (3) of section 106, establishes the exclusive right of publications. . . . Under this provision, the copyright owner would have the right to control the first public distribution of an authorized copy . . . of his work."

Id. at 62.

Though the right of first publication, like the other rights enumerated in § 106, is expressly made subject to the fair use provision of § 107, fair use analysis must always be tailored to the individual case. Id. at 65; 3 Nimmer § 13.05[A]. The nature of the interest at stake is highly relevant to whether a given use is fair. From the beginning, those entrusted with the task of revision recognized the

"overbalancing reasons to preserve the common law protection of undisseminated works until the author or his successor chooses to disclose them."

Copyright Law Revision, Report of the Register of Copyrights on the General Revision of the U.S. Copyright Law, 87th Cong., 1st Sess., 41 (Comm. Print 1961). The right of first publication implicates a threshold decision by the author whether and in what form to release his work. First publication is inherently different from other § 106 rights in that only one person can be the first publisher; as the contract with Time illustrates, the commercial value of the right lies primarily in exclusivity. Because the potential damage to the author from judicially enforced "sharing" of the first publication right with unauthorized users of his manuscript is substantial, the balance of equities in evaluating such a claim of fair use inevitably shifts.

The Senate Report confirms that Congress intended the unpublished nature of the work to figure prominently in fair use analysis. In discussing fair use of photocopied materials in the classroom the Committee Report states:

"A key, though not necessarily determinative, factor in fair use is whether or not the work is available to the potential user. If the work is 'out of print' and unavailable for purchase through normal channels, the user may have more justification for reproducing it. . . . The applicability of the fair use doctrine to unpublished works is narrowly limited, since, although the work is unavailable, this is the result of a deliberate choice on the part of the copyright owner. Under ordinary circumstances, the copyright owner's 'right of first publication' would outweigh any needs of reproduction for classroom purposes."

Senate Report at 64. Although the Committee selected photocopying of classroom materials to illustrate fair use, it emphasized that "the same general standards of fair use are applicable to all kinds of uses of copyrighted material." Id. at 65. We find unconvincing respondents' contention that the absence of the quoted passage from the House Report indicates an intent to abandon the traditional distinction between fair use of published and unpublished works. It appears instead that the fair use discussion of photocopying of classroom materials was omitted from the final Report because educators and publishers in the interim had negotiated a set of guidelines that rendered the discussion obsolete. House Report at 67. The House Report nevertheless incorporates the discussion by reference, citing to the Senate Report and stating: "The Committee has reviewed this discussion, and considers it still has value as an analysis of various aspects of the [fair use] problem." Ibid.

Even if the legislative history were entirely silent, we would be bound to conclude from Congress' characterization of § 107 as a "restatement" that its effect was to preserve existing law concerning fair use of unpublished works as of other types of protected works, and not to "change, narrow, or enlarge it." Id. at 66. We conclude that the unpublished nature of a work is "[a] key, though not necessarily determinative, factor" tending to negate a defense of fair use. Senate Report at 64. See 3 Nimmer § 13.05, at 13-62, n. 2; W. Patry, The Fair Use Privilege in Copyright Law 125 (1985) (hereinafter Patry).

We also find unpersuasive respondents' argument that fair use may be made of a soon-to-be-published manuscript on the ground that the author has demonstrated he has no interest in nonpublication. This argument assumes that the unpublished nature of copyrighted material is only relevant to letters or other confidential writings not intended for dissemination. It is true that common law copyright was often en-

listed in the service of personal privacy. See Brandeis & Warren, The Right to Privacy, 4 Harv.L.Rev.193, 198-199 (1890). In its commercial guise, however, an author's right to choose when he will publish is no less deserving of protection.

The period encompassing the work's initiation, its preparation, and its grooming for public dissemination is a crucial one for any literary endeavor. The Copyright Act, which accords the copyright owner the "right to control the first public distribution" of his work, House Report at 62, echos the common law's concern that the author or copyright owner retain control throughout this critical stage. See generally Comment, The Stage of Publication as a "Fair Use" Factor: Harper & Row, Publishers v. Nation Enterprises, 58 St. John's L.Rev. 597 (1984). The obvious benefit to author and public alike of assuring authors the leisure to develop their ideas free from fear of expropriation outweighs any short-term "news value" to be gained from premature publication of the author's expression. See Goldstein, Copyright and the First Amendment, 70 Colum.L.Rev. 983, 1004-1006 (1970) (The absolute protection the common law accorded to soon-to-be published works "[was] justified by [its] brevity and expedience"). The author's control of first public distribution implicates not only his personal interest in creative control, but his property interest in exploitation of prepublication rights, which are valuable in themselves and serve as a valuable adjunct to publicity and marketing. See Belshi v. Woodward, 598 F.Supp. 36 (DC 1984) (successful marketing depends on coordination of serialization and release to public); Marks, Subsidiary Rights and Permissions, in What Happens in Book Publishing 230 (C. Grannis ed.1967) (exploitation of subsidiary rights is necessary to financial success of new books). Under ordinary circumstances, the author's right to control the first public appearance of his undisseminated expression will outweigh a claim of fair use.

B

Respondents, however, contend that First Amendment values require a different rule under the circumstances of this case. The thrust of the decision below is that "[t]he scope of [fair use] is undoubtedly wider when the information conveyed relates to matters of high public concern." Consumers Union of the United States, Inc. v. General Signal Corp., 724 F.2d 1044, 1050 (CA2 1983) (construing 723 F.2d 195 (1983) (case below) as allowing advertiser to quote Consumer Reports), cert. denied, 469 U.S. 823 (1984). Respondents advance the substantial public import of the subject matter of the Ford memoirs as grounds for excusing a use that would ordinarily not pass muster as a fair use -- the piracy of verbatim quotations for the purpose of "scooping" the authorized first serialization. Respondents explain their copying of Mr. Ford's expression as essential to reporting the news story it claims the book itself represents. In respondents' view, not only the facts contained in Mr. Ford's memoirs, but "the precise manner in which [he] expressed himself [were] as newsworthy as what he had to say." Brief for Respondents 38-39. Respondents argue that the public's interest in learning this news as fast as possible outweighs the right of the author to control its first publication.

The Second Circuit noted, correctly, that copyright's idea/ expression dichotomy

"strike[s] a definitional balance between the First Amendment and the Copyright Act by permitting free communication of facts while still protecting an author's expression."

723 F.2d at 203. No author may copyright his ideas or the facts he narrates. 17 U.S.C. § 102(b). See, e.g., New York Times Co. v. United States, 403 U. S. 713, 403 U. S. 726, n. (1971) (BRENNAN, J., concurring) (Copyright laws are not restrictions on freedom of speech, as copyright protects only form of expression, and not the ideas expressed); 1 Nimmer § 1.10[B][2]. As this Court long ago observed:

"[T]he news element -- the information respecting current events contained in the literary production -- is not the creation of the writer, but is a report of matters that ordinarily are publici juris; it is the history of the day."

International News Service v. Associated Press, 248 U. S. 215, 248 U. S. 234 (1918). But copyright assures those who write and publish factual narratives such as "A Time to Heal" that they may at least enjoy the right to market the original expression contained therein as just compensation for their investment. Cf. Zacchini v. Scripps-Howard Broadcasting Co., 433 U. S. 562, 433 U. S. 575 (1977).

Respondents' theory, however, would expand fair use to effectively destroy any expectation of copyright protection in the work of a public figure. Absent such protection, there would be little incentive to create or profit in financing such memoirs, and the public would be denied an important source of significant historical information. The promise of copyright would be an empty one if it could be avoided merely by dubbing the infringement a fair use "news report" of the book. See Wainwright Securities Inc. v. Wall Street Transcript Corp., 558 F.2d 91 (CA2 1977), cert. denied, 434 U.S. 1014 (1978).

Nor do respondents assert any actual necessity for circumventing the copyright scheme with respect to the types of works and users at issue here. [Footnote 6] Where an author and publisher have invested extensive resources in creating an original work and are poised to release it to the public, no legitimate aim is served by preempting the right of first publication. The fact that the words the author has chosen to clothe his narrative may of themselves be "newsworthy" is not an independent justification for unauthorized copying of the author's expression prior to publication. To paraphrase another recent Second Circuit decision:

"[Respondent] possessed an unfettered right to use any factual information revealed in [the memoirs] for the purpose of enlightening its audience, but it can claim no need to 'bodily appropriate' [Mr. Ford's] 'expression' of that information by utilizing portions of the actual [manuscript]. The public interest in the free flow of information is assured by the law's refusal to recognize a valid copyright in facts. The fair use doctrine is not a license for corporate theft, empowering a court to ignore a copyright whenever it determines the underlying work contains material of possible public importance."

Iowa State University Research Foundation, Inc. v. American Broadcasting Cos., Inc., 621 F.2d 57, 61 (1980) (citations omitted). Accord, Roy Export Co. Establishment v. Columbia Broadcasting System, Inc., 503 F.Supp. 1137 (SDNY 1980) ("newsworthiness" of material copied does not justify copying), aff'd, 672 F.2d 1095 (CA2), cert. denied, 459 U.S. 826 (1982); Quinto v. Legal Times of Washington, Inc., 506 F.Supp. 554 (DC 1981) (same).

In our haste to disseminate news, it should not be forgotten that the Framers intended copyright itself to be the engine of free expression. By establishing a marketable right to the use of one's expression, copyright supplies the economic incentive to create and disseminate ideas. This Court stated in Mazer v. Stein, 347 U. S. 201, 209 (1954):

"The economic philosophy behind the clause empowering Congress to grant patents and copyrights is the conviction that encouragement of individual effort by personal gain is the best way to advance public welfare through the talents of authors and inventors in 'science and useful Arts.'"

And again in Twentieth Century Music Corp. v. Aiken:

"The immediate effect of our copyright law is to secure a fair return for an 'author's' creative labor. But the ultimate aim is, by this incentive, to stimulate [the creation of useful works] for the general public good."

It is fundamentally at odds with the scheme of copyright to accord lesser rights in those works that are of greatest importance to the public. Such a notion ignores the major premise of copyright, and injures author and public alike.

"[T]o propose that fair use be imposed whenever the 'social value [of dissemination] . . . outweighs any detriment to the artist' would be to propose depriving copyright owners of their right in the property precisely when they encounter those users who could afford to pay for it."

Gordon, Fair Use as Market Failure: A Structural and Economic Analysis of the Betamax Case and its Predecessors, 82 Colum.L.Rev. 1600, 1615 (1982). And as one commentator has noted:

"If every volume that was in the public interest could be pirated away by a competing publisher, . . . the public [soon] would have nothing worth reading."

Sobel, Copyright and the First Amendment: A Gathering Storm?, 19 ASCAP Copyright Law Symposium 43, 78 (1971). See generally Comment, Copyright and the First Amendment; Where Lies the Public Interest?, 59 Tulane L.Rev. 135 (1984).

Moreover, freedom of thought and expression "includes both the right to speak freely and the right to refrain from speaking at all." Wooley v. Maynard, 430 U. S. 705, 430 U. S. 714 (1977) (BURGER, C.J.). We do not suggest this right not to speak would sanction abuse of the copyright owner's monopoly as an instrument to suppress facts. But in the words of New York's Chief Judge Fuld:

"The essential thrust of the First Amendment is to prohibit improper restraints on the voluntary public expression of ideas; it shields the man who wants to speak or publish when others wish him to be quiet. There is necessarily, and within suitably defined areas, a concomitant freedom not to speak publicly, one which serves the same ultimate end as freedom of speech in its affirmative aspect."

Estate of Hemingway v. Random House, Inc., 23 N.Y.2d 341, 348, 244 N.E.2d 250, 255 (1968).

Courts and commentators have recognized that copyright, and the right of first publication in particular, serve this countervailing First Amendment value. See Schnapper v. Foley, 215 U.S.App.D.C. 59, 667 F.2d 102 (1981), cert. denied, 455 U.S. 948 (1982); 1 Nimmer § 1.10[B], at 1-70, n. 24; Patry 140-142.

In view of the First Amendment protections already embodied in the Copyright Act's distinction between copyrightable expression and uncopyrightable facts and ideas, and the latitude for scholarship and comment traditionally afforded by fair use, we see no warrant for expanding the doctrine of fair use to create what amounts to a public figure exception to copyright. Whether verbatim copying from a public figure's manuscript in a given case is or is not fair must be judged according to the traditional equities of fair use.

IV

Fair use is a mixed question of law and fact. Pacific & Southern Co. v. Duncan, 744 F.2d 1490, 1495, n. 8 (CA11 1984). Where the district court has found facts sufficient to evaluate each of the statutory factors, an appellate court

"need not remand for further factfinding . . . , [but] may conclude as a matter of law that [the challenged use] do[es] not qualify as a fair use of the copyrighted work."

Id. at 1495. Thus whether The Nation article constitutes fair use under § 107 must be reviewed in light of the principles discussed above. The factors enumerated in the section are not meant to be exclusive:

"[S]ince the doctrine is an equitable rule of reason, no generally applicable definition is possible, and each case raising the question must be decided on its own facts."

House Report at 65. The four factors identified by Congress as especially relevant in determining whether the use was fair are: (1) the purpose and character of the use; (2) the nature of the copyrighted work; (3) the substantiality of the portion used in relation to the copyrighted work as a whole; (4) the effect on the potential market for or value of the copyrighted work. We address each one separately.

Purpose of the Use. The Second Circuit correctly identified news reporting as the general purpose of The Nation's use. News reporting is one of the examples enumerated in § 107 to "give some idea of the sort of activities the courts might regard as fair use under the circumstances." Senate Report at 61. This listing was not intended to be exhaustive, see ibid.; § 101 (definition of "including" and "such as"), or to single out any particular use as presumptively a "fair" use. The drafters resisted pressures from special interest groups to create presumptive categories of fair use, but structured the provision as an affirmative defense requiring a case-by-case analysis. See H.R.Rep. No. 83, 90th Cong., 1st Sess., 37 (1967); Patry 477, n. 4.

"[W]hether a use referred to in the first sentence of section 107 is a fair use in a particular case will depend upon the application of the determinative factors, including those mentioned in the second sentence."

Senate Report at 62. The fact that an article arguably is "news," and therefore a productive use, is simply one factor in a fair use analysis.

We agree with the Second Circuit that the trial court erred in fixing on whether the information contained in the memoirs was actually new to the public. As Judge Meskill wisely noted, "[c]ourts should be chary of deciding what is and what is not news." 723 F.2d at 215 (dissenting). Cf. Gertz v. Robert Welch, Inc., 418 U. S. 323, 418 U. S. 345-346 (1974).

"The issue is not what constitutes 'news,' but whether a claim of newsreporting is a valid fair use defense to an infringement of copyrightable expression."

Patry 119. The Nation has every right to seek to be the first to publish information. But The Nation went beyond simply reporting uncopyrightable information and actively sought to exploit the headline value of its infringement, making a "news event" out of its unauthorized first publication of a noted figure's copyrighted expression.

The fact that a publication was commercial, as opposed to nonprofit, is a separate factor that tends to weigh against a finding of fair use.

"[E]very commercial use of copyrighted material is presumptively an unfair exploitation of the monopoly privilege that belongs to the owner of the copyright."

Sony Corp. of America v. Universal City Studios, Inc., 464 U.S. at 464 U. S. 451. In arguing that the purpose of news reporting is not purely commercial, The Nation misses the point entirely. The crux of the profit/nonprofit distinction is not whether the sole motive of the use is monetary gain, but whether the user stands to profit from exploitation of the copyrighted material without paying the customary price. See Roy Export Co. Establishment v. Columbia Broadcasting System, Inc., 503 F.Supp. at 1144; 3 Nimmer § 13.05[A][1], at 13-71, n. 25.3.

In evaluating character and purpose, we cannot ignore The Nation's stated purpose of scooping the forthcoming hardcover and Time abstracts. [Footnote 7] App. to Pet. for Cert. C-27. The Nation's use had not merely the incidental effect, but the intended purpose, of supplanting the copyright holder's commercially valuable right of first publication. See Meredith Corp. v. Harper & Row, Publishers, Inc., 378 F.Supp. 686, 690 (SDNY) (purpose of text was to compete with original), aff'd, 500 F.2d 1221 (CA2 1974). Also relevant to the "character" of the use is "the propriety of the defendant's conduct." 3 Nimmer § 13.05[A], at 13-72. "Fair use presupposes good faith' and `fair deal-

ing.'" Time Inc. v. Bernard Geis Associates, 293 F.Supp. 130, 146 (SDNY 1968), quoting

Schulman, Fair Use and the Revision of the Copyright Act, 53 Iowa L.Rev. 832 (1968). The trial court found that The Nation knowingly exploited a purloined manuscript. App. to Pet. for Cert. B-1, C-20 - C-21, C-28 - C-29. Unlike the typical claim of fair use, The Nation cannot offer up even the fiction of consent as justification. Like its competitor newsweekly, it was free to bid for the right of abstracting excerpts from "A Time to Heal." Fair use "distinguishes between `a true scholar and a chiseler who infringes a work for personal profit.'" Wainwright Securities Inc. v. Wall Street Transcript Corp., 558 F.2d at 94, quoting from Hearings on Bills for the General Revision of the Copyright Law before the House Committee on the Judiciary, 89th Cong., 1st Sess., ser. 8, pt. 3, p. 1706 (1966) (statement of John Schulman).

Nature of the Copyrighted Work. Second, the Act directs attention to the nature of the copyrighted work. "A Time to Heal" may be characterized as an unpublished historical narrative or autobiography. The law generally recognizes a greater need to disseminate factual works than works of fiction or fantasy. See Gorman, Fact or Fancy? The Implications for Copyright, 29 J.Copyright Soc. 560, 561 (1982).

"[E]ven within the field of fact works, there are gradations as to the relative proportion of fact and fancy. One may move from sparsely embellished maps and directories to elegantly written biography. The extent to which one must permit expressive language to be copied, in order to assure dissemination of the underlying facts, will thus vary from case to case."

Id. at 563. Some of the briefer quotes from the memoirs are arguably necessary adequately to convey the facts; for example, Mr. Ford's characterization of the White House tapes as the "smoking gun" is perhaps so integral to the idea expressed as to be inseparable from it. Cf. 1 Nimmer § 1.10[C]. But The Nation did not stop at isolated phrases, and instead excerpted subjective descriptions and portraits of public figures whose power lies in the author's individualized expression. Such

Page 471 U. S. 564

use, focusing on the most expressive elements of the work, exceeds that necessary to disseminate the facts.

The fact that a work is unpublished is a critical element of its "nature." 3 Nimmer § 13.05[A]; Comment, 58 St. John's L.Rev. at 613. Our prior discussion establishes that the scope of fair use is narrower with respect to unpublished works. While even substantial quotations might qualify as fair use in a review of a published work or a news account of a speech that had been delivered to the public or disseminated to the press, see House Report at 65, the author's right to control the first public appearance of his expression weighs against such use of the work before its release. The right of first publication encompasses not only the choice whether to publish at all, but also the choices of when, where, and in what form first to publish a work.

In the case of Mr. Ford's manuscript, the copyright holders' interest in confidentiality is irrefutable; the copyright holders had entered into a contractual undertaking to "keep the manuscript confidential" and required that all those to whom the manuscript was shown also "sign an agreement to keep the manuscript confidential." App. to Pet. for Cert. 1C-20. While the copyright holders' contract with Time required Time to submit its proposed article seven days before publication, The Nation's clandestine publication afforded no such opportunity for creative or quality control. Id. at C-18. It was hastily patched together, and contained "a number of inaccuracies." App. 300b-300c (testimony of Victor Navasky). A use that so clearly infringes the copyright holder's interests in confidentiality and creative control is difficult to characterize as "fair."

Amount and Substantiality of the Portion Used. Next, the Act directs us to examine the amount and substantiality of the portion used in rela-

tion to the copyrighted work as a whole. In absolute terms, the words actually quoted were an insubstantial portion of "A Time to Heal." The District Court, however, found that "[T]he Nation took what was essentially the heart of the book." 557 F.Supp. at 1072. We believe the Court of Appeals erred in overruling the District Judge's evaluation of the qualitative nature of the taking. See, e.g., Roy Export Co. Establishment v. Columbia Broadcasting System, Inc., 503 F.Supp. at 1145 (taking of 55 seconds out of 1 hour and 29-minute film deemed qualitatively substantial). A Time editor described the chapters on the pardon as "the most interesting and moving parts of the entire manuscript." Reply Brief for Petitioners 16, n. 8. The portions actually quoted were selected by Mr. Navasky as among the most powerful passages in those chapters. He testified that he used verbatim excerpts because simply reciting the information could not adequately convey the "absolute certainty with which [Ford] expressed himself," App. 303, or show that "this comes from President Ford," id. at 305, or carry the "definitive quality" of the original, id. at 306. In short, he quoted these passages precisely because they qualitatively embodied Ford's distinctive expression.

As the statutory language indicates, a taking may not be excused merely because it is insubstantial with respect to the infringing work. As Judge Learned Hand cogently remarked, "no plagiarist can excuse the wrong by showing how much of his work he did not pirate." Sheldon v. Metro-Goldwyn Pictures Corp., 81 F.2d 49, 56 (CA2), cert. denied, 298 U.S. 669 (1936). Conversely, the fact that a substantial portion of the infringing work was copied verbatim is evidence of the qualitative value of the copied material, both to the originator and to the plagiarist who seeks to profit from marketing someone else's copyrighted expression.

Stripped to the verbatim quotes, [Footnote 8] the direct takings from the unpublished manuscript constitute at least 13% of the infringing article. See Meeropol v. Nizer, 560 F.2d 1061, 1071 (CA2 1977) (copyrighted letters constituted less than 1% of infringing work but were prominently featured). The Nation article is structured around the quoted excerpts which serve as its dramatic focal points. See Appendix to this opinion, post p. 471 U. S. 570. In view of the expressive value of the excerpts and their key role in the infringing work, we cannot agree with the Second Circuit that the "magazine took a meager, indeed an infinitesimal, amount of Ford's original language." 723 F.2d at 209.

Effect on the Market. Finally, the Act focuses on "the effect of the use upon the potential market for or value of the copyrighted work." This last factor is undoubtedly the single most important element of fair use. [Footnote 9] See 3 Nimmer § 13.05[A], at 13-76, and cases cited therein. "Fair use, when properly applied, is limited to copying by others which does not materially impair the marketability of the work which is copied." 1 Nimmer § l.10[D], at 1-87. The trial court found not merely a potential, but an actual, effect on the market. Time's cancellation of its projected serialization and its refusal to pay the $12,500 were the direct effect of the infringement. The Court of Appeals rejected this factfinding as clearly erroneous, noting that the record did not establish a causal relation between Time's nonperformance and respondents' unauthorized publication of Mr. Ford's expression, as opposed to the facts taken from the memoirs. We disagree. Rarely will a case of copyright infringement present such clear-cut evidence of actual damage. Petitioners assured Time that there would be no other authorized publication of any portion of the unpublished manuscript prior to April 23, 1979. Any publication of material from chapters 1 and 3 would permit Time to renegotiate its final payment. Time cited The Nation's article, which contained verbatim quotes from the unpublished manuscript, as a reason for its nonperformance. With respect to apportionment of profits flowing from a copyright infringement, this Court has held that an infringer who commingles infringing and noninfringing elements "must abide the consequences, unless he can make a separation of the profits so as to assure to the injured party all that justly belongs to him." Sheldon v. Metro-Goldwyn Pictures Corp., 309 U. S. 390, 309 U. S. 406 (1940). Cf. 17 U.S.C. § 504(b) (the infringer is required to prove elements of profits attributable to other than the in-

fringed work). Similarly, once a copyright holder establishes with reasonable probability the existence of a causal connection between the infringement and a loss of revenue, the burden properly shifts to the infringer to show that this damage would have occurred had there been no taking of copyrighted expression. See 3 Nimmer § 14.02, at 14-7 - 14-8.1. Petitioners established a prima facie case of actual damage that respondents failed to rebut. See Stevens Linen Associates, Inc. v. Mastercraft Corp., 656 F.2d 11, 15 (CA2 1981). The trial court properly awarded actual damages and accounting of profits. See 17 U.S.C. § 504(b).

More important, to negate fair use, one need only show that, if the challenged use "should become widespread, it would adversely affect the potential market for the copyrighted work." Sony Corp. of America v. Universal City Studios, Inc., 464 U.S. at 464 U. S. 451 (emphasis added); id. at 464 U. S. 484, and n. 36 (collecting cases) (dissenting opinion). This inquiry must take account not only of harm to the original, but also of harm to the market for derivative works. See Iowa State University Research Foundation, Inc. v. American Broadcasting Cos., 621 F.2d 57 (CA2 1980); Meeropol v. Nizer, supra, at 1070; Roy Export v. Columbia Broadcasting System, Inc., 503 F.Supp. at 1146.

"If the defendant's work adversely affects the value of any of the rights in the copyrighted work (in this case the adaptation [and serialization] right) the use is not fair."

3 Nimmer § 13.05[B], at 13-77 - 13-78 (footnote omitted).

It is undisputed that the factual material in the balance of The Nation's article, besides the verbatim quotes at issue here, was drawn exclusively from the chapters on the pardon. The excerpts were employed as featured episodes in a story about the Nixon pardon -- precisely the use petitioners had licensed to Time. The borrowing of these verbatim quotes from the unpublished manuscript lent The Nation's piece a special air of authenticity -- as Navasky expressed it, the reader would know it was Ford speaking, and not The Nation. App. 300c. Thus it directly competed for a share of the market for prepublication excerpts. The Senate Report states:

"With certain special exceptions . . . a use that supplants any part of the normal market for a copyrighted work would ordinarily be considered an infringement."

Senate Report at 65.

Placed in a broader perspective, a fair use doctrine that permits extensive prepublication quotations from an unreleased manuscript without the copyright owner's consent poses substantial potential for damage to the marketability of first serialization rights in general.

"Isolated instances of minor infringements, when multiplied many times, become in the aggregate a major inroad on copyright that must be prevented."

Ibid.


V

The Court of Appeals erred in concluding that The Nation's use of the copyrighted material was excused by the public's interest in the subject matter. It erred, as well, in overlooking the unpublished nature of the work and the resulting impact on the potential market for first serial rights of permitting unauthorized prepublication excerpts under the rubric of fair use. Finally, in finding the taking "infinitesimal," the Court of Appeals accorded too little weight to the qualitative importance of the quoted passages of original expression. In sum, the traditional doctrine of fair use, as embodied in the Copyright Act, does not sanction the use made by The Nation of these copyrighted materials. Any copyright infringer may claim to benefit the public by increasing public access to the copyrighted work. See Pacific & Southern Co. v. Duncan, 744 F.2d at 1499-1500. But Congress has not designed, and

we see no warrant for judicially imposing, a "compulsory license" permitting unfettered access to the unpublished copyrighted expression of public figures.

The Nation conceded that its verbatim copying of some 300 words of direct quotation from the Ford manuscript would constitute an infringement unless excused as a fair use. Because we find that The Nation's use of these verbatim excerpts from the unpublished manuscript was not a fair use, the judgment of the Court of Appeals is reversed, and the case is remanded for further proceedings consistent with this opinion.

It is so ordered.


**JUSTICE BRENNAN, with whom JUSTICE WHITE and JUSTICE MARSHALL join, dissenting.**

The Court holds that The Nation's quotation of 300 words from the unpublished 200,000-word manuscript of President Gerald R. Ford infringed the copyright in that manuscript, even though the quotations related to a historical event of undoubted significance -- the resignation and pardon of President Richard M. Nixon. Although the Court pursues the laudable goal of protecting "the economic incentive to create and disseminate ideas," ante at 471 U. S. 558, this zealous defense of the copyright owner's prerogative will, I fear, stifle the broad dissemination of ideas and information copyright is intended to nurture. Protection of the copyright owner's economic interest is achieved in this case through an exceedingly narrow definition of the scope of fair use. The progress of arts and sciences and the robust public debate essential to an enlightened citizenry are ill-served by this constricted reading of the fair use doctrine. See 17 U.S.C. § 107. I therefore respectfully dissent.

I

A

This case presents two issues. First, did The Nation's use of material from the Ford manuscript in forms other than direct quotation from that manuscript infringe Harper & Row's copyright. Second, did the quotation of approximately 300 words from the manuscript infringe the copyright because this quotation did not constitute "fair use" within the meaning of § 107 of the Copyright Act. 17 U.S.C. § 107. The Court finds no need to resolve the threshold copyrightability issue. The use of 300 words of quotation was, the Court finds, beyond the scope of fair use, and thus a copyright infringement. [Footnote 3/1] Because I disagree with the Court's fair use holding, it is necessary for me to decide the threshold copyrightability question.

B

"The enactment of copyright legislation by Congress under the terms of the Constitution is not based upon any natural right that the author has in his writings . . . , but upon the ground that the welfare of the public will be served and progress of science and useful arts will be promoted by securing to authors for limited periods the exclusive rights to their writings."

H.R.Rep. No. 2222, 60th Cong., 2d Sess., 7 (1909). Congress thus seeks to define the rights included in copyright so as to serve the public welfare, and not necessarily so as to maximize an author's control over his or her product. The challenge of copyright is to strike the

"difficult balance between the interests of authors and inventors in the control and exploitation of their writings and discoveries, on the one hand, and society's competing interest in the free flow of ideas, information, and commerce, on the other hand."

Sony Corp. of America v. Universal City Studios, Inc., 464 U. S. 417, 464 U. S. 429 (1984).

The "originality" requirement now embodied in § 102 of the Copyright Act is crucial to maintenance of the appropriate balance between these competing interests. [Footnote 3/2] Properly interpreted in the light of the legislative history, this section extends copyright protection to an author's literary form, but permits free use by others of the ideas and information the author communicates. See S.Rep. No. 93-983, pp. 107-108 (1974) ("Copyright does not preclude others from using the ideas or information revealed by the author's work. It pertains to the literary . . . form in which the author expressed intellectual concepts"); H.R.Rep. No. 94-1476, pp. 56-57 (1976) (same); New York Times Co. v. United States, 403 U. S. 713, 403 U. S. 726, n. (1971) (BRENNAN, J., concurring) ("[T]he copyright laws, of course, protect only the form of expression, and not the ideas expressed"). This limitation of protection to literary form precludes any claim of copyright in facts, including historical narration.

"It is not to be supposed that the framers of the Constitution, when they empowered Congress"

"to promote the progress of science and useful arts, by securing for limited times to authors and inventors the exclusive right to their respective writings and discoveries"

"(Const., Art I, § 8, par. 8), intended to confer upon one who might happen to be the first to report a historic event the exclusive right for any period to spread the knowledge of it."

International News Service v. Associated Press, 248 U. S. 215, 248 U. S. 234 (1918). Accord, Rosemont Enterprises, Inc. v. Random House, Inc., 366 F.2d 303, 309 (CA2 1966), cert. denied, 385 U.S. 1009 (1967). See 1 Nimmer § 2.11[A], at 2-158. [Footnote 3/3]

The "promotion of science and the useful arts" requires this limit on the scope of an author's control. Were an author able to prevent subsequent authors from using concepts, ideas, or facts contained in his or her work, the creative process would wither and scholars would be forced into unproductive replication of the research of their predecessors. See Hoehling v. Universal City Studios, Inc., 618 F.2d 972, 979 (CA2 1980). This limitation on copyright also ensures consonance with our most important First Amendment values. Cf. Zacchini v. Scripps-Howard Broadcasting Co., 433 U. S. 562, 433 U. S. 577, n. 13 (1977). Our "profound national commitment to the principle that debate on public issues should be uninhibited, robust, and wide-open," New York Times Co. v. Sullivan, 376 U. S. 254, 376 U. S. 270 (1964), leaves no room for a statutory monopoly over information and ideas.

"The arena of public debate would be quiet, indeed, if a politician could copyright his speeches or a philosopher his treatises, and thus obtain a monopoly on the ideas they contained."

Lee v. Runge, 404 U. S. 887, 893 (1971) (Douglas, J., dissenting from denial of certiorari). A broad dissemination of principles, ideas, and factual information is crucial to the robust public debate and informed citizenry that are "the essence of self-government." Garrison v. Louisiana, 379 U. S. 64, 379 U. S. 74-75 (1964). And every citizen must be permitted freely to marshal ideas and facts in the advocacy of particular political choices. [Footnote 3/4]

It follows that infringement of copyright must be based on a taking of literary form, as opposed to the ideas or information contained in a copyrighted work. Deciding whether an infringing appropriation of literary form has occurred is difficult for at least two reasons. First, the distinction between literary form and information or ideas is often elusive in practice. Second, infringement must be based on a substantial appropriation of literary form. This determination is equally challenging. Not surprisingly, the test for infringement has defied precise formulation. [Footnote 3/5] In general, though, the inquiry proceeds along two axes: how closely has the second author tracked the first author's particular language and structure of presentation; and how much of the first author's language and structure has the second author appropriated. [Footnote 3/6]

In the present case the infringement analysis must be applied to a historical biography in which the author has chronicled the events of his White House tenure and commented on those events from his unique perspective. Apart from the quotations, virtually all of the material in The Nation's article indirectly recounted Mr. Ford's factual narrative of the Nixon resignation and pardon, his latter-day reflections on some events of his Presidency, and his perceptions of the personalities at the center of those events. See ante at 471 U. S. 570-579. No copyright can be claimed in this information qua information. Infringement would thus have to be based on too close and substantial a tracking of Mr. Ford's expression of this information. [Footnote 3/7]

The Language. Much of the information The Nation conveyed was not in the form of paraphrase at all, but took the form of synopsis of lengthy discussions in the Ford manuscript. [Footnote 3/8] In the course of this summary presentation, The Nation did use occasional sentences that closely resembled language in the original Ford manuscript. [Footnote 3/9] But these linguistic similarities are insufficient to constitute an infringement for three reasons. First, some leeway must be given to subsequent authors seeking to convey facts because those "wishing to express the ideas contained in a factual work often can choose from only a narrow range of expression." Landsberg v. Scrabble Crossword Game Players, Inc., 736 F.2d 485, 488 (CA9 1984). Second, much of what The Nation paraphrased was material in which Harper & Row could claim no copyright. [Footnote 3/10] Third, The Nation paraphrased nothing approximating the totality of a single paragraph, much less a chapter or the work as a whole. At most, The Nation paraphrased disparate isolated sentences from the original. A finding of infringement based on paraphrase generally requires far more close and substantial a tracking of the original language than occurred in this case. See, e.g., Wainwright Securities Inc. v. Wall Street Transcript Corp., 558 F.2d 91 (CA2 1977).

*The Structure of Presentation.* The article does not mimic Mr. Ford's structure. The information The Nation presents is drawn from scattered sections of the Ford work, and does not appear in the sequence in which Mr. Ford presented it. [Footnote 3/11] Some of The Nation's discussion of the pardon does roughly track the order in which the Ford manuscript presents information about the pardon. With respect to this similarity, however, Mr. Ford has done no more than present the facts chronologically and cannot claim infringement when a subsequent author similarly presents the facts of history in a chronological manner. Also, it is difficult to suggest that a 2,000-word article could bodily appropriate the structure of a 200,000-word book. Most of what Mr. Ford created, and most of the history he recounted, were simply not represented in The Nation's article. [Footnote 3/12]

When The Nation was not quoting Mr. Ford, therefore, its efforts to convey the historical information in the Ford manuscript did not so closely and substantially track Mr. Ford's language and structure as to constitute an appropriation of literary form.

## II

The Nation is thus liable in copyright only if the quotation of 300 words infringed any of Harper & Row's exclusive rights under § 106 of the Act. Section 106 explicitly makes the grant of exclusive rights "[s]ubject to section 107 through 118." 17 U.S.C. § 106. Section 107 states:

"Notwithstanding the provisions of section 106, the fair use of a copyrighted work . . . for purposes such as criticism, comment, news reporting, teaching (including multiple copies for classroom use), scholarship or research, is not an infringement of copyright."

The question here is whether The Nation's quotation was a noninfringing fair use within the meaning of § 107.

Congress "eschewed a rigid, bright-line approach to fair use." Sony Corp. of America v. Universal City Studios, Inc., 464 U.S. at 464 U. S. 449, n. 31. A court is to apply an "equitable rule of reason" analysis, id. at 464 U. S. 448, guided by four statutorily prescribed factors:

"(1) the purpose and character of the use, including whether such use is of a commercial nature or is for nonprofit educational purposes;"

"(2) the nature of the copyrighted work;"

"(3) the amount and substantiality of the portion used in relation to the copyrighted work as a whole; and"

"(4) the effect of the use upon the potential market for or value of the copyrighted work."

17 U.S.C. § 107. These factors are not necessarily the exclusive determinants of the fair use inquiry, and do not mechanistically resolve fair use issues; "no generally applicable definition is possible, and each case raising the question must be decided on its own facts." H.R.Rep. No. 94-1476, at 65. See also id. at 66 ("[T]he endless variety of situations and combinations of circumstances that can arise in particular cases precludes the formulation of exact rules in the statute"); S.Rep. No. 94-473, p. 62 (1975). The statutory factors do, however, provide substantial guidance to courts undertaking the proper fact-specific inquiry.

With respect to a work of history, particularly the memoirs of a public official, the statutorily prescribed analysis cannot properly be conducted without constant attention to copyright's crucial distinction between protected literary form and unprotected information or ideas. The question must always be: was the subsequent author's use of literary form a fair use within the meaning of § 107, in light of the purpose for the use, the nature of the copyrighted work, the amount of literary form used, and the effect of this use of literary form on the value of or market for the original?

Limiting the inquiry to the propriety of a subsequent author's use of the copyright owner's literary form is not easy in the case of a work of history. Protection against only substantial appropriation of literary form does not ensure historians a return commensurate with the full value of their labors. The literary form contained in works like "A Time to Heal" reflects only a part of the labor that goes into the book. It is the labor of collecting, sifting, organizing, and reflecting that predominates in the creation of works of history such as this one. The value this labor produces lies primarily in the information and ideas revealed, and not in the particular collocation of words through which the information and ideas are expressed. Copyright thus does not protect that which is often of most value in a work of history, and courts must resist the tendency to reject the fair use defense on the basis of their feeling that an author of history has been deprived of the full value of his or her labor. A subsequent author's taking of information and ideas is in no sense piratical, because copyright law simply does not create any property interest in information and ideas.

The urge to compensate for subsequent use of information and ideas is perhaps understandable. An inequity seems to lurk in the idea that much of the fruit of the historian's labor may be used without compensation. This, however, is not some unforeseen byproduct of a statutory scheme intended primarily to ensure a return for works of the imagination. Congress made the affirmative choice that the copyright laws should apply in this way:

"Copyright does not preclude others from using the ideas or information revealed by the author's work. It pertains to the literary . . . form in which the author expressed intellectual concepts."

H.R.Rep. No. 94-1476, at 56-57. This distinction is at the essence of copyright. The copyright laws serve as the "engine of free expression,"

ante at 471 U. S. 558, only when the statutory monopoly does not choke off multifarious indirect uses and consequent broad dissemination of information and ideas. To ensure the progress of arts and sciences and the integrity of First Amendment values, ideas and information must not be freighted with claims of proprietary right. [Footnote 3/13]

In my judgment, the Court's fair use analysis has fallen to the temptation to find copyright violation based on a minimal use of literary form in order to provide compensation for the appropriation of information from a work of history. The failure to distinguish between information and literary form permeates every aspect of the Court's fair use analysis, and leads the Court to the wrong result in this case. Application of the statutorily prescribed analysis with attention to the distinction between information and literary form leads to a straightforward finding of fair use within the meaning of § 107.

The Purpose of the Use. The Nation's purpose in quoting 300 words of the Ford manuscript was, as the Court acknowledges, news reporting. See ante at 471 U. S. 561. The Ford work contained information about important events of recent history. Two principals, Mr. Ford and General Alexander Haig, were, at the time of The Nation's publication in 1979, widely thought to be candidates for the Presidency. That The Nation objectively reported the information in the Ford manuscript without independent commentary in no way diminishes the conclusion that it was reporting news. A typical news story differs from an editorial precisely in that it presents newsworthy information in a straightforward and unelaborated manner. Nor does the source of the information render The Nation's article any less a news report. Often books and manuscripts, solicited and unsolicited, are the subject matter of news reports. E.g., New York Time Co. v. United States, 403 U. S. 713 (1971). Frequently, the manuscripts are unpublished at the time of the news report. [Footnote 3/14]

Section 107 lists news reporting as a prime example of fair use of another's expression. Like criticism and all other purposes Congress explicitly approved in § 107, news reporting informs the public; the language of § 107 makes clear that Congress saw the spread of knowledge and information as the strongest justification for a properly limited appropriation of expression. The Court of Appeals was therefore correct to conclude that the purpose of The Nation's use -- dissemination of the information contained in the quotations of Mr. Ford's work -- furthered the public interest. 723 F.2d 195, 207-208 (CA2 1983). In light of the explicit congressional endorsement in § 107, the purpose for which Ford's literary form was borrowed strongly favors a finding of fair use.

The Court concedes the validity of the news reporting purpose, [Footnote 3/15] but then quickly offsets it against three purportedly countervailing considerations. First, the Court asserts that, because The Nation publishes for profit, its publication of the Ford quotes is a presumptively unfair commercial use. Second, the Court claims that The Nation's stated desire to create a "news event" signaled an illegitimate purpose of supplanting the copyright owner's right of first publication. Ante at 471 U. S. 562-563. Third, The Nation acted in bad faith, the Court claims, because its editor "knowingly exploited a purloined manuscript." Ante at 471 U. S. 563.

The Court's reliance on the commercial nature of The Nation's use as "a separate factor that tends to weigh against a finding of fair use," ante at 471 U. S. 562, is inappropriate in the present context. Many uses § 107 lists as paradigmatic examples of fair use, including criticism, comment, and news reporting, are generally conducted for profit in this country, a fact of which Congress was obviously aware when it enacted § 107. To negate any argument favoring fair use based on news reporting or criticism because that reporting or criticism was published for profit is to render meaningless the congressional imprimatur placed on such uses. [Footnote 3/16]

Nor should The Nation's intent to create a "news event" weigh against a finding of fair use. Such a rule, like the

Court's automatic presumption against news reporting for profit, would undermine the congressional validation of the news reporting purpose. A news business earns its reputation, and therefore its readership, through consistent prompt publication of news -- and often through "scooping" rivals. More importantly, the Court's failure to maintain the distinction between information and literary form colors the analysis of this point. Because Harper & Row had no legitimate copyright interest in the information and ideas in the Ford manuscript, The Nation had every right to seek to be the first to disclose these facts and ideas to the public. The record suggests only that The Nation sought to be the first to reveal the information in the Ford manuscript. The Nation's stated purpose of scooping the competition should, under those circumstances, have no negative bearing on the claim of fair use. Indeed the Court's reliance on this factor would seem to amount to little more than distaste for the standard journalistic practice of seeking to be the first to publish news.

The Court's reliance on The Nation's putative bad faith is equally unwarranted. No court has found that The Nation possessed the Ford manuscript illegally or in violation of any common law interest of Harper & Row; all common law causes of action have been abandoned or dismissed in this case. 723 F.2d at 199-201. Even if the manuscript had been "purloined" by someone, nothing in this record imputes culpability to The Nation. [Footnote 3/17] On the basis of the record in this case, the most that can be said is that The Nation made use of the contents of the manuscript knowing the copyright owner would not sanction the use.

At several points the Court brands this conduct thievery. See, e.g., ante at 471 U. S. 556, 471 U. S. 563. This judgment is unsupportable, and is perhaps influenced by the Court's unspoken tendency in this case to find infringement based on the taking of information and ideas. With respect to the appropriation of information and ideas other than the quoted words, The Nation's use was perfectly legitimate, despite the copyright owner's objection, because no copyright can be claimed in ideas or information. Whether the quotation of 300 words was an infringement or a fair use within the meaning of § 107 is a close question that has produced sharp division in both this Court and the Court of Appeals. If the Copyright Act were held not to prohibit the use, then the copyright owner would have had no basis in law for objecting. The Nation's awareness of an objection that has a significant chance of being adjudged unfounded cannot amount to bad faith. Imputing bad faith on the basis of no more than knowledge of such an objection, the Court impermissibly prejudices the inquiry and impedes arrival at the proper conclusion that the "purpose" factor of the statutorily prescribed analysis strongly favors a finding of fair use in this case.

The Nature of the Copyrighted Work. In Sony Corp. of America v. Universal City Studios, Inc., we stated that "not . . . all copyrights are fungible" and that "[c]opying a news broadcast may have a stronger claim to fair use than copying a motion picture." 464 U.S. at 464 U. S. 455, n. 40. These statements reflect the principle, suggested in § 107(2) of the Act, that the scope of fair use is generally broader when the source of borrowed expression is a factual or historical work. See 3 Nimmer § 13.05[A][2], at 13-73 - 13-74. "[I]nformational works," like the Ford manuscript, "that readily lend themselves to productive use by others, are less protected." Sony Corp. of America v. Universal City Studios, Inc., 464 U.S. at 464 U. S. 496-497 (BLACKMUN, J., dissenting). Thus the second statutory factor also favors a finding of fair use in this case.

The Court acknowledges that "[t]he law generally recognizes a greater need to disseminate factual works than works of fiction or fantasy," ante at 471 U. S. 563, and that "[s]ome of the briefer quotations from the memoir are arguably necessary to convey the facts," ibid. But the Court discounts the force of this consideration, primarily on the ground that "[t]he fact that a work is unpublished is a crucial element of its nature.'" Ante at 471 U. S. 564. [Footnote 3/18] At this point, the Court introduces into analysis of this case a categorical presumption against prepublication fair use. See ante at 471 U. S. 555 ("Under ordinary circumstances, the author's right to control the first public appear-

ance of his undisseminated expression will outweigh a claim of fair use").

This categorical presumption is unwarranted on its own terms and unfaithful to congressional intent. [Footnote 3/19] Whether a particular prepublication use will impair any interest the Court identifies as encompassed within the right of first publication, see ante at 471 U. S. 552-555, [Footnote 3/20] will depend on the nature of the copyrighted work, the timing of prepublication use, the amount of expression used, and the medium in which the second author communicates. Also, certain uses might be tolerable for some purposes but not for others. See Sony Corp. of America v. Universal City Studios, Inc., supra, at 464 U. S. 490, n. 40. The Court is ambiguous as to whether it relies on the force of the presumption against prepublication fair use or an analysis of the purpose and effect of this particular use. Compare ante at 471 U. S. 552-555, with ante at 471 U. S. 564. To the extent the Court relies on the presumption, it presumes intolerable injury -- in particular the usurpation of the economic interest [Footnote 3/21] -- based on no more than a quick litmus test for prepublication timing. Because "Congress has plainly instructed us that fair use analysis calls for a sensitive balancing of interests," we held last Term that the fair use inquiry could never be resolved on the basis of such a "two-dimensional" categorical approach. See Sony Corp. of America v. Universal City Studios, Inc., 464 U.S. at 464 U. S. 455, n. 40 (rejecting categorical requirement of "productive use").

To the extent the Court purports to evaluate the facts of this case, its analysis relies on sheer speculation. The quotation of 300 words from the manuscript infringed no privacy interest of Mr. Ford. This author intended the words in the manuscript to be a public statement about his Presidency. Lacking, therefore, is the "deliberate choice on the part of the copyright owner" to keep expression confidential, a consideration that the Senate Report -- in the passage on which the Court places great reliance, see ante at 553 --recognized as the impetus behind narrowing fair use for unpublished works. See S.Rep. No. 94-473, at 64.

See also 3 Nimmer § 13.05[A], at 13-73 ("[T]he scope of the fair use doctrine is considerably narrower with respect to unpublished works which are held confidential by their copyright owners") (emphasis added). What the Court depicts as the copyright owner's "confidentiality" interest, see ante at 471 U. S. 564, is not a privacy interest at all. Rather, it is no more than an economic interest in capturing the full value of initial release of information to the public, and is properly analyzed as such. See infra at 471 U. S. 602-603. Lacking too is any suggestion that The Nation's use interfered with the copyright owner's interest in editorial control of the manuscript. The Nation made use of the Ford quotes on the eve of official publication.

Thus, the only interest The Nation's prepublication use might have infringed is the copyright owner's interest in capturing the full economic value of initial release. By considering this interest as a component of the "nature" of the copyrighted work, the Court's analysis deflates The Nation's claim that the informational nature of the work supports fair use without any inquiry into the actual or potential economic harm of The Nation's particular prepublication use. For this reason, the question of economic harm is properly considered under the fourth statutory factor -- the effect on the value of or market for the copyrighted work, 17 U.S.C. § 107(4) -- and not as a presumed element of the "nature" of the copyright.

The Amount and Substantiality of the Portion Used. More difficult questions arise with respect to judgments about the importance to this case of the amount and substantiality of the quotations used. The Nation quoted only approximately 300 words from a manuscript of more than 200,000 words, and the quotes are drawn from isolated passages in disparate sections of the work. The judgment that this taking was quantitatively "infinitesimal," 723 F.2d at 209, does not dispose of the inquiry, however. An evaluation of substantiality in qualitative terms is also required. Much of the quoted material was Mr. Ford's matter-of-fact representation of the words of others in conversations with him; such quotations are "arguably necessary adequately to convey the

facts," ante at 471 U. S. 563, and are not rich in expressive content. Beyond these quotations, a portion of the quoted material was drawn from the most poignant expression in the Ford manuscript; in particular The Nation made use of six examples of Mr. Ford's expression of his reflections on events or perceptions about President Nixon. [Footnote 3/22] The fair use inquiry turns on the propriety of the use of these quotations with admittedly strong expressive content.

The Court holds that, "in view of the expressive value of the excerpts and their key role in the infringing work," this third statutory factor disfavors a finding of fair use. [Footnote 3/23] To support this conclusion, the Court purports to rely on the District Court factual findings that The Nation had taken "the heart of the book." 557 F.Supp. 1062, 1072 (SDNY 1983). This reliance is misplaced, and would appear to be another result of the Court's failure to distinguish between information and literary form. When the District Court made this finding, it was evaluating not the quoted words at issue here, but the "totality" of the information and reflective commentary in the Ford work. Ibid. The vast majority of what the District Court considered the heart of the Ford work, therefore, consisted of ideas and information The Nation was free to use. It may well be that, as a qualitative matter, most of the value of the manuscript did lie in the information and ideas The Nation used. But appropriation of the "heart" of the manuscript in this sense is irrelevant to copyright analysis because copyright does not preclude a second author's use of information and ideas.

Perhaps tacitly recognizing that reliance on the District Court finding is unjustifiable, the Court goes on to evaluate independently the quality of the expression appearing in The Nation's article. The Court states that "[t]he portions actually quoted were selected by Mr. Navasky as among the most powerful passages." Ante at 471 U. S. 565. On the basis of no more than this observation, and perhaps also inference from the fact that the quotes were important to The Nation's article, [Footnote 3/24] the Court adheres to its conclusion that The Nation appropriated the heart of the Ford manuscript.

At least with respect to the six particular quotes of Mr. Ford's observations and reflections about President Nixon, I agree with the Court's conclusion that The Nation appropriated some literary form of substantial quality. I do not agree, however, that the substantiality of the expression taken was clearly excessive or inappropriate to The Nation's news reporting purpose.

Had these quotations been used in the context of a critical book review of the Ford work, there is little question that such a use would be fair use within the meaning of § 107 of the Act. The amount and substantiality of the use -- in both quantitative and qualitative terms -- would have certainly been appropriate to the purpose of such a use. It is difficult to see how the use of these quoted words in a news report is less appropriate. The Court acknowledges as much:

"[E]ven substantial quotations might qualify as a fair use in a review of a published work or a news account of a speech that had been delivered to the public."

See ante at 471 U. S. 564. With respect to the motivation for the pardon and the insights into the psyche of the fallen President, for example, Mr. Ford's reflections and perceptions are so laden with emotion and deeply personal value judgments that full understanding is immeasurably enhanced by reproducing a limited portion of Mr. Ford's own words. The importance of the work, after all, lies not only in revelation of previously unknown fact, but also in revelation of the thoughts, ideas, motivations, and fears of two Presidents at a critical moment in our national history. Thus, while the question is not easily resolved, it is difficult to say that the use of the six quotations was gratuitous in relation to the news reporting purpose.

Conceding that even substantial quotation is appropriate in a news report of a published work, the Court would seem to agree that this quotation was not clearly inappropriate in relation to The Nation's news reporting purpose. For the Court, the determinative factor is again that the substantiality of the use was inappropriate in relation to the prepub-lication timing of that use. That is really an objection to the effect of this use on the market for the copyrighted work, and is properly evaluated as such.

The Effect on the Market. The Court correctly notes that the effect on the market "is undoubtedly the single most important element of fair use." Ante at 471 U. S. 566, citing 3 Nimmer § 13.05[A], at 13-76, and the Court properly focuses on whether The Nation's use adversely affected Harper & Row's serialization potential and not merely the market for sales of the Ford work itself. Ante at 471 U. S. 566-567. Unfortunately, the Court's failure to distinguish between the use of information and the appropriation of literary form badly skews its analysis of this factor.

For purposes of fair use analysis, the Court holds, it is sufficient that the entire article containing the quotes eroded the serialization market potential of Mr. Ford's work. Ante at 471 U. S. 567. On the basis of Time's cancellation of its serialization agreement, the Court finds that "[r]arely will a case of copyright infringement present such clear-cut evidence of actual damage." Ibid. In essence, the Court finds that, by using some quotes in a story about the Nixon pardon, The Nation "competed for a share of the market of prepublication excerpts" ante at 471 U. S. 568, because Time planned to excerpt from the chapters about the pardon.

The Nation's publication indisputably precipitated Time's eventual cancellation. But that does not mean that The Nation's use of the 300 quoted words caused this injury to Harper & Row. Wholly apart from these quoted words, The Nation published significant information and ideas from the Ford manuscript. If it was this publication of information, and not the publication of the few quotations, that caused Time to abrogate its serialization agreement, then whatever the negative effect on the serialization market, that effect was the product of wholly legitimate activity.

The Court of Appeals specifically held that "the evidence does not support a finding that it was the very limited use of expression per se which led to Time's decision not to print excerpts." 723 F.2d at 208. I fully agree with this holding. If The Nation competed with Time, the competition was not for a share of the market in excerpts of literary form, but for a share of the market in the new information in the Ford work. That the information, and not the literary form, represents most of the real value of the work in this case is perhaps best revealed by the following provision in the contract between Harper & Row and Mr. Ford:

"Author acknowledges that the value of the rights granted to publisher hereunder would be substantially diminished by Author's public discussion of the unique information not previously disclosed about Author's career and personal life which will be included in the Work, and Author agrees that Author will endeavor not to disseminate any such information in any media, including television, radio and newspaper and magazine interviews prior to the first publication of the work hereunder."

App. 484. The contract thus makes clear that Harper & Row sought to benefit substantially from monopolizing the initial revelation of information known only to Ford.

Because The Nation was the first to convey the information in this case, it did perhaps take from Harper & Row some of the value that publisher sought to garner for itself through the contractual arrangement with Ford and the license to Time. Harper & Row had every right to seek to monopolize revenue from that potential market through contractual arrangements, but it has no right to set up copyright as a shield from competition in that market, because copyright does not protect information. The Nation had every right to seek to be the first to publish that information. [Footnote 3/25]

Balancing the Interests. Once the distinction between information and literary form is made clear, the statutorily prescribed process of weighing the four statutory fair use factors discussed above leads naturally to a conclusion that The Nation's limited use of literary form was not an infringement. Both the purpose of the use and the nature of the copyrighted work strongly favor the fair use defense here. The Nation appropriated Mr. Ford's expression for a purpose Congress expressly authorized in § 107 and borrowed from a work whose nature justifies some appropriation to facilitate the spread of information. The factor that is perhaps least favorable to the claim of fair use is the amount and substantiality of the expression used. Without question, a portion of the expression appropriated was among the most poignant in the Ford manuscript. But it is difficult to conclude that this taking was excessive in relation to the news reporting purpose. In any event, because the appropriation of literary form -- as opposed to the use of information -- was not shown to injure Harper & Row's economic interest, any uncertainty with respect to the propriety of the amount of expression borrowed should be resolved in favor of a finding of fair use. [Footnote 3/26] In light of the circumscribed scope of the quotation in The Nation's article and the undoubted validity of the purpose motivating that quotation, I must conclude that the Court has simply adopted an exceedingly narrow view of fair use in order to impose liability for what was in essence a taking of unprotected information.

III

The Court's exceedingly narrow approach to fair use permits Harper & Row to monopolize information. This holding "effect[s] an important extension of property rights and a corresponding curtailment in the free use of knowledge and of ideas." International News Service v. Associated Press, 248 U.S. at 248 U. S. 263 (Brandeis, J., dissenting). The Court has perhaps advanced the ability of the historian -- or at least the public official who has recently left office -- to capture the full economic value of information in his or her possession. But the Court does so only by risking the robust debate of public issues that is the "essence of self-government." Garrison v. Louisiana, 379 U.S. at 379 U. S. 74-75. The Nation was providing the grist for that robust debate. The Court imposes liability upon The Nation for no other reason than that The Nation succeeded in being the first to provide certain information to the public. I dissent.

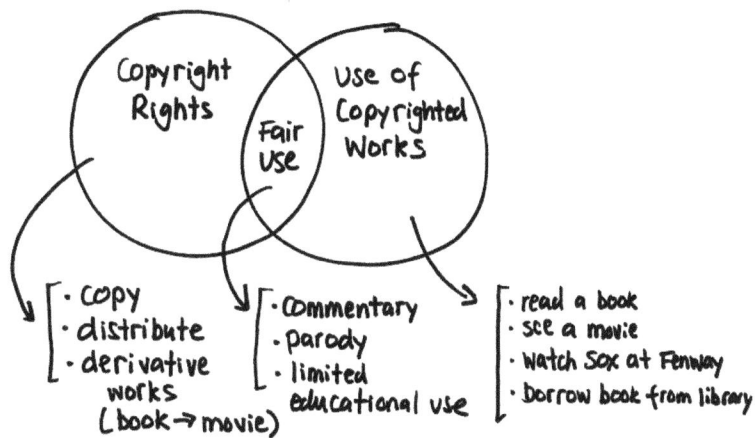

Source: http://www.erikjheels.com/2007-07-18-drawing-that-explains-copyright-law.html

# Creative commons

**creative commons**
*Explained*

*In Plain English*

sarahhawkins.com

One of the best ways to find usable copyrighted works, especially images, is to find someone who wants to share their work under a Creative Commons license. Since 2002, Creative Commons has been giving creators a way to share their work without having to relinquish copyright or individually license their work. These licenses have provided the public with the ability to use works under set circumstances without needing to pay for a license or pass along royalties.

Unfortunately, most people don't know what all these little icons mean and how the licenses work. This has led to challenges for creators who find their work being used in ways not intended, as well as users who pluck out a work and use it only to find that the creator is unhappy and seeing a DMCA Takedown. Neither situation is ideal and is contrary to what the creators of the Creative Commons license program set out to do.

Many people who find works that are covered by one of the following license want to do right and not upset the original creator of the work. Few people purposefully ignore a license and just do whatever they wish. But what do the little icons mean? And once I understand the icons, are there certain rules I need to follow?

Key things to know:

- **Every Creative Commons license requires giving** *appropriate credit*. It's important to understand this, and to also know what this phrase "*appropriate credit*" means.

- A Creative Commons licensor (the person granting you the license) may not revoke your license so long as you are following the terms of the license. This is often a sticking point because many do not provide credit as required.

- There are 6 Creative Commons license and they apply worldwide.

- The license, once granted, lasts as long as the copyright on the work so long as the license is used properly.

Note: These specifically reference Creative Commons 4.0, but the explanations also apply to prior versions.

**Attribution Only**– This one is likely the most straightforward of all the Creative Commons licenses because it's the one they all build from. This license requires anyone who uses the copyrighted work to provide "*appropriate credit*" AND indicate what, if any, changes were made. In plain English, it means you have to give credit. According to the Creative Commons the credit must be in a certain way. Interesting that this is one of the most broad categories but most people actually get it wrong.

Creative Commons defines "appropriate credit" as (a) the name of the creator and attribution parties, (b) a copyright notice, (c) a license notice, (d) a disclaimer notice, and (e) a link to the material.

Once you understand that then you can do whatever else you wish with the work, regardless of whether it is for commercial, non-commercial, non-profit, educational, internal purposes at work, etc. Doesn't matter how you use or distribute the work, give credit and say how you've changed the work and you're good to go.

In reality, though, what I usually see is a "photo courtesy of" remark with a name. Sometimes the name is hyperlinked to the original work, but not always. And, to be honest, I don't think I've ever seen a use where the user indicated what changes they made.

Bottom Line: every CC license user needs to get better at giving credit!

**Attribution, ShareAlike** – This license is often confusing to many people. It carries with it all the same flexibility as the Attribution Only license but it brings along with it the rights YOU have to give to YOUR new work. In plain English, this license means that once you complete your changes to the underlying work then your new work, when shared, carries with it the exact same license and you can not prohibit others from changing or sharing your work. This license is the foundation for the idea of open-source works where various people "improve" upon others work. It's like hitting the 'Save' instead of the 'Save As' button.

271

**Attribution, No Derivatives** – This license is kind of the opposite of what you can do with the Attribution Only license. You have to give credit, or used in the Creative Commons license "appropriate credit", but you can't change the work in any way. Want to crop it? No. Lighten it up a bit? Nope. Make it black and white? Again, No. In plain English, this license means you can use the work for ANY – commercial, non-commercial, educational, work, gaming, or what have you – purpose, so long as you provide the license-required credit and not alter the work in any way.

**Attribution, Non-Commercial** – This license is a little trickier because there is no clear definition of what "commercial" means as far as Creative Commons licenses go and thus "non-commercial" is not as black and white as you may think. Under the Creative Commons license, **"commercial" is defined as "primarily intended for commercial advantage or monetary gain"**. When Creative Com-

mons licenses were created we didn't have the concept of social media sharing that we do now. The value placed on posting photos on social networks may be to gain a commercial advantage in the form of likes or pins or tweets, etc. It hasn't been further defined from when the original understanding of commercial advantage had a decidedly different paradigm than it does now.

Of course, as with all Creative Commons licenses, with this one you must provide attribution, as defined by the license. However, you are able to add to, modify, change, etc., the underlying work so long as YOU are not doing it in a commercial way. THEN if you were to share or distribute the work you may only do so in a non-commercial manner. Put that in to plain English, please!

We've got a number of things going on here.

A – provide attribution
B – you changing the underlying work in a non-commercial way
C – you sharing the new work in a non-commercial way
D – licensing the new work

So let's tackle these separately.

A – provide attribution. That's easy enough, you've got this! (Note: see above)

B – you changing the underlying work in a non-commercial way. If you plan to make changes you can not do it in a commercial manner. Obviously, that means you can't charge for your work. This is important if you're a designer and need to create something for a client or if you work in-house and are modifying something for use within your own organization. Those are obvious "commercial" activities – getting paid for your work. While it would only be speculation, as there is no case law or commons commentary, as to whether "in kind" compensation would amount to "commercial" if you're not normally in the business of charging or being paid for your work. But, for the most post, I don't think this is the sticking point with this license, it's the next part.

C – you sharing the new work in a non-commercial way. Obviously, you **can't** put it up for sale or charge clients for this new work. But can you ask for donations but make it available whether or not someone gives? Can you include it on your website where you have ads, affiliate links, and/or other paid business relationships? Can you include it on your website if your website is basically an advertisement to hire you? These are all gray areas and if a problem arises you'd need to deal with it on an individual basis. The difficulty is that just because one creator may see a means of sharing as commercial doesn't mean others necessarily do.

D – licensing your new work. You may attach any Creative Commons license you wish to the new work. This may seem crazy. You can't sell your new work, but you can license it to someone else (for no money) and they can use it for either commercial or non-commercial purposes. That doesn't sound right, does it? You can't make money off the new work, but someone else can. But, yes, that's exactly what this means.

**Attribution, Non-Commercial, and Share Alike** – Now that we've established the basics, this one starts to put them together. This one makes a change from the prior Attribution, Non-Commercial and adds on the Share Alike license.

Again, in plain English it's the *same as the prior license except when it comes to how YOU share the new work.* The new work MUST be licensed in the same manner as the work you started with. So, since you started with an "Attribution, Non-Commercial" license you must license your new work in the same way. Whereas with the "Attribution, Non-Commercial" you can license your new work as either commercial or non-commercial, with this Share Alike license you may not provide a different license on your new work than you had on the underlying work. It's that idea of fairness, really.

**Attribution, Non-Commercial, No Derivatives** – Basically, with this license all you're able to do is share the work. Of course, you must provide "appropriate credit", but you can not modify the work in any manner then distribute it even if the distribution is not for commercial gain. With this license, all you're allowed to do is share it for free with other people and in doing so give credit to the original creator.

Added 2/15/14:

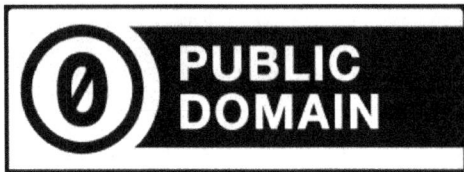

**Public Domain (CC0)** – I had a number of people ask me about public domain works. While that's a separate discussion, I want you to know there is a Creative Commons designation (CC0 1.0 Universal) for works someone wants to place in the public domain. Since the assumption is all works are subject to copyright unless otherwise designated or known, if a creator wants to make their work available without any restrictions they can add what is called the "CC0" or "CCZero" designation. A work that carries this designation has "No Rights Reserved" and is free of copyright restrictions, and likely other restrictions (i.e., moral, publicity, and privacy rights). This is **a very broad designation** and it is clearly understood within the Creative Commons community that *no work carries this designation unless it is explicitly marked as a CC0 work*.

Source: http://sarafhawkins.com/creative-commons-licenses-explained-plain-english/

# CHAPTER 13

# The free flow of information

# Nadezhda Tolokonnikova (2012)

Nadezhda Tolokonnikova

Closing Statement

**8 August 2012**, Khamovnichesky Courthouse, Moscow

**Essentially, it is not three singers from Pussy Riot who are on trial here**. If that were the case, what's happening would be totally insignificant. It is the entire state system of the Russian Federation which is on trial and which, unfortunately for itself, thoroughly enjoys advertising its cruelty towards human beings, its indifference to their honour and dignity, the very worst that has happened in Russian history to date. To my deepest regret, this mock trial is close to the standards of the Stalinist troikas. Thus, we have our investigator, lawyer and judge. And then, what's more, what all three of them do and say and decide is determined by a political demand for repression. Who is to blame for the performance at the Cathedral of Christ the Saviour and for our being put on trial after the concert? The authoritarian political system is to blame. What Pussy Riot does is oppositional art or politics that draws upon the forms art has established. In any event, it is a form of civil action in circumstances where basic human rights, civil and political freedoms are suppressed by the corporate state system.

Since the turn of the millennium many people, relentlessly and methodically flayed alive by the systematic destruction of liberties, have rebelled.

We were looking for authentic genuineness and simplicity and we found them in the holy foolishness of our punk performances. Passion, openness and naivety are superior to hypocrisy, cunning and a contrived decency that conceals crimes. The state's leaders stand with saintly expressions in church but, in their deceit, their sins are far greater than ours. We've put on our political punk concerts because the Russian state system is dominated by rigidity, closedness and caste and the policies pursued serve only narrow corporate interests to the extent that even the air of Russia makes us ill.

We are absolutely not happy with—and have been forced into acting and living politically by—the use of coercive, strong-arm measures to handle social processes, a situation in which the most important political institutions are the disciplinary structures of the state - the security agencies, the army, the police, the special forces and the accompanying means of ensuring political stability: prisons, preventive detention and mechanisms to closely control public behaviour. Nor are we happy with the enforced civic passivity of the bulk of the population or the complete domination of executive structures over the legislature and judiciary. Moreover, we are genuinely angered by the fear-based and scandalously low standard of political culture, which is constantly and knowingly maintained by the state system and its accomplices. Look at what Patriarch Kirill has to say: "The Orthodox don't go to rallies." We are angered by the appalling weakness of horizontal relationships within society. We don't like the way in which the state system easily manipulates public opinion through its tight control of the overwhelming majority of media outlets. A perfect example is the unprecedentedly shameless campaign against Pussy Riot, based on the distortion of facts and words, which has appeared in nearly all the Russian media, apart from the few independent media there are in this political system.

Even so, I can now state—despite the fact that we currently have an authoritarian political situation—that I am seeing this political system collapse to a certain extent when it comes to the three members of Pussy Riot, because what the system was counting on, unfortunately for that system, has not come to pass. Russia as a whole does not condemn us. Every day more and more people believe us and believe in us, and think we should be free rather than behind bars. I can see this from the people I meet. I meet people who represent the system, who work for the relevant agencies. I see people who are in prison. And every day there are more and more people who support us, who hope for our success and especially for our release, who say our political act was justified. People tell us, "To start with, we weren't sure you could have done this," but every day there are more and more people who say, "Time is proving to us that your political gesture was correct. You have exposed the cancer in this political system and dealt a blow to a nest of vipers who then turned on you." These people are trying to make life easier for us in whatever way they can and we are very grateful to them for that…

We are grateful to all those who, free themselves, speak out in our support. There are a vast number, I know. I know that a huge number of Orthodox people are standing up for us. They are praying for us outside the courtroom, for the members of Pussy Riot who are incarcerated. We've seen the little booklets Orthodox people are handing out with prayers for those in prison. This alone shows that there isn't a unified social group of Orthodox believers as the prosecution is trying to assert. No such thing exists. More and more believers are starting to defend Pussy Riot. They don't think what we did deserves even five months in detention, much less the three years in prison the prosecutor would like. And every day, more and more people realize that if this political system has ganged up to this extent against three girls for a 30-second performance in the Cathedral of Christ the Saviour, it means the system is afraid of the truth and afraid of our sincerity and directness. We haven't dissembled, not for a second, not for a minute during this trial, but the other side is dissembling too much and people can sense it. People can sense the truth. Truth really does have some kind of ontological, existential superiority over lies and this is written in the Bible, in the Old Testament, in particular. In the end, the ways of truth always triumph over the ways of wickedness, guile and lies. And with each day that passes, the ways of truth are more and more triumphant even though we are still behind bars and are likely to be here a lot longer yet.

Madonna performed yesterday (7 August). She appeared with "Pussy Riot" written on her back. More and more people can see that we are being held here unlawfully and on a completely false charge – I'm overwhelmed by this. I am overwhelmed that truth really does triumph over lies even though physically we are here in a cage. We are freer than the people sitting opposite us for the prosecution because we can say everything we like, and we do, but those people sitting there say only what political censorship allows them to say. They can't speak words like "punk prayer" or "Virgin Mary, Banish Putin!" They can't say the lines from our punk prayer that have to do with the political system. Perhaps they think it wouldn't be a bad thing to send us to jail because we are rising up against Putin and his system as well but they can't say so because that's not allowed either. Their mouths are sewn shut. Unfortunately, they are mere puppets. I hope they realize this and also take the road to freedom, truth and sincerity because these are superior to stasis, contrived decency and hypocrisy. Stasis and the search for truth are always in opposition to one another and, in this case, at this trial, we can see people who are trying to find the truth and people who are trying to enslave those who want to find the truth.

Humans are beings who always make mistakes. They are not perfect. They strive for wisdom but never actually have it. That's precisely why philosophy came into being, precisely because philosophers are people who love wisdom and strive for it, but never actually possess it and it is what makes them act and think and, ultimately, live the way they do. This is what made us go into the Cathedral of Christ the Saviour. I think that Christianity, as I've understood it from studying the Old and New Testaments, supports the search for truth and a constant overcoming of the self, overcoming what you used to be. It is not for nothing that Christ associated with prostitutes. He said we should help those who stumble, saying, "I forgive them" but for some reason I can't see any of that at our trial, which is taking place under the banner of Christianity. I think the prosecutor is defying Christianity. The lawyers want nothing to do with the injured parties. Here's how I understand this: Two days ago, Lawyer Taratukhin made a speech in which he wanted everyone to understand that he does not identify with the people he is representing. This means he's not ethically comfortable representing people who want to send the three members of Pussy Riot to jail. Why they want to do this, I don't know. Perhaps it is their right. The lawyer was embarrassed, the shouts of "Shame! Executioners!" had got to him, which goes to show that truth and goodness always triumph over lies and evil.

I think some higher powers are guiding the speeches of the lawyers for the other side when, time after time, they make mistakes in what they say and call us the "injured parties". Almost all the lawyers are doing it, including Lawyer Pavlova who is very negatively disposed towards us. Nevertheless, some higher powers are causing her to say "the injured parties" about us rather than the people she's defending, us. I wouldn't give people labels. I don't think there are winners or losers here, injured parties or accused. We just need to make contact, to establish a dialogue and a joint search for truth, to seek wisdom together, to be philosophers together, rather than stigmatizing and labelling people. This is one of the worst things people can do and Christ condemned it.

We have been subjected to abuse during this trial. Who would have thought that one man and the state system he controls would once again be capable of entirely wanton evil? Who would have thought that history and Stalin's fairly recent Great Terror, in particular, would teach us nothing at all? It makes you want to weep to see how the methods of the medieval inquisition are brought out by the law-enforcement and judicial system of the Russian Federation, which is our country. Since the time of our arrest, however, we can no longer weep. We've forgotten how to cry. At our punk concerts we used to shout out in desperation to the best of our abilities about the iniquities of the authorities and now we've been robbed of our voice.

Throughout this whole trial, they have refused to hear us and I mean *hear us*, which involves understanding and, moreover, thinking. I think every individual should strive to attain wisdom, to be a philosopher, not just people who happen to have studied philosophy. That's nothing. Formal education is nothing in itself and Lawyer Pavlova is constantly trying to accuse us of not being sufficiently well-educated. I think though that the most important thing is the desire to know and to understand, and that's something people can do for themselves outside of educational establishments. The trappings of academic degrees don't mean anything in this instance. Someone can have a vast fund of knowledge and for all that not be human. Pythagoras said that 'the learning of many things does not teach understanding'. Unfortunately, that's something we are forced to observe here. We're just part of the scenery, a bit of wildlife, just bodies brought into the courtroom. If, after many days of asking, talking and doing battle our petitions are examined, they are inevitably rejected.

The court, on the other hand—and unfortunately for us and for our country—listens to the prosecutor who repeatedly distorts our comments and statements with impunity in a bid to neutralize them. There is no attempt to conceal this breach in an adversarial system. They even seem to be showing it off. On 30th July, the first day of the trial, we presented our response to the charges against us. Prior to that we were in prison, in confinement. We can't do anything there: we can't make statements, we can't film, we don't have Internet. We can't even give our lawyer any papers because that's banned too. Our first chance to speak came on 30th July. The document we'd written was read out by defence lawyer Volkova because the court refused outright to let the defendants speak. We called for contact and dialogue rather than conflict and opposition. We reached out a hand to those who, for some reason, assume we are their enemies. In response they laughed at us and spat in our outstretched hands. "You're disin-genuous," they told us. But they needn't have bothered. Don't judge others by your own standards. We were, as always, sincere in saying exactly what we thought, out of childish naïvety, sure, but we don't regret anything we said, even on that day. We are reviled but we do not intend to speak evil in return. We are in desperate straits but do not despair. We are persecuted but not forsaken. It's easy to humiliate and crush people who are open, but when I am weak, then I am strong.

Listen to us rather than to Arkady Mamontov talking about us. Don't twist and distort everything we say. Let us enter into dialogue and contact with the country, which is ours too, not just Putin's and the Patriarch's. Like Solzhenitsyn, I believe that in the end, words will shatter concrete. Solzhenitsyn wrote, "the Word is more ancient than concrete. The Word is not to be taken lightly. In just the same way, noble people will suddenly spring up and their word will shatter concrete."

Katya, Masha and I are in jail but I don't consider that we've been defeated. Just as the dissidents weren't defeated. When they disappeared into psychiatric hospitals and prisons, they passed judgement on the country. The art of creating an image of an era knows no winners or losers. The OBERIU poets remained artists to the very end, impossible to explain or understand. They were purged in 1937. Vvedensky wrote: "We like what can't be understood, What can't be explained is our friend." According to the death certificate, Aleksandr Vvedensky died on 20 December 1941. We don't know the cause, whether it was dysentery in the train after his arrest or a bullet from a guard. It was somewhere on the railway line between Voronezh and Kazan. Pussy Riot are Vvedensky's disciples and his heirs. His principle of 'bad rhyme' is our own. He wrote: "It happens that two rhymes will come into your head, a good one and a bad one and I choose the bad one. It will be the right one." What can't be explained is our friend. The elitist, sophisticated occupations of the OBERIU poets, their search for sense at the edge of meaning was ultimately realized at the cost of their lives, swept away in the senseless Great Terror that's impossible to explain. At the cost of their own lives, the OBERIU poets unintentionally demonstrated that their feeling of meaninglessness and alogism as the raw nerve of the period was correct, but at the same time led art into the realm of history. The cost of taking part in creating history is always staggeringly high for people, for their very lives. But that taking part is the very spice of human life. Being poor while bestowing riches on many; having nothing but possessing everything. It is believed that the OBERIU dissidents are dead, but they live on. They are persecuted but they do not die.

Do you remember why the young Dostoyevsky was given the death sentence? All he had done was to get carried away with socialist theories—and at the Friday meetings of a friendly circle of free thinkers at Petrashevsky's, he became acquainted with works by Charles Fourier and George Sand. At one of the last meetings, he read out Belinsky's letter to Gogol, which was packed, according to the court, and, please note, "with childish utterances against the Orthodox Church and the supreme authorities". After all his preparations for the death penalty and ten dreadful, impossibly frightening minutes waiting to die, as Dostoyevsky himself put it, the announcement came that his sentence had been commuted to four years hard labour followed by military service.

Socrates was accused of corrupting youth through his philosophical discourses and of not recognizing the gods of Athens. Socrates had a connection to a divine inner voice and was by no means a theomachist, something he often said himself. What did that matter, however, when he had angered the influential people of the city with his critical, dialectical and unprejudiced thinking? Socrates was sentenced to death and, refusing to run away, although he was given that option, he calmly drank down a cup of hemlock and died.

Have you forgotten the circumstances under which Stephen, follower of the Apostles, ended his earthly life? "Then they secretly induced men to say, 'We have heard him speak blasphemous words against Moses and against God.' And they stirred up the people, the elders and the scribes, and they came upon him and dragged him away, and brought him before the Council. And they put forward false witnesses who said, 'This man incessantly speaks against this holy place, and the Law.'" He was found guilty and stoned to death.

And I hope everyone remembers what the Jews said to Christ: "We're stoning you not for any good work, but for blasphemy." And finally it would be well worth remembering this description of Christ: "He is possessed of a demon and out of his mind."

I believe that if leaders, tsars, elders, presidents and prime ministers, the people and the judges really understood what "I desire mercy, not sacrifice" meant, they would not condemn the innocent. Our leaders are currently in a hurry only to condemn and not at all to show mercy. Incidentally, we thank Dmitry Anatolievich Medvedev for his latest wonderful aphorism. If Medvedev gave his presidency the slogan: "Freedom is better than non-freedom", then, thanks to Medvedev's felicitous saying, Putin's third term has a good chance of being known by a new aphorism: "Prison is better than stoning."

I would like you to think carefully about the following reflection by Montaigne from his *Essays* written in the 16th century. He wrote: "You are holding your opinions in too high a regard if you burn people alive for them." Is it worth accusing people and putting them in jail on the basis of totally unfounded conjectures by the prosecution?

Since in actual fact we never were, and are not, motivated by religious hatred and hostility, there is nothing left for our accusers to do other than to draw on the aid of false witnesses. One of them, Motilda Ivashchenko, was ashamed and didn't show up in court. That left false witness by [Vsevolod] Troitsky, [Igor] Ponkin and Mrs [Vera] Abramenkova. And there is no evidence of any hatred or enmity on our part other than this expert examination. For this reason, if it is honourable and just, the court must rule the evidence inadmissible because it is not a strictly scientific or objective text but a filthy, lying bit of paper from the medieval days of the inquisition. There is no other evidence that can even remotely suggest a motive.

The prosecution is reluctant to produce excerpts from the texts of Pussy Riot interviews because they are primary evidence of this lack of motive. For the umpteenth time, I will quote this excerpt. I think it's important. It was from an interview with "Russky Reporter", given the day after the concert at the Cathedral of Christ the Saviour: "Our attitude toward religion, and toward Orthodoxy in particular, is one of respect, and for this very reason we are distressed that the great and lumi-nous Christian philosophy is being used so shabbily. We are very angry that at this abuse of the sublime". It still makes us angry and we find it very painful to watch.

The lack on our part of any show of hatred or enmity has been attested by all the character witnesses examined by the defence. In addition to all the other character statements, I'd like you to consider the findings of the investigation's psychiatric and psychological tests I had to undergo in detention. The expert's findings were as follows: the values to which I am committed in my life are justice, mutual respect, humanity, equality and freedom. That's what the expert said, someone who doesn't know me and Investigator Ranchenko would probably have very much liked him to write something different. It would appear, however, that there are more people who love and value the truth, and the Bible's right about that.

Finally, I'd like to quote a Pussy Riot song because, strange as it may seem, all our songs have turned out to be prophetic, including the one that says: "The KGB chief, their number one saint, will escort protestors off to jail" – that's about us. What I'd like to quote now, however, is the next line: "Open the doors, off with the military insignia, join us in a taste of freedom."

(Project team: Agnes Parker: translation/Eja Werner: coordination)

282

# Punk Prayer: Virgin Mary, Mother of God, banish Putin

*On February 21, 2012, five members of the Russian feminist collective Pussy Riot staged an performance in Moscow's Cathedral of Christ the Savior. They were arrested and charged was "hooliganism, motivated by religious hatred." The formal allegations against the group were presented on June 4, with the indictment running to 2,800 pages. After a highly publicized trial, two members including Nadezhda Tolokonnikova were convicted and sentenced to two years of hard labor in a remote penal colony.*

### Virgin Mary, Mother of God, banish Putin

Banish Putin, Banish Putin!

Congregations genuflect

Black robes brag, golden epaulettes

Freedom's phantom's gone to heaven

Gay Pride's chained and in detention

The head of the KGB, their chief saint

Leads protesters to prison under escort

Don't upset His Saintship, ladies

Stick to making love and babies

Crap, crap, this godliness crap!

Crap, crap, this holiness crap!

[Chorus]

Virgin Mary, Mother of God

Become a feminist, we pray thee

Become a feminist, we pray thee

Bless our festering bastard-boss

Let black cars parade the Cross

The Missionary's in class for cash

Meet him there, and pay his stash

Patriarch Gundyaev believes in Putin

Better believe in God, you vermin!

Fight for rights, forget the rite –


Join our protest, Holy Virgin


[Chorus]

Virgin Mary, Mother of God, banish Putin, banish Putin

Virgin Mary, Mother of God, we pray thee, banish him!